NEW YORK

LONDON

TORONTO

SYDNEY

NEW DELHI

SCHOOL OF *Fish*

BEN POLLINGER

EXECUTIVE CHEF *of* OCEANA

and STEPHANIE LYNESS

G

Gallery Books
A Division of Simon & Schuster, Inc.
1230 Avenue of the Americas
New York, NY 10020

First Gallery Books hardcover edition September 2014

GALLERY BOOKS and colophon are registered trademarks of Simon & Schuster, Inc.

For information about special discounts for bulk purchases, please contact Simon & Schuster Special Sales at 1-866-506-1949 or business@simonandschuster.com.

The Simon & Schuster Speakers Bureau can bring authors to your live event. For more information or to book an event, contact the Simon & Schuster Speakers Bureau at 1-866-248-3049 or visit our website at www.simonspeakers.com.

Designed by Jaime Putorti

Manufactured in the United States of America

3   5   7   9   10   8   6   4   2

Library of Congress Cataloging-in-Publication Data
Pollinger, Ben.
School of fish / Ben Pollinger.
pages cm
1. Cooking (Seafood) I. Title.
TX747.P626 2014
641.6'92,—dc23

ISBN 978-1-4516-6513-0
ISBN 978-1-4516-6515-4 (ebook)

CONTENTS

For Christine

YOUR LOVE, FRIENDSHIP,

PATIENCE, AND SACRIFICE

HAVE MADE MY JOURNEY POSSIBLE.

INTRODUCTION

In June, 1997, I boarded a plane at Kennedy Airport and flew to Monaco to work under Chef Alain Ducasse at Le Louis XV, which at the time was considered to be the best restaurant in the world. I'd earned the yearlong apprenticeship in the final months of my education at The Culinary Institute of America. This extraordinarily expensive restaurant redefined my concept of perfection. The kitchen was as clean as an operating room, and rigorously ordered. The cooking was intensely professional and pressured. All of the work was surgically precise, including the use of a ruler to cut the food to an exact size and shape. Nothing ever went out of that kitchen that wasn't absolutely flawless. As the year went on, I felt grateful for the excruciating and exacting training I'd received at the hands of chefs Jean-Jacques Rachou and Christian Delouvrier for whom I'd worked in Manhattan. The experience in Monaco pushed me to my limit.

It also sparked my passion for fish. Picture the fish station in the kitchen at Le Louis XV. All of the seafood was pristine. Sometimes the locally caught bass was so fresh that I was pleading for it to get through rigor mortis just so I could get it filleted and into the pan on time. Shrimp from the Gulf of Genoa came in still quivering. There were mountains of tiny fresh squid called *pistes* to clean, live spider and tortoise crabs to cook and pick for their meat. In the course of that year, I experienced a quality and variety of seafood I'd never seen before. And I really learned. By the time I returned home a year later, I had my culinary chops.

Now imagine me couple of years later, still fairly new to my career, at home in New Jersey. It's Friday night and I'm in the kitchen because we're having people over for dinner. My wife, Christine—who has married a chef, after all—is expecting some good food on the table. Everyone's been here since about 7:00 p.m., here I am at nine o'clock, still cooking, and there's no way I'll get the food out before 10:00 p.m. The kitchen is a disaster. I'm used to having staff to take care of this stuff. Every pot and pan is dirty, and the stovetop's a mess.

The guests loved the food. But Christine was unhappy. "This is how it always goes when you cook," she said later that evening. "I don't understand how a guy who's worked at some of the best restaurants in the world can't get dinner on the table at home!"

. . .

I didn't start out to be a chef. Growing up in New Jersey, I enjoyed my mother's cooking though it wasn't exactly haute cuisine. I definitely enjoyed eating, but I wasn't one of those guys who learned to cook at his grandmother's knee. In fact, I didn't learn to cook at home at all. When I went to college at Boston University, it was to be an economics major. But during my sophomore year, I got a job in the cafeteria kitchen in my dorm. Suddenly I was getting up early on Sundays to cook eggs to order for 600 students. And I realized that I liked it. I liked it a lot. Cooking was a lot of fun.

It was a tough conversation with the parents. "I know what I'm going to do after I graduate," I said. "Great!" they replied. "Law school? Wall Street?"

"I want to cook."

The silence went on for a long time. We made it through that moment, and of course they agreed that what was most important was that I be happy. Then: "And please be successful." Great. No pressure.

So as you can imagine, succeeding has been rewarding in a variety of ways. My apprenticeship in Europe was followed by jobs at several great restaurants in Manhattan. I worked again with Christian Delouvrier at Les Célébrités and Lespinasse; with Michael Romano at Union Square Cafe; and with Floyd Cardoz at Tabla. Experiences at Union Square Cafe and Tabla helped my French training evolve toward a more global repertoire. Fish became my specialty. And in 2006, I took my current job as executive chef at Oceana, an upscale fish restaurant in midtown Manhattan.

I love running my kitchen at Oceana, turning out great food in an orderly environment. But I like to cook for my family, too. So after that Friday night cooking for friends at home, I decided that it was important to make it work in my kitchen across the river. Adapting my restaurant training to the home kitchen turned out to be a discovery process. It was a "School of Fish" for me. I realized that there were certain things that you can do in a restaurant that just don't work at home. Like complicated garnishes and dishes that require twelve pans. And I appreciated that there are things to do at home that you wouldn't necessarily want to do in a restaurant. Nice things. At home it makes sense to serve things very simply. To do it all in one pan.

And that was the inspiration for this book.

. . .

What do I love about fish? There's so much variety and there are so many things you can do with it. Compare a fish fillet with a New York strip steak. For the steak, you're going to grill it, broil it, or pan-roast it. But with seafood, you've got lots of choices. Techniques like poaching and steaming deliver the pure flavor of the fish. Sauté for a rich, caramelized taste; grill for a pleasant char and smokiness. Bake with herbs, braise in a red pepper stew, or broil with an Asian-style glaze. And that's just the cooked preparations; raw fish is another fantastic universe. So once you know the techniques, you have a lot of options to play with. And that's the fun of it.

Most of us grow up with cooking traditions for meat and poultry, but not necessarily for fish. I have terrible memories of fish, which, at my mother's table, meant frozen fish sticks. I wouldn't eat them. (I remember sitting at the table until 9:00 p.m. one night because my parents wouldn't let me get up until I'd eaten my dinner.) At the restaurant, customers tell me all the time that they don't cook fish at home. They'd like to, if only they

knew what to do with it. So the goal of this book is to give you recipes for family and friends—even some really great fish sticks children will like—and to demystify fish by teaching you approaches that give you the confidence to cook it well.

The book is called *School of Fish* because it's more than just a collection of recipes. I want to really teach you to cook fish, and the best way to do that is to break the cooking down by technique: I will teach you to bake, braise, broil, steam, poach, grill, fry, and sauté fish. I recommend cooking through those chapters sequentially. They are organized by degree of difficulty: I believe you'll find baking the easiest technique and a good introduction to the subject, while sautéing fish offers the most challenges.

But before you start cooking, get oriented by reading the chapters on "How to Buy and Store Fish" and "How to Season Fish" that apply to all recipes. "Is It Done Yet?," the next chapter, will teach you the all-important skill of testing fish for doneness.

Begin your *School of Fish* education with baking, which is an easy, forgiving method. The recipes in this chapter will give you a chance to hone your proficiency at testing for doneness. Braising is not much more difficult. The next chapter, Broiled Fish, is my favorite home-cooking technique. As you progress through these chapters, you'll build on your skills until you arrive at sautéing, by which time you'll be cooking like a pro.

Feel free to dig into the nontechnique chapters along the way. Chapter 2, Dressed Fish, recipes for raw fish, requires no cooking at all. There's a chapter for soups and chowders, and another for appetizers, salads, pasta, and rice. Vegetable recipes to accompany your fish entrées are interspersed throughout the book, and there's a chapter at the end with more.

I've chosen recipes to provide satisfaction to cooks with a broad range of cooking expertise. But primarily, I used my wife as my muse. Like a lot of people I talk to, she wants to cook fish more often, doesn't have much experience with it, has to get dinner on the table for herself and our three young children almost every night, and is bored with her repertoire. She needs some practical choices with variety, and doesn't have a lot of time to mess around.

Each chapter contains a collection of nonintimidating recipes labeled "101." The idea behind these 101 recipes is that they are quick, with familiar ingredients that won't distract you from focusing on the technique. Once you've cooked your way through the 101 group, I expect you'll feel confident enough to attack the recipes at the ends of the chapters, many of which

may introduce you to some cool new ingredients. (If you come across an ingredient that's new to you, turn to page 395, where you'll find an alphabetical guide to unusual ingredients. I also give ingredient substitutions in the recipes where possible. The taste won't be exactly the same, but your food will still be great!) These recipes will also appeal to more experienced cooks who want to try their hand at dishes that are a little more restaurant style. But the recipes are still doable for the novice. They simply have more steps and take more time. Most of the recipes are intended to serve as entrées, including the soups and pastas. You can, of course, cut the recipes in half to serve as appetizers if you're having people over for a more formal meal.

Throughout the book, sidebars labeled "Equip Yourself" offer recommendations for cooking equipment as it relates to each technique; "Kitchen Notebook" sidebars discuss ingredients and offer cooking tips. "Extra Credit" sidebars tell you how I do it at the restaurant, or give instructions for dressing up the recipes if you have the time and want to impress your guests.

Since some techniques, such as opening clams and filleting a fish, are best presented visually, page 378 begins a section of step-by-step technique photographs. At the end of the book, you'll find a dictionary of fish (Fish-ionary on page 405), briefly describing all the fish used in the book. My goal here is to give you a short introduction to each of them. I want to let you know where it's fished, how it's typically sold, tips for buying and cooking, whether to eat the skin, what to substitute, and my recommendation for best degree of doneness.

School of Fish represents a synthesis of my professional culinary training with a real-life understanding of the pressures of putting dinner on the table at home. It will teach you great technique so that you can serve the very best, most flavorful fish possible. Have fun with it!

HOW TO BUY AND STORE FISH

The only real criterion when buying fish is that it be as fresh as possible. If you go to the market looking for swordfish and the flounder looks better, get the flounder. If it's super fresh, you may discover that you really like flounder much better than you thought.

Your best line of defense is a quality fish market that does a brisk business. Rapid turnover doesn't guarantee fresh fish, but it doesn't hurt. Whether you are shopping at a Japanese seafood market, an upscale fish store, or your local supermarket, develop a relationship with the person behind the counter. Find out what days the store receives deliveries and shop then. Ask for help in choosing, and complain pleasantly if you're not satisfied.

It's also a good idea to learn to judge freshness yourself. People feel intimidated by this, but with a little practice it's actually fairly obvious. Fresh fish really *looks* fresh, appetizing, and appealing, even through the glass of the refrigerated case. Not so fresh, and fish begins to look dejected, like the last kid picked for the baseball team. Here are some specifics to look for.

• Whether you're buying whole fish, fillets, or steaks, look for fish that sparkles. As fish ages, the sparkle dulls noticeably. On whole fish, the skin should be shiny. Pull open the flap that covers the gills and take a look—the gills should be bright red, not brown. The eyes should be bright, not clouded. Fillets and steaks should gleam. They should look moist and translucent; as they age, the translucence turns opaque.

- Look at the dark areas (the bloodline) on white-fleshed fish such as swordfish, shark, mahi mahi, and striped bass. The color should be a bright, lively-looking red. As fish ages, those areas turn brown.

- As fish ages, it also dries out. The flakes on a fillet of flakey fish such as cod will begin to separate.

- Touch the fish if you can. The flesh of whole fish, steaks, and fillets should feel firm.

- If you have any questions, ask to smell the fish. Really fresh fish has no odor to speak of.

You can also tell a lot about the fish by the way it's stored in the case. Fish deteriorates more quickly than other proteins and must be kept iced, at 32°F.

- Fillets and steaks should be stored in containers on top of flaked or shaved ice; direct contact with the ice will damage the flesh.

- Whole fish should be buried in the ice.

- Shellfish should also be stored on ice. Shells of clams, oysters, and mussels should be tightly closed or should close when you tap them.

- Neither fish nor shellfish should be sitting in water or melted ice.

- Clawed lobsters and crabs should be alive (spiny lobsters without claws will be frozen tails only). They will die if stored on ice; they need a warmer temperature. Lobsters will likely be stored in tanks. Live crabs should be refrigerated.

HOW TO STORE FISH

Once you have your catch, get it home as soon as possible. If you have a ways to go, ask if your fish can be packed with a plastic bag of ice.

At home, given that the optimum temperature for storing fish is 32°F and your refrigerator is about 40°F, unless you're cooking the fish immediately it will stay fresher if you store it on ice. Wrap fillets and steaks in resealable plastic bags. Fill a baking dish with ice and place the fish on top of the ice. Whole fish can be stored directly in the ice. Replace the ice as it melts.

Clams: Refrigerate, covered with a wet towel, in a colander set in a baking dish. Top the towel with a layer of ice. Do not store in sealed plastic bags; it will kill them.

Mussels: Refrigerate, covered with a wet towel, in a colander set in a baking dish. Top the towel with a layer of ice. Do not store in a sealed plastic bag; it will kill them.

Oysters: Store oysters flat to prevent their liquor from leaking out. Cover with a wet towel and top the towel with a layer of ice. Do not store in a sealed plastic bag; it will kill them.

Sea scallops: Refrigerate as you would fish fillets and steaks.

Shrimp: Refrigerate shrimp in the shell on ice in a colander in a baking dish. Refrig-erate shelled shrimp as you would fish fillets and steaks.

Lobster: If you can, cook lobster the day you buy it. Otherwise, store it in the refrigerator, wrapped in wet newspaper, for no more than 2 days.

Blue crabs: Cook blue crabs, hard and soft-shell, as soon as possible. Until then, refrigerate live crabs in a baking dish or on a tray, covered with a wet towel to keep them moist, for no more than 2 days.

Squid: Enclose squid in a resealable plastic bag and refrigerate as you would fish fillets and steaks.

Octopus: Enclose octopus in a resealable plastic bag and refrigerate as you would fish fillets and steaks.

HOW TO SEASON FISH

In order to give seasoning a chance to pen-etrate before cooking, season the fish on both sides with salt and pepper, place it on a plate and let stand at room temperature for 5 minutes (15 minutes for poaching). For thin fillets, prevent overseasoning by sea-soning only one side or by seasoning both sides minimally. Thin fillets need stand only a few minutes before cooking. For dry-heat cooking methods (roasting, broiling, grilling, sautéing, and most frying) in which you're looking to develop a crust, pat the fish dry very well with paper towels just before cooking to blot up the liquid wicked out by the salt. It's not important for poaching, steaming, and braising, which we call "wet-heat" methods for obvious reasons, because the fish will not brown anyway.

IS IT DONE YET?

Whatever cooking technique you're playing with, knowing when the fish is done is key. There are several ways to test doneness. I'll walk you through them here. You may use all of them or find that one or another is more practical for you, depending on the fish you're cooking. But know going in that learning this is a process of trial and error. That's why I chose baking as the first technique chapter in this book; because doneness is basically all you need to focus on. You can pull the fish out of the oven as many times as you need to check on it. In fact, I encourage you to do just that. Then when you graduate to a more involved technique like grilling or sautéing, in which you will also be paying attention to browning and developing a crust, you'll already feel comfortable with the doneness question.

Let's start with what your hands can tell you. I don't know any better way to demonstrate the feeling of correctly cooked fish than to use the old trick I learned at cooking school. Put your hand out in front of you and make a loose fist. Don't squeeze; just hold your hand in the shape of a fist. Gently press the flesh between your thumb and forefinger. It should feel soft and relaxed: That's what it feels like to press on fish that has been cooked to rare. Now pull your fingers closed a bit more so that the fist closes but doesn't really tighten. That area still feels soft but there's a little resistance: That's what medium-rare feels like. Put a little more effort into closing the fingers— that's medium. Now squeeze the fist so that it feels intentional but not clenched: that's cooked through. Medium-well done is a subtle step between the feelings of medium and cooked through. (As I said, it's about trial and error.)

Another excellent way to test for doneness is with a metal cake tester, a tool with a long, thin metal wire attached to a small plastic grip. (I always have an Ateco cake tester in the pocket of my chef's jacket.) Insert the tester through the side of the fish fillet or steak, the thickest part of the fish (this will be at or near the center), until the tester just breaks through the other side. Hold it for 3 to 5 seconds. Remove the tester from the fish and quickly touch the center portion of the wire to the area below your lower lip. For fish that is cooked through, the tester should feel hot enough to be uncomfortable. For fish that is medium, the tester should feel hot—hotter than body temperature—but not uncomfortable. For medium-rare, the tester will feel a little warmer than body temperature. Rare will feel a little cooler than body temperature. Additionally, you can feel for the way the texture of the fish changes as it cooks: when the fish is cooked through, you will feel no resistance as you slide the tester into the fish. (If you like, you can sanitize the tester in a weak bleach solution as we do at the restaurant; see page 31. Keep a bowl of the solution at the ready and dip the tester into it—handle and all—each time after touching the tester to your body.)

A third way to gauge doneness is with your eyes. The look of the flesh changes from translucent to opaque as it cooks. If you're sautéing or grilling a piece of fish, you can assess the cooking progress as the opaqueness rises from the bottom of the fillet, where it touches the pan or grill, toward the center. And there's no harm in cutting into the fish to check it. If you cut into a piece of fish that's been cooked through, the flesh will be completely opaque. Cut into a fish cooked to medium-well, and there's a shade of translucence at the core. For medium, the central quarter of the fish is translucent; medium-rare, the center third. Rare fish is mostly translucent.

For tips on checking the doneness of lobster, see Kitchen Notebook: Is It Cooked? on page 251.

EQUIP YOURSELF: CAKE TESTERS

Cake testers are sold at kitchen supply stores and online at amazon.com.

1.

BASICS

This is a chapter of stocks, seasonings, flavored oils, vinaigrettes, and my homemade hot sauce, which punch up the flavor of simply cooked fish and make serving it even easier.

Don't be put off by the recipes for Fish Fumet (opposite) and Clam Broth (page 15). In general, I've tried to limit the necessity for stocks in the book because they do add another step. But for really professional results, they also add incomparable flavor to soups, braises, and pastas. These are the recipes we use at the restaurant in much larger batches. I make Low-Stress Chicken Stock (page 16) at home with carcasses from roast chicken dinners, saved in the freezer until I've collected enough to make the stock. (These carcasses may be from deli or supermarket roast chickens, too.) You'll find it used throughout the recipes, sometimes as a substitute for fumet or clam broth.

If you don't have any of these homemade options, you can always substitute store-bought low-sodium chicken stock in the recipes. But stocks freeze very well, so I recommend making a batch when you've got a moment and dividing it into 1- and 2-cup containers to stash in the freezer. For easy access to smaller amounts, freeze some in ice cube trays, then pop out the cubes and store in resealable freezer bags.

Most of the flavored oils and vinaigrettes, and my hot sauce, will last for several weeks—even several months—so you can have them at the ready to turn the plainest weekday fish dinner into something a little more special. Recipes throughout the book call for Blackening Spice (page 23), Sofrito (page 24), and Preserved Lemons (page 25); headnotes let you know how to use these flavoring elements to liven up basic recipes quickly and easily.

· FISH FUMET ·

MAKES ABOUT 4 QUARTS

The key to making a great-tasting fish fumet is twofold: The fish bones must be carefully rinsed and soaked to clean them of blood, and the cook must be vigilant about skimming the foam as it rises to the surface of the stock. The foam is simply coagulated protein, but along with the blood, it can make the stock bitter. Unlike the boiled broth for bouillabaisse (page 115), fish fumet is cooked at a low simmer to maintain its clarity.

With a little notice, your fishmonger will be able to supply you with the bones.

5 pounds bones from lean white fish (such as flounder, sole, halibut, cod, striped bass, hake, black sea bass, and/or snapper)

1 tablespoon canola oil

½ onion, sliced

¼ bulb fennel, trimmed, sliced

1 stalk celery, sliced

1 clove garlic, peel-on, crushed with the heel of your hand

2 cups dry white wine

2 sprigs fresh Italian parsley

2 sprigs fresh tarragon

2 sprigs fresh thyme

1 bay leaf

Fine sea salt

½ teaspoon whole black peppercorns

1. Rinse the bones well under cold running water to remove all traces of blood. Drain. Cut the bones into 3-inch sections with a heavy knife or kitchen scissors.

2. Place an 8-quart pot over medium heat. Add the oil and heat until fluid enough to coat the bottom of the pot when swirled. Add the onion, fennel, celery, and garlic and cook without coloring, stirring occasionally, until the vegetables are aromatic, about 5 minutes.

3. Add the fish bones, wine, 4 quarts water, the parsley, tarragon, thyme, bay leaf, 1 teaspoon salt, and the peppercorns. Bring to a boil, reduce the heat, and simmer gently about 45 minutes, skimming off the foam with a slotted spoon as it rises.

4. Strain the fumet through a fine-mesh strainer into a large container.

recipe continued on next page

5. Use immediately or prepare an ice bath: fill your sink with ice and cold water. Set the container with the fumet in the sink and let stand, stirring the fumet every 10 to 15 minutes, until chilled. Divide among containers refrigerate, and use within 3 days or freeze for up to 6 months.

EXTRA CREDIT: FOR UTMOST CLARITY

At the restaurant, where the clarity of the stock is of utmost importance, the bones are soaked overnight in the refrigerator with 1 tablespoon salt per 5 pounds bones in water to cover. The cold water and salt help to draw out blood and impurities that can cloud the fumet and make it bitter. The finished stock is also carefully ladled—not poured—through the strainer so as not to disturb its clarity.

· CLAM BROTH ·

MAKES ABOUT 5 CUPS

Clam broth is made with chowder clams, also called quahogs, which are a larger version of the same species as littlenecks and cherrystones. Same flavor, but bigger and tougher. Too tough to serve steamed, they're perfect for a broth. If chowder clams aren't available, use cherrystones.

2 tablespoons extra virgin olive oil

2 shallots, sliced

2 cloves garlic, sliced

½ finger chile, cut lengthwise, seeds removed, sliced crosswise

2 sprigs fresh Italian parsley

1 sprig fresh basil

1 sprig fresh thyme

1 tablespoon whole black peppercorns

1 bay leaf

15 chowder clams or 25 cherrystones, scrubbed

2½ cups dry white wine

1. Place a 4-quart pot over medium heat. Add the oil and heat until fluid enough to coat the bottom of the pot when swirled. Add the shallots, garlic, and chile and cook without coloring, stirring often, until the shallots are translucent, about 3 minutes. Add the parsley, basil, and thyme and cook, stirring often, 1 minute. Add the peppercorns and bay leaf and cook, stirring often, about 30 seconds.

2. Add the clams and cook, stirring, 1 minute. Add the wine and bring to a boil. Reduce the heat and simmer just until the clams open, 5 to 8 minutes. Strain the broth through a fine-mesh strainer into a clean container, holding back the last of the liquid in case of grit.

3. Use immediately or prepare an ice bath: Fill your sink with ice and cold water. Set the container with the broth in the sink and let stand, stirring the broth every 10 to 15 minutes, until chilled. Divide among containers, refrigerate and use within 3 days or freeze for up to 6 months.

EXTRA CREDIT: DON'T WASTE THE CLAMS

At the restaurant, where nothing is wasted, we pull the clams out of the shells, being careful to avoid the tough muscles that attach the meat to the shells. We finely chop them and add them to the finished broth for extra flavor.

· LOW-STRESS CHICKEN STOCK ·

MAKES 3½ QUARTS

At home, I make chicken stock with roast chicken carcasses that I save in the freezer. When I've collected seven or eight, I whack them into pieces with a chef's knife or cut them up with poultry shears, put them in a pot with some vegetables and water to cover, and make chicken stock. You could also make this the way we do in the restaurant, with raw chicken bones, such as backs and necks, rinsed well under cold running water to remove blood.

7 or 8 roast chicken carcasses, cut into pieces, or 8 pounds raw chicken bones (such as necks and backs), rinsed well under cold running water to remove blood

1 medium onion, cut into ½-inch dice (about 2 cups)

2 medium carrots, cut into ½-inch dice (about 2 cups)

2 stalks celery, cut into ½-inch dice (about 1 cup)

1 teaspoon whole black peppercorns

1 bay leaf

2 sprigs fresh Italian parsley

2 sprigs fresh thyme

1 teaspoon fine sea salt

1. Put the chicken bones in a large pot with the onion, carrots, celery, peppercorns, bay leaf, parsley, thyme, salt, and 4 quarts water. Bring to a boil, skimming the foam with a slotted spoon as it rises. Reduce the heat and simmer very gently, skimming as needed, about 4 hours. If the bones stick up out of the water, add 2 cups more water.

2. Toward the end of cooking, fat will rise to the surface; remove it with a ladle. (Refrigerate and save for cooking; it's delicious.)

3. Strain the stock through a fine-mesh strainer into a clean container, holding back the last of the liquid in case of grit. Use immediately or prepare an ice bath: Fill your sink with ice and cold water. Set the container with the stock in the sink and let stand, stirring the stock every 10 to 15 minutes, until chilled. Divide among containers, refrigerate and use within 3 days or freeze for up to 6 months.

· HOMEMADE HOT SAUCE ·

MAKES ABOUT 2 CUPS

Hot sauce is my go-to sauce for just about any kind of fish, cooked any way. This recipe is made with finger chiles but you can use any variety; for a milder version, replace some of the finger chiles with red bell pepper. The longer the chiles are refrigerated in the salt and vinegar, the more flavor they develop. And they develop more flavor at room temperature than in the fridge.

Because there are no emulsifiers, the hot sauce will separate and a clear, watery layer will collect on the bottom; just shake it up before using.

8 ounces red finger chiles, stems removed, halved lengthwise, seeds left in, sliced crosswise ½ inch thick

1 tablespoon fine sea salt

1 cup white distilled vinegar

1. Place the chiles in a bowl. Add the salt and toss to coat. Let stand at room temperature for 1 hour, until the chiles begin to exude their juices. Toss again. Transfer to a 1-pint container and seal with the cover.

2. Let stand in the refrigerator or at room temperature for 4 days, gently shaking the container twice daily.

3. Transfer the chiles with their liquid to a blender. Add the vinegar. Begin on low speed and gradually move to high speed; purée 30 seconds at high speed. Scrape down the sides of the blender and purée until smooth, about 30 seconds more. Pour into a bottle and seal. Store at room temperature for up to 6 months or refrigerate for up to 1 year.

EXTRA CREDIT: LOUISIANA-STYLE FERMENTED HOT SAUCE

Tabasco and other Louisiana-style fermented hot sauces are made by holding the salted peppers at room temperature until they begin to ferment, to develop a more complex, slightly fermented flavor. You can do the same by leaving the peppers out for as long as a week to 10 days. In that case, don't shake the container as in the recipe for Homemade Hot Sauce. Instead, place a doubled layer of plastic wrap directly over the chiles and weight them with a clean glass jar or nest a second bowl, filled with water, inside so that the chiles stay submerged in their juices. Then proceed with step 3 of the recipe for Homemade Hot Sauce.

· LEMON ZEST OIL ·

MAKES ABOUT 2 TABLESPOONS

Drizzle this on any fish for a blast of lemon.

1 lemon, rinsed and dried   2 tablespoons extra virgin olive oil

Use a Microplane to grate the zest of the lemon into a small bowl. Add the olive oil and stir. Use within a few hours.

EQUIP YOURSELF: MICROPLANES

A Microplane—a very sharp metal grater—is the easiest, quickest way to grate lemon zest. Once a strictly professional tool, Microplanes are available at most kitchen stores and online now. They work so well that you need to be careful, particularly if your Microplane is new, not to grate so hard so that you grate through the colored exterior and into the bitter white pith.

· CHILE OIL ·

MAKES ABOUT 1½ CUPS

Chile oil will last at room temperature indefinitely. Just keep topping off the oil once you've used about half of it. I've had the same bottle—a glass vinegar bottle I saved for this purpose—for a few years. Note that chile oil takes just a few minutes to put together but will need to sit for at least 2 months before the oil takes on the flavor of the chiles.

¾ cup whole dried Thai bird chiles (¾ ounce)   1½ cups extra virgin olive oil

1. Place the chiles in a glass bottle and cover with the oil. Seal. The chiles are hollow so they'll float. Once a day, overturn the jar, then turn it upright; repeat once.

2. Once the chiles sink below the level of the oil, top off the oil if necessary to cover them entirely. Let stand in a cool, dark place until the oil tastes strongly of the chiles, 2 to 3 months.

· ROSEMARY OIL ·

MAKES ABOUT 1½ CUPS

I make herb oils the simplest possible way: Just pour the cold oil over the herbs and set aside in a dark place for a couple of months. You can make thyme and lavender oils the same way; substitute the same quantity of the herb and oil.

¾ ounce fresh rosemary sprigs (about 6)   1½ cups extra virgin olive oil

1. Place the rosemary sprigs in a glass bottle with a cap and pour the olive oil over them. Seal. Let stand in a cool, dark place for about 2 months.

2. Remove the rosemary with tweezers. The oil will keep for about 2 months at room temperature.

· SHERRY VINAIGRETTE ·

MAKES ABOUT 1 CUP

As a rule, vinaigrettes are made with a ratio of one part acid to three parts oil. Sherry vinegar has a higher percentage of acid than most other vinegars, so a one-to-four ratio is better. If you want to make a larger batch, this will hold fine at room temperature for several months. Store in a bottle or jar with a lid and shake before using to reemulsify.

3 tablespoons sherry vinegar   ¾ cup extra virgin olive oil
Fine sea salt and freshly ground black pepper

In a small bowl, whisk the vinegar with a pinch each of salt and pepper. Drizzle in the oil, whisking to emulsify. Taste for seasoning and add salt and/or pepper as necessary.

· HOT SAUCE VINAIGRETTE ·

MAKES ABOUT 1 CUP

The addition of olive and grapeseed oils tempers the heat of the hot sauce so that the flavor of the chiles carries through without the searing heat.

½ cup Homemade Hot Sauce (page 17) or
your favorite store-bought hot sauce

¼ cup extra virgin olive oil
¼ cup grapeseed or other neutral oil

Place the hot sauce in a blender. With the motor running, gradually pour in the oils to emulsify. (If you have a variable-speed blender, blend on medium-high speed.) Pour into a bottle, cover, and refrigerate for up to several months. Shake before using to reemulsify.

· ORANGE VINAIGRETTE ·

MAKES ABOUT 1¼ CUPS

If you're not squeezing your own, look for unpasteurized juice in the refrigerated section of your supermarket for this delicately sweet vinaigrette.

1½ cups freshly squeezed orange juice or
unpasteurized store-bought

6 tablespoons extra virgin olive oil
½ teaspoon fine sea salt

1. In a 10-inch sauté pan, bring the orange juice to a boil. Reduce the heat and simmer over medium-high heat until reduced to ¾ cup, 3 to 5 minutes.

2. Pour into a bowl and let cool to room temperature. Whisk in the olive oil in a thin stream, then the salt.

3. Transfer to a bottle, cover, and refrigerate for up to 1 month.

· HOMEMADE MAYONNAISE ·

MAKES ABOUT 1 CUP

Mayonnaise is traditionally made by hand with a whisk and bowl. But it's so incredibly easy to make in a blender that I provide blender instructions here instead. (A mini food processor will also do the job.) I use a whole egg, in part because I don't like to waste the egg white. But also because egg white is largely water, and egg yolk–only mayonnaise usually needs to be thinned with a little water anyway.

1 large egg (see Kitchen Notebook, page 22)   ¼ teaspoon fine sea salt

1 teaspoon fresh lemon juice   1 cup canola oil

1. Combine the egg, lemon juice, and salt in a blender. With the blender running, drizzle in the oil in a slow, steady stream until thick and smooth. (If you have a variable-speed blender, blend on medium-high or high.) This should take about 1 minute maximum.

2. Transfer to a container, cover, and refrigerate for up to 2 days.

KITCHEN NOTEBOOK: MAYONNAISE TRICKS OF THE TRADE

The enemies of blender mayonnaise are overmixing and the heat generated by the friction of the blender. The trick is to add the oil slowly enough to emulsify, but not so slowly that the mayonnaise "breaks," a term used to mean that it stops looking thick and creamy and starts looking loose, curdled, and liquidy. If the mayonnaise does break, however, it's easy to fix: Simply empty the contents of the blender into a liquid cup measure (with a spout). Add a second yolk to the blender, turn it on, and drizzle in the contents of the measuring cup in a slow, steady stream.

As an extra precaution, chill the blender jar and oil for 30 minutes before making the mayonnaise.

· ROASTED RED PEPPER AIOLI ·

MAKES ABOUT 2 CUPS

This makes a great sauce for steamed, fried, or poached fish, and a delicious dip for crudités. I also serve it as an alternative to rouille in Monkfish Bouillabaisse (page 115).

1 red bell pepper

1 teaspoon plus 1 cup canola oil

1 large egg yolk (see Kitchen Notebook, below)

1 teaspoon fresh lemon juice

½ teaspoon fine sea salt

1. To roast the pepper, rub it all over with 1 teaspoon of the oil. If you have a gas burner, turn the heat to high, place the pepper directly on the burner, and roast it, turning it with tongs as the skin blackens, until the skin is blackened all over. Blacken the top and bottom of the pepper, too. This should take about 5 minutes total.

2. If your burners are electric, instead preheat the oven to 400°F. Place the oiled pepper on a baking sheet and roast, turning from time to time, until the skin is blistered all over, about 40 minutes.

3. Place the pepper in a bowl and cover with plastic until it's cool enough to handle, at least 5 minutes. Place the cooled pepper on a paper towel and scrape off all of the blackened skin with a paring knife. Cut the pepper in half through the stem end, cut out the stem, and scrape out the seeds. Coarsely chop the pepper. (See Kitchen Notebook: Peeling Roasted Peppers, page 240.)

4. Combine the chopped pepper, egg yolk, lemon juice, and salt in a blender. With the blender running, drizzle in the remaining 1 cup oil in a slow, steady stream. (If you have a variable-speed blender, blend on medium-high or high speed.) This process should take about 1 minute maximum.

KITCHEN NOTEBOOK: RAW EGG SAFETY

If you're concerned about raw eggs, substitute 2 tablespoons pasteurized yolks for the 1 egg yolk in this recipe; 2 tablespoons pasteurized yolks plus 2 tablespoons water for 1 whole egg. Your supermarket may also sell pasteurized eggs in the shell.

· BLACKENING SPICE ·

I developed this spice mix for Blackened Swordfish 101 (page 339), my take on Paul Prud-homme's famous blackened redfish recipe. The swordfish is sautéed, but the spice mix can just as easily be used on broiled or grilled fish (see Kitchen Notebook, below). And it's a quick way to make a Cajun aioli (page 323).

¼ cup smoked paprika

4 teaspoons onion powder

4 teaspoons garlic powder

2 teaspoons cayenne pepper

1 teaspoon ground white pepper

1 teaspoon ground black pepper

Mix all the ingredients together in a bowl. Store in an airtight container at room temperature.

KITCHEN NOTEBOOK: GRILLING AND BROILING WITH BLACKENING SPICE

For 4 portions, coat the fish very lightly with a thin sheen of oil, dredge in about ¼ cup of the spice mix, and broil or grill according to the recipe.

· SOFRITO ·

MAKES 1 ¼ CUPS

Sofrito is a traditional mixture of cooked aromatic ingredients, used as a flavoring base in Italian, Spanish, Caribbean, and Latin cuisines. You'll find it spelled in a variety of ways and made with a variety of vegetables. My version is made with onion, garlic, and tomato cooked in olive oil. It's a great way to perk up any boiled or steamed vegetable. Have it on hand to toss with green beans, as on page 369, or with broccoli, cauliflower, broccoli rabe, or sautéed zucchini. Or stir it into soups, braises, and sauces.

½ cup extra virgin olive oil

2 medium or 1 large onion, cut into ¼-inch dice (about 1 ½ cups)

4 cloves garlic, sliced

1 ½ cups diced cored tomatoes (2 to 3 medium; ¼-inch dice)

1. Place a 10-inch skillet over medium heat. Add the olive oil and heat until fluid enough to coat the bottom of the pot when swirled. Add the onion and cook without coloring, stirring, about 5 minutes.

2. Add the garlic and cook without coloring, stirring often, about 5 minutes more.

3. Add the tomatoes and cook until they start to break down, about 5 minutes.

4. Let cool. If not using immediately, refrigerate in a tightly closed container for up to 1 week.

· PRESERVED LEMONS ·

MAKES 16 LEMON QUARTERS, ABOUT 1 QUART

Preserved lemons are not hard to make, and they're a wonderful thing to have on hand in the fridge. The salt cure transforms their citrus flavor into something very aromatic and floral, and makes the otherwise bitter white pith palatable. Just a little bit of the rind, chopped or sliced, will make other flavors more distinctive. Cut out the pulp with a paring knife and add thinly sliced preserved lemon rind to salads, to fish cooked *en papillote* (see page 211), to pastas, or to tuna salad. Or finely mince some and add to vinaigrettes, raw fish preparations, salsas, and cooked vegetables.

4 lemons, rinsed and dried   2 cups kosher salt, plus more as needed

1. Trim both ends and quarter each lemon through the stem ends. Lay each quarter on its side and cut off the line of pith. Use the tip of a paring knife to pick out the seeds.

2. Line the bottom of a 1-quart plastic container with about ½ inch salt. Arrange 4 lemon quarters on top. Add salt to completely cover. Arrange 4 more lemon quarters on top and add more salt to completely cover. Make 2 more layers of lemon and salt, ending with a layer of salt. Seal tightly with a lid.

3. Tap the container lightly on a counter to tamp down the salt. Refrigerate for 1 month, turning once or twice over the course of the month. As the salt draws out the juice, some of the salt will dissolve and you may see a layer of thick liquid developing at the bottom of the container. That's fine. But if you notice the lemons beginning to poke out of the salt, flip the container over so the top is now the bottom, and tap it down a bit. If any lemons still stick out, turn it back upright, add more salt to cover, and cover again tightly. Return the container to the fridge.

4. After 1 month, when the lemons are cured, take them out of salt to use as needed. Brush or scrape the excess salt back into the container. Ideally, soak the lemon overnight in cold water in the refrigerator to draw out excess salt before using. But if you're pressed for time, just give the lemon a rinse under cold running water, cut off a small piece and taste it. If it tastes very salty, soak it for 20 minutes in cold water to cover. Be sure to taste the dish before seasoning; you may need to decrease the amount of salt.

5. Store the lemons in the salt in the refrigerator for up to 6 months. After that, the lemons will soften and deteriorate.

2.
DRESSED FISH

*T*I'm a sometimes fisherman. For me, a day of fishing means casting off the beach on the ocean side of Long Beach Island, spending several hours in the hopes of catching a striped bass for dinner, probably coming home empty handed. My kids love fishing, too, but they don't have the patience for that. It's the excitement of catching something—anything—that counts. I take them to the bay side of Long Beach Island, where the water is calmer, and they can catch a dozen 4-inch spots in the hour between dinner and dessert. The fish are too small to keep so we throw them all back. But the kids don't care—they're into the action!

My son, Nathaniel, got a real treat last summer when my father-in-law, Joel, and I took him out fluke fishing on a boat in Barnegat Bay. Joel snagged a nice big fluke that day and he wanted Nathaniel to have the experience of pulling in something big enough to take home. So when he felt the pull, he didn't let on that he had a fish on the line. He called Nathaniel over and asked him to take the rod while he went "to get some water." Nathaniel was thrilled to reel in the big fish (and he'll never know it wasn't really his catch unless he reads this book).

Back at the house, I turned the fluke into sashimi. All it took was skinning the fillets, cutting them into thin slices, and dressing them with a little lemon juice, olive oil, and salt. It tasted great. Nathaniel wouldn't touch it—raw fish isn't big on my kids' list of favorite foods—but for the grownups the fluke, just four hours out of the water, was awesome.

Whether you're fishing on Barnegat Bay or your fish store, putting together raw fish dishes at home is not as intimidating as it sounds. I talk to people all the time who say that they'd like to serve raw fish; they just don't know what to do with it. This chapter will answer that question.

I call this type of preparation "dressed fish" because most of the recipes—whether you're making Scallop Crudo 101 with Lemon and Parsley (page 35), Striped Bass Tartare 101 with Tomato and Basil (page 39), or Halibut Ceviche with Coconut, Lime, and Mint (page 50)—are like salads. What do you do with salads? You just dress them. I define these preparations (crudo, tartare, sashimi, carpaccio, and ceviche) in Raw Fish Lingo on page 30. But like my son's fluke, though they look very fashionable, the recipes are for the most part very simple. The fish already tastes fantastic. You just toss it with this or drizzle it with that and it tastes even more fantastic.

Like salads, raw fish is a great way to start a meal. Light and fresh, it makes sense as an appetizer. And because portions are small, once you get the hang of it you can experiment with flavors that are bolder, spicier, or more acidic than you and your guests might like in an entrée-size portion. Just remember that the focus should be on the fish. Whatever sauce or garnish ingredients you choose are simply to accent its flavor and texture. This is particularly true when it comes to mild fish like halibut, snapper, and fluke; you don't want to mask their delicate taste. You can be much more aggressive with stronger flavored fish like tuna, mackerel, and salmon. Borrow the formula I've developed over the years: As a rule of thumb, ingredients for my dressed fish dishes include something tart, something sweet, something spicy, a little crunch, and a little salt.

Beyond "dressed fish" preparations, I've also got a few recipes for curing fish that are easy to do at home. You've probably eaten gravlax at some point, but there are also some cool Japanese cures for fluke, tuna, and mackerel that are worth trying.

For all these recipes, I have allotted 2 ounces of fish per person for an appetizer portion. You can vary that amount, depending on your dinner guests, serving as much or as little fish as you like; just increase or decrease the dressing amounts accordingly. And if you really want to impress, serve two or three of these preparations together as an appetizer course. You'll definitely get some oohs and ahs, and it's a blast to taste the range of flavors and textures.

The raw fish preparations in this chapter may be roughly divided into four categories:

1. Sashimi, crudo, and carpaccio are all names for fish that is served thinly sliced on an angle or straight down, about ¼ inch thick. It may be sliced several hours ahead, covered with plastic wrap, and refrigerated until you're ready to serve.

2. Tartare is fish cut into small cubes, then mixed with flavorful ingredients right before serving. The fish may be diced several hours ahead, covered with plastic, and refrigerated separately from the other ingredients. When you're ready to serve, just toss it all together.

3. Ceviche is fish that is diced, then marinated in a citrus juice preparation for 45 minutes to 1 hour to "cook" the fish. It's not really cooked because no heat is applied. But the acid in the marinade causes the protein to denature, turning the flesh opaque and firming it up some-what so that the texture resembles cooked fish. Once the fish has been marinated, I drain off the liquid and add fresh garnish ingredients. The fish may be marinated, drained, covered with plastic, and refrigerated for up to several hours ahead of time. When it's time to serve, toss with the fresh ingredients.

4. Finally, before refrigeration became widespread, most traditional cuisines developed methods for curing fish to preserve it. Now that we have refrigerators, we still make these dishes because they taste so good. In this chapter you'll find recipes for the popular Swedish dry-cure called gravlax (Gravlax with Mustardy Celery Root Salad, page 51) as well as three Japanese cures: one with soy sauce, one with seaweed, a third with salt and vinegar.

TIPS FOR WORKING WITH RAW FISH

• The fish should be as fresh as possible, obviously, but it's fine to buy it the day before you plan to serve and refrigerate it overnight. Don't get hung up on the species of fish. Get something fresh. Step-by-step photos starting on page 384 show you how to slice raw fish for recipes in this chapter.

• You need to work impeccably clean. Make sure to wash your hands. Work on a clean cutting board. And keep your fish refrigerated as much as possible.

• When we're working with raw fish in the restaurant, we sanitize the cutting board every 15 to 20 minutes with a commercial sanitizing agent. You can simply scrub your cutting board, bowls, and utensils with soap and hot water before using them, or sanitize them with a weak bleach solution: Combine 1 teaspoon of chlorine bleach with 1 quart of water.

Wash your board, bowls, and utensils as usual, then dip a sponge or paper towel in the bleach solution and scrub again. Rinse under warm running water, wipe dry with a paper towel and go to work. When you're done work, repeat without the final rinse in fresh water; set the equipment aside to air dry. (I recommend wearing disposable gloves while bleaching, to protect your hands.) In the restaurant, we wear gloves when handling raw fish, and you may want to do that, too.

EQUIP YOURSELF: YOUR KNIFE

You're going to need a sharp chef's knife or slicing knife (I use a Japanese slicer called a *sujihiki*). Other than that, have cutting board, will travel.

·TUNA CRUDO 101·
WITH SUNFLOWER SEEDS, LEMON, AND CHIVES

SERVES 4 AS AN APPETIZER

This is the recipe I give people who tell me they want to serve raw fish at home but don't know how to begin. The ingredients are available at the supermarket; and the sunflower seeds, which you can buy roasted, add a nice nuttiness and crunch. It's so easy but when it's on the plate, the dish looks a lot more complicated than it really is. If you end up buying a wide, thin tuna steak, cut it in half crosswise before slicing so your pieces are not insanely long.

8 ounces skinless tuna steak, bloodline removed

2 teaspoons fresh lemon juice

4 teaspoons extra virgin olive oil

Fine sea salt and freshly ground black pepper

4 teaspoons roasted shelled sunflower seeds

1 teaspoon thinly sliced fresh chives

Cutting straight down, cut the tuna into slices about ¼ inch thick. Arrange one quarter of the tuna slices, overlapping, on each of four serving plates. Drizzle each plate of fish with ½ teaspoon lemon juice and 1 teaspoon olive oil. Sprinkle lightly with salt and pepper. Sprinkle each with 1 teaspoon sunflower seeds and ¼ teaspoon chives.

KITCHEN NOTEBOOK: EASY SLICING

If you have access to a Japanese market, look for neatly trimmed rectangular blocks of tuna, called *neta*, ready to cut for sushi. These regularly shaped blocks of fish make it easier to cut even, attractive slices for crudo.

· SPICY TUNA TARTARE 101 ·
WITH TOGARASHI AND LIME

SERVES 4 AS AN APPETIZER

Shichimi togarashi, also called *togarashi*, is a Japanese spice blend (see Guide to Unusual Ingredients, page 403). It's got a lot of flavor and though not excessively spicy, also packs some heat. You may have tasted it in spicy tuna rolls. It's a great accent for a fish like tuna that has enough flavor to stand up to it. Finely diced carrot, daikon, and cucumber add a little crunch.

8 ounces skinless tuna steak, bloodline removed

2 tablespoons finely diced carrot (¼ inch or a little smaller)

2 tablespoons finely diced peel-on seedless cucumber (¼ inch or a little smaller)

2 tablespoons finely diced peeled daikon or peel-on radish (¼ inch or a little smaller)

1 tablespoon fresh lime juice, plus more if needed

2 tablespoon extra virgin olive oil

1 teaspoon shichimi togarashi

Fine sea salt

1. Cutting straight down, cut the tuna into slices about ¼ inch thick. Cut the slices into ¼-inch-wide strips. Cut the strips crosswise into ¼-inch dice. Place in a bowl.

2. Add the carrot, cucumber, daikon or radish, lime juice, olive oil, togarashi, and a sprinkle of salt. Stir gently to combine. Taste for salt and lime and adjust if necessary.

3. To serve, divide among four bowls.

EXTRA CREDIT: SHICHIMI TOGARASHI

Try a sprinkle of shichimi togarashi on cooked or raw scallops and on sautéed vegetables—it adds a nice kick.

· SCALLOP CRUDO 101 ·
WITH LEMON AND PARSLEY

SERVES 4 AS AN APPETIZER

Raw sea scallops have a very silky texture, low fat content, and a sweet flavor. They're easy to work with because they slice evenly into rounds. Make sure to cut the lemon segments into small pieces so as not to overwhelm the taste of the scallop.

1 lemon, rinsed and dried

2 tablespoons extra virgin olive oil

8 ounces large sea scallops (U10, meaning fewer than 10 scallops to the pound, if you can get them), tough white side muscles removed

Fine sea salt and freshly ground black pepper

2 teaspoons very finely slivered fresh Italian parsley

1. Use a Microplane to grate the zest of the lemon into a small bowl. Stir in the olive oil; set aside.

2. Slice off the top and bottom of the lemon. Set it on a cutting board on one end and slice off the bitter white pith with a paring knife. Working over a bowl to catch the juices, cut between the membranes with the knife to cut out 2 segments. Cut the segments in half lengthwise and then crosswise into small, regular pieces; set aside. Squeeze the juice from the rest of the lemon into the bowl—you'll need 2 teaspoons juice; set aside.

3. Set the scallops on their sides and cut into thin disks (⅛ to ¼ inch thick).

4. Arrange one quarter of the scallop slices, overlapping, on each of four serving plates. Drizzle each with ½ teaspoon lemon juice, then 1 teaspoon of the lemon zest oil. (Cover and refrigerate the remaining oil for up to 2 weeks to sauce baked, grilled, or other simply cooked fish.) Sprinkle lightly with salt and pepper. Scatter one quarter of the lemon pieces over each serving. Sprinkle each with about ½ teaspoon parsley.

· SALMON SASHIMI 101 ·
WITH PONZU

SERVES 4 AS AN <u>APPETIZER</u>

Ponzu is a thin, tart Japanese sauce based on juices from various citrus fruits. I like to serve a simplified version of ponzu with salmon because the lime juice cuts the richness of the fish. A garnish of crushed toasted seaweed sheets called nori adds a smoky dimension of flavor, but you can skip it if you like. Cover and refrigerate leftover ponzu sauce to use as a dipping sauce. Or using a ratio of one to four, ponzu to vegetable oil, whisk ponzu with oil to make a vinaigrette to dress salad or sauce simply cooked fish.

FOR THE PONZU SAUCE

4 teaspoons soy sauce

4 teaspoons rice vinegar

2 teaspoons fresh lime juice

FOR THE SALMON SASHIMI

½ of an 8 by 7½-inch sheet nori (optional)

8 ounces boneless, skinless salmon fillet

1 scallion (white and green parts), sliced into thin rounds

Fine sea salt

1. For the ponzu, stir together 3 tablespoons plus 1 teaspoon water, the soy sauce, vinegar, and lime juice in a small bowl; set aside.

2. If using nori, heat a dry skillet over medium heat for 30 seconds. Add the nori and toast until it turns a grayish color, about 5 seconds. Turn with tongs and toast 5 seconds more. Remove from the pan and let cool. Crush with your fingers into smallish pieces.

3. Cutting straight down, cut the salmon crosswise into long, thin rectangular slices.

4. Arrange one quarter of the salmon slices, overlapping, on each of four serving plates. Drizzle each with about 1 teaspoon ponzu. Sprinkle with the crushed nori, if using, and the scallion. Sprinkle lightly with salt.

· SALMON TARTARE 101 ·
WITH HORSERADISH AND MUSTARD

SERVES 6 TO 8 AS AN HORS D'OEUVRE

This makes a great, simple party dish.

1 pound boneless, skinless salmon fillet

⅓ cup extra virgin olive oil

4 teaspoons whole-grain mustard

4 teaspoons prepared white horseradish

2 teaspoons slivered fresh tarragon

½ teaspoon sugar

Fine sea salt and freshly ground black pepper

Rye bread toast or pumpernickel bagel chips, for serving

1. Cutting straight down, cut the salmon into slices about ¼ inch thick. Cut the slices into strips ¼ inch wide. Cut the strips crosswise into ¼-inch dice.

2. Combine the salmon, oil, mustard, horseradish, tarragon, sugar, 1 teaspoon salt, and ¼ teaspoon pepper in a medium bowl. Toss gently to coat.

3. Place the tartare in the center of a serving platter and arrange toast or bagel chips around.

· STRIPED BASS TARTARE 101 ·
WITH TOMATO AND BASIL
SERVES 4 AS AN APPETIZER

This simple tartare of striped bass combines a handful of Italian flavors—black olives, tomato, pine nuts, and basil. Ask your fishmonger to remove most of the dark-colored bloodline; some is fine as long as it is bright red, not black. The taste is a little strong but that's not necessarily a bad thing. The Japanese like a little bloodline, particularly on hamachi; they appreciate its flavor, and a rosy color demonstrates that the fish is fresh.

8 ounces boneless, skinless striped bass fillet (about ½ inch thick), bloodline removed

1 medium plum tomato

2 tablespoons pine nuts

2 rounded tablespoons halved pitted black olives (preferably oil-packed such as Taggiasche)

3 tablespoons extra virgin olive oil

4 teaspoons fresh lemon juice

4 teaspoons slivered fresh basil

½ teaspoon fine sea salt

½ teaspoon red pepper flakes

1. Cutting straight down, cut the bass into slices about ¼ inch thick. Cut the slices into ¼-inch-wide strips. Cut the strips crosswise into ¼-inch dice. Place in a medium bowl.

2. Quarter the tomato lengthwise. Cut out the core and scoop out and discard the seeds. Flatten the tomato flesh with the palm of your hand. Cut each piece into slices ¼ inch wide. Cut the slices crosswise into ¼-inch dice. Add to the fish. Add the pine nuts, olives, oil, lemon juice, basil, salt, and red pepper flakes. Stir well and divide among four serving plates or bowls.

· SCALLOP CEVICHE 101 ·
WITH APPLE AND CUCUMBER

SERVES 4 AS AN APPETIZER

Here's a very easy ceviche, marinated simply in lemon and lime with a little salt for flavor. Once "cooked" in the marinade (and you'll see that the scallops will be almost entirely opaque), the scallops are drained and tossed with diced cucumber for crunch and apple for sweetness, then moistened with a little of the citrus marinade and olive oil.

8 ounces sea scallops, any size, tough white side muscles removed

Fine sea salt

¼ cup fresh lemon juice

¼ cup fresh lime juice

¼ peel-on apple, preferably Gala

2-inch section peel-on seedless cucumber

2 tablespoons plus 2 teaspoon extra virgin olive oil

4 teaspoons slivered fresh mint

2 teaspoons slivered, seeded finger chile, preferably red

Freshly ground black pepper

1. Set the scallops on edge and slice each into two equal disks. Cut each disk into ¼-inch-wide strips. Cut the strips crosswise into ¼-inch dice. Place in a medium bowl. Add ½ teaspoon salt and the lemon and lime juices. Stir well. Cover with plastic wrap and refrigerate 45 minutes.

2. Place a strainer over another medium bowl and drain the scallops; set aside the marinade and scallops separately.

3. Cut the apple quarter lengthwise into slices ¼ inch thick. Cut the slices into strips ¼ inch wide. Cut the strips crosswise into ¼-inch dice. Add to the scallops.

4. Stand the cucumber on its end on the cutting board and cut into 4 wedges. Lay each wedge on its side and slice off the core in a strip. Cut the trapezoidal wedges lengthwise into 2 thinner strips. Cut each strip crosswise into ¼-inch dice. Add to the scallops and apple.

5. Add the olive oil and 2 tablespoons of the reserved marinade; discard the remaining marinade. Add the mint and chile, ¼ teaspoon salt, and pepper to taste. Stir well. Divide among four serving plates or bowls.

KITCHEN NOTEBOOK: SEEDLESS CUCUMBERS

There's no need to peel the thin skin from seedless cucumbers. But if you substitute the regular shorter garden variety, peel them.

· SNAPPER CARPACCIO ·
WITH GUASACACA

SERVES 4 AS AN APPETIZER

Cookbook author (and my friend) Rozanne Gold introduced me to *guasacaca*, a cool green avocado sauce from Venezuela. In Venezuela, they put it on everything, the way we use ketchup. It tastes more of cilantro than avocado, but the ripe avocado gives the sauce richness and body. With a tart kick from the lime juice and vinegar, it's great with snapper. You'll have some sauce left over. Refrigerate it and serve with grilled fish or meat within 3 to 4 days.

FOR THE GUASACACA SAUCE

½ avocado, seed removed, in the skin

1 tablespoon fresh lime juice

2 tablespoons red wine vinegar

1 clove garlic, coarsely chopped (see Kitchen Notebook, opposite)

½ shallot, coarsely chopped

¾ finger chile, cut lengthwise, seeds removed, coarsely chopped

¼ cup plus 2 tablespoons firmly packed fresh cilantro leaves

¼ teaspoon fine sea salt

¼ cup extra virgin olive oil

FOR THE SNAPPER

8 ounces boneless, skinless snapper fillet

Extra virgin olive oil, for drizzling

Fine sea salt and freshly ground black pepper

1. For the sauce, use a large spoon to scoop the avocado flesh into a blender. Add the lime juice, vinegar, garlic, shallot, chile, cilantro, salt, oil, and ½ cup water. Blend until smooth. (If you have a variable-speed blender, start on low and work up to high speed.) With the blender running, drizzle in another ½ cup water until emulsified. Transfer to a container, cover, and refrigerate.

2. To serve, starting at the edge of the plate, spoon about 2 tablespoons of the sauce onto each of four serving plates, and with the back of the spoon, spread the sauce across the plate.

3. Cut the snapper on an oblique angle into pieces slightly less than ¼ inch thick (they should not be paper thin). The size of the slices will vary depending on the size and shape of the fillet.

4. On each plate, arrange one quarter of the slices next to the sauce, overlapping the slices slightly. Drizzle the fish very lightly with oil and sprinkle lightly with salt and pepper.

KITCHEN NOTEBOOK: CHOPPING GARLIC

Garlic tastes best when it's chopped with clean, precise cuts. This preserves its fresh, sweet flavor; mashing through a garlic press can cause the garlic to become strong and bitter-tasting. It's not hard: Peel the garlic and cut it into thin slices. Arrange the slices in a loose pile and cut the slices into thin strips. Then turn the cutting board 90 degrees (or I just turn my body) so that the knife is perpendicular to the strips and cut the strips crosswise into small dice. You're done.

· HAMACHI SASHIMI ·
WITH KUMQUATS AND
ORANGE-CHILE VINAIGRETTE

SERVES 4 AS AN APPETIZER

With its high oil content and velvety texture, hamachi (also called yellowtail) tastes amazing against the sharp, bright taste of kumquats. Crushed Brazil nuts and coarse Hawaiian sea salt lend contrasting crunch.

Piment d'Espelette is a variety of chile pepper grown in the Basque region of southern France. Its slightly sweet, smoky flavor accentuates the taste of the orange juice and zest in the vinaigrette. If Brazil nuts are hard to get hold of, pine nuts and macadamia nuts make a good substitute; count on about 2 teaspoons crushed nuts per serving.

FOR THE ORANGE-CHILE VINAIGRETTE

Finely grated zest of ½ orange

Juice of ½ orange (about ¼ cup)

Fine sea salt and freshly ground black pepper

¼ cup extra virgin olive oil

⅛ teaspoon piment d'Espelette, Aleppo pepper, hot paprika, or cayenne pepper

FOR THE SASHIMI

4 blanched Brazil nuts

4 kumquats

8 ounces boneless, skinless hamachi fillet, halved lengthwise (see Kitchen Notebook, opposite)

Hawaiian red sea salt or other coarse sea salt such as fleur de sel

1. For the vinaigrette, in a bowl combine the orange zest and juice, a scant ½ teaspoon salt, and a pinch of pepper. Stir in the olive oil and season with the piment d'Espelette. Set aside.

2. For the sashimi, crush the Brazil nuts one at a time with the side of a large chef's knife until coarsely crumbled. Cut the kumquats crosswise into thin rounds. Pop out and discard the seeds.

3. Set out four serving plates. Cut the fish on a shallow angle into slices slightly less than ¼ inch thick. Arrange one-quarter of the slices, overlapping slightly, in a line on each

plate. Sprinkle one-quarter of the nuts on top of each line of fish. Arrange the kumquat slices in a line on top of the nuts.

4. Stir the vinaigrette to blend and drizzle about 1 tablespoon around the fish on each plate. Drizzle a little more on top. Finish with a tiny pinch of Hawaiian sea salt, sprinkled on top of the fish.

KITCHEN NOTEBOOK: SLICING HAMACHI

Hamachi fillets are often large, wide, and thick. If so, cut the fillet in half lengthwise before slicing so that your sashimi slices are not too wide. Notice that the thinner belly half is fattier; it's normally more desirable. But hamachi is so rich that either half is delicious.

· FLUKE TARTARE ·
WITH CASHEWS, MANGO, AND COCONUT

SERVES 4 AS AN APPETIZER

Sweet, sharp mango plus coconut water infused with the Southeast Asian trio of cilantro, mint, and Thai basil complement the delicate taste of fluke. At the restaurant, we crack open young coconuts, drain the water, and scrape out the mild, gelatinous meat to use as a garnish. For home cooks, it's easier to buy the coconut water in supermarkets—a good if not perfect substitute for the fresh stuff. (I hear that the leftover herb-infused coconut water is a particularly good hangover helper.) Unsweetened dried coconut substitutes for coconut meat.

FOR THE HERB-INFUSED COCONUT WATER

1½ cups coconut water

½ sprig fresh Thai basil

½ sprig fresh mint

2 sprigs fresh cilantro

¼ red finger chile, cut lengthwise, seeds removed

⅛-inch-thick coin peel-on fresh ginger

½ teaspoon fine sea salt

FOR THE FLUKE

16 raw cashews

1 mango, ripe but still firm

8 ounces boneless, skinless fluke fillet

2 teaspoons slivered seeded finger chile

2 teaspoons firmly packed slivered fresh cilantro

1 teaspoon chopped fresh chives

¼ teaspoon minced peeled fresh ginger

2 tablespoons extra virgin olive oil

2 teaspoons fresh lime juice, plus more if needed

Fine sea salt and freshly ground black pepper

2 teaspoons dried unsweetened coconut

1. For the coconut water, combine all the ingredients in a bowl. Cover and refrigerate for several hours or overnight to infuse.

2. For the fluke, crush the cashews, one at a time, with the side of a large chef's knife until coarsely crumbled; transfer to a medium bowl.

3. Peel the mango with a paring knife. Cut the flesh off both sides of the large, flat seed. Place each half flat side down on a cutting board and slice lengthwise ¼ inch thick. Cut each slice lengthwise into ¼-inch-wide strips. Cut the strips crosswise into ¼-inch dice; you should have about ½ cup. Add the mango to the cashews.

4. Cutting straight down, cut the fluke lengthwise into strips about ¼ inch thick. Cut the strips crosswise into ¼-inch dice. Add to the cashews and mango. Add the chiles, cilantro, chives, ginger, oil, lime juice, ¼ teaspoon salt, and ⅛ teaspoon pepper. Gently stir to combine. Taste for salt, pepper, and lime and adjust if necessary.

5. To serve, divide among four shallow bowls, spooning the tartare into the center of each bowl. Sprinkle each with ½ teaspoon unsweetened coconut. Spoon about 3 tablespoons of the coconut water around each serving, leaving the herbs, chile, and ginger in the bowl.

EXTRA CREDIT: A FASHIONABLE SHAPE

At Oceana, we shape this tartare into a disk with a ring mold, as shown in the photo below. To create this presentation at home, place a 3-inch ring mold in the center of a serving bowl, loosely pack with one-quarter of the tartare, then carefully lift off the mold. Sprinkle the top with unsweetened coconut to cover. Repeat for the other three bowls.

EQUIP YOURSELF: RING MOLDS

Ring molds are available from Williams-Sonoma and at amazon.com.

· HIRAMASA TARTARE WITH PEARS ·

SERVES 4 AS AN APPETIZER

Hiramasa is a firm, oily fish related by species to hamachi, which it resembles. I think of it as "hamachi light" because while both are rich fish, hiramasa has a lighter mouthfeel. We served this tartare at the restaurant during the fall and winter with persimmons and it was such a big hit that when persimmons went out of season, we substituted pears—even easier for the home cook. Use any variety of pear that looks good.

1 pear, peeled, halved lengthwise, and stemmed

8 ounces boneless, skinless hiramasa fillet

2 teaspoons slivered seeded finger chile

2 teaspoons slivered fresh basil, preferably Thai basil

1 teaspoon thinly sliced fresh chives

1 tablespoon fresh lime juice

2 tablespoons extra virgin olive oil

Hawaiian red sea salt or other coarse sea salt such as fleur de sel

Fine sea salt and freshly ground black pepper

8 teaspoons crushed toasted pistachios (preferably Sicilian)

1. Core the pear halves with a melon baller or paring knife. Cut one of the pear halves lengthwise into ¼-inch-thick slices. Cut the slices lengthwise into ¼-inch-wide strips. Cut the strips crosswise into ¼-inch dice. Measure ¼ cup diced pear; if you need more, cut into the second half.

2. Cutting straight down, cut the hiramasa into slices about ¼ inch thick. Cut the slices into ¼-inch-wide strips. Cut the strips crosswise into ¼-inch dice.

3. Place the pear and fish in a medium bowl. Add the chiles, basil, chives, lime juice, and olive oil, a big pinch of Hawaiian sea salt, and sea salt and black pepper to taste.

4. Divide the tartare among four serving plates or shallow bowls. Sprinkle each with about 2 teaspoons of the crushed pistachios.

EXTRA CREDIT: FUYU AND HACHIYA PERSIMMONS

If you want to try this with persimmons, use the Fuyu variety, which is flatter than the heart-shaped Hachiya. Fuyu persimmons can be eaten firm—not rock hard, but firm—and you do want a little texture in this dish. The Hachiya variety, on the other hand, must be consumed completely ripened, by which point the flesh will have turned almost to purée and be impossible to dice. Persimmon skin is edible but astringent: Cut off the top leaves in a cone shape. Set the persimmon on the stem end and cut the skin off the persimmon the way you cut the pith off a lemon before segmenting (see Scallop Crudo 101 with Lemon and Parsley, page 35). Then dice the flesh just like you would dice the pear.

· HALIBUT CEVICHE ·
WITH COCONUT, LIME, AND MINT

SERVES 4 AS AN APPETIZER

Coconut, lime, and mint evoke a Thai flavor palette in this ceviche. It's mild and a bit sweet; the flavors and textures play off each other without overpowering the delicate taste of the fish. The natural sweetness and richness of the coconut is countered with the acidity of the lime. Mint adds a floral note and brightens the coconut. And the lean halibut welcomes the velvety avocado.

8 ounces boneless, skinless halibut fillet

Juice of 3 limes (about ½ cup)

½ cup unsweetened coconut milk

1 Hass avocado, halved, pit removed, peeled, cut into ¼-inch dice

½ red bell pepper, cored, stem, seeds, and ribs removed, cut into ¼-inch dice

1 tablespoon extra virgin olive oil

1 tablespoon slivered seeded finger chile

Leaves from 1 sprig fresh mint (about 10 leaves), torn

1 teaspoon fine sea salt

4 teaspoons unsweetened dried coconut

1. Cutting straight down, cut the halibut into slices about ¼ inch thick. Cut the slices into ¼-inch-wide strips. Cut the strips crosswise into ¼-inch dice. Place the fish in a medium bowl.

2. Add the lime juice and stir. Cover with plastic, and refrigerate for 35 minutes.

3. Drain the fish and discard the juice. Return the fish to the bowl. Add the coconut milk, avocado, bell pepper, olive oil, chile, mint, and salt. Toss to combine.

4. To serve, divide among four shallow serving bowls or plates. Sprinkle 1 teaspoon of the coconut over the top of each.

· GRAVLAX WITH MUSTARDY ·
CELERY ROOT SALAD
SERVES 4 TO 6 AS AN APPETIZER

Gravlax is a Swedish method of curing fish by packing it in a mixture of salt, sugar, and dill. The salt and sugar draw out the moisture, so that the texture is slightly firmer than the raw fish, but because of salmon's high fat content is just as silky. My version adds a drizzle of gin to infuse with a light juniper taste. (I like the complexity of Tanqueray No. 10, if you can get it.) I thinly slice the fish on a long bias and serve it with a celery root salad. But it's also scrumptious on crackers as an hors d'oeuvre, in which case it's better sliced straight down for smaller bite-size pieces that'll fit the crackers (this way, the recipe will serve 8 to 12). Once you've cut into it, eat the gravlax within a day or two.

Before curing, make sure you or your fishmonger removes the pin bones, the small, flexible bones that run the length of the fillet (see page 379).

FOR THE GRAVLAX

1½ cups kosher salt

¾ cup sugar

1½ pounds boneless, skin-on salmon fillet (cut from the wide end, closer to the head; 1¼ to 1½ inches thick)

2 tablespoons gin

2 teaspoons coarsely ground black pepper

4 large sprigs fresh dill, plus picked dill (just the soft, feathery leaves) for serving

FOR THE CELERY ROOT SALAD

6 tablespoons crème fraîche

1 tablespoon whole-grain mustard

1½ tablespoons extra virgin olive oil

1½ teaspoons sugar

½ teaspoon fine sea salt

4 teaspoons picked (just the soft, feathery leaves) fresh dill

½ large celery root

1. For the gravlax, in a medium bowl, stir together the salt and sugar.

2. Place the salmon on a plate and drizzle both sides with the gin. Sprinkle each side with 1 teaspoon of the pepper.

3. Open a 1-gallon resealable plastic bag. Hold the top of the bag in one hand, allowing the bottom edge to rest on the counter. Press down the inside of the bag with your other hand to make as flat a bottom as possible. Dump about half of the salt-sugar mixture into

recipe continued on next page

the bag, spreading it out to a layer about the size of the fillet. Place 4 of the dill sprigs on top. Set the fish on top and arrange the remaining 4 dill sprigs on top. Cover with the remaining salt-sugar mixture.

4. Press the air out of the bag and seal. Poke several small holes in the bag to allow the liquid to drain. Place on a cooling rack over a plate or in a baking dish and refrigerate for 48 hours, turning the bag over every 12 hours for even curing.

5. Remove the salmon from the cure and rinse under cold running water. Pat dry with paper towels. Air-dry on a cooling rack in the refrigerator overnight.

6. Wrap in plastic and refrigerate until you're ready to serve.

7. For the celery root salad, in a medium bowl, stir together the crème fraîche and mustard. Gradually stir in the olive oil, then the sugar and salt. Stir in the dill; set aside.

8. Cut the brown skin off the celery root. Cut the celery root piece in half. Cut each piece into slices ⅛ inch thick, preferably on a Japanese mandoline. Cut the slices into ⅛-inch-wide strips. (Or grate the celery root on the large holes of a box grater.) Add to the dressing and toss to coat.

9. To serve, cut the gravlax on an angle into very thin slices, cutting the fish off the skin. Divide among serving plates or arrange overlapping slices on a platter and garnish with picked dill. Serve with the celery root salad.

EXTRA CREDIT: GRAVLAX FOR A CROWD

Gravlax makes a killer party dish. It's beautiful, impressive, and delicious—but practical, too, because it can be made ahead of time. And it's no harder to make in large quantities.

To double the recipe above, ask your fishmonger for two 1½-pound sections, cut from the wider (head) end of two salmon fillets of fairly equal size. Double the quantities for the cure and the gin; you can go with 12 sprigs of dill. Spread one third of the cure over the bottom of a 1½-gallon resealable bag. Lay 4 sprigs of dill on top. Lay one piece of salmon, skin side down, on top of the dill. Top the salmon with 4 more dill sprigs and another third of the cure. Top with the second fillet, flesh side down. Top that with the remaining 4 dill sprigs and the rest of the cure. Seal. Poke several holes in the top and bottom of the bag (for drainage). Place on a cooling rack in a baking dish and refrigerate for 48 hours, flipping the bag every 12 hours.

Here are three traditional Japanese techniques for lightly curing fish. I was introduced to them in a Japanese cooking class that I attended with two dozen of New York City's top chefs. I've gone on to serve the dishes in the restaurant, where they have become real crowd pleasers. I'm sure you'll like them, too. If you're not familiar with Japanese cuisine, don't be put off by some of the ingredients (you'll find sources for everything you need in the Guide to Unusual Ingredients starting on page 395). Although I learned these recipes in a professional context, all three are simple enough to make at home. You can serve them individually with a spoonful of store-bought seaweed salad or some edamame, or plate all three together for a sensational starter.

Kombu-Cured Fluke   Tuna Zuke

· KOMBU-CURED FLUKE ·

SERVES 4 AS AN APPETIZER

You may know kombu as the base of the classic Japanese broth dashi. A nutritious variety of dried seaweed, full of minerals and salt, it comes in large sheets. In this preparation, the salt in the kombu cures the fluke (pictured on page 54, left), contributing a mild, briny, almost nutty flavor without making the fish taste at all salty. It also firms the fish to a pleasantly chewy texture. If you can't find fluke, any thin flatfish fillets—flounder, gray sole, plaice, or turbot—will substitute nicely.

2 sheets dashi kombu (dried seaweed)

Four 2-ounce boneless, skinless fluke fillets

Store-bought seaweed salad or edamame in the pod, for serving

1. Run 1 sheet of seaweed under cold running water for 2 to 3 seconds, until pliable. Pat dry on paper towels and place on a cutting board. Arrange 1 fillet crosswise about 3 inches from the bottom edge of the seaweed. Fold the bottom edge up over the fillet to completely cover it; adjust the placement of the fillet as needed. Place a second fillet on top so that the fillets are stacked one on top of the other with seaweed in between. Now roll the package over and away from you so that both fillets are enclosed in seaweed. Set aside. Repeat to enclose the remaining 2 fillets in the second sheet of seaweed.

2. Place the seaweed packages on a plate or in a baking dish. Cover with plastic wrap and refrigerate for 24 hours.

3. To serve, carefully unroll the packages. The seaweed will stick a little; be careful not to tear the fillets. Place 1 fillet on the cutting board with the wide (head) end of the fillet to one side. Starting at the head end of the fillet, with a sharp knife cut the fish into thin slices at a 45 degree angle. Discard the skinny end of the fillet.

4. Arrange the slices, overlapping, on a serving plate. Slice the remaining 3 fillets, arranging each on a serving plate. Arrange a neat pile of seaweed salad or edamame next to the fish on each plate.

· TUNA ZUKE ·

SERVES 4 AS AN APPETIZER

For this traditional cure, tuna is scalded in boiling water, then marinated briefly in a mixture of soy sauce, mirin, and sake. The scalding firms the surface of the fish slightly, creating a barrier that allows the marinade to penetrate just the edge of the flesh. This process contributes a mild soy flavor that doesn't eclipse the delicate taste of the tuna. Once marinated, the tuna (pictured on page 54, right) may be served immediately or wrapped in plastic wrap and refrigerated overnight.

1 cup soy sauce

⅓ cup mirin

⅓ cup sake

8 ounces tuna steak (about 1 inch thick)

Store-bought seaweed salad or cooked
edamame in the pod, for serving

1. In a container slightly larger than the tuna steak, combine the soy sauce, mirin, and sake; refrigerate until chilled.

2. Bring 1 quart water to a boil in a medium saucepan. Prepare an ice bath by filling a large bowl with ice and cold water; set aside. Set the chilled soy mixture on the counter.

3. Place the tuna in a colander in the sink and cover with a doubled piece of paper towel. Pour about half of the boiling water over the tuna. Fold back the paper towel, flip the fish, and then re-cover the fish with the towel. Pour the rest of the boiling water over the fish.

4. Remove the paper towel and plunge the tuna immediately into the ice bath to stop the cooking. Let stand 1 minute. Remove the tuna from the ice bath and pat dry with fresh paper towels. Place the fish in the chilled soy mixture to cover; if the liquid doesn't cover the fish, use a different container. Cover and refrigerate 45 minutes.

5. Drain the tuna. Cutting straight down, cut the tuna into slices about ¼ inch thick. Divide the slices among four serving plates, overlapping them slightly. Place a neat mound of seaweed salad or edamame next to the fish on each plate.

• MACKEREL SUJIME •

SERVES 4 TO 6 AS AN APPETIZER

If you think mackerel is too strong for your taste, this recipe is for you. The traditional Japanese cure of sugar, salt, rice vinegar, and sake softens the mackerel's "fishy" taste so you end up with a mild, buttery flavor that I think will surprise you.

The pin bones are removed from the fillet after curing (see page 379); pulling out the bones opens the flesh and would allow the vinegary marinade to penetrate too deeply.

1 cup plus 2 tablespoons rice vinegar

2 tablespoons sake

One 8- to 10-ounce skin-on mackerel fillet with pin bones

1 teaspoon sugar

1 teaspoon fine sea salt

Store-bought seaweed salad or cooked edamame in the pod, for serving

1. In a medium bowl, combine the vinegar and sake; refrigerate.

2. Place a cooling rack on a rimmed baking sheet and place the mackerel fillet on the rack, skin side down. Stir together the sugar and salt in a small bowl. Sprinkle the fillet evenly with about half of the sugar-salt mixture. Turn the fillet skin side up and sprinkle evenly with the remaining mixture. Turn the fillet skin side down again. Cover with plastic wrap and refrigerate for 45 minutes.

3. Rinse the mackerel under cold running water. Place it skin side down directly in a baking dish just large enough to hold it. Pour the chilled vinegar marinade over to cover. Cover again with the plastic wrap and refrigerate for 45 minutes.

4. Remove the mackerel from the vinegar marinade and pat dry. Run your fingers down the center of the fillet from the head end to feel the pin bones. Pull the bones out with tweezers.

5. To serve, place the fillet on a cutting board, skin side down, with the wide (head) end of the fillet to one side. Starting at the head end, with a sharp knife cut the fillet with the skin at a 45 degree angle into thin slices; discard the skinny ends of the fillet. (If you're not ready to serve, wrap the mackerel in plastic wrap; serve within 48 hours.)

6. Arrange overlapping slices of mackerel on serving plates, with a neat pile of seaweed salad beside them.

3.

APPETIZERS, SALADS, PASTA, AND RICE

Here's a chapter of seafood hors d'oeuvres, appetizers, salads, and light meals. I know that most people aren't serving hors d'oeuvres and appetizers on an everyday basis. But every now and then, an opening nibble is in order when you want to put on a show with a special celebration meal.

To begin, I've given you a recipe for the ultimate seafood spread: a Raw Bar (opposite) featuring raw clams and oysters, cooked mussels and lobster, and shrimp cocktail, poached the professional way in court bouillon (a wine and vegetable broth). If you choose to serve it with the three different sauces we offer at Oceana, it's pretty much guaranteed to blow away your guests. Asparagus Tonnato 101 with Frisée Lettuce and Pistachios (page 66) is a play on the traditional cold Italian dish of veal with tuna sauce called *vitello tonnato*. And Oysters Rockefeller (page 68) is still a classic for a reason—it's delicious.

Salmon and shrimp salads (pages 70 and 73) make nice, light summer meals

and delicious appetizers in half portions. The same goes for three simple pastas: Spaghetti 101 with Flaked Cod, Arugula, and Golden Raisins (page 76), Rigatoni with Clams, Zucchini, Preserved Lemon, and Basil (page 78), and Orecchiette 101 with Shrimp, Rosemary, and Green Olives (page 80). All are quick and easy enough for weeknight dining but sophisticated enough in a simple, rustic Italian way to serve to guests. And the Korean-style rice flour pancake Paejun (page 91), while not exactly light, tastes great any time day or night.

Extra Credit tips elevate the dishes from excellent to exceptional. Make my Sicilian-inspired Risotto with King Crab, Pistachios, and Blood Orange (page 88) with store-bought chicken stock when you want something stylish that doesn't require a lot of time in the kitchen; replace the chicken stock with a homemade blue crab stock when your schedule allows you the latitude to play around. Cristina's Spanish Chicken, Shrimp, and Rice (page 85) is dynamite with store-bought chicken stock but homemade stock tastes even better. Pollinger Tuna Noodle Casserole (page 83) redefines the classic with home-poached tuna and a homemade mushroom sauce. There are no shortcuts there; it's made from scratch all the way, and worth it.

· RAW BAR ·

SERVES 4 GENEROUSLY AS AN APPETIZER
OR 8 AS AN HORS D'OEUVRE

This is a real special occasion dish. Add a salad, and it's substantial enough for a light meal. At the restaurant, we serve this on a seafood tower. If you have a two- or three-tiered serving stand (sometimes called an *étagère*), use that, mixing up the seafood among the layers. Otherwise divide the seafood among a couple of large platters; put the lobster front and center, where you can show it off. King crab legs make a nice addition; cut the shells open with kitchen scissors so your guests can get at the meat. A bed of seaweed will keep the clams and oysters level so you don't lose the juices. Your fishmonger should be able to get some for you, with a little notice.

Two 1¼-pound live lobsters

½ cup dry white wine

1 pound mussels, rinsed, beards removed if necessary

8 littleneck clams, scrubbed

8 oysters, scrubbed

½ recipe Shrimp Cocktail (page 64), chilled, or store-bought cocktail sauce

Piquillo Pepper Aioli (page 244; optional)

Curry Leaf Vinaigrette (page 224; optional)

Lemon wedges, for serving

Seaweed, for serving

Shaved iced (see Extra Credit, page 65; optional), for serving

1. For the lobsters, prepare an ice bath by filling your sink with ice and cold water. Bring about 6 quarts water to a boil in a large pot. Add the lobsters to the water and boil for 7 minutes.

2. With tongs, remove the lobsters from the pot and place in the ice bath to stop the cooking and chill them. Twist off the claws and knuckles, remove the rubber bands, and remove the meat from the shells (see page 392); discard the shells. Twist the tails from

recipe continued on next page

the heads; discard the heads or save them to make Lobster Broth (page 329). Cut the tails (still in the shells) in half lengthwise with a large heavy knife. Remove the meat, reserving the shells. Remove the vein that runs the length of the tail and return each tail half to its halved shell. Cover and refrigerate the claw and knuckle meat, and the tail meat in the tail shells.

3. For the mussels, bring the wine to a boil in a large saucepan over high heat. Add the mussels and give them a stir. Cover and cook, stirring every minute for even cooking, until the mussels open, 2 to 3 minutes. If the pan looks dry, add a little water. Place a colander in a large bowl and drain the mussels, holding back the last of the liquid in case of grit.

Save the cooking liquid, if you like (see Extra Credit, below). Chill the mussels in their shells for at least 1 hour.

4. Line a multitiered serving stand or two platters with seaweed and shaved ice, if you like. Remove the lobster tail meat from the shells and cut crosswise into bite-size pieces. Reconstruct the pieces, colored side up for presentation, in opposing tail halves. (Because you're turning the pieces over, they'll fit perfectly in the shells this way.) Arrange the lobster on the serving stand.

5. Open the oysters and clams (see pages 387 and 388), being careful not to lose the juices. Arrange on the serving stand along with the chilled mussels and shrimp.

6. Serve with lemon wedges, cocktail sauce, and either or both of the other two sauces, if you choose.

EXTRA CREDIT: MUSSEL COOKING LIQUID
Boil the mussel cooking liquid to reduce it by half, chill, and add to the vinaigrette and aioli for extra flavor.

· SHRIMP COCKTAIL ·

SERVES 4 AS AN APPETIZER

Making shrimp cocktail can be as easy as putting shrimp into boiling water, draining, and chilling. But if you want the shrimp to taste really great, it's worth the effort to poach them in a court bouillon, a briefly cooked white wine–vegetable broth. The cooked shrimp cool completely in the court bouillon, which adds flavor and keeps the shrimp moist. Serve the shrimp simply with a store-bought cocktail sauce, or give your guests a choice of sauces as we do in the restaurant: cocktail sauce, a curry leaf vinaigrette, and a rich-flavored, brick-red piquillo aioli.

If you can find them, here's a place to go all-out with very large shrimp sold as U15, meaning fewer than 15 shrimp to the pound. If not, 16–20 shrimp, meaning 16 to 20 to the pound, will taste just fine.

FOR THE CLASSIC COURT BOUILLON

½ onion, sliced ¼ inch thick

½ carrot, sliced ¼ inch thick

½ stalk celery, sliced ¼ inch thick

¼ bulb fennel, trimmed and sliced ¼ inch thick

2 cloves garlic, halved lengthwise

¼ lemon

1 sprig fresh thyme

1 sprig fresh Italian parsley

1 bay leaf

¼ teaspoon whole black peppercorns

¼ teaspoon coriander seeds

¼ teaspoon mustard seeds

¼ teaspoon fennel seeds

1 whole clove

1 allspice berry

½ small, dried red chile, such as a Thai or cayenne chile

2 cups dry white wine

4 teaspoons fine sea salt

FOR THE SHRIMP COCKTAIL

1 pound very large (U15) or large (16–20) shrimp, shelled, tails on, deveined (see page 385)

Store-bought cocktail sauce, for serving

Seaweed, for serving

Shaved iced (see Extra Credit, opposite; optional), for serving

Piquillo Pepper Aioli (page 244; optional)

Curry Leaf Vinaigrette (page 224; optional)

1. For the court bouillon, combine the onion, carrot, celery, fennel, garlic, lemon, thyme, parsley, bay leaf, peppercorns, coriander, mustard and fennel seeds, clove, allspice, and chile in an 8-quart pot. Add 3 quarts water, the wine, and salt. Bring to a boil, reduce the heat and simmer, uncovered, 20 minutes.

2. Prepare an ice bath by filling your sink with ice and cold water. Fill a quart container with more ice.

3. Add the shrimp to the simmering court bouillon. Return to a simmer and cook until the shrimp are firm and cooked through, about 45 seconds for large shrimp, about 40 seconds for medium. Remove from the heat and add 1 quart ice to the pot to cool down the court bouillon. Put the pot into the ice bath and let the shrimp cool in the court bouillon for at least 1 hour.

4. Remove the cooled shrimp from the liquid and refrigerate until you're ready to serve. Discard the court bouillon.

5. To serve, cover the bottom of a large, deep serving platter with seaweed. Arrange the shrimp on top. Spoon the sauce(s) into ramekins and serve with the shrimp.

EXTRA CREDIT: SHAVED ICE

At Oceana, shrimp cocktail and the raw bar are served on a bed of shaved ice. To make it at home, fill your blender or food processor no more than half full with ice cubes. Pulse to chop the ice into small bits, stopping once or twice to remove the processor bowl or blender from the motor, and shake to evenly distribute the cubes. To serve, cover the serving platter with a layer of paper towels to prevent the ice from sliding. Cover the towels with ice, and cover the ice with a layer of seaweed. Arrange the shrimp on top.

· ASPARAGUS TONNATO 101 ·
WITH FRISÉE LETTUCE
AND PISTACHIOS

SERVES 4 AS AN APPETIZER

It turns out that asparagus tastes great with the classic Italian tuna-flavored sauce that's traditionally served with cold sliced veal. The mayonnaise-like sauce is typically made with canned tuna, but I like the clean flavor that fresh tuna delivers. It's difficult to make the sauce in a smaller batch, so you'll have leftovers. Refrigerate and use within 3 days on sandwiches or as a cold sauce on any grilled, poached, or steamed fish.

FOR THE TONNATO SAUCE

5 ounces tuna steak, cut into 1-inch cubes

Fine sea salt and freshly ground black pepper

1 tablespoon capers (preferably salted, not brined), soaked at least 2 hours or overnight, drained, and rinsed

¼ cup red wine vinegar

1 large egg (see Kitchen Notebook, page 22)

½ cup extra virgin olive oil

½ cup canola oil

FOR THE ASPARAGUS

1 pound medium asparagus, woody ends snapped off

1 cup firmly packed frisée lettuce

4 teaspoons Sherry Vinaigrette (page 19)

Fine sea salt and freshly ground black pepper

4 teaspoons crushed pistachios (see Kitchen Notebook, opposite)

1. For the sauce, on a plate, sprinkle the tuna on both sides with salt and pepper and let stand 5 minutes to allow the seasonings to penetrate.

2. Bring 2 cups water to a boil with 1 teaspoon salt in a 2-quart pot. Add the tuna, return to a boil, then reduce the heat so that the water simmers. Simmer the tuna until just cooked through, about 3 minutes. Remove to a bowl with a slotted spoon or spatula. Measure ¼ cup of the poaching liquid and pour over the tuna; discard the rest. Set aside the tuna in the poaching liquid to cool to room temperature.

3. Combine the cooled tuna, reserved poaching liquid, capers, and vinegar in a blender. Pulse on low speed until almost smooth. Add the egg and blend until smooth. With the blender running on medium-high or high speed, drizzle in the oils in a thin stream to

emulsify. Season to taste with salt and pepper. Transfer to a container, cover, and refrigerate until you're ready to serve.

4. For the asparagus, line a baking dish with paper towels. Bring about 1 inch water to a simmer in the bottom of a steamer pot. Place the asparagus in a steamer basket over the simmering water, cover, and steam until the asparagus is tender, about 15 minutes. Transfer the asparagus to the paper towel–lined baking dish to cool to room temperature.

5. To serve, toss the frisée in a bowl with 2 teaspoons of the vinaigrette. Season with salt and pepper. Remove the paper towels from the baking dish and drizzle the asparagus with the remaining 2 teaspoons vinaigrette; season with salt and pepper.

6. Place a mound of dressed frisée on each of four serving plates. Spoon 2 to 3 tablespoons of the tonnato sauce next to each salad. Arrange one quarter of the asparagus on each plate, placing it on top of the sauce so that the tips balance on top of the lettuce. Scatter 1 teaspoon pistachios over each serving.

KITCHEN NOTEBOOK: CRUSHED PISTACHIOS

To crush pistachios and other nuts, put the nuts in a resealable bag and roll over with a rolling pin.

· OYSTERS ROCKEFELLER ·

SERVES 4 TO 6 AS AN HORS D'OEUVRE, DEPENDING ON WHAT ELSE YOU'RE SERVING

Oysters Rockefeller, created at Antoine's restaurant in New Orleans, is one of those dishes that has been reinterpreted and copied with much controversy. I don't make any claim that mine is an accurate representation of the original—it's simply inspired by it. More important, it's delicious.

I prefer East Coast oysters for this dish because they're a little firmer and brinier than other varieties. The topping is flavored with Pernod, an anise-flavored liqueur, and hot sauce, so you feel the heat a little. If you like it less spicy, cut the hot sauce by ¼ teaspoon. Or cut it entirely and substitute an equal amount of lemon juice or white vinegar for the required acidity. You'll need seaweed or rock salt to steady the oysters during cooking. With a little notice, your fishmonger should be able to hook you up with seaweed.

2 tablespoons unsalted butter

1 scallion (white and green parts), sliced into thin rounds

1 medium stalk celery, thinly sliced

2 cups gently packed rinsed, dried watercress, heavy stems trimmed (about 1½ ounces)

6 cups gently packed rinsed, dried, stemmed spinach (5 ounces)

12 medium-to-large (2½- to 3-inch) oysters (preferably East Coast), scrubbed

2 tablespoons sour cream

1 tablespoon dried breadcrumbs (preferably panko)

1 tablespoon Pernod or other anise-flavored liqueur such as Ricard

¾ teaspoons Homemade Hot Sauce (page 17) or store-bought hot sauce

¼ teaspoon fine sea salt

Rock salt or seaweed

1. Melt the butter in a 12-inch skillet or straight-sided sauté pan over medium heat. Add the scallion and celery and cook without coloring, stirring often, for 1½ minutes. Add the watercress and cook, stirring often, 30 seconds. Turn the heat to high. Add the spinach. Cook, stirring often, until the spinach has wilted, about 1 minute. Spread the greens on a wide plate or shallow bowl and let cool to room temperature, about 5 minutes.

2. Meanwhile, preheat the oven to 400°F. Line a baking sheet with a thin layer of rock salt or seaweed. Open the oysters (see page 387), leaving them on the half shell. Arrange them on the baking sheet in a single layer as you open them.

3. Place the cooled, cooked greens on a cutting board and chop well or pulse in a food processor until well chopped. Place in a medium bowl. Add the sour cream, breadcrumbs, anise liqueur, hot sauce, and salt and mix well. Divide the topping among the oysters.

4. Bake the oysters for 6 minutes, until warmed through but not cooked.

5. Adjust a rack about 4 inches below the broiler element. Turn the broiler to high. Broil the oysters until the topping browns very slightly, about 1 minute. Set a trivet on the table or wherever you're planning on serving and place the hot baking sheet on the trivet. Allow the oysters to cool for a few minutes, then dig in.

· SALMON SALAD 101 ·
WITH SPINACH, DILL,
AND MUSTARD VINAIGRETTE

SERVES 4 AS A LIGHT ENTRÉE

This salad is inspired by the unbeatable Scandinavian flavor combination of salmon, fresh dill, and mustard. It's about as easy as it gets.

FOR THE VINAIGRETTE

3 tablespoons red wine vinegar

½ cup plus 1 tablespoon extra virgin olive oil

1 tablespoon Dijon mustard

Fine sea salt and freshly ground black pepper

FOR THE SALMON SALAD

Four 5- to 6-ounce boneless, skinless salmon fillets (about 1 inch thick)

4 teaspoons extra virgin olive oil

12 ounces white mushrooms (about 28 medium), wiped clean, stem ends trimmed

12 ounces stemmed spinach, rinsed and dried (two 5-ounce bags, or one 11-ounce container)

½ cup loosely packed picked (just the soft, feathery leaves) fresh dill

1. For the vinaigrette, combine the vinegar, olive oil, mustard, ⅜ teaspoon salt and ⅜ teaspoon pepper in a small bowl and whisk with a fork to emulsify; set aside.

2. For the salmon, preheat the oven to 350°F. Line a baking sheet with foil. On the baking sheet, sprinkle the fillets on both sides with salt and pepper and let stand 5 minutes to allow the seasonings to penetrate.

3. Coat the fillets on both sides with about 1 teaspoon oil each. Bake the salmon until medium-rare and just translucent in the center, 13 to 15 minutes. Let cool to room temperature, then refrigerate if not using immediately.

4. Cut a thin slice off the top of each mushroom cap to stabilize it. Set the mushrooms, cut side down on the cutting board and cut into ¼-inch-thick slices.

5. In a large bowl, combine the spinach, sliced mushrooms, and dill. Give the vinaigrette a stir with a fork to re-emulsify it and add to the bowl (see Kitchen Notebook, page 249). Break the salmon into pieces and add to the bowl. Season with a pinch more salt and

pepper. With fingers splayed as if you had two spatulas on the ends of your arms, toss the salad very gently until everything is lightly coated with vinaigrette.

6. Divide among four shallow serving bowls or deep serving plates.

KITCHEN NOTEBOOK: LET'S GO STEADY

When slicing round vegetables such as mushroom caps, carrots, and potatoes, stabilize them by cutting off a thin slice first. Rest the vegetable on the flat side and slice.

· GRILLED SHRIMP SALAD ·
WITH HEARTS OF PALM, CASHEWS,
AND HONEY-BASIL VINAIGRETTE

SERVES 4 AS AN ENTRÉE

This is a nice summer dish for when you don't want to spend time in the kitchen. The dressing is a little sweet and sour, and the Thai basil will give it a bit of an Asian flavor. (You'll have some left over for your next salad; cover and refrigerate for up to 3 days.) Hearts of palm (see page 399 for sources), the edible inner core of a palm tree, add some crunch and the natural sweetness of raw cashew—very different than the flavor of roasted cashews—pairs well with the rest of the ingredients. Leave the seeds in the chiles if you like a little kick. Farmed shrimp are a great product and available all over, but if you can get hold of them, I recommend wild-caught Gulf shrimp for their incredible flavor.

FOR THE HONEY-BASIL VINAIGRETTE

½ cup plus 2 tablespoons canola or grapeseed oil

¼ cup plus 2 tablespoons extra virgin olive oil

1 tablespoon slivered seeded finger chile

½ cup fresh lime juice (from about 4 limes)

2 tablespoons rice vinegar

¼ cup honey

Fine sea salt and freshly ground black pepper

½ cup gently packed Thai basil or basil leaves

FOR THE SHRIMP SALAD

1 pound large (16–20) shrimp, shelled, tails removed, deveined (see page 385)

Fine sea salt and freshly ground black pepper

2 tablespoons extra virgin olive oil

Vegetable oil, for the grill grates

1 pound mixed baby lettuces (6 quarts not packed)

1 cup sliced fresh hearts of palm (⅛-inch-thick slices, from about two 5-inch pieces)

5 large radishes, trimmed, sliced very thin on a Japanese mandoline (about 2 cups)

1 cup unsalted, raw cashews

1. For the dressing, chill the canola (or grapeseed) and olive oils for 20 to 30 minutes, if possible; this will prevent the bright green color of the basil from darkening.

2. Combine the chile, lime juice, vinegar, honey, 1 teaspoon salt, and a pinch of black pepper in a blender and process until blended. (If you have a variable-speed blender, use

recipe continued on next page

medium-high or high speed.) With the blender running, gradually add the oils in a thin stream to emulsify. Add the basil and purée (on high, if using a variable-speed blender) until smooth, about 30 seconds; transfer to a container and set aside.

3. For the shrimp, preheat a gas grill to high. Scrub the grill grates with a grill brush.

4. Put the shrimp in a bowl and season lightly with salt and pepper. Add the olive oil and toss to coat evenly. Oil the grill grates. Place the shrimp on the grill so they won't fall through the grates and grill until cooked about halfway, 1½ minutes. Flip with tongs and grill until just firm, pink, and cooked through, about 1½ minutes longer.

5. With the tongs, remove the shrimp to a large bowl. Let cool for a few minutes to room temperature.

6. Add the lettuces, hearts of palm, radishes, cashews, 1 cup of the vinaigrette (see Kitchen Notebook, page 249), ½ teaspoon salt, and a pinch of pepper. Toss to coat.

7. Divide among four deep serving plates or shallow serving bowls, making sure that each serving gets an equal number of shrimp.

KITCHEN NOTEBOOK: HEARTS OF PALM

When I need hearts of palm for the restaurant, I order them from a supplier in Hawaii who simply goes out and cuts down a palm tree for me. She strips the outside bark down to the heart and ships it to me in a couple of pieces. I may need to trim some of the woody exterior around the thick bottom end, but I'm basically dealing with the whole tree. You won't need to do even that much to prepare the vegetable for this salad.

• SMOKED SALMON SANDWICHES 101 •

SERVES 4 AS A HEARTY SNACK

When I worked the day shift at La Côte Basque under Jean-Jacques Rachou, we made our own smoked salmon. The fish was cured with salt and sugar for a day or two, then cold smoked. The salmon was served as an appetizer, thin slices completely covering the plate, topped with a garnish. The chef in charge of slicing the salmon was amazing—because he'd been doing it forever, he could cut slices that were practically as long as the whole side of fish.

Salmon trimmings were saved in a container in the fridge to use in other dishes. Those of us on the morning crew would get in a few minutes early and sit on the kitchen counter drinking our coffee before the shift. And we'd make these incredible smoked salmon sandwiches. We'd rip the day-old mini walnut-raisin loaves in half (one of the restaurant's bread selections from Tom Cat Bakery), slather them with Dijon mustard, and pack on so much salmon that the sandwiches barely fit in our mouths. We were eating the best breakfast of anyone in New York City. The sous chef would yell at us from time to time when the chef gave him a hard time, wanting to know where all that smoked salmon trim was going.

Whether you're enjoying breakfast, lunch, or a snack, these simple sandwiches are the best.

8 slices good-quality walnut-raisin bread

Dijon mustard

1 pound thinly sliced smoked salmon

Toast the bread. Slather four slices with mustard and pile with salmon. Top with the remaining toast.

· SPAGHETTI 101 ·
WITH FLAKED COD, ARUGULA,
AND GOLDEN RAISINS

SERVES 4 AS AN ENTRÉE

This is the epitome of simple Italian cooking, which means that the result far exceeds the plainness of the everyday ingredients. In addition to the pasta, there are really just three things going on here—cod, raisins, and arugula—with a few herbs and aromatics plus breadcrumbs for texture. If you have a choice, there's no need to spend the money for thick cod fillets; this works just as well with thinner tail sections, which are likely to be less expensive.

Two 8-ounce boneless, skinless cod fillets

Fine sea salt and freshly ground black pepper

3 tablespoons extra virgin olive oil, plus extra for serving

½ cup firmly packed golden raisins

1 pound spaghetti

2 cloves garlic, chopped

¼ teaspoon red pepper flakes

2 cups gently packed arugula

Juice of 1 lemon

¼ cup gently packed slivered fresh basil

4 heaping teaspoons toasted breadcrumbs

1. Bring a large pot of water to a boil for the pasta. Set a colander in the sink to drain it.

2. On a plate, season the cod on both sides with salt and pepper. Let stand 5 minutes to allow the seasonings to penetrate.

3. Place a skillet (with a lid) large enough to hold the cod in a single layer over medium heat. Add 2 tablespoons of the oil and heat until fluid enough to coat the bottom of the pan when swirled. Add the cod, ¾ cup water, and the raisins. Bring to a boil, reduce the heat, cover, and simmer until the cod is cooked through, about 5 minutes for thick fillets, 3 to 4 minutes for skinny tail ends. With a slotted spoon or spatula, remove the cod to a plate to cool to room temperature. Set aside the poaching liquid with the raisins in a container. Wipe out the skillet with paper towels.

4. When the cod is cool enough to handle, flake it into large pieces.

5. When the pasta water boils, add enough salt to make it taste like seawater. Add the spaghetti and cook until al dente, about 8 minutes.

6. When the spaghetti is just about cooked (6 to 7 minutes in), place the skillet over medium heat. Add the remaining 1 tablespoon oil and heat until fluid enough to coat the bottom of the skillet when swirled. Add the garlic and red pepper flakes and cook, stirring constantly, until the garlic is aromatic and just beginning to turn golden, about 1 minute. Add the cod poaching liquid and raisins.

7. Drain the spaghetti in the colander, saving 1 cup of the cooking water. Return the spaghetti and cooking water to the pasta pot. Add the contents of the skillet. Bring to a boil and cook 1 minute. Add the arugula and toss to wilt. Season to taste with salt and pepper. Add the lemon juice, basil, and the flaked cod and toss gently.

8. Divide among four deep serving plates or shallow serving bowls. Sprinkle each with a heaping teaspoon of breadcrumbs and drizzle with olive oil.

· RIGATONI WITH CLAMS, ZUCCHINI, · PRESERVED LEMON, AND BASIL

SERVES 4 AS AN ENTRÉE

Sautéed zucchini and slivers of preserved lemon dress up this Italian classic. You want to time the clams to be open by the time the rigatoni is about halfway cooked so that the clams go immediately into the pot with the pasta. That way, it continues to cook while it soaks up the flavorful white wine-clam broth. The pasta initially cooks for only about 8 minutes. Get all your ingredients next to the stove, ready to go before you drop the pasta into the boiling water.

2 quarters Preserved Lemons (page 25), pulp scraped out and discarded, rinds rinsed well or soaked overnight in the refrigerator with water to cover

Fine sea salt

1 pound rigatoni

⅓ cup extra virgin olive oil

Two 10-inch zucchini, trimmed, quartered lengthwise, seeds removed (see Kitchen Notebook, opposite) sliced on the bias into 2-inch sections

½ teaspoon red pepper flakes

40 littleneck clams, rinsed (and scrubbed, if necessary)

½ cup dry white wine

1 cup Clam Broth (page 15), bottled clam juice, or store-bought low-sodium chicken stock

2 teaspoons unsalted butter

¼ cup slivered fresh basil

1. Bring a large pot of water to a boil for the pasta. Set a colander in the sink to drain the pasta.

2. Thinly slice the preserved lemon rinds crosswise; set aside.

3. When the pasta water boils, add enough salt to make it taste like seawater. Add the rigatoni and cook for 8 minutes. It won't be al dente yet, but that's okay; it will finish cooking in the clam liquid.

4. Meanwhile, heat a 12-inch skillet (with a lid) over high heat. Add the olive oil and heat until it shimmers. Add the zucchini and stir to coat it with the oil. Sprinkle with ½ teaspoon salt and cook, stirring twice, until the color changes and the zucchini no longer looks raw, 1 to 2 minutes. Add the red pepper flakes and stir. Add the clams and

cook, stirring occasionally, 1½ minutes. Add the wine, broth, and preserved lemon, cover, and simmer until all the clams open, 4 to 5 minutes.

5. When the pasta is cooked, drain it in the colander. Return it to the pasta pot. Add the contents of the skillet, holding back the last of the liquid in case of grit, and simmer until the pasta is tender, 4 to 6 minutes. Add the butter and toss to melt. Stir in the basil.

6. Divide the pasta, clams, and zucchini among four deep serving plates or shallow serving bowls.

KITCHEN NOTEBOOK: SEEDING ZUCCHINI

The centers of larger zucchini are likely to be spongy, full of seeds, and without much flavor. To remove the centers, quarter the zucchini lengthwise. Lay the quarters on a cutting board. Slice off and discard the spongy edge portion that contains the seeds. (Small, young zucchini needn't be seeded.)

The same technique may be used to seed standard garden cucumbers. Seedless cucumbers usually don't need usually to be seeded.

· ORECCHIETTE 101 ·
WITH SHRIMP, ROSEMARY,
AND GREEN OLIVES

SERVES 4 AS AN ENTRÉE

Here's another simple pasta, this one made with the small round, indented shapes called *orecchiette*, meaning "little ears." Given their small size, orecchiette, which are typical of the region of Puglia, are perfect with small shrimp.

Fine sea salt

1 pound orecchiette

1½ pounds small (31–40) shrimp, shelled, tails removed, deveined (see page 385)

2 tablespoons canola oil

4 tablespoons extra virgin olive oil

1 teaspoon red pepper flakes

2 teaspoons finely chopped fresh rosemary

8 ounces pitted Picholine olives (2 cups), quartered

¼ cup dry white wine

1½ cups Low-Stress Chicken Stock (page 16) or store-bought low-sodium chicken stock

1. Bring a large pot of water to a boil for the pasta. Place a colander in the sink to drain the pasta.

2. When the pasta water boils, add enough salt to make it taste like seawater. Add the orecchiette and cook until al dente, 10 to 11 minutes.

3. Meanwhile, on a baking sheet, season the shrimp with salt.

4. Place a 12-inch skillet over high heat. Add 1 tablespoon of the canola oil and heat until it shimmers. Add about half the shrimp to the oil and cook 1 minute. Turn over with a spatula and cook 1 minute more. Remove to a large plate or platter. Add the remaining tablespoon of canola oil and repeat to cook the rest of the shrimp.

5. Return the first batch of shrimp to the skillet. Add 1 tablespoon of the olive oil, the red pepper flakes, 1 teaspoon of the rosemary, and the olives and stir to coat. Add the white wine and chicken stock and bring to a simmer.

6. When the pasta is al dente, drain it in the colander. Return it to the pasta pot. Add the contents of the skillet. Stir over high heat to reduce the liquid and coat the pasta, about

1 minute. Add the remaining teaspoon rosemary and the remaining 3 tablespoons olive oil and stir to combine.

7. Divide the pasta among four deep serving plates or shallow serving bowls, making sure each serving gets an equal amount of shrimp.

· POLLINGER TUNA NOODLE CASSEROLE ·

SERVES 8 TO 10 GENEROUSLY AS AN ENTRÉE

While I was growing up, my mom's culinary library consisted, in good portion, of recipes from the backs of boxes and on labels from Campbell's soup cans. (What can I say? It was the '70s.) Her tuna noodle casserole was a Pollinger household staple: canned cream of mushroom soup, canned tuna, and cooked elbow macaroni, stirred together in a casserole and topped with crushed potato chips. It was my favorite fish dinner—far better than the despised fish sticks.

When I was invited to cook at an event at Rockefeller Plaza to benefit Citymeals on Wheels, the other chefs and I were asked to serve dishes we had grown up with. I decided to dignify my mom's dinnertime staple by making it from scratch. Tuna noodle casserole was a hit at the Pollinger household, it was a hit at Rockefeller Center, and it'll be a hit at your home, too. This is a good make-ahead meal: You can poach the fish, make the sauce, and cook the macaroni ahead of time. Put it all together and bake it when you're ready to eat.

FOR THE TUNA

1¾ pounds tuna steak, cut into ½-inch dice

Fine sea salt

FOR THE MUSHROOM SAUCE

6 tablespoons (¾ stick)
　　unsalted butter

1 small onion, minced

1 clove garlic, minced

Two 10-ounce packages white button
　　mushrooms, wiped clean,
　　stems trimmed, thinly sliced

Fine sea salt

½ cup all-purpose flour

7 cups whole milk

Freshly ground black pepper

FOR THE CASSEROLE

1 pound elbow macaroni

Unsalted butter, softened, for buttering the
　　casserole

One 10-ounce bag potato chips

1. On a baking sheet, season the tuna with ¾ teaspoon salt. Let stand 15 minutes to allow the salt to penetrate.

recipe continued on next page

2. Prepare an ice bath by filling your sink with ice and cold water. Bring 2 quarts water to a boil in a medium pot. Add 4 teaspoons salt. Add the tuna, shaking the pot gently so the tuna doesn't stick to the bottom. Lower the heat and simmer until the tuna is just cooked through, about 5 minutes. Set the pot in the ice bath and let stand, shaking the pan every 10 to 15 minutes, until the tuna is cool.

3. For the sauce, melt the butter in a 4-quart saucepan over medium heat. Add the onion and garlic and cook without coloring, stirring often, until translucent, about 3 minutes. Add the mushrooms and 1 teaspoon salt. Cook without coloring, stirring often, until tender, 5 to 6 minutes. Add the flour and cook, stirring often, 3 minutes. Add the milk and stir well to combine,. Bring to a boil, reduce the heat, and simmer, stirring frequently, until the taste of the raw flour has cooked out, about 20 minutes. Season with 1 teaspoon salt, and pepper to taste; set aside.

4. For the macaroni, bring a large pot of water to a boil. Place a colander in the sink. When the water boils, add enough salt to make it taste like seawater. Add the macaroni and cook until tender, 6 to 8 minutes. Drain in the colander.

5. Preheat the oven to 350°F. Butter a 3-quart (9 by 13-inch Pyrex) casserole or baking dish.

6. When the tuna has cooled, drain it and gently flake. Discard the poaching liquid. Transfer the tuna to a very large bowl. Add the sauce and cooked macaroni and stir well to combine and break up the clumps of macaroni. Season to taste with salt and pepper. Spoon into the prepared casserole or baking dish. Cover with aluminum foil and bake until heated through, 20 to 30 minutes.

7. Break the seal on the bag of chips, empty half the chips to eat at another time, and pass a rolling pin over the bag to coarsely crush the chips. (Or crush the chips in your hands.) Remove the foil and top the casserole with the crushed chips. Return to the oven and bake, uncovered, 10 minutes more until the crushed topping is lightly browned.

· CRISTINA'S SPANISH CHICKEN, · SHRIMP, AND RICE

SERVES 4 GENEROUSLY AS AN ENTRÉE

I owe this recipe to Cristina Mosquera, a friend of the family and a fantastic Spanish cook. I always look forward to dinner when she cooks, as much for the food as for the company. From the spread she and her husband, Victor, set out for us you'd think she was cooking for an army. This is one of my favorites. If it's more convenient, make the dish up to an hour ahead, cover with foil, and hold in a warm oven. When you're ready to serve, heat ½ cup stock and stir it in to moisten the rice.

1 pound boneless, skinless chicken thighs, cut into ½-inch dice

3 cloves garlic, peeled

1 tablespoon slivered fresh Italian parsley

4 tablespoons extra virgin olive oil

1 pound small or medium (31–40 or 21–30) shrimp, shelled, tails removed, deveined (see page 385)

1 cup chopped onion (about 1 medium)

½ cup chopped red bell pepper (about ¼ pepper)

½ cup chopped fresh tomatoes (about 1 medium)

½ cup dry white wine

½ cup Clam Broth (page 15) or bottled clam juice

⅛ teaspoon saffron threads

1 bay leaf

3 cups Low-Stress Chicken Stock (page 16) or store-bought low-sodium chicken stock

Fine sea salt

1½ cups basmati rice

1. Place the chicken in a medium bowl or baking dish. Chop 2 of the garlic cloves and add to the chicken along with the parsley and 1 tablespoon of the olive oil. Toss to coat the chicken; cover with plastic wrap and set aside at room temperature (see Kitchen Note-book: Prevent Sticking, page 87).

2. Place the shrimp in another medium bowl or baking dish and toss with 1 tablespoon of the olive oil; cover with plastic wrap and set aside at room temperature.

3. Place a 10-inch skillet over medium-low heat. Add the remaining 1 tablespoon olive oil and heat until fluid enough to coat the bottom of the pan when swirled. Add the onion and the remaining whole garlic clove. Cook without coloring, stirring often, until the onion is tender and translucent, about 5 minutes.

recipe continued on next page

4. Add the bell pepper and cook without coloring, stirring often, until tender, about 4 minutes more.

5. Add the tomato and cook, stirring occasionally, until it has softened and begun to break down, about 5 minutes.

6. Add the wine, clam broth or clam juice, saffron, bay leaf, 1 cup of the chicken stock, and ½ teaspoon salt. Simmer, uncovered, to allow the flavors to meld, 6 to 7 minutes.

7. Add the rice, stir, and then simmer without stirring, uncovered for 5 minutes.

8. Add another 1 cup of the chicken stock and stir gently. Simmer 5 minutes more, until the liquid has been mostly absorbed (the pan will not be dry).

9. Add another ½ cup chicken stock, stir gently, and continue cooking until the rice is tender and the stock has been almost completely absorbed, about 10 minutes more. Keep in mind that the rice will continue to absorb liquid after you've removed it from the heat; make sure some liquid remains or the rice will be dry. Add a bit more, if necessary. Fish out and discard the bay leaf.

10. About 5 minutes into the previous step, heat a 12-inch skillet over high heat. Add the remaining 1 tablespoon olive oil and heat until it shimmers. Add the chicken in a single layer. Let it brown without stirring, 1 minute. Season with ½ teaspoon salt, stir, and cook 1 minute more. Stir in the shrimp. Cook 1 minute more. Remove from the heat and set aside until the rice is done.

11. Add the chicken and shrimp to the rice. Pour the remaining ½ cup chicken stock into the pan in which the chicken and shrimp were cooked and let stand off the heat for 1 minute to soften the browned bits on the bottom of the pan. Scrape up the browned bits with a spatula or wooden spoon and pour with the liquid into the rice. Stir to combine. Serve from the pan in which the rice was cooked.

KITCHEN NOTEBOOK: PREVENT STICKING

Room-temperature meat and seafood are less likely to stick to the pan while cooking. They won't lower the temperature of the pan significantly, so they will develop a crust more quickly. So it makes sense to bring the shrimp and chicken to room temperature while you cook the rice.

· RISOTTO WITH KING CRAB, · PISTACHIOS, AND BLOOD ORANGE

SERVES 4 AS AN ENTRÉE

This recipe is inspired by a Sicilian flavor palette. I use king crab because its large size stands out nicely against the rice, and blood orange juice and homemade blue crab stock accentuate the crab flavor. If you're pressed for time, go ahead and substitute store-bought chicken stock—it makes this a pretty easy dish to put together. If you do make the crab stock, you'll almost certainly have a bit left over; freeze it for soup.

A note about stirring: Traditionally, risotto is stirred constantly, and that *is* the correct way to make it. But I don't always have time for that, and I like risotto too much to leave it to days when I've got a leisurely 16 to 18 minutes to do nothing but stir. So I'll give it a good stir, turn my attention elsewhere, and come back to it as often as I can.

2 oranges (preferably blood oranges)

2 tablespoons plus 2 teaspoons extra virgin olive oil, plus extra for serving

2 teaspoons plus 1 tablespoon unsalted butter

1 tablespoon chopped shallot (about ½ small)

2 large cloves garlic, minced

1½ cups Carnaroli rice

Fine sea salt and freshly ground black pepper

½ cup dry white wine

4 cups Crab Stock (see Extra Credit, page 90), Low-Stress Chicken Stock (page 16), or store-bought low-sodium chicken stock, brought to a bare simmer

1½ pounds cooked king crab in the shell, meat removed and cut into ½-inch pieces, or about 1 pound jumbo lump crabmeat

½ cup shelled pistachios

¼ cup grated pecorino cheese

⅓ cup gently packed slivered fresh basil

1. Finely grate the orange zest into a small bowl, preferably with a Microplane. Stir in 2 tablespoons of the olive oil; set the orange zest oil aside.

2. With a chef's knife, cut both ends off the orange. Stand the orange on one end on a cutting board and cut off the bitter white pith. Working over a bowl to catch the juices, cut between the membranes of the orange with a paring knife to release the segments into the bowl. Squeeze the juice from the membrane into the bowl and discard the membrane. Set aside.

3. Place a large pot or 10- to 11-inch sauté pan over medium-low heat. Add the remaining 2 teaspoons oil and 2 teaspoons of the butter and heat to melt the butter. Add the shallot and garlic and cook without coloring, stirring often with a heatproof spatula, until aromatic, 30 to 60 seconds. Add the rice and cook, stirring often, until it smells toasted, about 2 minutes. Season with 1 teaspoon salt, and pepper to taste.

4. Remove the pan from the heat and add the wine. Return the pan to the heat and simmer, stirring constantly, about 1 minute, until the wine reduces enough that when you draw a line through the center of the rice with your spatula, the remaining liquid returns only very slowly to refill the space. This visual cue is key because it is your indication throughout the cooking process that's it's time to add more liquid.

5. Add ½ cup simmering crab or chicken stock. Cook, stirring constantly (ideally), and scraping down the sides of the pan often with the spatula, until reduced as in step 3. Add

recipe continued on next page

another ½ cup stock and repeat. Continue adding the stock in ½-cup increments, stirring constantly and adding more stock only when the liquid is reduced as in step 3. You'll use about 3½ cups stock total. The rice is done when it has lost the chalky center but still has tooth. (Bite into a grain or two to test it.) This should take 16 to 18 minutes once you start adding the stock.

6. After the rice has cooked for about 15 minutes, fold the crab, pistachios, and orange segments and juice into the rice; continue cooking.

7. Off the heat, stir in the remaining 1 tablespoon butter and the cheese and basil.

8. To serve, divide among four deep serving plates or shallow serving bowls. Drizzle with the orange zest oil.

EXTRA CREDIT

· CRAB STOCK ·

MAKES ABOUT 5 ⅓ CUPS

1 tablespoon plus 1 teaspoon canola oil	1½ pounds (about 6) live blue crabs (see Kitchen Notebook, below)

Heat the oil in an 8-quart pot over medium heat until it shimmers With a large, heavy knife, cut the crabs in half lengthwise. Add them to the pot and cook, stirring often, until they turn orange, about 5 minutes. Add 2 quarts water and bring to a boil. Reduce the heat and simmer 25 minutes. Strain through a fine-mesh strainer into a bowl. Use immediately or prepare an ice bath: fill your sink with ice and cold water. Set the container with the broth in the sink and let stand, stirring the broth every 10 to 15 minutes, until chilled. Divide among containers, refrigerate and use within 3 days or freeze for up to 6 months.

KITCHEN NOTEBOOK: WORKING WITH LIVELY BLUE CRABS

The crabs must be alive, and they may be lively. To make them easier to handle safely, stick them in the freezer for a few minutes. The cold will slow them down.

· PAEJUN ·
(KOREAN-STYLE SEAFOOD PANCAKES)

SERVES 4 AS AN ENTRÉE, 8 AS AN APPETIZER (MAKES 4 PANCAKES)

We're blessed to have lots of great Korean restaurants in midtown Manhattan not far from Oceana. Many are open late, until 1:00 or 2:00 a.m. at least (some are open 24 hours), which makes them the perfect late-night after-work hangout for chefs. One of my favorite dishes is a type of green scallion–rice pancake called *paejun*. Tender with a bit of chew, and a little crisp at the edges, the pancakes are usually made with squid or—my favorite— octopus. But if you don't have a Japanese market nearby for octopus, they're tasty with cooked shrimp, squid, or scallops, too (see the variation).

These pancakes go great with the spicy pickled cabbage, called *kimchee*, available at Asian markets. If you have two nonstick pans, it's not difficult to make two pancakes at a time. The pancakes will hold for a few minutes if you want to complete the cooking before serving, but I usually serve them right out of the pan as they come off the heat.

FOR THE DIPPING SAUCE

¼ cup soy sauce

4 teaspoons rice vinegar

1 tablespoon sugar

FOR THE BATTER

1 cup all-purpose flour

½ cup rice flour

½ cup cake flour

1 teaspoon fine sea salt

1 teaspoon baking powder

2 cups cold water

FOR THE FILLING

1 pound cooked octopus tentacles, sliced ¼ inch thick

2 tablespoons Korean chile paste or *gochujang*

1 tablespoon soy sauce

¼ teaspoon toasted sesame oil

¼ teaspoon sugar

½ clove garlic, minced

½ teaspoon minced peeled fresh ginger

FOR THE PANCAKES

4 tablespoons canola oil

2 red bell peppers, halved lengthwise then crosswise, seeds and ribs removed, cut into thin strips

2 bunches scallions (white and green parts), thinly sliced on the bias

4 teaspoons unsalted butter

Kimchee, for serving

recipe continued on next page

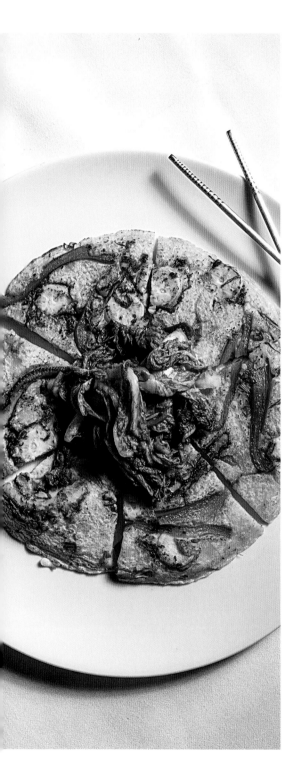

1. Preheat the oven to 350°F.

2. For the sauce, stir together the soy sauce, vinegar, and sugar in a small bowl; set aside at room temperature until you're ready to serve.

3. For the batter, in a medium bowl, stir together the all-purpose, rice, and cake flours, the salt, and baking powder. Add the water all at once and whisk until smooth. Set aside.

4. For the filling, in a medium bowl, stir together the octopus, chile paste, soy sauce, sesame oil, sugar, garlic, and ginger until the octopus is well coated; set aside.

5. For the pancakes, place a 10-inch ovenproof nonstick skillet over medium heat. Add 1 tablespoon of the oil and heat until fluid enough to coat the bottom of the skillet when swirled. Add one quarter each of the pepper strips, scallions, and octopus mixture. Cook, stirring often, until the vegetables are coated with the oil, 1 minute. Ladle about one quarter of the batter into the pan, tilting and swirling the batter so the bottom of the pan is completely covered. Cook 1 minute. Place the skillet in the oven and bake until the batter is set, about 4 minutes.

6. Remove from the oven. Add 1 teaspoon of the butter to the edge of the pan. Swirl the butter around the edge, shaking the pan so the melting butter runs under the pancake. Place over medium heat and cook 1 minute more, until lightly browned.

7. If you're feeling brave, flip the pancake in the pan and slide it onto a serving plate. If you're more cautious, overturn a serving plate on top of the skillet. Overturn both plate and skillet so that the pancake falls onto the plate. Cut the pancake into 8 wedges with kitchen scissors.

8. Repeat steps 5 through 7 to make three more pancakes.

9. Serve with the dipping sauce, topped with kimchee. Offer your guests chopsticks or knives and forks.

• VARIATION •
PAEJUN WITH SAUTÉED SHRIMP, SQUID, AND SCALLOPS

Shrimp, squid, and/or scallops are great in paejun. The cooking method is similar for all three. Shrimp should be shelled and deveined; scallops cut in half crosswise into thin disks (in thirds if they're very large); squid tubes cut into ¼-inch-wide rings. Season the seafood and pat it dry to prevent sticking.

Choose a skillet large enough to hold the seafood in a single layer; if you don't have one, cook the seafood in batches. Place the pan over high heat. Add a very small amount of canola oil, just enough to film the bottom of the pan. When the oil is just shy of smoking, add the seafood and let it sit there for at least 30 seconds without moving. You want it to sear slightly and develop color and flavor. After about 30 seconds, give the pan a shake—if the seafood doesn't release, let it cook some more. You want to cook it halfway through on the first side; it's ready to flip when you see that the flesh has changed from translucent to opaque from the bottom to about halfway up the side. This should take 30 to 60 seconds. If the seafood seems to be browning too quickly or the oil is smoking too much, turn down the heat.

Flip shrimp and scallops with a spatula or tongs. (Squid rings don't really have a side; just toss.) Then cook another 30 to 60 seconds until the flesh is opaque. Remove to a baking sheet or dish to stop the cooking. Use in place of the octopus in the filling in step 4.

4.

SOUPS AND CHOWDERS

About fifteen years ago, shortly after returning from my training in Monaco, I was on vacation on the Jersey Shore, fishing for black bass with a couple of my buddies. We got a tug on the line, pulled it up, and I recognized the fish hanging there as a *gurnard*, one of several small, boney species we used at Le Louis XV to make fish jus (a concentrated broth) for the Provençal fish soup *soupe de poissons*. Here, the fish is called sea robin, a close cousin of the fish I knew in France. Sea robin is incredibly underappreciated and underutilized here, though; it's what we call a trash fish. So my buddies threw it back. I was stunned: "Dude, what are you doing?"

"What do you mean?" they said. "It's trash. Why do you want to keep it?"

"Because it's a good-tasting fish!" I insisted.

We kept pulling them in, they kept throwing them back. I got obnoxious. "There goes dinner!" I'd say. Every time a sea robin went back into the water: "There goes dinner!"

Finally they said, "If we keep the fish, will you shut up?" I agreed, and I got to keep my fish. I took it home and proceeded to make a classic bouillabaisse for the guys and our wives. The guys thought it was wonderful—they said it was one of the most delicious things they'd ever eaten. My sea robin rescue was vindicated.

You'll find a recipe for that bouillabaisse in this chapter, made with monkfish instead of sea robin because monkfish is a lot easier to get hold of unless you're fishing on the Jersey Shore. (I give you instructions for using sea robin, too.) But I recommend starting with one of the easier recipes in the chapter that doesn't require making a fish stock. Cod Chowder 101 with Fennel and Roasted Red Peppers (page 97) is just an ultra simple vegetable broth, thickened with potato; the cod gets cooked into the broth at the end. Borscht 101 with Smoked Whitefish (page 101) is made with an infusion of grated beets and whole spices, no more difficult than making tea, topped with smoked whitefish. Chilled Corn Soup 101 with Smoked Trout and Cherry Tomatoes (page 105) is built on a corn stock and puréed corn. Ajo Blanco with Shrimp (page 107) is a traditional Spanish soup that requires no stock and tastes dynamite with shrimp. And summer gazpacho (page 102) is garnished with seared scallops.

The recipes for New England and Manhattan chowders are my rendition of the classics, both nice and light, with whole fresh clams. You'll need Fish Fumet (page 13) for both, and you'll make a clam broth for the New England chowder. By the time you get to the bouillabaisse at the end of the chapter, its saffron-scented fish broth should pose no difficulties.

Most of these recipes are made in entrée portions—I'd like you to have the satisfaction of sitting down to a full dinner after you've done the cooking. But for more formal meals, the recipes may also be halved to serve as appetizers.

· COD CHOWDER 101 WITH FENNEL · AND ROASTED RED PEPPERS

SERVES 4 AS AN ENTRÉE

While at college in Boston, I spent a lot of time eating New England chowders: clam, cod, hake, and haddock. This is my take on traditional New England cod chowder but with roasted red peppers, fennel, and spinach for something a little different. Like New England Clam Chowder (page 110), it's bound with potato; but without a fish fumet or clam broth, it's a snap to make.

1 small white onion, peeled

1 medium Yukon gold potato, peeled

Fine sea salt

2 tablespoons extra virgin olive oil

5 cloves garlic, thinly sliced

1 small bulb fennel, trimmed, cored, and cut in ¼-inch dice

¼ teaspoon red pepper flakes

¼ cup dry white wine

One 12-ounce jar roasted red peppers, drained, sliced into ½-inch-wide ribbons

Freshly ground black pepper

Eight 3-ounce boneless, skinless cod fillets

6 fresh basil leaves, torn into pieces

1 cup gently packed baby spinach

recipe continued on next page

1. Cut the onion into quarters through the root end, then thinly slice crosswise; set aside.

2. Cut the potato in half. Cut one half into ¼-inch dice and place in a bowl; set aside. Cut the other half into 1-inch chunks and place in a small pot. Add 2 cups water and 1 teaspoon salt. Bring to a boil, reduce the heat, and simmer until tender, about 10 minutes. Remove from the heat and set aside; do not drain.

3. Place a 4-quart pot over medium heat. Add the olive oil and heat until fluid enough to coat the bottom of the pot. Add the onion and garlic and cook without coloring, stirring often, until tender, 5 to 6 minutes.

4. Add the fennel and raw diced potato. Cook, stirring often, until the fennel is translucent, about 4 minutes. Add red pepper flakes and white wine and cook until almost all the liquid has evaporated.

5. Add 3 cups water and the red pepper strips. Pour in the water from the cooked potato. In the pot, mash the cooked potato well with a fork, then stir it into the soup. Bring to a simmer and cook until slightly thickened, about 12 minutes. Season to taste with salt and pepper.

6. Meanwhile, on a plate, season the fish on both sides with salt and pepper and let stand 5 minutes to allow the seasonings to penetrate.

7. Add the fish to the soup and simmer gently, covered, until just cooked through, about 5 minutes.

8. To serve, divide the cod among four serving bowls. Add the basil and spinach to the soup and stir to wilt. Ladle the soup over the fish.

· BORSCHT 101 WITH SMOKED WHITEFISH ·

SERVES 4 AS A LIGHT MEAL (MAKES ABOUT 6 CUPS)

The inspiration for this soup was a recent trip to Moscow where I tasted an incredible borscht made with goose stock. (The traditional Russian soup is based on beef stock.) In order to lighten up the traditional recipe and make it more suitable for seafood, I chose an unorthodox method that's more like making tea than soup: The beets are grated to maximize their surface area, and lots of sweet, earthy flavor is extracted when they're simmered in water. You get a very pure beet flavor, unadulterated by fat and other vegetables—sort of essence of beet. The smoke in the whitefish is a nice complement to the vegetable's natural sweetness. This tastes fantastic hot or cold.

At the restaurant, we wear disposable gloves when working with beets to keep from staining our hands.

2⅓ pounds red beets (about 6 medium), trimmed and peeled

1 teaspoon whole black peppercorns

½ teaspoon caraway seeds

½ teaspoon dill seeds

½ teaspoon anise seeds

½ cup red wine vinegar

1½ teaspoons fine sea salt, or as needed

6 to 8 ounces boneless, skinless smoked whitefish, broken into bite-size pieces

4 tablespoons sour cream, for serving

1 tablespoon thinly sliced fresh chives, for serving

1. Grate the beets on a box grater into a baking dish to save any juices; set aside.

2. In a dry 4-quart pot or larger, toast the peppercorns, caraway, dill, and anise seeds over medium heat until lightly toasted and aromatic, about 1 minute. Move the pot constantly so that the spices don't burn.

3. Add the vinegar, 2 quarts water, and the grated beets with any juices. Bring to a boil, reduce the heat, and simmer, covered, until the soup develops a good, deep beet flavor, about 45 minutes. Strain through a fine-mesh strainer into a bowl. Season with the salt. Chill, if you like.

4. Ladle the borscht into four serving bowls. Top each bowl with one quarter of the whitefish, a tablespoonful of the sour cream, and ¾ teaspoon of the chives.

· GAZPACHO 101 WITH SEARED SCALLOPS ·

SERVES 6 AS AN APPETIZER (MAKES ABOUT 7 CUPS)

This chilled bright orange soup makes even not-so-great tomatoes taste good; with better tomatoes, it's stunning. The secret to puréeing this baby is to put the tomatoes into the blender or food processor first. You need their liquid to get the soup moving. Once the vegetables are puréed, drizzle in olive oil to give the soup a rich, creamy consistency. This can be made several days ahead. The soup may separate; just stir it before serving to re-emulsify. And remember that once chilled, the soup will need to be reseasoned.

4 large ripe tomatoes (about 1¾ pounds), cored and coarsely chopped

1 large red bell pepper, stem, seeds, and ribs removed, coarsely chopped

½ seedless cucumber, peeled and coarsely chopped

½ small red onion, coarsely chopped

1 clove garlic, coarsely chopped

½ red finger chile, cut lengthwise, seeds removed, coarsely chopped

¼ cup sherry vinegar

1 teaspoon sugar

Fine sea salt

1 teaspoon Homemade Hot Sauce (page 17) or store-bought hot sauce

¾ cup plus 1 tablespoon extra virgin olive oil

6 large (U15) sea scallops (8 to 10 ounces total), tough white side muscles removed

Freshly ground black pepper

1. Put the tomatoes in a blender or food processor. Add the bell pepper, cucumber, onion, garlic, chile, vinegar, sugar, 1 tablespoon salt, and the hot sauce. Start the blender on low, if you have a choice of speed. When you see the tomatoes begin to liquefy, turn the blender to high and blend until smooth.

2. With the blender running on medium-high or high speed, drizzle in ¾ cup of the olive oil to emulsify. Transfer to a container, cover, and refrigerate until well chilled.

3. When you're ready to serve, sprinkle the scallops on both sides with salt and pepper and let stand 5 minutes to allow the seasonings to penetrate.

4. Taste the soup for seasoning. It may have separated: stir until smooth.

5. Place a skillet over medium heat. Add the remaining 1 tablespoon olive oil and heat until it shimmers. Remove the pan from the heat to avoid flare-ups and gently lay the scallops in the pan, placing the edge closest to you down first so as not to splatter yourself

with hot oil. Return the pan to the heat and cook until the scallops are a nice golden color on the pan side and the bottom third of the scallop is opaque, about 2 minutes. Carefully turn the scallops with a spatula and cook until the other side is golden brown and the scallops are medium-rare with all but the center third opaque, 1 to 2 minutes depending on size.

6. Center a scallop in the bottom of each of six shallow serving bowls. Pour the soup into a large measuring cup. Pour the soup around the scallops so that the scallops are visible.

EXTRA CREDIT: GAZPACHO GARNISH

For a more formal restaurant-style presentation that also gives the soup texture, peel and quarter a 3-inch chunk of seedless cucumber; cut into ⅛-inch dice. Very finely dice (⅛ inch) enough red bell pepper to make 6 tablespoons. Cut three 1-inch wedges of tomato and cut out the core and seeds; cut the flesh into ⅛-inch dice. Combine the vegetables in a small bowl with 1 tablespoon extra virgin olive oil, a pinch each of salt and black pepper, and 3 tablespoons slivered fresh cilantro. To serve, spoon this mixture into the serving bowls before adding the scallops.

· CHILLED CORN SOUP 101 ·
WITH SMOKED TROUT
AND CHERRY TOMATOES

SERVES 4 AS AN APPETIZER (MAKES ABOUT 4 CUPS)

Corn stock and buttermilk are the secrets to this recipe: The stock gives it a full, rich flavor and the buttermilk adds a tangy low-fat dairy component that backs up the sweet taste of the corn. Garnished with smoked trout, this soup is a good example of the way that fat and smoke play well with sweet.

FOR THE CORN STOCK

2 ears corn, husked and cut into quarters

2 teaspoons extra virgin olive oil

½ teaspoon fine sea salt

FOR THE SOUP

2 ears corn, husked

2 tablespoons extra virgin olive oil

2 cloves garlic, thinly sliced

½ cup firmly packed, thinly sliced onion

Fine sea salt

2 sprigs fresh thyme

1 ⅓ cups low-fat buttermilk

Freshly ground black pepper

FOR THE GARNISH

1 cup cherry tomatoes, quartered

6 ounces boneless smoked trout, skin removed, flaked (about 1 cup)

¼ cup loosely packed fresh Italian parsley leaves

4 teaspoons extra virgin olive oil

Fine sea salt and freshly ground black pepper

1. For the corn stock, preheat the oven to 350°F. Coat the corn with the oil on a baking sheet. Roast until golden brown, about 25 minutes.

2. Place the roasted corn in a medium pot. Add 3 cups water and the salt. Bring to a boil, reduce the heat, and simmer for 20 minutes.

3. Strain the stock and discard the corn. You should have about 2 cups stock. Set aside.

4. For the soup, stand the corn on end on a cutting board and slice off the kernels with a chef's knife; set the kernels aside and discard the cobs.

recipe continued on next page

5. Place the pot over medium heat. Add the oil and heat until fluid enough to coat the bottom of the pot when swirled. Add the garlic and cook without coloring for 15 seconds. Add the onion and ¾ teaspoon salt and cook without coloring, stirring often, for 1½ minutes. Add the corn kernels and thyme and cook without coloring, stirring often, about 4 minutes.

6. Add the buttermilk and corn stock. Bring to a boil, reduce the heat, and simmer gently for 10 minutes. (If it separates, don't worry; when you purée the mixture it will come together.)

7. Fish out and discard the thyme. Pour the soup into a blender. If your blender lid has a removable plug, remove it. Hold a folded kitchen towel over the top so that the lid stays put and to prevent the soup from splashing upward and blend until smooth. Season to taste with salt and pepper. Transfer to a container and let cool to room temperature. Refrigerate until well chilled, 3 to 4 hours.

8. For the garnish, combine the tomatoes, trout, parsley, and olive oil in a small bowl and toss gently to mix. Season to taste with salt and pepper.

9. To serve, divide the garnish among four large shallow serving bowls. Taste the soup for seasoning—it will probably need more salt. Ladle the soup around the garnish in the bowls.

KITCHEN NOTEBOOK: BLENDER BUSINESS

If your blender lid has a removable plug in the center, take it out. This will relieve some of the pressure that is created when blending hot mixtures, and prevent the blender lid from popping off. But then you *must* cover the lid with a folded kitchen towel to prevent the soup from splashing upward; added insurance, as well, that the lid will stay put.

· AJO BLANCO WITH SHRIMP ·

SERVES 4 TO 6 AS AN ENTRÉE (MAKES ABOUT 8 CUPS)

One of the differences between home and restaurant cooking is that at home, you don't necessarily want to deal with garnishing a dish the way it's done in the restaurant. But here's a recipe for which the garnish really makes the soup. *Ajo blanco* ("white garlic" in Spanish) is a traditional soup from Andalusia, Spain, made with bread, crushed almonds, garlic, and grapes. When it was on the menu at Oceana, we garnished it with sliced grapes, croutons, chopped Marcona almonds, and lightly cooked sea urchin. The urchin gave the soup a briny undercurrent, the grapes added a little sweetness, and the almonds gave it texture. If you can find sea urchin, go for it (see Extra Credit, page 109). But shrimp are much easier to get hold of at home—scallops would taste great, too—and can be grilled, broiled, or sautéed. The point is, garnish the soup with some type of seafood in addition to the grapes and almonds.

FOR THE SOUP

20 large cloves garlic, peeled

½ small white onion, cut through the root end

2 tablespoons extra virgin olive oil

1 tablespoon unsalted butter

½ finger chile, cut lengthwise, seeds removed

2 cups seedless green grapes

1 cup slivered blanched almonds

Fine sea salt

2 cups firmly packed diced sourdough bread without crust (1-inch dice)

2 tablespoons verjus (see Guide to Unusual Ingredients, page 404), or 2 tablespoons white wine vinegar plus ½ teaspoon sugar

FOR THE CROUTONS

5 tablespoons extra virgin olive oil

2 cups diced sourdough or other tight-crumbed bread, with crust (¼-inch dice)

⅛ teaspoon fine sea salt

FOR THE GARNISH

3 tablespoon slivered blanched almonds

30 seedless red grapes, halved

3 tablespoons extra virgin olive oil

1 tablespoon thinly sliced fresh chives

1 pound large (16–20) shrimp, shelled, tails removed, deveined (see page 385)

Fine sea salt and freshly ground black pepper

recipe continued on next page

1. Bring a small saucepan of water to a boil. Add the garlic cloves and simmer 30 seconds; drain. Bring fresh water to a boil in the saucepan, add the garlic and simmer 30 seconds. Repeat once more. Drain the garlic and set aside.

2. Quarter the onion piece lengthwise, through the root end. Slice crosswise; set aside.

3. Place a medium saucepan over medium heat. Add the oil and butter and heat to melt the butter. Add the onion and chile and cook without coloring, stirring often, until the onion is translucent, about 2 minutes. Add the grapes and sauté until the skins blister and pop, about 3 minutes more. Add the almonds and blanched garlic and cook for 2 minutes.

4. Add 6 cups water, 2 teaspoons salt, and the large-diced bread. Bring to a boil, reduce the heat and simmer gently, covered, until the bread is falling apart, about 20 minutes.

5. Fish out and discard the chile. Working in batches if necessary, pour the soup into a blender or food processor and purée until very smooth. (If using a blender, remove the removable plug from the blender lid, if there is one, and hold a folded towel over the lid so that the lid stays put and to prevent the hot soup from splashing upward.) Recombine the batches of puréed soup if necessary, and add the verjus or vinegar and sugar.

6. For the croutons, line a baking dish with a double layer of paper towels. Place a 12-inch skillet or straight-sided sauté pan over medium heat. Add the oil and heat until it shimmers. Add the small-diced bread and immediately toss or stir to coat the bread with the oil. Reduce the heat to medium-low and cook until the bread is crisp and golden brown, tossing or stirring often, about 5 minutes. Season with the salt and drain in the baking dish. (This will make more croutons than you need for this recipe; store extras in a covered container at room temperature for up to a couple of days to use in salads.)

7. For the garnish, preheat the oven to 350°F. Spread the slivered almonds on a baking sheet and toast until fragrant, 5 to 7 minutes. Transfer to a bowl and let cool a few minutes. Add 1 cup of the croutons, the grape halves, 1 tablespoon of the olive oil, and the chives. Stir to combine.

8. Cover a baking sheet with aluminum foil. Adjust the rack to the closest setting to the element and preheat the broiler to high.

9. In a bowl, season the shrimp with salt and pepper and toss with the remaining 2 tablespoons olive oil. Spread on the prepared baking sheet in a single layer. Broil until firm, opaque, and cooked through, about 3 minutes.

10. To serve, reheat the soup if it has cooled. Divide the crouton-grape garnish among six shallow serving bowls. Set 3 shrimp in each bowl and ladle the hot soup around so that the shrimp remain visible.

EXTRA CREDIT: SEA URCHIN ROE

Sea urchin roe (*uni* in Japanese) is sold in trays containing strips of the orange roe, referred to as "tongues." For each serving of soup, place 5 tongues in each bowl (3 if they're large) and pour the hot soup over. Your fishmonger or a Japanese fish market will be able to get the roe for you.

· NEW ENGLAND CLAM CHOWDER ·

SERVES 4 GENEROUSLY AS AN ENTRÉE

I wanted to come up with a lighter chowder that doesn't rely on heavy cream or flour as traditional recipes do. Since milk curdles when heated, I cook the milk with potato, then purée them together; the potato binds the milk and you get a light but creamy, silky chowder with a rich taste. The emulsion remains a little delicate so the chowder must not be boiled. If reheating, bring it just to a gentle simmer.

4 slender fingerling potatoes (about 4 ounces)

24 littleneck clams, scrubbed

1 cup dry white wine

1 tablespoon unsalted butter

2 tablespoons extra virgin olive oil

Bouquet garni (see Kitchen Notebook, page 112), or ¼ teaspoon dried thyme and 1 bay leaf

½ teaspoon yellow mustard seeds

1 clove garlic, sliced

1 cup coarsely chopped onion (about 1 medium)

1 pound Yukon gold potatoes, peeled, quartered lengthwise, and thinly sliced crosswise

4 to 5 cups Fish Fumet (page 13), Low-Stress Chicken Stock (page 16), or store-bought low-sodium chicken stock

3 cups whole milk

½ cup sliced linguiça or Spanish chorizo sausage (about 3 ounces, quartered lengthwise and sliced ⅛ inch thick)

1 cup firmly packed torn stemmed greens such as baby red mustard, Swiss chard, or spinach (1- to 2-inch pieces)

1 tablespoon slivered fresh Italian parsley

1 tablespoon thinly sliced fresh chives or scallion greens

Juice of ½ lemon (about 1½ tablespoons), plus more if needed

Fine sea salt and freshly ground black pepper

1. Put the potatoes in a small saucepan with cold water to cover. Bring to a boil, reduce the heat, and simmer until the potatoes are just tender when pierced with a paring knife, 20 to 30 minutes. Drain and set aside.

2. Place a colander in a large bowl and set it by the stove. Place a large heavy-bottomed pot over high heat. Add the clams and the wine. Cover and bring to a boil. Reduce the heat and simmer, stirring after 2 to 3 minutes for even cooking, until several of the clams have opened, about 5 minutes. Remove the open clams with tongs to the colander. Cover and continue cooking until the rest of the clams have opened, 3 to 5 minutes more.

Remove all the open clams to the colander and set aside until they're cool enough to handle. Discard any clams that didn't open. Pour the clam cooking liquid into a large liquid measuring cup, holding back the last of the liquid in case of grit; set aside. Wash and dry the pot.

3. Shell the cooled clams, avoiding the tough muscles that attach the meat to the shells. Discard the shells and set aside the clam meat in the bowl.

4. Place the pot over medium heat. Add the butter and 1 tablespoon of the oil and heat until the butter stops foaming. Add the bouquet garni or the dried thyme and bay leaf, the mustard seeds, and garlic. Cook without coloring, stirring often, until the mixture is fragrant, about 30 seconds. Add the onion and cook without coloring, stirring often, until softened, 4 to 5 minutes. (Turn down the heat if the onion begins to color.) Stir in the Yukon gold potato slices and cook 1 minute.

5. Add 4 cups of the fish fumet or chicken stock and 2 cups of the reserved clam cooking liquid to the onion and potatoes. Add the milk. Bring to a boil over medium-high heat, reduce the heat, and simmer, partially covered, until the potatoes are very soft, about 25 minutes. The milk will curdle—that's okay. Fish out and discard the bouquet garni or the bay leaf, whichever you used.

6. If your blender lid has a removable plug, remove it. Working in batches and holding a folded towel over the lid to make sure it stays put and to prevent the hot soup from splashing upward, purée the soup in a blender or food processor until smooth; pour into a large bowl. Wash and dry the pot; return the puréed soup to the pot.

7. To serve, bring the soup to a gentle simmer over medium-high heat. Do not boil. Place a small skillet over medium-high heat. Add the remaining 1 tablespoon olive oil and heat until fluid enough to coat the bottom of the skillet when swirled. Add the sausage and cook until lightly browned, about 2 minutes. Add to the hot soup along with the clams, greens, parsley, and chives. Thinly slice the cooked fingerling potatoes and add. Add the lemon juice, ½ teaspoon salt, and ⅛ teaspoon pepper. Taste for salt, pepper, and lemon juice and adjust if necessary. Divide among six shallow serving bowls, making sure everyone gets an equal serving of clams.

KITCHEN NOTEBOOK: BOUQUET GARNI

Bouquet garni is simply a French phrase for fresh herbs tied together in a bundle so that they are easy to remove from the pot. To make the bouquet garni for this soup, use 2 sprigs Italian parsley, 5 stems fresh thyme, and 1 bay leaf. Gather the parsley sprigs in your hand. Set the thyme and bay leaf on top and fold over the parsley to enclose. Wrap a couple of times with kitchen twine and tie to hold the bundle together. For soup that will be strained, there's no need to bundle the herbs because you'll be straining them out.

EXTRA CREDIT: THE RESTAURANT VERSION

When I make New England clam chowder at the restaurant, I use a combination of Clam Broth (page 15) and Fish Fumet (page 13). The clam broth represents a few more steps but it really hammers home the clam flavor. If you'd like to try it, substitute 3 cups clam broth for that much of the fumet.

· MANHATTAN CLAM CHOWDER ·

SERVES 4 GENEROUSLY AS AN ENTRÉE

This is basically a clam minestrone, a very flavorful vegetable soup with lots of tomato, whole clams, and clam broth. You can make it with fresh tomatoes if they are in season; otherwise, good-quality canned tomatoes work fine. I finish the soup with a handful of bonito flakes (a tuna-like fish belonging to the mackerel family; see Guide to Unusual Ingredients, page 395). The bonito adds a nice smokiness, but if you can't get hold of it, the soup has enough flavor to do without.

24 littleneck clams, scrubbed

1 cup dry white wine

1 tablespoon canola oil

½ cup diced chorizo (¼- to ½-inch dice; optional)

½ cup chopped onion (about ½ medium)

½ cup chopped carrot (about 1 medium)

½ cup chopped celery (about 1 medium stalk)

1 clove garlic, chopped

1 large Yukon gold potato, peeled and cut into ¼- to ½-inch dice (about 1¼ cups)

One 28-ounce can whole peeled tomatoes (preferably organic), drained (save the juice) and chopped, or 4 cups chopped, peeled, and cored ripe beefsteak tomatoes (see Kitchen Notebook, page 280)

2 to 3 cups Fish Fumet (page 13), Low-Stress Chicken Stock (page 16), or store-bought low-sodium chicken stock

2 tablespoons slivered fresh Italian parsley

1 teaspoon fresh thyme leaves

½ cup bonito flakes (optional)

Fine sea salt and freshly ground black pepper

1. Place a colander in a bowl and set it by the stove. Place a large heavy-bottomed pot over high heat. Add the clams and wine. Cover and bring to a boil. Reduce the heat and simmer, stirring after 2 to 3 minutes for even cooking, until several of the clams have opened, about 5 minutes. Remove the open clams with tongs to the colander. Cover and continue cooking until the rest of the clams have opened, 3 to 5 minutes more. Remove all the open clams to the colander and set aside until they're cool enough to handle. Discard any clams that didn't open. Pour the clam cooking liquid into a 1-quart liquid measuring cup, holding back the last of the liquid in case of grit; set the liquid aside. Wash and dry the pot.

2. Place the pot over medium heat. Add the oil. Add the chorizo, if using, and cook until lightly browned, about 1 minute. Add the onion, carrot, celery, and garlic and cook without coloring, stirring often, until the onion is translucent, about 2 minutes. Add the potato and cook 1 minute.

3. Add the tomatoes and juice. Bring to a simmer and cook for 2 to 3 minutes.

4. Add enough fish fumet or chicken stock to the clam cooking liquid to equal 4 cups total. Add to the vegetables, return the soup to a simmer, and cook, uncovered, until the potato is tender, 12 to 15 minutes.

5. Meanwhile, shell the cooled clams, avoiding the tough muscles that attach the meat to the shells. Discard the shells; set the clam meat aside in the bowl.

6. When the potatoes are cooked, add the clams, parsley, and thyme to the soup. If using them, crush the bonito flakes into small bits and stir into the soup. Season to taste with salt and pepper.

7. Divide among four serving bowls, making sure everyone gets an equal serving of clams.

· MONKFISH BOUILLABAISSE ·

Bouillabaisse, the classic Mediterranean French fish soup, is a great thing to serve to company because it looks really fancy and complicated—when in fact it's just fish poached in a homemade fish broth spiked with the anise liqueur Ricard. It's not hard, though it does take a little time. Sea robin (*gurnard* in French) is traditional in bouillabaisse because it poaches well; however, monkfish is more readily available and poaches well, too. For sea robin, you'll need 5 to 6 pounds whole fish; make the broth with the bones and leave fillets whole (they're likely to be 4 to 5 ounces each unless you get really large fish).

FOR THE BROTH

½ medium bulb fennel, trimmed, halved lengthwise, cored (save the core), and cut into ½-inch dice

½ large onion, cut through the root end, sliced crosswise (1 generous cup)

4 cloves garlic, crushed with the side of a chef's knife and peeled

Peel of ½ navel orange, removed in strips with a vegetable peeler with as little bitter white pith as possible

1 sprig fresh Italian parsley

1 sprig fresh basil

1 sprig fresh tarragon

1 sprig fresh thyme

1 bay leaf

1 teaspoon whole black peppercorns

¼ cup extra virgin olive oil

1 teaspoon fennel seeds

2 pounds bones from lean white fish such as striped bass, snapper, cod, halibut, hake, black bass, flounder, or sea robin, rinsed thoroughly under cold running water and cut into 3-inch sections with a heavy knife or kitchen scissors

1 medium plum tomato, cut into ½-inch dice

1 teaspoon fine sea salt

Juice of ½ orange

½ cup Ricard or other anise liqueur such as Pernod

1 cup dry white wine

FOR THE BOUILLABAISSE

⅛ teaspoon saffron threads

8 ounces fingerling potatoes, peel-on, sliced into ¼-inch-thick coins

Four 6- to 7-ounce skinless monkfish fillets, each cut crosswise into 4 equal pieces

Fine sea salt and freshly ground black pepper

1 tablespoon extra virgin olive oil

½ large bulb fennel, trimmed, halved lengthwise, cored, and sliced crosswise ¼ inch thick (about 1½ cups)

½ large zucchini, quartered lengthwise, seeds removed, sliced ⅛ to ¼ inch thick on the bias (see Kitchen Notebook, page 79)

1 tablespoon slivered fresh Italian parsley

Juice of ½ orange

recipe continued on next page

1. For the broth, slice the fennel core ¼ inch thick. Combine in a bowl with the fennel, onion, and garlic and set aside. Combine the orange peel, parsley, basil, tarragon, thyme, bay leaf, and peppercorns in another small bowl and set aside.

2. Place a large pot over medium-high heat. Add the olive oil and heat until fluid enough to coat the bottom of the pot when swirled. Add the fennel seeds and heat, swirling the pot until the seeds are fragrant and start to sizzle, 30 to 60 seconds. Add the onion, fennel, and garlic and cook without coloring, stirring often, until the onion is translucent, about 5 minutes. Add the fish bones and tomato and stir well. Cook, uncovered, until the bones begin to break apart and are simmering in their juices, about 3 minutes.

3. Add 1 teaspoon salt and the orange peel mixture and cook until aromatic, about 1 minute. Add the orange juice, Ricard, and white wine. Bring to a vigorous boil and boil for 2 minutes. Add 4 cups water and boil 20 minutes.

4. Add 2 cups more water and boil for 10 minutes more. Sip a little of the broth; the consistency should be unctuous and almost a little tacky when you press your lips together. If not, add ¼ cup water and boil 5 minutes more. Strain through a fine-mesh strainer into a large container. You should have 4 to 5 cups broth.

5. For the bouillabaisse, rinse out the pot and return the broth to the pot. Add the saffron and bring to a simmer. Add the potatoes and simmer until the potatoes are tender, 10 to 12 minutes.

6. On a plate, season the monkfish pieces on both sides with salt and pepper. Let stand 5 minutes to allow the seasonings to penetrate.

7. Meanwhile, heat a 12-inch straight-sided sauté pan or a medium pot (with a lid) over medium heat. Add the olive oil, fennel, and ½ teaspoon salt. Cook without coloring, stirring, until the fennel is translucent, about 1 minute. Add the zucchini, cover, and reduce the heat to medium-low. Cook without coloring, stirring often, until the zucchini is almost tender, about 5 minutes.

8. Add the broth and potatoes and bring to a simmer. Add the monkfish and simmer until cooked through, about 8 minutes (4 minutes for sea robin). Remove to a plate with a slotted spoon. Add the parsley and orange juice to the broth. Taste for salt and pepper and adjust if necessary.

9. To serve, use the slotted spoon to divide the vegetables among four serving bowls. Divide the soup among the bowls and place the fish in the center.

KITCHEN NOTEBOOK: BOILED, NOT SIMMERED

Technique is important here. Bouillabaisse is all about a very specific, richly flavored broth that's a bit more unctuous than standard fish broth. The broth must be boiled with the olive oil, not simmered, to create the correct emulsion.

EXTRA CREDIT

· ROUILLE ·

A traditional accompaniment to bouillabaisse is a saffron-flavored condiment called *rouille*, which is French for "rust." There are a million versions—some are bound with breadcrumbs, some with potato, some are mayonnaise-based. If you want to do your bouillabaisse up right, make this rouille, or Roasted Red Pepper Aioli (page 22). Serve with croutons made with baguette sliced ¼ inch thick, drizzled on one side with olive oil, and toasted on a baking sheet at 350°F for 7 to 10 minutes, until crisp. If you're concerned about raw eggs, substitute 2 tablespoons pasteurized yolks plus 2 tablespoons water for the whole egg.

Pinch of saffron threads	1 teaspoon fresh lemon juice
1 teaspoon hot water	¼ teaspoon fine sea salt
1 large egg	⅛ teaspoon cayenne pepper
2 cloves garlic, coarsely chopped	1 cup extra virgin olive oil

Put the saffron in a small glass, add the hot water, and let stand a few minutes. Combine the egg, garlic, lemon juice, salt, and cayenne in a blender. Holding a folded towel over the lid of the blender to prevent the lid from popping off, blend 30 seconds. (If you have a variable-speed blender, blend on medium or high speed. If you started on medium, turn to medium-high speed at this point.) With the blender running, drizzle in about half of the oil to emulsify. Blend in the saffron mixture. Drizzle in the rest of the oil and blend until thick and smooth. Transfer to a container, cover, and refrigerate for up to 2 days.

5.

BAKED AND
ROASTED FISH

If you're relatively new to cooking fish, baking is a good place to start. It's the easiest way to cook fish at home. You just season the fish, rub it with oil, set it in the preheated oven on an oiled baking sheet, and pull it out when it's done.

I end up doing a lot of baking at home, particularly when I'm short on time, in part because cleanup is easy. At the restaurant, I've got an army of people to wash dishes, but at home, I'm the guy doing it. Just line your baking sheet or baking dish with aluminum foil, and all it needs is a rinse when you're done. I often bake plain white fish for the kids (we call it New Jersey Baked Fish 101, page 122) because for a long time, that's all they'd eat. With a simple recipe like that, you get the pure, sweet flavor of the fish. Highlight it with a squeeze of lemon, one of the herb oils or vinaigrettes in the book, or my go-to favorite, Homemade Hot Sauce (page 17), and you're done.

Want to add a little sophistication with an additional layer of flavor? Rub the fish with a ground spice or combination of spices before baking. Try Coriander-Dusted Halibut 101 with Wheat Pilaf, Almonds, and Lemon (page 128). Or for a more complex taste, salmon coated with a Moroccan blend of herbs, spices, and olive oil called charmoula (page 133) is killer.

I also like to bake fish on a bed of vegetables, which contributes flavor to the vegetables and turns the fish into a one-pot meal. These dishes are easy to do on an everyday basis. Since fish cooks so quickly, I usually precook the vegetables. For example, I'll make a quick ratatouille, set halibut fillets on top, and put the whole thing in the oven (Baked Halibut 101 with 10-Minute Ratatouille, page 126). For One-Pot Baked Alaskan Cod 101 (page 124), you toss cut-up bell peppers, potatoes, and carrots with oil in a baking dish and bake for a few minutes to get them going. Then you set the cod on top and bake until both fish and vegetables are cooked through.

When you're ready to graduate from these very simple 101 baked dishes, move on to a whole fish like branzino, which tastes great with a fennel-chile vinaigrette (page 144) and a side of spinach and mushrooms. Serve an elegant fillet of dorade topped with an overlapping layer of potato slices arranged to look like fish scales. Or stuff a fresh cod fillet with a garlicky salt cod mixture called brandade for Cape Cod "Turkey" (page 141).

I have a couple of delicious lobster recipes in this chapter. Baking is practical for lobster because it's so much less cumbersome than dealing with the big pot you need for steaming or boiling. It's also easier than broiling because while you can bake a couple of lobsters at a time, a home broiler can really only handle one.

Roasted Lobster 101 with Basil-Garlic Butter (page 136) is very simple; directions for splitting the lobster are on page 389. Once you're comfortable with baking, Crab-Stuffed Roasted Lobster on page 147, with an herbed crab stuffing, is a little dressier and extremely tasty.

Baking is done at moderate heat (350°F) so that the fish doesn't color. Some fish, such as halibut and cod, taste great with no color. I'm good with snapper both ways—no color or with a crusty, caramelized exterior. Same with salmon. (On page 130, I show you how to bake salmon at an even lower heat, 250°F, so that it stays very silky and soft.) But I think some fish taste best with a little color—branzino, for example, and lobster—so I bake at a higher temperature, 400°F, which, if we are to be technically correct, is actually roasting.

BEST FISH FOR BAKING

You can pretty much bake everything, though meaty fish such as swordfish, tuna, and wahoo benefit from a really well caramelized exterior and are better seared, sautéed, grilled, or broiled. Whole fish, fillets, and steaks are great baked, as is lobster. I prefer to cook scallops, clams, and squid by other techniques.

EQUIP YOURSELF: BAKING

I'll bet you already have everything you need for baking in your kitchen.

• I use baking sheets and ovenproof glass baking dishes (when baked-on residue builds up on the handles, oven cleaner works well to clean it off).

- Aluminum foil.
- I use a slender metal spatula and a wider slotted plastic spatula. I prefer the plastic because it won't tear a flakey fish and if I'm using aluminum foil, it doesn't tear the foil, either.

· NEW JERSEY BAKED FISH 101 ·

SERVES 4 AS AN ENTRÉE

My kids are becoming more adventurous now but it was a long time before I could get them to eat anything but white fish. They didn't like to see grill marks. No browned crusts. They didn't even like to see little dots of black pepper. They just wanted the plain white fish. This recipe got its name one day when the kids were in for lunch at Oceana. Since they were very young and it was their first meal there, we'd carefully discussed what they might want to order. I'd recommended fish and chips, and that sounded good to them until it appeared on the table. "We don't like that," they said. I reminded them of our conversation. "No, we don't want it." Well, what did they want? "We want the New Jersey fish. Like you bake in the oven at home." So here's the recipe the way we've been serving it at home for years, sesasoned with salt and baked with a little olive oil. It goes great with Green Beans with Sofrito (page 369) or swiss chard (page 138). And I generally douse my portion with some of my Homemade Hot Sauce (page 17). This is as much a method as a recipe because it's a foolproof way to bake any 1-inch-thick fish fillet or steak.

Four 1-inch-thick boneless, skinless halibut fillets (6 to 8 ounces each)

Fine sea salt and freshly ground black pepper

4 teaspoons extra virgin olive oil or vegetable oil

Lemon wedges, for serving

Homemade Hot Sauce, for serving

1. Preheat the oven to 350°F. Cover a baking sheet with aluminum foil.

2. On the baking sheet, sprinkle the fish on both sides with salt and pepper, if your kids will go for it. Let stand 5 minutes to allow the seasonings to penetrate.

3. Pat the fish dry with paper towels. Coat each fillet all over with 1 teaspoon oil.

4. Bake the fish to medium-well, about 13 minutes. Serve with lemon wedges and/or hot sauce.

· ONE-POT BAKED ALASKAN COD 101 ·

Here's a nice, easy method for baking fish on a bed of vegetables. I developed this recipe for Oprah Winfrey, who was doing a feature on healthy cooking for her website. She asked me for something that was healthy, flavorful, and easy. This recipe has got it all. Alaskan and Pacific cods have a slightly different texture and flavor from Atlantic cod, but as far as this recipe goes, they're interchangeable.

Fine sea salt and freshly ground black pepper

4 tablespoons extra virgin olive oil

1 medium red bell pepper

1 medium green bell pepper

1 medium red onion, peeled

1 medium Yukon gold or other waxy potato, peel-on, scrubbed

2 medium carrots, peeled

1 clove garlic, thinly sliced

2 tablespoons slivered fresh Italian parsley

2 tablespoons slivered fresh basil

Four 8-ounce boneless, skinless Alaskan cod fillets

1. Preheat the oven to 350°F.

2. Cut the bell peppers in half lengthwise, remove and discard the stems, ribs, and seeds, and cut lengthwise into strips about ¼ inch wide. Set aside in a large bowl.

3. Cut the onion in half through the root end, cut off the root end. Slice lengthwise into strips about ¼ inch wide. Add to the bell pepper strips.

4. Cut the potato lengthwise into slices about ¼ inch thick. Cut the slices into strips about ¼ inch thick. Add to the peppers and onion.

5. Cut the carrots crosswise into three sections. Cut each section lengthwise into slices about ¼ inch thick. Cut the slices into strips about ¼ inch thick. Add to the other vegetables.

6. Add the garlic, parsley, and basil to the vegetables. Drizzle with 2 tablespoons of the oil, season with salt and pepper, and toss to coat with the oil. Spread the vegetables in a 9 by 13-inch baking dish, cover with aluminum foil, and bake 10 minutes.

7. On a plate or a sheet of aluminum foil, season the fish on both sides with salt and pepper. Drizzle with the remaining 2 tablespoons of oil; set aside while the vegetables bake.

8. Remove the dish from the oven, remove the foil, and place the fish on top of the vegetables in a single layer. Return the dish to the oven, uncovered, and bake until fish is cooked through, about 8 minutes. Serve the fish with the vegetables.

· BAKED HALIBUT 101 ·
WITH 10-MINUTE RATATOUILLE

SERVES 4 AS AN ENTRÉE

I remember making ratatouille at home for the first time. It was well over fifteen years ago and I was cooking dinner to impress my girlfriend. I was still a young cook, practicing the classics, so I made it the traditional way in which all the vegetables are cooked separately, then combined at the end. I remember thinking it was good (must have been—my then-girlfriend is now my wife) but a lot of work. I came to appreciate the combination but have since streamlined the process for cooking at home. It's a natural bed for baked halibut, cod, or grouper fillets.

½ small eggplant, trimmed

Fine sea salt

½ medium zucchini, trimmed

½ medium yellow squash, trimmed

½ medium red bell pepper, stem, seeds, and ribs removed

Four 6- to 8-ounce boneless, skinless halibut fillets (about 1 inch thick)

Freshly ground black pepper

2 tablespoons extra virgin olive oil

4 cloves garlic, thinly sliced

¼ large onion, cut through the root end, thinly sliced crosswise

½ large tomato, coarsely chopped

2 tablespoons dry white wine

⅓ cup gently packed coarsely torn fresh basil

1. Preheat the oven to 350°F.

2. Peel the eggplant and cut lengthwise into slices ¼ to ⅓ inch thick. Cut the slices lengthwise into strips ¼ to ⅓ inch wide. Cut the strips crosswise into ¼- to ⅓-inch dice. Place the eggplant in a bowl and rub with ¼ teaspoon salt. Set aside while you cut up the rest of the vegetables.

3. Quarter the zucchini and yellow squash pieces lengthwise and slice crosswise into ¼-inch-thick wedges; set aside together in a bowl. Cut the bell pepper lengthwise into ¼-inch-wide slices. Cut the slices crosswise into thirds; set aside with the squashes.

4. On a plate or a sheet of aluminum foil, sprinkle the fish on both sides with salt and pepper. Let stand 5 minutes to allow the seasonings to penetrate.

5. Place a 12-inch ovenproof skillet over medium-high heat. Add 1 tablespoon of the oil and heat until fluid enough to coat the bottom of the skillet when swirled. Add the garlic and cook until fragrant, about 30 seconds. Stir in the onion slices, season with ½ teaspoon salt, and cook, stirring often, until the onion is translucent, about 1½ minutes.

6. Add the remaining tablespoon of oil to the pan along with zucchini, yellow squash, and bell pepper. Cook, stirring frequently, until you see the color of the squash deepen, 1½ to 2 minutes. Add the diced eggplant and cook, stirring frequently, until it loses the raw look, about 1½ minutes.

7. Stir in the chopped tomato and season with a pinch of pepper. Cook until the mixture begins to look juicy, about 2 minutes. Stir in the wine and let it bubble for a few seconds.

8. Arrange the fish on top of the ratatouille in a single layer. Cover with aluminum foil and bake until the fish is cooked to medium-well, 13 to 15 minutes.

9. To serve, stir the basil into the ratatouille and taste for salt and pepper; adjust if necessary. Spoon onto four serving plates and set the fish on top.

KITCHEN NOTEBOOK: SALTING EGGPLANT

Salting the eggplant will break down the flesh so it will cook more consistently and absorb less oil.

· CORIANDER-DUSTED HALIBUT 101 ·
WITH WHEAT PILAF, ALMONDS,
AND LEMON

SERVES 4 AS AN ENTRÉE

I've always been a fan of Middle Eastern cuisine, and I love the way fish plays off the lively flavors of Middle Eastern bulgur wheat salads. Here, the bulgur is flavored with lemon, fresh herbs, scallions, and almonds, and the halibut is baked with a dusting of ground coriander to amplify the Middle Eastern flavor palette. This recipe is delicious with any lean white fish such as cod, black bass, flounder (fold it in thirds), or grouper. It's worth grinding whole coriander seed, if you have a spice grinder, for a burst of bright, citrusy flavor.

FOR THE PILAF

1 cup medium bulgur

½ teaspoon fine sea salt

1 lemon

3 tablespoons extra virgin olive oil

2 scallions (white and green parts), thinly sliced on the bias

3 tablespoons sliced, blanched almonds

1 tablespoon slivered fresh mint

1 tablespoon slivered fresh Italian parsley

Freshly ground black pepper

FOR THE HALIBUT

Four 6- to 8-ounce boneless, skinless halibut fillets (about 1 inch thick)

Fine sea salt and freshly ground black pepper

4 teaspoons extra virgin olive oil

1 teaspoon untoasted coriander seeds, ground medium-fine, or 1 teaspoon ground coriander

1. For the pilaf, turn the oven on for a minute and let it get a little warmer than room temperature, then turn it off. Place the bulgur in a wide heatproof bowl. Bring 1½ cups water and the salt to a boil in a small saucepan. Pour the boiling water over the wheat, stir, and cover tightly with plastic wrap. Place the bowl in the oven and let stand until the wheat has absorbed the water and is tender, about 30 minutes.

2. Meanwhile, finely grate the lemon zest into a medium bowl, preferably with a Microplane. Cut off the ends of the lemon with a chef's knife. Stand it on one end on a cutting board and slice off all the bitter white pith. Working over another bowl to catch the juices, cut between the membranes with a paring knife to release the segments. Cut the lemon segments crosswise into quarters. Add to the zest along with any juice. Squeeze the juice from the membrane into the bowl and discard the membrane. Set aside.

3. When the wheat is tender, gently fold in the lemon zest, segments, and juice, the olive oil, scallions, almonds, mint, parsley, and black pepper to taste; set aside until you're ready to serve. (The bulgur wheat may be rehydrated a day ahead and refrigerated; bring it to room temperature and add the remaining pilaf ingredients just before serving.)

4. For the halibut, preheat the oven to 400°F. Line a baking sheet with aluminum foil. On the foil-lined baking sheet, sprinkle the halibut on both sides with salt and pepper. Let stand 5 minutes to allow the seasonings to penetrate.

5. Pat the fish dry with paper towels. Coat each fillet with 1 teaspoon olive oil. Sprinkle the top of each fillet with about ¼ teaspoon of the ground coriander. Bake until the fish is cooked to medium-well, about 12 minutes.

6. Divide the pilaf between four serving plates. Set the fish on top.

KITCHEN NOTEBOOK: BULGUR

Bulgur is made from wheat that has been parboiled and dried. Since bulgur has already been cooked, it simply needs rehydrating; it's important that it rehydrate in a warm place because wheat best absorbs the water at a warm temperature. Bulgur is often confused with cracked wheat, which has *not* been parboiled; cracked wheat must be cooked, not rehydrated. Bulgur is sold in four "grinds": fine, medium, coarse, and extra coarse.

· SLOW-BAKED SALMON 101 ·
WITH ROASTED BEET
AND ORANGE SALAD

SERVES 4 AS AN ENTRÉE

Baking salmon at a very low temperature—250°F—does two things. Because the fish is cooking so slowly, it gives you a very comfortable margin of error for overcooking. It also produces a different taste and texture than you usually get with baked fish. The salmon firms up but remains silky, closer to the texture of the raw fish. The salad creates is own sauce for the fish, but if you're pressed for time, skip the salad and sauce the salmon with a quick Sherry Vinaigrette (page 19).

FOR THE ROASTED BEET AND ORANGE SALAD

2 medium red beets, trimmed, peel-on, rinsed, and dried

2 teaspoons canola oil

Fine sea salt

1 navel orange

Freshly ground black pepper

3 tablespoons extra virgin olive oil

2 teaspoons lemon juice

½ teaspoon sugar

1 rounded teaspoon slivered fresh mint

1 rounded teaspoon thinly sliced fresh chives

1 teaspoon slivered seeded finger chile

FOR THE SALMON

Four 6- to 8-ounce boneless, skinless salmon fillets (about 1 inch thick)

Fine sea salt and freshly ground black pepper

4 teaspoons extra virgin olive oil

1. For the beet salad, preheat the oven to 350°F. On a sheet of aluminum foil large enough to loosely wrap the beets, coat the beets with the canola oil and sprinkle with ¼ teaspoon salt. Seal the beets in the foil and bake until a paring knife penetrates the beets easily, 2 to 2¼ hours. Set aside at room temperature until cool enough to handle.

2. Turn the oven temperature down to 250°F.

3. Slip the skins off the cooled beets. Cut the beets in half through the stem ends. Place one half on the cutting board. Cut into thirds lengthwise, angling the knife blade toward the center for each cut—this will ensure relatively even wedges. Cut crosswise into ½-inch

dice, angling the blade toward the center again at both ends. Repeat to dice the remaining beet halves. Place in a bowl.

4. Use a Microplane to grate the orange zest into the beets. Cut off both ends of the orange with a chef's knife and set it on one end on a cutting board. Slice off the bitter white pith in sections. Working over the bowl to catch the juices, cut between the membranes with a paring knife to release the orange segments. Squeeze the juice from the membrane into the bowl and discard the membrane. Add the orange segments and juice to the beets. Add ¾ teaspoon salt, ⅛ teaspoon black pepper, the olive oil, lemon juice, sugar, mint, chives, and chile. Stir to coat and taste for seasoning. Cover and set aside at room temperature until you're ready to serve.

5. For the salmon, cover a baking sheet with aluminum foil. On the foil-lined baking sheet, season the fish on both sides with salt and pepper and let stand 5 minutes to allow the seasonings to penetrate.

6. Pat the fish dry with paper towels. Coat each fillet all over with 1 teaspoon olive oil. Bake, uncovered, until the salmon firms up and is medium-rare, about 25 minutes. The ends of the fillets will feel cooked through but the centers will still feel soft to the touch.

7. Serve the salmon alongside the beet salad.

KITCHEN NOTEBOOK: BEETS

When preparing beets for roasting, trim the ends close to the flesh but don't cut into the beet itself or it will bleed during cooking. At the restaurant, we wear disposable gloves when working with beets to keep from staining our hands.

· MOROCCAN BAKED SALMON ·
WITH CHICKPEAS, BLACK OLIVES,
AND RAISINS

SERVES 4 AS AN ENTRÉE

This dish can be as easy or challenging as you like. If you just want a sensational-tasting piece of salmon, coat the fish with the charmoula (a mix of fresh herbs, lemon zest, garlic, and smoky Spanish paprika), add a salad, and you're done. But if you want to do the whole thing blown out the way we do it in the restaurant, serve the salmon with a Moroccan-spiced chickpea purée and finish the plate with a garnish of whole chickpeas warmed with black olives, chopped almonds, and raisins. Guaranteed to knock your guests' socks off. If you're on the fence about which way to go, the more challenging version of this recipe isn't really hard; there are just a lot of steps. But you'll need to get going the day before by soaking the chickpeas overnight. In a pinch, you can use canned chickpeas but the flavor doesn't compare with the ones you cook yourself.

FOR THE CHICKPEAS

1 ½ cups dried chickpeas

Fine sea salt

FOR THE CHARMOULA

2 small cloves garlic, minced

2 tablespoons slivered fresh Italian
  parsley

1 tablespoon plus 1 teaspoon slivered
  fresh cilantro

Grated zest of ½ lemon

1 teaspoon sweet smoked Spanish
  paprika

½ teaspoon ancho chile powder

Scant ½ teaspoon ground cumin

¼ cup extra virgin olive oil

FOR THE BOHARAT

½ teaspoon ground allspice

½ teaspoon ground cinnamon

¼ teaspoon freshly grated ground nutmeg

⅛ teaspoon ground cardamom

⅛ teaspoon ground cloves

⅛ teaspoon ground ginger

FOR THE CHICKPEA PURÉE

2 cups drained cooked chickpeas

1 cup chickpea cooking liquid

1 tablespoon extra virgin olive oil

⅓ cup chopped onion

recipe continued on next page

1 clove garlic, minced

½ teaspoon slivered seeded finger chile

1 teaspoon boharat

Fine sea salt

FOR THE SALMON

Four 7- to 8-ounce boneless, skinless salmon fillets (preferably king or coho, 1 to 1¼ inches thick)

Freshly ground black pepper

FOR THE CHICKPEA-OLIVE GARNISH

1 tablespoon plus 1 teaspoon extra virgin olive oil

2 teaspoons chopped shallot

2 teaspoons slivered seeded finger chile

1 cup drained cooked chickpeas

¼ cup halved pitted black olives (preferably Taggiasche)

16 raw blanched almonds (preferably Marcona), coarsely chopped

2 tablespoons firmly packed golden raisins, soaked in boiling water to cover 5 minutes and drained

1 teaspoon thinly sliced fresh chives

1 teaspoon slivered fresh cilantro

Pinch each of fine sea salt and freshly ground black pepper

boharat, for garnish

1. For the chickpeas, in a bowl, cover the chickpeas with cold water by about 3 inches. Cover and set aside at room temperature to soak overnight.

2. Drain the chickpeas and rinse under cold running water. Transfer to a medium saucepan and add fresh water to cover by about 3 inches. Bring to a boil, reduce the heat, and simmer until the chickpeas are tender. This could take as little as 25 minutes or as much as 3 hours, depending on the age of the chickpeas. Add 1 teaspoon salt. Set aside in the cooking liquid.

3. For the charmoula, in a bowl, combine the garlic, parsley, cilantro, lemon zest, paprika, chile powder, cumin, and olive oil. Stir to blend. Set aside.

4. For the boharat, stir all the spices together in a small bowl; set aside.

5. For the chickpea purée, drain the chickpeas, saving the cooking water. Measure out 2 cups chickpeas and 1 cup cooking liquid. Return the rest of the chickpeas to the cooking liquid and set aside. Place a small saucepan over medium heat. Add the olive oil and heat until fluid enough to coat the bottom of the pan when swirled. Add the onion, garlic, and chile and cook without coloring, stirring often, until the onion is softened and translucent, 2 to 3 minutes. Add the chickpeas, cooking liquid, boharat, and a pinch of salt. Bring to a simmer. Transfer to a blender. If your blender has a removeable plug, remove it. Holding a folded kitchen towel over the top to prevent the lid from popping off and the purée from splashing upward, blend until smooth. Taste for salt and adjust if necessary. Scrape into a small saucepan; set aside.

6. Preheat the oven to 350°F. Cover a baking sheet with aluminum foil. On the baking sheet, season the salmon fillets on both sides with salt and pepper and let stand 5 minutes to allow the seasonings to penetrate.

7. Pat the fish dry with paper towels. Spread one quarter (about 1 tablespoon) of the charmoula over the top and sides of each fillet, pressing gently with the spoon to adhere. Bake until medium-rare, 13 to 15 minutes.

8. Meanwhile, gently rewarm the chickpea purée over low heat until heated through, adding 1 tablespoon of the remaining chickpea cooking liquid.

9. For the chickpea-olive garnish, while the fish is baking and the purée reheating, heat a large skillet over medium heat. Add 1 tablespoon of the olive oil, shallot, and chile and cook 1 minute without coloring. Add the chickpeas and cook to warm through, about 2 minutes. Remove from the heat and stir in the olives, almonds, raisins, chives, cilantro, salt and pepper.

10. To serve, spoon a mound of chickpea purée in the center of each of four deep serving plates; add a spoonful of the chickpea-olive garnish. Place a salmon fillet off-center on the purée and garnish. Stir the rest of the boharat with the remaining 1 teaspoon olive oil; use a spoon to garnish each plate with a little of the boharat oil.

· ROASTED LOBSTER 101 ·
WITH BASIL-GARLIC BUTTER

This is a dead simple way to make great-tasting roast lobster, focusing on the sweetness of the meat. Serve with Olive Oil Crushed Potatoes (page 370) and sautéed zucchini.

FOR THE BASIL-GARLIC BUTTER

8 tablespoons (1 stick) unsalted butter, cubed

3 cloves garlic, chopped

1 generous tablespoon slivered fresh basil

FOR THE LOBSTER

Four 1¼-pound live lobsters

Fine sea salt and freshly ground black pepper

1. For the basil-garlic butter, melt about one quarter of the butter (2 tablespoons) in a small pan over low heat. Add the garlic and cook without coloring, about 3 minutes. Add the remaining butter and heat until melted, about 3 minutes more. Remove from the heat. Add the basil and let stand 10 minutes to infuse the broth.

2. Place the lobsters on a cutting board. Kill the lobsters by driving the point of a chef's knife through the center point of the line that bisects the tails from the heads; pull off the claws and knuckles, split the lobster tails in half lengthwise, and remove the vein from the tail and the grain sac from the head (see page 390). Crack the claws just as you would for a cooked lobster (see pages 393–394).

3. Arrange two racks in the oven and preheat the oven to 400°F. Line two rimmed baking sheets with aluminum foil.

4. Arrange 4 lobster halves cut side up on each baking sheet. Sprinkle the tail meat of each lobster half lightly with salt and pepper and drizzle with ½ tablespoon basil-garlic butter. Cover with foil and bake 5 minutes.

5. Remove from the oven and remove the foil. Drizzle each lobster tail half with about ½ teaspoon more of the butter. Cover again with foil and roast 5 minutes more, switching racks this time for even cooking. Remove the foil and continue roasting until the lobsters are cooked through and lightly browned, about 8 minutes more.

6. Serve drizzled with the rest of the basil-garlic butter.

EXTRA CREDIT: RESTAURANT PRESENTATION

Once you feel confident cutting up a raw lobster, try making this recipe the way it's shown in the photo, using the technique for butterflying lobster on page 390. The presentation is a little neater and more impressive. Butterfly the lobster as shown, sprinkle each butterflied tail with salt and pepper as in step 4, then drizzle each with 1 tablespoon of the garlic-basil butter. Bake as in step 4. In step 5, drizzle each butterflied tail with 1 teaspoon more of the butter; continue on with the recipe as written.

· BAKED DORADE FILLET · WITH POTATO "SCALES" AND SWISS CHARD

SERVES 4 AS AN ENTRÉE

This dish reminds me of the old-style haute cuisine recipes that fascinated me when I was beginning my culinary training, dishes in which cooked fish was made to mimic the look of a live whole fish, decorated with "scales" made of pastry or cucumber slices. Here's a simplified, contemporary version decorated with sliced potato. It's not hard to do, and it brings a little restaurant elegance to your dinner table. You can cook the chard ahead and reheat it. Or preheat the oven and get the fish all ready, start the chard, then put the fish in the oven. The dorade and the chard will be ready at the same time.

FOR THE DORADE

Fine sea salt

8 large fingerling potatoes, peel-on, sliced into coins about ⅛ inch thick (preferably on a Japanese mandoline), rounded ends discarded

Four 6- to 7- ounce boneless, skin-on dorade fillets

Freshly ground black pepper

9 tablespoons (1 stick plus 1 tablespoon) unsalted butter, melted

FOR THE SWISS CHARD

2 bunches Swiss chard (about 1¾ pounds total), stems trimmed, rinsed in a sinkful of cold water, changing the water until no grit remains

2 tablespoons extra virgin olive oil

2 cloves garlic, sliced

1. For the dorade, line a baking sheet with paper towels. Fill a large pot with water and bring to a boil. Add 3 tablespoons salt and the potato slices. Simmer until the slices are cooked through, 1½ to 2 minutes. With a skimmer or a slotted spoon, remove the slices to the paper towel–lined baking sheet, arranging them in a single thin layer. Set aside to dry as much as possible.

2. Preheat the oven to 400°F. Line a second baking sheet with aluminum foil and brush the foil with about one-third of the butter. On the baking sheet, sprinkle the fillets on both sides with salt and pepper. Let stand 5 minutes to allow the seasonings to penetrate.

3. Pat the fish dry with paper towels and arrange the fillets skin side down in a single layer. Brush the fillets with butter, using about half of what you have left. Arrange the potato slices over the fillets in overlapping rows so that they look like fish scales. Brush the "scales" with the rest of the melted butter; set aside while you get the chard going.

4. For the chard, cut the leaves from the stems. Stack a few leaves at a time. Roll tightly like a cigar and cut crosswise into ¼-inch-wide strips; repeat until all the leaves are cut. Set aside. Cut the stems on a thin bias; set aside separately from the leaves

5. Place a 12-inch skillet over medium heat. Add the olive oil and garlic and cook without coloring, stirring often, until fragrant, about 3 minutes.

6. Put the fish in the oven and bake until the fish is cooked through and the potatoes are lightly browned at the edges, about 10 minutes.

7. Meanwhile, add the chard stems to the skillet, 1 teaspoon salt, and pepper to taste.

recipe continued on next page

Cook without coloring, stirring often, until the stems are softened, 5 to 7 minutes. Add the leaves and 2 tablespoons water. Cook, stirring constantly, until the leaves wilt, about 2 minutes more.

8. Divide the chard among four serving plates. Place the fillets on top, angling the fillets a bit so that they rest half on the plate, half on the chard.

EQUIP YOURSELF: JAPANESE MANDOLINES

A Japanese mandoline, also called a Benriner (after one of the companies that makes them), is an inexpensive kitchen tool for slicing and cutting vegetables into thin strips. It's indispensable in a professional kitchen and useful at home because it's far easier to slice thinly with a mandoline than with a knife. You can choose among a variety of models, sizes, and prices. For home, I recommend a less expensive plastic model. Make sure it has a finger guard to protect you.

Japanese mandolines are simple to use. Use the knob underneath the plate to set the blade opening to the thickness you want: Cut a slice of vegetable to check, then adjust the opening as needed. Set the food to be sliced on the Benriner and place the finger guard on top. Press gently on the finger guard with the palm of your hand, stretching your fingers out so that they keep clear of the blade, and slide the vegetable over the blade.

· CAPE COD "TURKEY" ·

SERVES 4 AS AN ENTRÉE

Looking for a seafood dish one year to evoke the spirit of Thanksgiving, I stumbled across a recipe for something called "Cape Cod Turkey" in a 1941 New England cookbook called *Vittles for the Captain: Cape Cod Sea-Food Recipes,* compiled by Harriet Adams. Hers was a sturdy dish of salt cod with a flour-bound salt pork and milk gravy. It inspired this recipe for fresh cod stuffed with the garlicky Provençal potato-and-salt-cod purée called brandade. We serve it at Oceana every Thanksgiving.

FOR THE BRANDADE STUFFING

6-ounce piece salt cod (preferably skinless and boneless; see Kitchen Notebook, page 143)

1 large Yukon gold potato (6 ounces), peeled and left whole

½ cup whole milk

2 cloves garlic, peeled

2 tablespoons extra virgin olive oil

2 teaspoons fresh lemon juice

Finely grated zest of 1 lemon

1 tablespoon slivered fresh Italian parsley

Freshly ground black pepper

FOR THE COD

Four 6- to 8-ounce boneless, skinless fresh cod fillets (1¼ to 1½ inches thick)

Fine sea salt and freshly ground black pepper

4 teaspoons extra virgin olive oil, plus extra for the baking sheet

1. For the brandade, in a bowl, cover the salt cod with cold water. Cover the bowl and soak for 24 hours in the refrigerator, changing the water four times during the soaking time.

2. The next day, in a medium saucepan, combine the potato and 2 quarts water. Bring to a boil, reduce the heat, and simmer until the potato is tender when pierced with a paring knife, about 30 minutes. Remove from the heat and set the potato aside in the cooking water.

3. Meanwhile, bring 1 quart water to a boil in a medium saucepan. Drain the soaked cod and add it, reduce the heat, and simmer gently for 5 minutes.

4. Drain the cod in a colander, then return it to the pot. Add the milk and garlic. Bring to a boil, reduce the heat, cover, and simmer 10 minutes. Remove from the heat and set aside.

recipe continued on next page

5. Place the cooked potato in a medium bowl, saving the cooking water. Crush the potato with a fork to coarsely mash, with some chunks remaining. With a slotted spoon, remove the cod and garlic from the milk and add to the potato; save the milk. Flake the cod with the fork and mash it and the garlic into the potato. Add the reserved milk, the olive oil, lemon juice and zest, parsley, and pepper to taste. Mix with the fork until the brandade looks like chunky mashed potatoes. If it looks stiff, add a touch of the potato cooking water to loosen it.

6. Preheat the oven to 400°F. Line a baking sheet with aluminum foil and brush lightly with olive oil. Make a lengthwise cut through the center line of each cod fillet, but do not cut all the way through; this will make a pocket for the stuffing. On the baking sheet, sprinkle the cod on both sides with salt and pepper and let stand 5 minutes to allow the seasonings to penetrate.

7. Pat the cod dry with paper towels and drizzle each fillet with 1 teaspoon olive oil. Divide the brandade among the fillets, stuffing it into the pockets and mounding in the center. Bake until the cod is cooked through, about 10 minutes. Remove from the oven.

8. Adjust the rack to 2 to 3 inches from the broiler element and preheat the broiler to high. Broil the fish, still on the baking sheet, until both fish and brandade are lightly browned, about 2 minutes.

KITCHEN NOTEBOOK: SALT COD

Salt cod is fresh cod that has been preserved by salting and drying. Before cooking, it must be rehydrated and desalted by soaking for 24 hours. It was an important staple on Cape Cod when fresh cod wasn't available, as it was throughout European, West African, Caribbean, and Brazilian cuisines. Ms. Adams's recipe notes that the virtuous Cape Codders eventually convinced themselves that they liked salt cod better than the fresh. (For more information, see Guide to Unusual Ingredients, page 397.)

· WHOLE ROASTED BRANZINO ·
WITH MUSHROOMS, SPINACH,
AND FENNEL-CHILE VINAIGRETTE

SERVES 4 AS AN ENTRÉE

This is an adaptation of one of my signature dishes at Oceana, in which branzino is boned, stuffed with mushrooms and spinach, and roasted. In this simplified version, the fish is roasted whole, then filleted, and the vegetables are served on the side. It's got all the flavor with far less hassle.

FOR THE BRANZINO

Two 2-pound whole branzino, scaled, gutted, fins and gills removed

Fine sea salt and freshly ground black pepper

8 thin (⅛-inch) slices lemon (from 2 lemons)

4 sprigs fresh Italian parsley

4 sprigs fresh thyme

4 sprigs fresh oregano

2 tablespoons extra virgin olive oil

FOR THE FENNEL-CHILE VINAIGRETTE

½ cup extra virgin olive oil

2 small cloves garlic, sliced

½ teaspoon crushed fennel seeds (see Kitchen Notebook, page 146)

½ teaspoon crushed coriander seeds (see Kitchen Notebook, page 146)

¼ teaspoon red pepper flakes

2 tablespoons plus 2 teaspoons white wine vinegar

½ teaspoon fine sea salt

FOR THE MUSHROOM-SPINACH SAUTÉ

¼ cup canola oil

8 ounces honshimeiji mushrooms (about 4 cups), stem bottoms trimmed, clusters pulled apart, or 8 ounces white mushrooms, stem bottoms trimmed, quartered

½ cup pitted small black olives (preferably Taggiasche)

1 tablespoon fresh thyme leaves

8 ounces stemmed mature or baby spinach (about 8 cups gently packed)

8 ounces arugula, heavy stems removed (about 14 cups gently packed)

Fine sea salt and freshly ground black pepper

½ teaspoon piment d'Espelette, Aleppo pepper, or hot paprika, or ⅛ teaspoon cayenne pepper

1½ teaspoons finely grated lemon zest (from 1 to 2 lemons)

1 tablespoon fresh lemon juice

1. For the branzino, preheat the oven to 400°F. Cut three evenly spaced 1-inch slits on the bias on each side of both fish. Cut a shallow slit down both sides of the spine of the fish. On a plate or a sheet of aluminum foil, season the inside of each fish with ½ teaspoon salt and ½ teaspoon pepper. Line each cavity with 4 lemon slices, 2 parsley sprigs, 2 thyme sprigs, and 2 oregano sprigs. Sprinkle each fish all over with 1 teaspoon salt and ½ teaspoon pepper. Let stand 5 minutes to allow the seasonings to penetrate.

2. Pat the fish dry with paper towels. Rub each fish all over with 1 tablespoon olive oil.

3. Cut a sheet of 15½-inch-wide parchment paper so that it is about 4 inches longer than the length of one of the fish and place on the counter. Center a fish crosswise on the paper. Bring the top and bottom edges of the paper up to meet over the top of the fish and roll down the edges to seal, just like you were rolling down the top of a paper bag. Roll in both ends the same way—you'll have a nice neat package. Wrap in a sheet of aluminum foil the same way. (Foil accelerates the cooking and the paper keeps the fish from sticking to the foil.) Repeat to wrap the second fish. Place the packets side by side on a baking sheet and roast 22 minutes.

4. Open the foil and parchment (roll back but do not remove) and continue roasting until the fish are nicely browned and cooked through, 4 to 5 minutes. The flesh along the back of the fish should begin to separate from the bone and a paring knife or cake tester stuck into the thickest part of the fish should encounter no resistance. Set aside to keep warm.

5. For the vinaigrette, heat ¼ cup of the oil in a small saucepan over medium-low heat. When warm, add the garlic and cook until very lightly golden but not browned, about 1 minute. Add the fennel and coriander seeds and the red pepper flakes and cook until aromatic, about 15 seconds. Remove from the heat and immediately add the remaining ¼ cup oil and the vinegar to stop the cooking of the garlic and spices. Whisk in the salt and set aside.

6. For the mushroom-spinach sauté, heat a large saucepan over high heat. Add the oil and heat until just smoking. Add the mushrooms and cook without stirring for 2 to 3 minutes, then stir and cook until moderately browned, about 5 minutes total. Stir in the olives and thyme. Add the spinach and arugula, season with 1½ teaspoons salt, ½ teaspoon black pepper, and the piment d'Espelette. Cook, stirring, until the spinach and arugula are wilted, about 3 minutes. Stir in the lemon zest and juice.

recipe continued on next page

7. To serve, divide the vegetables among four deep serving plates. Use a fork and serving spoon to fillet the fish (see page 382), placing a fillet on top of the mound of vegetables on each of two plates. Repeat to fillet and serve the second fish. Spoon any juices over the fish.

8. Rewarm the vinaigrette over low heat and drizzle over the fillets.

KITCHEN NOTEBOOK: CRUSHING WHOLE SEEDS

To crush whole seeds such as coriander and fennel, place the seeds on a cutting board and crush with the bottom of a saucepan. Or pulse very briefly in a spice grinder.

· CRAB-STUFFED ROASTED LOBSTER ·

SERVES 4 AS AN ENTRÉE

Every fish house menu has some kind of fish—flounder, shrimp, or sole—stuffed with crab. Here's my take on that classic. The lobster is butterflied—split lengthwise but not quite in half; just enough to crack it open for stuffing. The crab is aggressively flavored with fresh herbs and lemon and topped with an herbed panko crust for texture. This is a special occasion recipe but absolutely worth the trouble.

For even more flavor, drizzle the tails with basil-garlic butter (page 136) instead of plain melted butter.

FOR THE CRAB STUFFING

5 tablespoons Homemade Mayonnaise (page 21) or good-quality store-bought mayonnaise

3 tablespoons chopped shallot (about 1 small)

2 teaspoons slivered seeded finger chile

1 tablespoon thinly sliced fresh chives

1 tablespoon slivered fresh Italian parsley

1 tablespoon slivered fresh tarragon

1 teaspoon finely grated lemon zest

1 tablespoon plus 1 teaspoon fresh lemon juice

Fine sea salt and freshly ground black pepper

1 pound lump crabmeat, picked through for shell and cartilage

FOR THE SEASONED PANKO

½ cup panko breadcrumbs

½ teaspoon thinly sliced fresh chives

½ teaspoon slivered fresh Italian parsley

½ teaspoon slivered fresh tarragon

2 teaspoons extra virgin olive oil

Fine sea salt and freshly ground black pepper

FOR THE LOBSTER

Four 1¼-pound live lobsters

Fine sea salt and freshly ground black pepper

8 tablespoons (1 stick) unsalted butter, melted

1. For the stuffing, stir together the mayonnaise, shallot, chile, chives, parsley, tarragon, lemon zest and juice, ¾ teaspoon salt, and ⅛ teaspoon pepper in a medium bowl. Gently fold in the crab so as to not break it into pieces. Taste for salt and pepper and adjust if necessary. Cover and refrigerate.

2. For the panko, stir together the breadcrumbs, chives, parsley, tarragon, and olive oil in a medium bowl. Season with ¼ teaspoon salt and a pinch of pepper; set aside.

recipe continued on next page

3. Place the lobsters on a cutting board, underside facing up, and butterfly as shown on pages 390–91. Pull off the claws and knuckles. Remove the vein from the tails and the grain sacs from the heads; crack the claws as you would a cooked lobster (page 394).

4. Arrange two racks in the top and center of the oven and preheat the oven to 400°F. Line two rimmed baking sheet with aluminum foil. Arrange 2 lobsters cut side up on each baking sheet. Stuff each head cavity with one quarter of the crab mixture. Season the lobster tails with salt and pepper and drizzle each tail with 1 tablespoon of the melted butter. Cover with foil and roast the lobsters for 20 minutes, switching the baking sheets between the oven racks halfway through roasting for even cooking.

5. Remove from the oven. Remove the foil and set aside the claws. Return the lobsters to the oven to continue roasting for 6 minutes more.

6. Remove from the oven and sprinkle about 1 tablespoon of the panko mixture over the stuffing in each lobster. Drizzle each with 1 tablespoon of the melted butter. Return to the oven and roast until the breadcrumbs are golden brown, about 4 minutes more.

KITCHEN NOTEBOOK: SLIVERING FRESH HERBS

Rather than chopping, I prefer to thinly slice fresh herbs for a nice clean cut that avoids bruising the delicate leaves. Thin slivers are also attractive, and integrate well into the food. Just gather the herbs into a loose pile and, holding the pile together with one hand, slice thinly.

6.

BRAISED FISH

Once you've got a handle on baking, it's an easy next step to braising.

Braising means cooking the fish partially submerged in liquid in a covered container. So it's a lot like baking but with liquid. You season the fish, put it in a cooking vessel with the liquid, and don't mess with it until it's cooked. Easy.

You can braise in the oven or on the stovetop. The liquid can be as simple as white wine or something with a few more ingredients—Blackfish 101 Braised with Oyster Mushrooms, Crème Fraîche, and Tarragon (page 160), for example. Either way, braising is a great way to get some flavor into the fish. And the fish stays moist. The cooking liquid gets a shot of flavor, too, because while the fish cooks, its juices meld with the liquid. In almost all cases, the braising liquid is served with the fish. Lemon Sole 101 with Ben's All-Purpose Seasoning Mix on page 155 is an example of a recipe in which the liquid reduces and thickens enough during cooking to serve as a sauce. It's a good place to start because the preparation is so simple.

Braised Sea Robin 101 Basque-Style (page 164)—also easy—was inspired by a dish from the kitchen at La Côte Basque. There, we wrapped a fillet of black bass in prosciutto, cooked it on the stovetop, and served it with a piperade, a Basque-style bell pepper stew that works great as a braise. Braised Cod 101 Garbure (page 161) is based on a hearty French soup I serve at Oceana. These make excellent weekday meals because the cooking all happens in one pot.

In this chapter you'll find several such recipes adapted from the restaurant kitchen. Every once in a while I cook a restaurant-style meal in a private home because I've donated my time for a charity event. When I do that sort of thing, I'm often feeding a large group of people out of a small Manhattan apartment kitchen. I want to do something that's representative of the restaurant, but have to adapt to the small kitchen. Braising is a great way to incorporate a range of interesting flavors into a simple dish.

Another advantage to braising is that it allows you to build layers of flavor into the dish. Each ingredient is cooked to develop its flavor before the next ingredient is added. Braised Cod 101 Garbure is a good example of this structure. The ingredients are cooked in sequence—first the bacon, then the aromatics (onion and garlic), then the longer-cooking root vegetables, and finally the Brussels sprouts. Then you add the water, and eventually the fish. If you were just to put bacon and vegetables in a pot and boil until the vegetables were tender, then add the fish, you wouldn't end up with the same intensity of flavor. Try it. On second thought, don't; you'll likely be disappointed.

When you're feeling confident with the technique and you've got some time to fool around, try a Thai-style bouillabaisse (page 172), in which ocean perch fillets are braised in fish stock flavored with tamarind and kaffir lime leaves and served over glass noodles. Braised Monkfish Avgolemono (page 176) has a few more steps; it relies on a fish stock in which the monkfish is braised. That fortified braising liquid is used in a last minute egg-lemon sauce. Not exactly a dish for the novice cook but insanely delicious. Just follow the steps and you'll get there.

Techniques of braising and steaming overlap. We talk about steaming shellfish but technically we're braising it: the shellfish is cooked partially submerged in a flavorful liquid that is served with the fish. So this chapter also includes a few recipes for steamed clams and mussels. Steamed Clams 101 with Garlic and Oregano (page 175) is a basic method for braising/steaming shellfish. Steamer Clams with Red Miso Broth (page 168) introduces Japanese flavors, and Mussels 101 with Curry and Yogurt (page 167) fills your kitchen with the fragrance of Indian cuisine.

BEST FISH FOR BRAISING

Choose leaner, white-fleshed fish such as flatfish (sole, flounder, halibut, and turbot), snapper, cod, striped bass, black bass, blackfish, perch, and monkfish. They come out of the pot moist, with their subtle flavors accented. They also add great flavor to the cooking base. Oilier fish such as salmon, trout, and bluefish are less desirable because they will impart a very strong flavor and oiliness to the braising liquid. Clams and mussels are excellent braised, as are scallops.

EQUIP YOURSELF: BRAISING

• For braising on top of the stove, you'll need pots that are large enough to hold the fish in a single layer. Some recipes can be done in a deep skillet.

• For braising in the oven, you'll need an ovenproof glass baking dish large enough to hold the fish in a single layer.

• In either case, use a large kitchen spoon for scooping the garnish and sauce out of the pot onto the serving plates.

• For stirring, heatproof silicone spatulas or composite nylon-fiberglass "wooden" spoons made by MIU France, available online at amazon.com.

• Wooden spoons are traditional; the downside of wood is that it absorbs foods and their smells.

KITCHEN NOTEBOOK: BEN'S ALL-PURPOSE SEASONING MIX

Ask any of my sous chefs how I like to cook zucchini and they'll rattle if off: "Extra virgin olive oil in pan. Add zucchini, season, cook a minute. Push zucchini to the side. In space left open, add butter; let melt. Add shallot, slivered chile; swirl to coat with butter and cook 10 seconds. Stir into zucchini. Add chicken stock and simmer until zucchini is cooked. Off heat, add chopped parsley and chives." It's my all-purpose seasoning mix. It's terrific with most vegetables, and with braised fish, too.

The technique will work with any vegetable, but I might augment the seasoning mix to suit the vegetable. Try basil with zucchini, savory with green beans, tarragon with mushrooms, or epazote with corn.

· LEMON SOLE 101 ·
WITH BEN'S ALL-PURPOSE SEASONING MIX

SERVES 4 AS AN ENTRÉE

This is my version of a traditional French, home-cook method for braising fish, seasoned with my go-to seasoning mix (see Kitchen Notebook, page 154). The flounder and wine create a killer sauce while they cook. It's as simple as it gets but looks fancy enough that if you've got people coming over for dinner, it will seem special. As much a method as a recipe, this is a great way to cook any lean white fish, including other flatfish such as flounder and fluke, also cod, snapper, black sea bass, and halibut. If you're working with thin fillets, be sure to season only one side, or both sides very lightly. Serve with rice or another grain to soak up the sauce.

Four 6-ounce boneless, skinless lemon sole fillets

Fine sea salt and freshly ground black pepper

¼ cup finely chopped shallots (about 1 medium)

¼ cup dry white wine

2 tablespoons extra virgin olive oil

2 teaspoons slivered seeded finger chile

2 teaspoons slivered fresh Italian parsley

2 teaspoons thinly sliced fresh chives

1. Preheat the oven to 350°F.

2. On a plate or a sheet of aluminum foil, sprinkle the fillets on one side only with salt and pepper. Let stand about 5 minutes to allow the seasonings to penetrate.

3. Fold the fillets crosswise in half or thirds, depending on thickness; you want the folded "packages" to be 1 to 1¼ inch thick.

4. Choose a baking dish or ovenproof skillet large enough to hold the folded fish in a single layer. Scatter the shallots over the bottom of the dish or skillet. Add the wine and oil. Set the fish on top and sprinkle with the slivered chile, parsley, and chives. Cover with aluminum foil and bake until the fish is cooked through but still looks a little underdone when you poke a paring knife in the center, about 20 minutes.

5. Use a spatula to place the fish on each of four serving plates. Spoon the shallots and herbs on top. Spoon over the sauce.

· HALIBUT 101 BRAISED ·
WITH PEAS, CARROTS, AND POTATOES

SERVES 4 AS AN ENTRÉE

Here's another very easy weeknight braise featuring a roster of old-fashioned flavors—carrots, potatoes, pearl onions, and peas. It's great to make in the spring when you can get fresh peas in the pod. Otherwise, frozen peas are always acceptable.

6 slender carrots, peeled

15 pearl onions, peel-on

Four 7- to 8-ounce boneless, skinless halibut fillets

Fine sea salt and freshly ground black pepper

¼ cup extra virgin olive oil

4 cloves garlic, sliced

12 fingerling potatoes, peel-on, cut on an oblique angle into 1-inch pieces

3 cups Low-Stress Chicken Stock (page 16) or store-bought low-sodium chicken stock

2 cups shelled fresh peas (2 pounds in the pod) or one 9- to 10-ounce package frozen peas (without sauce)

¼ cup slivered fresh Italian parsley

1. Cut the carrots on an angle into 1-inch pieces, rolling the carrots slightly after each cut to achieve oblique pieces (see page 378); set aside.

2. Place the onions in a heatproof bowl. Bring 2 cups water to a boil. Pour over the onions and let stand 2 minutes. Drain the onions and peel with a paring knife. Cut into halves, or quarters if larger than ¾-inch diameter.

3. On a plate or a sheet of aluminum foil, season the halibut on both sides with salt and pepper. Let stand at least 5 minutes to allow the seasonings to penetrate.

4. Meanwhile, heat the oil in a large, deep skillet or a pot large enough to hold the fish in a single layer (with a lid) over medium heat. Add the garlic and cook without coloring, stirring often, for 2 minutes. Add the carrots and potatoes and mix well. Season with 1 teaspoon salt and a pinch of pepper and cook, stirring often, 1½ minutes more.

5. Add the chicken stock, cover, and simmer until the carrots and potatoes are almost tender, about 6 minutes. Add the peas, stir, cover, and cook 2 minutes more. If using frozen peas, stir to break up any remaining frozen clumps.

6. Nestle the halibut on top of the vegetables, spooning some of the liquid over. Cover and simmer until the halibut is cooked to medium-well, about 5 minutes. Remove from the heat and let stand 1 minute.

7. Remove the halibut to a sheet of aluminum foil. Stir the parsley into the vegetables and adjust the seasoning. Divide the vegetables and broth among four shallow serving bowls or deep serving plates and place the fish on top.

· STRIPED BASS 101 BRAISED ·
WITH GREEN BEANS STRACOTTO

SERVES 4 AS AN ENTRÉE

This rustic Italian dish is something I've been making at home for a long time. I adapted it last summer for the restaurant to serve with tuna *a la plancha*. But at home, it makes a simple, tasty one-pot dish. *Stracotto* means "extra cooked" in Italian, so don't expect the beans to be bright green. Extra cooked until gray-green and extra tender, their taste and texture are very different from the bright green crunch of quickly steamed green beans, but I love them cooked this way. During the summer, you can use fresh tomatoes in place of canned—coarsely chop about 1¾ pounds tomatoes. And if you live in the Carolinas, substitute local channel bass. Make sure to remove the skin; its gelatinous texture doesn't improve with braising.

The beans may be cooked several hours ahead. Just bring them to a simmer before adding the fish.

¼ cup extra virgin olive oil

4 cloves garlic, thinly sliced crosswise

½ large onion, cut through the root end, thinly sliced lengthwise (1 generous cup)

1¼ pounds green beans, stem ends trimmed, cut into 2-inch lengths

Fine sea salt

One 28-ounce can whole peeled plum tomatoes with juice (preferably organic)

2 sprigs fresh basil, plus ½ cup gently packed whole fresh basil leaves

Four 6- to 8-ounce boneless, skinless striped bass fillets (1¼ to 1½ inches thick)

Freshly ground black pepper

1. Place a pot large enough to hold the fish in a single layer (with a lid) over medium heat. Add the oil and heat until fluid enough to coat the bottom of the pan when swirled. Add the garlic and cook without coloring, about 1 minute. Add the onion and cook until the onion is translucent and the garlic has begun to develop some golden color, about 2 minutes. Add the beans and 2 teaspoons salt and cook, stirring often, until the color of the beans brightens, about 3 minutes. Add the tomatoes with their juices, crushing the tomatoes in your hand as you add them. Add the basil sprigs. Cover and simmer gently until the beans are very tender, about 40 minutes.

2. On a plate or a sheet of aluminum foil, sprinkle the fish on both sides with salt and pepper. Let stand 5 minutes to allow the seasonings to penetrate.

3. Return the beans to a simmer. Nestle the fillets in the beans in a single layer and spoon some of the liquid over. Cover and simmer until the fish is cooked through, 8 to 10 minutes.

4. Remove the fish to four deep serving plates or shallow serving bowls. Stir the basil leaves into the beans. Season to taste with pepper, and taste for salt; adjust if necessary. Serve the beans alongside the fish.

KITCHEN NOTEBOOK: GREEN BEANS, BRAISED VS. BOILED

For a good demonstration of just how big an impact cooking technique has on flavor, compare the taste of the braised beans in this dish against the boiled beans on page 369 (Green Beans with Sofrito). Same ingredient; entirely different flavor.

· BLACKFISH 101 BRAISED ·
WITH OYSTER MUSHROOMS,
CRÈME FRAÎCHE, AND TARRAGON

SERVES 4 AS AN ENTRÉE

This simple, French-inspired braise demonstrates the practicality and elegance of the technique. You make what amounts to a creamy mushroom sauce, add the blackfish, and 5 minutes later, you've got perfectly moist fish with a sophisticated-tasting sauce. With just a few ingredients yielding great flavor, this is a classy, quick way to prepare any lean white fish such as black sea bass, snapper, flounder, and grouper. Blackfish, also called tautog, is similar to black sea bass but less expensive. With this sauce, some people might be fooled into thinking they're enjoying the more expensive bass.

Four 6-ounce boneless, skin-on blackfish fillets (½ to ¾ inch thick)

Fine sea salt and freshly ground black pepper

1 tablespoon unsalted butter

2 cloves garlic, sliced

1 large shallot, halved through the root end and thinly sliced crosswise (about ½ cup)

8 ounces oyster mushrooms, clusters pulled apart, wiped clean, base discarded

1¼ cups Low-Stress Chicken Stock (page 16) or store-bought low-sodium chicken stock

¼ cup crème fraîche, or sour cream

1 tablespoon slivered fresh tarragon

1. On a plate or a sheet of aluminum foil, season the fish on both sides with salt and pepper. Let stand 5 minutes to allow the seasonings to penetrate.

2. Heat a 12-inch skillet (with a lid) over medium heat. Add the butter and heat to melt. Add the garlic and shallot and cook without coloring, stirring often, about 1 minute. Add the mushrooms, ½ teaspoon salt, and pepper to taste and cook without coloring, stirring often, 2 to 3 minutes, until the mushrooms are softened.

3. Add the stock and crème fraîche and stir well to blend. Cover and simmer gently for 5 minutes to allow the mushrooms to flavor the liquid. Place the fish on top, cover, and simmer gently until the fish is cooked through, about 5 minutes. Remove from the heat.

4. Remove the fish to a plate. Off the heat, add the tarragon to the braising liquid and stir. Divide the mushrooms and braising liquid among four shallow serving bowls or deep serving plates. Set a piece of fish on top.

· BRAISED COD 101 GARBURE ·

SERVES 4 AS AN ENTRÉE

There is no one authentic recipe for the soulful, rustic French country soup called garbure, but cabbage is a usual ingredient along with preserved meats (usually ham, sometimes duck confit), shell beans, and whatever vegetables are available. I serve a more contemporary version with Brussels sprouts at the restaurant. Here, I've reduced the liquid to turn the soup into a stew, adding the starch from the potatoes to lightly thicken the broth. Try this recipe with hake, too.

4 strips thin-cut bacon (2 ounces)

3 medium carrots, peeled

2 small turnips, trimmed, peeled, quartered through the stem end, and sliced crosswise ½ inch thick

1 teaspoon canola oil

½ large onion, cut into ½-inch dice

2 cloves garlic, thinly sliced

Fine sea salt

One 10-ounce package fresh Brussels sprouts, trimmed and halved through the stalk end

8 ounces fingerling potatoes, peel-on, halved lengthwise if thick, sliced crosswise ⅓ to ½ inch thick

Freshly ground black pepper

Four 6- to 8-ounce boneless, skinless cod fillets (1 to 1¼ inches thick)

1. Cut the bacon strips in half crosswise, stack, and cut crosswise into ¼-inch-wide pieces; set aside.

2. Cut the carrots in half crosswise. Slice the skinny halves into ½-inch-thick coins. Cut the fatter halves in half lengthwise, then slice into ½-inch-thick half-rounds; set aside with the turnips.

3. Place a pot large enough to hold the fish in a single layer over medium-low heat. Add the oil and heat until fluid enough to coat the bottom of the pot when swirled. Add the bacon and cook, stirring often, until the fat is rendered and the bacon begins to brown, 2 to 3 minutes. Add the onion and garlic and cook, stirring often, until the onion is translucent, 4 to 5 minutes.

4. Add the carrots, turnips, and 1 teaspoon salt and stir. Reduce the heat to low and cook the vegetables without coloring, stirring often, for 5 minutes to begin developing flavor. Add the Brussels sprouts and potatoes and cook, stirring often, 3 minutes more, until they begin to cook.

recipe continued on next page

5. Add 4 cups water, season with pepper, and bring to a simmer, scraping up any caramelized juices that have collected on the bottom of the pot. Cover and simmer vigorously until the vegetables are tender, 25 to 30 minutes. The liquid may reduce over the vegetables; add ½ cup to 1 cup water, as needed (see Kitchen Notebook, below).

6. Meanwhile, on a plate, season the cod on both sides with salt and pepper and let stand 5 minutes to allow the seasonings to penetrate.

7. When the vegetables are tender, nestle the cod into them in a single layer and spoon some of the liquid over. Cover and simmer gently until the cod is cooked through, 5 to 6 minutes.

8. Remove the fish carefully with a slotted spatula to four shallow bowls or deep serving plates. Taste and adjust the seasoning in the garbure. Spoon the vegetables and sauce around the fish.

KITCHEN NOTEBOOK: BRAISING LIQUIDS

The amount of water required for this recipe depends on the speed of the reduction. And that depends on a number of factors including the heat, the size of your pot, and how vigorous a simmer you've got going. By the end of cooking, the solids should no longer be fully submerged—they should poke out a little (about one sixth) from under the liquid. If you find the liquid reducing too quickly, add another ½ to 1 cup water during cooking.

· BRAISED SEA ROBIN 101 ·
BASQUE-STYLE

SERVES 4 AS AN ENTRÉE

Piperade is a typical Basque preparation of bell peppers stewed with onion, garlic, and tomato. It's flavored with *jambon de Bayonne* (Bayonne ham), a raw cured ham that tastes similar to prosciutto, and the Basque chile pepper, piment d'Espelette. The bell peppers are sweet, soft, and saucy, and the rich, salty ham complements their flavor. I like sea robin or perch for this because the smaller fillets are easy to tuck into the piperade and the flavors meld into the dish. Both fish are a good value, too.

¼ cup extra virgin olive oil

½ large onion (cut through the root end), thinly sliced crosswise (about 1 cup)

2 cloves garlic, thinly sliced crosswise

2 ounces Bayonne ham or prosciutto (thinly sliced but preferably not paper-thin), cut into thin strips

2 red bell peppers, halved through the stem end, stems, seeds, and ribs removed, cut into 3- to 4-inch-long strips about ¼ inch thick

2 yellow bell peppers, halved through the stem end, stems, seeds, and ribs removed, cut into 3- to 4-inch-long strips about ¼ inch thick

Fine sea salt and freshly ground black pepper

One 14.5-ounce can whole peeled tomatoes in juice (preferably organic)

½ teaspoon piment d'Espelette, Aleppo pepper, or hot paprika, or ⅛ teaspon cayenne pepper

1½ pounds boneless, skin-on sea robin or ocean perch fillets

1. Place a deep 12-inch skillet or a pot large enough to hold the fish in a single layer over medium-high heat. Add the oil, onion, and garlic and cook without coloring, stirring often, for 3 minutes.

2. Add the ham and cook, stirring often, until the fat renders and the ham is aromatic, 30 seconds to 1 minute.

3. Add the pepper strips, ½ teaspoon salt, and ⅛ teaspoon pepper and stir to coat the peppers with the oil. Reduce the heat to medium and cook, stirring often, until the peppers give off their liquid and begin to stew in their juices, about 2 minutes.

4. Add the tomatoes with their juice, crushing the tomatoes in your hand as you add them. Add the piment d'Espelette, stir well. Cover, reduce the heat to low, and cook, stirring once or twice during cooking, until the peppers are tender, 13 to 15 minutes.

5. Meanwhile, on a plate or a sheet of aluminum foil, season the fillets on both sides with salt and pepper. Let stand 5 minutes to allow the seasonings to penetrate.

6. Add the fillets to the piperade in as close to a single layer as possible (it doesn't matter if the fish is crowded) and spoon on some of the liquid. Cover and cook until the fillets are cooked through, about 5 minutes. Divide the peppers among four shallow serving bowls or deep serving plates and place the fillets on top.

· MUSSELS 101 ·
WITH CURRY AND YOGURT

SERVES 4 AS AN ENTRÉE

This recipe employs the same basic technique for shellfish as the one for Steamed Clams 101 with Garlic and Oregano (page 175). The yogurt adds depth of flavor and acidity, as well as a little richness to balance the curry spices. Serve with crusty bread to sop up the sauce.

2 teaspoons cornstarch

½ cup plain Greek yogurt

2 tablespoons canola oil

3 tablespoons chopped shallot (about 1 medium)

4 cloves garlic, sliced

2 tablespoons slivered seeded finger chile

4 teaspoons curry powder

4 pounds cultivated mussels, scrubbed, beards removed if necessary

¼ cup firmly packed fresh cilantro leaves

1. In a small bowl, stir together the cornstarch and yogurt; set aside.

2. Place a large pot over medium heat. Add the oil and heat until fluid enough to coat the bottom of the pot when swirled. Add the shallots, garlic, and chiles and cook until fragrant and the garlic is translucent but not colored, about 30 seconds. Add the curry powder and cook, stirring constantly, 15 seconds. Add ½ cup water and stir.

3. Turn the heat to high. Add the mussels and give them a stir. Cover and cook, stirring every minute for even cooking, until the mussels open, 2 to 3 minutes. Discard any mussels that didn't open.

4. Stir in the yogurt mixture and bring to a boil for 10 seconds. Remove from the heat. Add the cilantro and stir to wilt.

5. Use a slotted spoon to divide the mussels among four shallow serving bowls or deep serving plates. Pour the cooking liquid over the mussels, holding back the last of the liquid in case of grit.

· STEAMER CLAMS ·
WITH RED MISO BROTH

SERVES 2 AS AN ENTRÉE

I recently attended a series of Japanese cooking classes for professional chefs where I discovered red miso, a fermented soybean paste with a much deeper, nuttier flavor than white or yellow miso. That nutty taste pairs very well with the sweetness of clams. So if you want to do something interesting with your classic steamer clam recipe, this is a great option. Still very simple, but with a little twist. Littlenecks can be substituted for steamers.

1 tablespoon canola oil

1 small shallot, thinly sliced crosswise (about 2 tablespoons)

1 clove garlic, thinly sliced (about 1 teaspoon)

¾-inch piece fresh ginger, peeled and minced (about 2 teaspoons)

½ finger chile (cut lengthwise), seeds removed, slivered

One 12-ounce bottle wheat beer

3 tablespoons red miso

2 teaspoons sugar

24 steamer clams, rinsed (and purged, if necessary; see page 421)

1. Place a medium pot over medium heat. Add the oil, shallot, and garlic and cook without coloring, stirring often for 2 minutes. Add the ginger and chile and cook without coloring stirring often, for 3 minutes more.

2. In a medium bowl, stir together the beer, 1 cup water, the red miso, and the sugar until blended. Add to the aromatics and simmer 3 to 4 minutes.

3. Add the clams, cover, and cook until they open, about 3 minutes. Discard any clams that didn't open.

4. Use a slotted spoon to divide the clams between two deep serving plates or shallow serving bowls. Pour the cooking liquid over, holding back the last of the liquid in case of grit.

· CARIBBEAN FISH CHOWDER ·

SERVES 4 AS AN ENTRÉE

I make this Caribbean-inspired braise with mahi mahi, but you can use any firm, meaty white fish such as swordfish and striped bass, or a combination of fish. Though it's simple enough for weeknight cooking, it's not your usual weekday fare, at least in my household. It's a fun dish for a party.

1 medium sweet potato (about 12 ounces), peeled and quartered

Fine sea salt

1 poblano pepper

One 13.5-ounce can unsweetened coconut milk

1¼ pounds boneless, skinless mahi mahi fillet, bloodline removed, cut into 1-inch dice

Freshly ground black pepper

1 tablespoon canola oil

1 medium red onion, quartered through the root end and sliced crosswise medium-thin (about 1 cup)

1 cup water

½ teaspoon ground allspice

1 teaspoon ground toasted coriander

Finely grated zest and juice of 1 lime

¾ cup gently packed fresh cilantro leaves (about 2 small bunches)

1. Bring 2 quarts water to a boil in a 3- to 4-quart saucepan. Cut each sweet potato quarter lengthwise into 4 equal wedges; cut each wedge crosswise into 4 even pieces. Add 1 tablespoon salt to the boiling water. Add the sweet potato. Return the water to a boil, reduce the heat, and simmer until the sweet potato is cooked through but not falling apart, about 7 minutes. Drain in a colander; set aside.

2. Lightly rub the pepper all over with oil. If you have a gas burner, turn the heat to high, place the pepper directly on the burner and roast, turning with tongs as the skin blackens, until the pepper is blackened all over. Blacken the top and bottom of the pepper, too. This should take about 5 minutes total. (If your burners are electric, instead preheat the oven to 400°F. Place the oiled pepper on a baking sheet and roast, turning from time to time, until the skin is blistered all over, about 40 minutes.)

3. Place the pepper in a bowl and cover with plastic until cool enough to handle, at least 5 minutes. Place the cooled pepper on a paper towel and scrape off all of the blackened skin with a paring knife. Cut the pepper in half through the stem end, cut out the stem, and scrape out the seeds. Coarsely chop the pepper and place in a blender. Add the coconut milk and purée until smooth; set aside.

4. On a plate or a sheet of aluminum foil, season the fish with salt and pepper. Let stand 5 minutes to allow the seasonings to penetrate.

5. Pat the fish dry with paper towels.

6. Place a large saucepan over medium heat. Add the oil. Add the onion and cook, stirring often, 2 minutes, until very lightly golden.

7. Turn the heat to high. Add the cubed fish, and cook, stirring once or twice, 1 minute. Add the water and coconut milk-poblano mixture. Bring slowly to a simmer but do not boil—the coconut milk will separate. Add the allspice, coriander, and ¼ teaspoon salt. Simmer 4 minutes more.

8. Stir in the zest and cooked sweet potatoes and simmer 1 minute. Remove from the heat. Stir in the lime juice and cilantro. Taste for seasoning.

9. Divide among four deep serving plates or shallow serving bowls.

· THAI-STYLE BOUILLABAISSE · WITH OCEAN PERCH, TAMARIND, AND GLASS NOODLES

SERVES 4 AS AN ENTRÉE

The technique for making this dish is similar to a classic bouillabaisse (page 115). The fish broth is boiled, not simmered, in order to create the correct emulsion that thickens the broth slightly. I've put an Asian spin on the French classic with tamarind, ginger, lime leaves, Thai herbs, and a little sugar to balance the acidity of the tamarind. Silky glass noodles, sour tamarind, crunchy lotus root, and tender, delicate-flavored fish give the dish a range of contrasting textures and flavors. With a little notice, your fishmonger should be able to supply you with bones for broth.

Though this recipe calls for 4 ounces, you're probably going to be buying a larger package of glass noodles (also called cellophane noodles). Use kitchen scissors to cut off the appropriate amount—just eyeball it. Put the noodles in an airtight container and store with the rest of your pastas.

FOR THE BROTH

1 tablespoon canola oil

2 cloves garlic, crushed with the side of a chef's knife and peeled

2 medium shallots, sliced crosswise ½ inch thick

¾-inch piece peel-on fresh ginger, thickly sliced

½ cup coarsely chopped white mushrooms (2 to 3 large mushrooms, stems trimmed)

½ red finger chile with seeds (cut lengthwise), sliced crosswise ½ inch thick

2 pounds bones from any lean white fish such as striped bass, cod, halibut, hake, black bass, sole, or flounder, rinsed thoroughly under cold running water and cut into 3-inch sections with a heavy knife or kitchen scissors

Fine sea salt

2 kaffir lime leaves, or grated zest of ½ lime

¾ cup dry white wine

2 tablespoons light brown sugar

2 tablespoons tamarind paste

1 sprig fresh Thai basil

FOR THE BOUILLABAISSE

4 ounces dried glass noodles

1½ pounds boneless, skin-on ocean perch fillets

Fine sea salt and freshly ground black pepper

One 7-ounce piece fresh lotus root

1 tablespoon canola oil

4 ounces honshimeiji mushrooms, stem
    bottoms trimmed, clusters pulled apart
    (about 2 cups)

½ seedless cucumber (cut lengthwise),
    peel-on, quartered lengthwise and sliced
    crosswise into ¼-inch-thick wedges

1 teaspoon chopped shallot

1 teaspoon chopped peeled fresh ginger

1 teaspoon chopped seeded finger chile

1 tablespoon slivered fresh mint

1 tablespoon slivered fresh Thai basil

1. For the broth, heat a large pot over medium heat. Add the oil and heat until fluid enough to coat the bottom of the pot when swirled. Add the garlic, shallots, ginger, mushrooms, and chile, and cook, stirring often, until fragrant, about 2 minutes. Add the fish bones and stir well. Cook without coloring, uncovered, until the bones begin to fall apart and are simmering in their juices, 5 to 6 minutes.

2. Stir in 1 teaspoon salt and the kaffir lime leaves. Add the wine and simmer 1 minute. Add 8 cups water, bring to a boil, and boil vigorously, uncovered, for 25 minutes. The solids should remain almost completely submerged. If you find the water evaporating too quickly, add ½ to 1 cup more (see Kitchen Notebook: Braising Liquids, page 163).

3. Strain the broth through a fine-mesh strainer into another large pot. Place over medium heat. Add the brown sugar and tamarind paste and whisk to blend. Whisk in 1 teaspoon salt. Remove from the heat. Add the Thai basil, cover, and let stand 20 minutes to allow the basil to infuse the broth.

4. For the bouillabaisse, fill a large bowl with hot tap water. Add the noodles and let stand 10 minutes to soften. Drain through a fine-mesh strainer; return to the bowl and set aside.

5. When the broth has been infused, remove the basil sprig. Set the broth aside.

6. On a baking sheet or a sheet of aluminum foil, season the perch fillets on both sides with salt and pepper. Let stand at least 5 minutes to allow the seasonings to penetrate.

7. To prepare the lotus root, fill a medium bowl with cold water (once peeled and cut, the root must be stored in water or it will turn brown). Trim the ends of the lotus root and peel with a vegetable peeler. Quarter the root lengthwise, then cut it crosswise into ¼-inch-thick wedges. Set aside in the water.

8. Bring a medium pot of water to a boil. Fill a large bowl with cold water. Set out a baking sheet for the noodles. Spread the drained noodles on your cutting board and cut them with kitchen scissors into approximately 6-inch lengths. (This makes them easier to eat.)

recipe continued on next page

Add the noodles to the boiling water. Count 10 seconds. Drain in a fine-mesh strainer or remove from the boiling water with a skimmer and transfer to the bowl of cold water to cool. When they're cool, drain again and spread out on the baking sheet.

9. Score the skin of the fillets on an angle at 1-inch intervals to inhibit curling (they will curl somewhat anyway).

10. Return the broth to a boil. Drain the lotus root, and add it to the broth. Remove the broth from the heat.

11. Place a large, deep skillet or a pot large enough to hold the fish in a single layer (with a lid) over high heat. Add the canola oil and heat until fluid enough to coat the bottom of the skillet when swirled. Add the mushrooms and 1 teaspoon salt. Cook, stirring often, 2 minutes. Add the cucumber wedges, shallot, ginger, and chile, and cook, stirring often, about 30 seconds. Add the broth and lotus root and adjust the heat so the broth simmers. Arrange the fish on top in a single layer, skin side up. Cover and braise the fish until the flesh is opaque but not yet falling apart, 2 to 4 minutes.

12. Using a slotted spatula, remove the fish to a large plate. Remove the broth from the heat. Stir in the mint and basil.

13. Divide the noodles among four deep serving plates or shallow serving bowls. Pour the broth over. Divide the fillets among the servings.

· STEAMED CLAMS 101 ·
WITH GARLIC AND OREGANO

SERVES 2 AS AN ENTRÉE

I've always loved clams. I enjoy that little bit of chewiness, and they have a good, full flavor that tastes of the sea. I'm also a big fan of fresh oregano, and this combination of garlic, butter, and oregano just screams "ITALIAN COOKING" for me. If you prefer, you can substitute extra virgin olive oil for the butter. This recipe is easily doubled—just use two pots. The clams also taste great tossed with linguine; cook 8 ounces of pasta for two people.

- 2 tablespoons unsalted butter
- 2 tablespoons chopped garlic (about 7 cloves)
- 24 littleneck clams (3½ pounds), scrubbed well (see Equip Yourself, below)
- 1 cup dry white wine
- 1 tablespoon slivered fresh oregano
- Warm crusty bread, for serving

1. In a deep 12-inch skillet (with a lid) or a large pot, gently warm the butter with the garlic over low heat until the butter melts. Raise the heat to medium and cook without coloring, swirling the pan frequently so that the garlic doesn't burn, about 2 minutes.

2. Add the clams, stir, and cook 30 seconds. Add the wine and cover the pot. Raise the heat to high and cook until the clams begin to open, about 4 minutes. Add the oregano, cover again, and continue cooking until all the clams are open, about 4 minutes more. Once you've added the oregano, check about once a minute to remove clams that have opened.

3. Use a slotted spoon to divide the clams between two serving bowls. Discard any clams that didn't open. Pour the cooking liquid over the clams, holding back the last of the liquid in case of grit. Serve with warm bread to sop up the juices.

EQUIP YOURSELF: POTATO BRUSH

A potato brush, available at kitchen supply stores and most supermarkets, is perfect for scrubbing the shells of clams, oysters, and mussels to remove sand and grit.

· BRAISED MONKFISH AVGOLEMONO ·

SERVES 4 AS AN ENTRÉE

Avgolemono means "egg-lemon" in Greek, and usually refers to a chicken and rice soup thickened slightly with eggs whisked with lemon juice. The tart egg-lemon combo tastes good with chicken and lamb; it's a natural with a nice, rich fish broth, too. And with its meaty texture, monkfish is the perfect fish. Note that this is not a starter recipe. You make a fish fumet, braise the fish in it, and at the last minute, while your guests are breathing down your neck, bind the braising liquid with an egg-lemon sauce. This preparation certainly requires a little more focus, but the end result is more than worth it.

FOR THE FUMET

1 tablespoon extra virgin olive oil

½ cup diced onion (½-inch dice; about ½ small onion)

¼ cup diced carrot (½-inch dice; about 1 small carrot)

¼ cup diced celery (½-inch dice; about ½ medium stalk celery)

2 cloves garlic, crushed with the side of a chef's knife and peeled

2 pounds bones from lean, white-fleshed fish, such as striped bass, cod, halibut, hake, black bass, sole, or flounder, rinsed thoroughly under cold running water and cut into 3-inch sections with a heavy knife or kitchen scissors

1 cup dry white wine

FOR THE AVGOLEMONO

Fine sea salt

12 ounces fingerling potatoes (about 6), peel-on

¼ medium head savoy cabbage (cut through the root end), cored, leaves separated

¼ cup plus 2 tablespoons fresh lemon juice

2½ teaspoons all-purpose flour

6 large eggs

Four 6- to 7-ounce pieces skinless, trimmed monkfish fillet, each cut crosswise into 4 equal pieces

Freshly ground black pepper

2 teaspoons ground dill seed

2 teaspoons ground fennel seed

½ cup gently packed chopped fresh dill

¼ cup gently packed slivered fresh mint

¼ cup gently packed slivered fresh Italian parsley

1. For the fumet, heat a large pot over medium heat. Add the olive oil and heat until fluid enough to coat the bottom of the pot when swirled. Add the onion, carrot, celery, and garlic, and cook without coloring, stirring often, until the onion is translucent, about 5 minutes. Add the fish bones and stir well. Cook without coloring, uncovered, until the bones begin to fall apart and are simmering in their juices, 5 to 6 minutes. Add the wine and 6 ½ cups water. Bring to a boil, reduce the heat and simmer, uncovered, over medium-high heat for 40 minutes. (You'll have 4 to 5 cups broth.) Strain through a fine-mesh strainer. Measure out and set aside 2½ cups of the fumet. Freeze the remaining broth for another use.

2. For the avgolemono, in a 4-quart or larger saucepan, bring 3 quarts water to a boil with 2 teaspoons salt. Add the potatoes and cook until tender when pierced with a paring knife, 20 to 30 minutes.

3. Drain the potatoes and let cool. Slice into ⅓-inch-thick coins; set aside.

4. Meanwhile, prepare an ice bath by filling a very large bowl with ice and water. In a 4-quart or larger saucepan, bring 3 quarts water to a boil with 2 teaspoons salt. Add the cabbage leaves and boil 2 minutes. Drain the cabbage and place in the ice bath. When cool, drain. Cut the cabbage into ½-inch-wide strips.

5. In a small bowl, whisk the lemon juice with the flour; set aside. Separate the eggs, placing the whites in the top of a double boiler (do not place over the simmering water yet) and the yolks in a medium bowl.

6. On a plate or a sheet of aluminum foil, season the monkfish pieces on both sides with salt and pepper. Let stand 5 minutes to allow the seasonings to penetrate.

7. Bring the reserved 2½ cups fumet to a simmer in a deep 12-inch skillet (with a lid). Add the sliced potatoes, cabbage, and monkfish. Cover and braise gently over medium heat until the fish is cooked through, about 8 minutes. Remove the fish with a slotted spatula or spoon and divide among four shallow serving bowls or deep serving plates. Divide the cabbage and potatoes equally among the bowls or plates. Keep the braising liquid hot.

8. Finish the avgolemono broth: Bring 1 inch water to a simmer in the bottom of the double boiler. Add 1 teaspoon salt to the egg whites and whisk until frothy, about 1 minute. Whisk the lemon juice mixture into the yolks to blend, then add to the whites. Place on top of the simmering water and whisk until the mixture thickens and whitens, about 4 minutes.

9. Once the fish and vegetables have been removed, gradually whisk the hot braising liquid into the egg-lemon mixture. Whisk for 2 minutes more to stabilize the mixture. Remove from the heat. Whisk in the ground dill and fennel seed, the fresh dill, mint, parsley, ½ teaspoon salt, and a pinch of pepper.

10. Spoon the sauce over the fish and vegetables.

7.

BROILED FISH

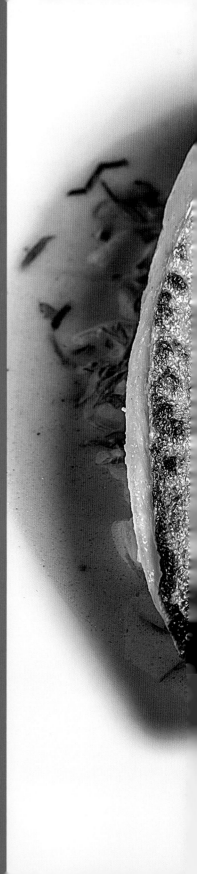

Broiling is a method by which the food is cooked *under* the heat source. To me, it's the ultimate home-cook method for fish. It happens a little faster than baking and braising, but it's almost as easy. There's still no flipping, no sticking to the pan, no hot fat. You don't need to touch the fish once you start cooking. You just season it, rub it with oil, put it on a baking sheet or broiler pan, and go. The broiler does all the work.

Along with grilling, it's also the method that demands the least cleanup. There are no pots, pans, or poaching liquids. So if you line your baking sheet or broiler pan with aluminum foil as I do, you just need to give the pan a light wash when you're done.

From the perspective of taste, a major advantage to broiling is that it produces a nice, crisp browned surface, which means concentrated flavor. You can brown the fish quite simply by rubbing it with a little olive or canola oil, as in the recipes for

Broiled Trout 101 with Yellow Rice and Radicchio (page 183) and Broiled Scallops 101 with Garlicky Spinach (page 189). Almost all fish lend themselves well to broiling and are delicious served with nothing more than lemon wedges or a vinaigrette.

Once you've got the hang of broiling, you can get a little fancier and coat the fish with what the French call a *glaçage*, which means "glaze." The intense heat from the broiler browns the glaze, building in a nice look and an additional layer of flavor. A mayonnaise glaze, as in the recipe for Broiled Cod 101 with Fulton Fish Market Glaçage (page 193), will caramelize nicely under the broiler. Glazes made with a sweet ingredient like orange juice and chile sauce (as in Orange Chile Glazed–Tilefish, page 199) or the natural sugar in coconut milk (Plantain Curry with Coconut-Glazed Shark, page 197) will caramelize especially well. Thicker fillets are broiled for a few minutes before glazing so the glaze doesn't burn before the fish cooks. But cooking time will depend in part on your broiler.

This is the only catch to broiling: You need to get to know your broiler. You need to learn how hot it is, how fast it cooks, and how close to the element you can get your fish in order to brown it up well. All broilers are not the same. My broiler at home, for example, is in a broiler box—a separate compartment below my oven. I can move the rack as close as 2 inches or as far away as 6 inches from the element. For a thicker piece of fish, such as swordfish, salmon, or cod, I set the rack to the 6-inch setting; the fillet cooks through nicely in the same amount of time that it takes to brown the top. Thinner fillets such as trout or flounder need more intense heat for a shorter period of time to brown well; they cook best about 2 inches from the element. And my broiler is a little hotter at the back of the oven, so if I have fillets of different thicknesses, I put the thicker ones toward the back.

The broiler element in my writing partner's oven, however, is at the top of the oven, and the top rack cannot be moved closer than 5 inches to the element. She uses a broiling pan to raise the fish toward the heat.

So there's an element of trial and error in all this, but it's not insurmountable. Take some notes and adjust: If the fish is cooked through before it browns, raise the fish toward the element. If the fish browns up before it's cooked through, lower the fish. Just takes practice. You're up!

SEVEN STEPS TO FOOLPROOF BROILING

1. If you have the option, adjust a rack to 5 to 6 inches from the broiler element for thicker fillets or 2 to 3 inches from the element for thinner fillets. If the rack cannot be raised closer than 5 to 6 inches, use a broiler rack to raise thin fillets. If the rack is only 3 inches from the element, you may have a hard time broiling thick fillets.

2. Preheat your broiler to high for 5 to 15 minutes, until the entire broiling box or oven gets hot.

3. Season the fish (see How to Season Fish, page 7).

4. Line a baking sheet or broiling pan, bottom and sides, with aluminum foil. Rub it very lightly with oil or spray with nonstick cooking spray. (For salmon, be

particularly careful not to use too much oil; the salmon will release a great deal of fat on its own.)

5. Damp seafood will not brown well, so it's key that the fish be dry. Blot it well, skin and flesh sides, with paper towels to absorb any moisture.

6. Place the fish on the baking sheet, skin side up if there's skin. Rub with about 1 teaspoon oil (less for salmon) or spread skinless fillets with a glaze, if you like. Place the baking sheet under the broiler and broil away.

7. Using whichever method you're comfortable with, check the fish for doneness as often as you need to. When cooked, remove the fish to plates with a spatula.

EQUIP YOURSELF: BROILING

- You can broil on any kind of baking sheet, but I recommend using heavy-gauge metal because thinner baking sheets will buckle under the heat of the broiler.
- If you want to raise the food toward the element, a broiling pan will give you a couple of inches.
- Aluminum foil for wrapping the baking sheet or pan.
- A plastic spatula is best because plastic won't rip the aluminum foil.
- Nonstick spray, if you like, for coating the aluminum foil.

· BROILED TROUT 101 ·
WITH YELLOW RICE AND RADICCHIO

SERVES 4 AS AN ENTRÉE

My wife, Christine, inspired this recipe. Sometimes when she's in a pinch, she makes yellow rice for the kids out of a box, the kind with the packet of salty bouillon. This dish is made from scratch and it's not much harder for her to get on the table. Yellow rice, colored with turmeric and flavored with onion, tastes scrumptious with trout. The radicchio softens up a little as it sits in the vinaigrette but retains a little crunch, for a nice textural and color contrast, and its bitterness offsets the fat in the trout. If you've got a hungry crowd, broil a couple more trout fillets in a second batch.

FOR THE YELLOW RICE

1 tablespoon unsalted butter

½ medium onion, coarsely chopped
    (about ¾ cup)

⅛ teaspoon turmeric

1 cup long grain rice

2 cups Low-Stress Chicken Stock (page 16),
    store-bought low-sodium chicken stock, or
    water

½ teaspoon fine sea salt

FOR THE FISH

½ head radicchio

Fine sea salt and freshly ground pepper

2 tablespoons Sherry Vinaigrette (page 19)

Four 5-ounce boneless, skin-on trout fillets

4 teaspoons extra virgin olive oil

1. For the rice, place a 1- to 2-quart saucepan over medium heat. Add the butter and heat to melt. Add the onion and cook, stirring often, until translucent, 3 to 5 minutes. Stir in the turmeric. Stir in the rice and cook, stirring often, until the rice smells toasty, 1 to 2 minutes. Add the chicken stock or water and the salt. Bring to a boil, reduce the heat, cover, and simmer very gently until the rice is just tender and the liquid has been absorbed, 15 to 16 minutes. Let stand, covered, at least 5 minutes before serving.

2. Meanwhile, for the fish, cut the radicchio in half through the root end. Cut out the wedges of white core in each piece. Slice the radicchio crosswise about ⅓ inch thick. Place in a large bowl and toss to separate the leaves. Sprinkle with a pinch each of salt and pepper. Add the vinaigrette and toss to coat. Set aside to soften.

recipe continued on next page

3. Adjust the rack to 2 to 3 inches from the element and preheat the broiler to high. Line a baking sheet with aluminum foil. On the foil, season the trout fillets on the flesh side with salt and pepper. Let stand 5 minutes to allow the seasonings to penetrate.

4. Pat the fillets dry with paper towels. Rub each fillet all over with 1 teaspoon olive oil and place skin side up on the baking sheet. Broil, rotating the baking sheet about halfway through for even cooking, until the flesh is opaque, 4 to 6 minutes. (Pull the baking sheet out from the broiler so that you can lift the fillets to see if the fish is cooked.)

5. To serve, arrange a spoonful of rice on each of four serving plates. Lean a fillet, skin side up, on top of each spoonful of rice. Spoon the salad on top.

· BROILED SALMON STEAKS 101 ·
WITH BRAISED RED CABBAGE AND CHESTNUTS

SERVES 4 AS AN ENTRÉE

This was conceived as a fall dish, when chestnuts are in season. But great-quality, cooked, peeled chestnuts are available year round (see Guide to Unusual Ingredients, page 396); a 7.05-ounce package from D'Artagnan yields about 1 cup chestnuts, perfect for this recipe. The mildly spiced, sweet-sour flavor of German-style braised red cabbage balances the rich fat flavor of salmon—it's a great combination. Salmon steaks work well here, but if you prefer boneless, skinless fillet, I don't notice an appreciable difference in taste (although steaks offers more surface area for browning). Monkfish or grouper are good substitutes, too. A 1¼- to 1½-inch-thick fillet will take 8 to 10 minutes to broil.

FOR THE CABBAGE

2 teaspoons canola oil

½ large onion (cut through the root end), thinly sliced lengthwise (about 1 cup)

1 small head red cabbage (about 1¾ pounds), tough outer leaves removed, quartered through the root end, cored, and sliced crosswise ¼ inch thick (about 8 cups)

¾ teaspoon fine sea salt

3 tablespoons maple syrup

3 tablespoons red wine vinegar

1 bay leaf

1-inch cinnamon stick or ¼ teaspoon ground cinnamon

1 piece whole star anise or ¼ teaspoon ground star anise

4 whole allspice berries or ⅛ teaspoon ground allspice

4 whole cloves or ⅛ teaspoon ground cloves

1 cup cooked chestnuts

FOR THE SALMON

Canola oil, for the fish and baking sheet

Four 6- to 8-ounce salmon steaks, pin bones removed

Fine sea salt and freshly ground black pepper

1. Place a large pot over medium heat. Add the oil and heat until it shimmers. Add the onion and cook without coloring, stirring often, until wilted, about 2 minutes. Add the cabbage and salt. Cook 3 minutes, stirring frequently.

2. Add ½ cup water, the maple syrup, vinegar, bay leaf, cinnamon, star anise, allspice, and cloves and stir to coat the cabbage. Cover and cook, stirring occasionally, until the cabbage

recipe continued on next page

is softened and wilted but still has texture, 10 to 12 minutes. Fish out and discard the bay leaf and whole spices, if using.

3. Add the chestnuts and stir. Cover and cook 3 minutes more. Remove from the heat and set aside.

4. Meanwhile, adjust the rack to 4 to 6 inches from the element and preheat the broiler to high. Line a baking sheet or broiling pan with aluminum foil and brush very lightly with oil. On the foil, season the salmon steaks on both sides with salt and pepper. Let stand 5 minutes to allow the seasonings to penetrate.

5. Pat the steaks dry with paper towels. Rub each with ½ teaspoon oil and broil, rotating the baking sheet about halfway through for even cooking, until the steaks are medium-rare, 5 to 6 minutes.

6. To serve, spoon the cabbage and chestnuts into the center of four serving plates. Set the steaks on top, a little off-center so that they lean on the cabbage.

KITCHEN NOTEBOOK: CHESTNUTS IN ITALY

Chestnuts are one of my favorite foods. They're very underappreciated in America, though they used to be a crucial food source for people living in mountainous regions of Italy. They were the base of all sorts of sweet and savory dishes, and ground into flour for pasta and bread. When I was getting my culinary training in Alain Ducasse's kitchen in Monaco, I used to spend my days off traveling around exploring. I'd take the train to Ventimiglia in Italy. From there, I'd take a bus through the little villages in the Val de Nervia in Liguria. There'd be a village every 15 to 20 minutes, and I'd get off the bus and just spend a few hours exploring the town, usually starting with the town square where the action was. During the late fall, I walked into one of those town squares lined with chestnut trees. A group of old Italian ladies was walking around with bags picking up the chestnuts that were falling off the trees. What a cool sight.

· BROILED SCALLOPS 101 ·
WITH GARLICKY SPINACH

SERVES 4 AS AN ENTRÉE

Scallops come out great from under the broiler—sweet and creamy inside, with nice, golden brown tops. They're delicious with a side of garlicky spinach (baby spinach works perfectly well in this recipe). If your scallops are smaller, start checking them after 2 minutes.

FOR THE SCALLOPS

1½ pounds large sea scallops (about 20), tough white side muscles removed

Fine sea salt and freshly ground black pepper

4 teaspoons extra virgin olive oil

FOR THE GARLICKY SPINACH

2 cloves garlic, thinly sliced

1 tablespoon extra virgin olive oil

10 ounces spinach from 2 bunches loose spinach (about 1 pound, large stems removed) or one 11-ounce bag spinach, rinsed well

1. For the scallops, adjust the rack to 2 to 3 inches from the element and preheat the broiler to high. Line a baking sheet with aluminum foil. Place the scallops on the foil and sprinkle with salt and pepper. Let stand 5 minutes to allow the seasonings to penetrate.

2. Meanwhile, for the spinach, heat the garlic with the olive oil in a large pot over medium heat until the garlic is aromatic but doesn't color, about 1 minute. Turn the heat to high, add the spinach, ¼ teaspoon salt, and pepper to taste. Cook, stirring every couple of seconds, until the spinach wilts, 1½ to 2 minutes.

3. Pat the scallops dry with paper towels. Drizzle with the oil and toss with your hands to coat. Spread the scallops in a single layer, one flat side facing up. Broil to medium-rare, about 3 minutes.

4. Serve the scallops with the spinach.

· BROILED BLUEFISH 101 WITH · BROILED TOMATOES, BASIL, AND TAPENADE

SERVES 4 AS AN ENTRÉE

The key to cooking bluefish is a vinegar marinade, because bluefish is strong-tasting and the vinegar softens the flavor. Change up the basil for another herb, if you like, and feel free to leave out the garlic. Though it's not traditional, I season my tapenade with vinegar because it heightens the flavor. Leftover tapenade will last indefinitely in a covered container in the refrigerator. Bring to room temperature before serving.

If you're using olive oil-packed Taggiasche olives, use that olive oil in the tapenade.

FOR THE BLUEFISH

2 tablespoons extra virgin olive oil

1 tablespoon sherry wine vinegar

2 cloves garlic, crushed with the flat blade of a chef's knife and peeled

2 sprigs fresh basil

1½ pounds boneless, skinless bluefish fillets (about ½ inch thick), bloodlines removed

Fine sea salt and freshly ground black pepper

FOR THE TAPENADE

1 cup pitted black olives (preferably Taggiasche packed in extra virgin olive oil; second choice, Gaeta)

10 oil-packed anchovy fillets (preferably in extra virgin olive oil), drained and coarsely chopped

2 tablespoons large capers (preferably salted, not brined), soaked at least 2 hours or overnight, drained, rinsed, and coarsely chopped

1 clove garlic, coarsely chopped

3 teaspoons red wine vinegar

½ cup extra virgin olive oil

FOR THE TOMATOES

1 tablespoon extra virgin olive oil

3 medium beefsteak tomatoes, each cored and cut crosswise into 4 thick slices

1. For the bluefish, mix the oil, vinegar, garlic, and basil in an ovenproof glass dish large enough to hold the bluefish fillets (they don't need to be in a single layer). Add the bluefish and turn it in the marinade to coat. Cover with plastic wrap and refrigerate for 1 hour. Most of the marinade will be absorbed.

2. For the tapenade, put the olives in a food processor with the anchovies, capers, and garlic, and pulse until well chopped, scraping down the sides of the bowl a few times. Add the vinegar and oil and pulse, scraping down the sides of the bowl, to a coarse purée; set aside.

3. For the tomatoes, adjust the rack to 2 inches from the element and preheat the broiler to high. Line a baking sheet or broiler pan with aluminum foil. Drizzle half the oil over the foil. Arrange the tomato slices in a single layer on the baking sheet and season with salt and pepper. Drizzle the slices with the remaining oil. Broil 4 minutes, until lightly browned. Remove to a plate and set aside.

4. For the bluefish, move the rack to 4 inches from the element. Reline the baking sheet or with clean aluminum foil and arrange the fillets in a single layer. Season on both sides with salt and pepper to taste. Let stand 5 minutes to allow the seasonings to penetrate.

5. Pat the fish very dry with paper towels and broil until it is cooked through and browned on top, 4 to 5 minutes. Serve with the tomatoes and the tapenade.

· BROILED COD 101 · WITH FULTON FISH MARKET GLAÇAGE

SERVES 4 AS AN ENTRÉE

Glaçage just means "glaze" in French. The title of this recipe is a little tongue-in-cheek because I got the idea from a fish vendor at the Fulton Fish Market who pulled me aside one morning to show me the fish fillet he was cooking, slathered with mayonnaise, on a George Foreman grill. He thought it was hysterical to be teaching *me* how to cook fish. But it turned out to be a fantastic idea for a home broiler; I just amped up the flavor of the mayonnaise with some fresh herbs. This recipe is written for 1- to 1¼-inch-thick cod fillets. If your fillets are thinner, cut the unglazed broiling time by a few minutes. You'll still need to count on about 4 minutes to brown the glaze. Serve with Green Beans with Sofrito (page 369) or boiled or steamed asparagus.

¼ cup plus 2 tablespoons Homemade Mayonnaise (page 21), or good-quality store-bought mayonnaise

2 rounded teaspoons coarsely chopped fresh dill

2 rounded teaspoons coarsely chopped fresh tarragon

Vegetable oil, for the baking sheet

Four 6-ounce boneless, skinless cod fillets, 1 to 1¼ inches thick

Fine sea salt and freshly ground black pepper

1. Stir the mayonnaise with the herbs in a small bowl; set aside.

2. Adjust the rack to 4 to 6 inches from the element and preheat the broiler to high. Line a baking sheet or broiler pan with aluminum foil and lightly coat with oil.

3. On the baking sheet or broiler pan, sprinkle the fish on both sides with salt and pepper. Let stand 5 minutes to allow the seasonings to penetrate

4. Pat the fish very dry with paper towels. Broil the fish 6 minutes.

5. Remove the fish from the broiler and evenly spread each fillet with about one quarter of the mayonnaise. Broil, rotating the baking sheet about halfway through for even browning, until the cod is cooked through and the glaze is golden brown, about 4 minutes.

· TAMARIND-GLAZED SABLEFISH ·

SERVES 4 AS AN ENTRÉE

Sablefish, also called black cod, is about the fattiest fish out there. Unctuous and silky, its luscious texture and flavor are incomparable. Sablefish takes to the spices and the acid in this sweet and spicy tamarind glaze. Serve it with something on the plainer side—steamed cauliflower is delicious—since the tamarind glaze is so flavorful. If you can't find sablefish, substitute salmon or arctic char and cook to medium-rare.

1½ teaspoons canola oil, plus more for the baking sheet

1 tablespoon minced shallot

¾ teaspoon minced garlic

½ cup tamarind paste

2 tablespoons firmly packed light brown sugar

½ teaspoon ground coriander

¼ teaspoon freshly ground black pepper

¼ teaspoon Colman's mustard powder

⅛ teaspoon ground ginger

Fine sea salt

Four 6- to 8-ounce boneless, skinless sablefish fillets (about 1 inch thick)

1. For the glaze, heat a small saucepan over medium heat. Add the oil and heat until fluid when the pan is swirled. Add the shallot and garlic and cook without coloring, 2 to 3 minutes. Off the heat, add the tamarind paste, brown sugar, coriander, pepper, mustard, ginger, and a scant ½ teaspoon salt and stir well to blend. Stir in ½ cup water until smooth. Bring to a simmer and cook 1 minute to bring the ingredients together. Remove from the heat and let cool.

2. Adjust the rack to about 3 inches from the element and preheat the broiler to high. Cover a baking sheet or broiler pan with aluminum foil and lightly oil the foil. On the foil, season the fish on both sides with salt. Let stand 5 minutes to allow the salt to penetrate.

3. Pat the fish dry with paper towels. Spread the glaze liberally over the top and sides. Broil, rotating the baking sheet halfway through for even browning, until the fish is cooked through, about 8 minutes.

· PLANTAIN CURRY ·
WITH COCONUT-GLAZED SHARK

SERVES 4 AS AN ENTRÉE

I use the word "curry" here as it's used in Indian cuisine. Not as something spiced with the standard curry powder you find in supermarkets, but as a dish of meat or vegetables—plantains in this case—cooked in sauce, incorporating a unique combination of spices. Plantains are pretty bland; traditionally they're fried or stewed in a bold-flavored sauce like this one to boost their flavor. Cooked with coconut, lime, chiles, and spices, this tropical curry is a little sweet, a little hot, and a little sour—making it a delicious accompaniment to the meaty taste of the shark.

If you can't get shark, the texture of which is similar to swordfish but meatier, try swordfish, mahi mahi, cobia, or a firm Hawaiian fish like marlin, spearfish, wahoo (ono), opah (moonfish), or monchong.

FOR THE COCONUT GLAZE

One 13.5-ounce can unsweetened coconut milk

½ teaspoon ground ginger

¼ teaspoon ground toasted coriander seeds

¼ teaspoon ground toasted cumin seeds

¼ teaspoon freshly ground pepper (preferably white)

1 teaspoon fresh lime juice

¼ teaspoon fine sea salt

FOR THE PLANTAIN CURRY

2 medium green plantains

1 tablespoon sugar

Fine sea salt

2 tablespoons canola oil

1 teaspoon black or brown mustard seeds

1 cup diced onion (⅓-inch dice; about 1 large)

1½ teaspoons slivered seeded red finger chile

½ cup sweetened shredded coconut

1 teaspoon ground toasted cumin seeds

¼ teaspoon turmeric

¼ teaspoon garam masala, or a mix of ⅛ teaspoon ground cinnamon, ⅛ teaspoon ground black pepper, and ⅛ teaspoon ground allspice

2½ teaspoons fresh lime juice

2 tablespoons gently packed fresh cilantro leaves

FOR THE SHARK

Four 6- to 8-ounce boneless, skinless shark fillets (¾ to 1 inch thick)

Canola oil, for the baking sheet

Fine sea salt and freshly ground black pepper

recipe continued on next page

1. For the glaze, in a small or medium saucepan, simmer the coconut milk over medium heat until it has reduced to 1¼ cups, about 5 minutes. Let cool to room temperature. Whisk in the ginger, coriander, cumin, pepper, lime juice, and salt; set aside.

2. For the curry, preheat the oven to 400°F. Cut off the tips of the plantains and score the skin with a knife along the length of the plantain. Put in a baking dish and bake until the skin blackens a bit and loosens from the flesh, 5 to 7 minutes. Let cool.

3. When cool enough to handle, peel, cut the plantains in half crosswise, and quarter each half lengthwise. Slice the quarters crosswise into ½-inch-thick wedges.

4. In a medium saucepan, combine the plantains, 1 quart water, the sugar, and 2 teaspoons salt. Bring to a boil, reduce the heat, and simmer until the plantains are almost tender when pierced with a paring knife, about 20 minutes

5. Place a 10-inch skillet over medium heat. Add the oil and heat until fluid enough to coat the bottom of the skillet when swirled. Add the mustard seeds, cover, and cook until you hear the mustard seeds pop, 1 to 2 minutes. Add the onions and ¼ teaspoon salt and cook without coloring, stirring often, until the onions are translucent, about 5 minutes. Add the chile and cook, stirring often, until fragrant, about 15 seconds. Add the coconut, mustard, and cumin and stir to combine. Add to the plantains and simmer until the plantains are tender and the sauce has thickened to a loose stew-like consistency. Remove from the heat. Add the turmeric, garam masala, lime juice, and cilantro and stir to combine. Keep warm.

6. For the shark, adjust the rack to 4 to 6 inches from the element and preheat the broiler to high. Line a baking sheet or broiler pan with aluminum foil and lightly oil the foil. On the foil, season the fish on both sides with salt and pepper. Let stand 5 minutes to allow the seasonings to penetrate.

7. Pat the fish dry with paper towels. Spoon or brush about 2 tablespoons of the glaze over the top and sides of each fillet (cover and refrigerate the remaining glaze for another meal). Broil, rotating the baking sheet about halfway through for even cooking, until the fish is cooked through and the glaze is lightly caramelized, about 8 minutes. Serve with the plantain curry.

· ORANGE CHILE–GLAZED TILEFISH ·

SERVES 4 AS AN ENTRÉE

Tilefish is a mild, flakey white fish with a sweet, moist flesh that goes nicely with this sweet and spicy glaze. I make my own sweet chili sauce at the restaurant, but Mae Ploy is a good-quality brand that is readily available. This glaze also goes great with snapper, black bass, and cod.

2 cups orange juice

½ cup sweet chili sauce (Mae Ploy or other good-quality brand)

2 tablespoons plus 2 teaspoons soy sauce

1½ teaspoons minced peeled fresh ginger

Four 6- to 8-ounce boneless, skinless tilefish fillets (about 1 inch thick)

Fine sea salt

Canola or vegetable oil, for the baking sheet

1. In a 3-quart saucepan, bring the orange juice to a gentle boil and cook until reduced to ⅔ cup, 7 to 10 minutes. Off the heat, stir in the chili sauce, soy sauce, and ginger. Let cool to room temperature. Pour the glaze into a container just large enough to hold the fish in a single layer.

2. Meanwhile, on a plate or a sheet of aluminum foil, sprinkle the fish on both sides with salt. Let stand 5 minutes to allow the salt to penetrate

3. Pat the fish dry with paper towels. Place the fish in the glaze and marinate 30 minutes at room temperature, turning occasionally.

4. Adjust the rack to 4 to 6 inches from the element and preheat the broiler to high. Line a baking sheet or broiler pan with aluminum foil and lightly coat with oil. Arrange the fish on the baking sheet and spread a little more glaze on top of each fillet.

5. Broil, rotating the baking sheet about halfway through for even browning, until the fish is cooked through and the glaze is browned, about 8 minutes. Halfway through the cooking, spoon a little more of the glaze over each fillet.

· BROILED MAHI MAHI ·
WITH SPICED SQUASH PURÉE
AND MARIA'S MOLE

SERVES 4 AS AN ENTRÉE

One of my cooks, Maria Gonzalez, makes this mole for staff meal. She serves it with chicken and it's really tasty. I asked her to teach me to make it so that I could put it on the menu. When she returned from shopping for the ingredients at her local Latin American grocer, I noticed a box of animal crackers in the bag. I said, "What's with the animal crackers? Is that for your kid?"

"No, it's for the mole—you fry them up and put them in the sauce," she said.

I said, "We're not putting animal crackers in the sauce!"

Well, she put me in my place: "Who's asking who to make the sauce?" she said. She had a point. So I shut up and let her cook. This is a great mole. The crackers thicken it and add a subtle sweetness.

I made some minor adjustments to the recipe to make it more home cook–friendly but it's essentially Maria's family recipe. (Which, of course, really *is* a home-cook recipe.) I adapted it for Oceana by serving it with meaty, full-flavored mahi mahi and a rustic, Mexican-inspired pumpkin-bean mash. You'll have leftover mole. Freeze it; when you want to use it, thaw, and reheat in a saucepan over medium heat, whisking. If it doesn't smooth out, pop it back into the blender with a few tablespoons of water (or use an immersion blender) and buzz until it's smooth again.

FOR THE MOLE

1½ ounces whole dried mulato chiles (5 medium), stems removed, seeds left in

1 ounce whole dried pasilla chiles (7 medium), stems removed, seeds left in

1 medium shallot, peeled

2 cloves garlic, crushed with the side of a chef's knife and peeled

¼ cup white sesame seeds

¼ cup unsalted dry-roasted peanuts

¾ cup canola oil

¾ cup golden raisins

¾ cup blanched, sliced almonds

¼ cup animal crackers (about 6)

¼ medium plantain, on the turn from yellow to black (almost ripe), peeled and cut lengthwise into 4 slices

3 tablespoons dark brown sugar

⅛ teaspoon ground cloves

recipe continued on next page

1 teaspoon ground cinnamon

1 teaspoon ground anise seed

1 quart boiling water

1 tablespoon fine sea salt

FOR THE SPICED SQUASH PURÉE

1 cup dried adzuki or red beans

Fine sea salt

One 2-pound kabocha squash or other winter squash such as butternut

¼ cup plus 1 tablespoon extra virgin olive oil

Freshly ground black pepper

1 small onion, cut into ¼-inch dice (about 1 cup)

2 cloves garlic, sliced

1 teaspoon ground cumin

1 teaspoon ground coriander

1 teaspoon fresh lime juice

FOR THE MAHI MAHI

Four 6- to 8-ounce boneless, skinless mahi mahi fillets (about ½ inch thick)

Fine sea salt and freshly ground black pepper

4 teaspoons canola oil

1. For the mole, heat a heavy stainless-steel or cast-iron skillet over medium heat for 4 minutes until hot Add the mulato chiles and toast on both sides, pressing them flat with a spatula, until they're fragrant and warm enough to be pliable, about 1½ minutes. Remove to a 2-quart or larger heatproof bowl. Put the pasilla chiles in the hot skillet and toast 1½ minutes; add to the mulato chiles. Put the shallot and garlic cloves in the hot skillet and toast, stirring a couple of times, until charred, about 1 minute. Add to the chiles. Put the sesame seeds in the skillet and toast, stirring constantly, 1 minute; add to the bowl along with the peanuts. Set aside.

2. Place a large skillet over medium heat. Add ½ cup of the canola oil and heat until a few raisins added to the oil bubble gently. Add the remaining raisins and fry until plump, about 1 minute. Remove with a slotted spoon to the bowl. Add the almonds to the oil and cook until golden, about 1 minute. (Remove from the heat if they brown too quickly.) Remove with a slotted spoon to the bowl. Add the animal crackers to the oil and fry until golden brown, about 1 minute; remove to the bowl. Let the oil cool, then discard it.

3. Place a small skillet over medium heat. Add the remaining ¼ cup canola oil and heat until it shimmers. Add the plantain quarters and fry until golden on one side, about 1 minute. Turn with a spatula and fry until golden on the other side, about 1 minute more. Use the slotted spoon to remove to the bowl. Add the brown sugar, cloves, cinnamon, and anise to the oil and cook, stirring constantly, until aromatic, about 45 seconds. Do not burn.

Pour into the bowl. Pour the boiling water into the bowl. Cover the bowl with plastic wrap and let stand at room temperature for 3 hours to soften the chiles.

4. Transfer the mixture to a blender or food processor and blend on high speed until smooth. Season with the salt. Store in a container at room temperature or in the refrigerator until needed.

5. For the purée, in a bowl, cover the beans with cold water by about 3 inches. Cover with plastic wrap and set aside to soak overnight at room temperature.

6. Drain the beans in a colander and rinse under cold running water. Transfer the beans to a medium saucepan and add fresh water to cover by about 3 inches. Bring to a boil, reduce the heat, and simmer until the beans are tender, about 40 minutes.

7. Remove the beans from the heat, add 1 teaspoon salt, and let stand at least 15 minutes to allow the salt to penetrate. (If not using immediately, set the beans aside in the cooking liquid; the beans can be cooked the night before and refrigerated.)

8. Preheat the oven to 450°F. Line a baking sheet with aluminum foil. Cut the squash in half through the stem end and scrape out the seeds and fibers. Place the squash on the baking sheet cut side up and rub the interior with ¼ cup of the olive oil. Sprinkle with ¼ teaspoon salt and pepper to taste. Roast until a paring knife encounters no resistance when piercing the squash, about 50 minutes. Set aside to cool to room temperature.

9. Scoop the squash flesh out of the skin. Discard the skin and set aside the flesh.

10. Place a 12-inch skillet over medium heat. Add the remaining 1 tablespoon olive oil and heat until fluid enough to coat the bottom of the skillet when swirled. Add the onion and garlic and cook without coloring until the onions are translucent, about 3 minutes. In a small bowl, stir together the cumin, coriander, and 2 tablespoons water; add to onions pan and cook, stirring constantly to prevent the spices from burning, for 1 minute.

11. Drain the beans. Add the squash flesh, beans, and ¼ cup water to the onions. Stir with a spatula, mashing, until the squash has broken down to a coarse purée and the mixture is heated through. Season with ½ teaspoon salt, pepper to taste, and the lime juice. Keep warm.

recipe continued on next page

12. For the mahi mahi, adjust the rack about 4 inches from the element and preheat the broiler to high. Line a baking sheet or broiler pan with aluminum foil. On the foil, season the fish on both sides with salt and pepper. Let stand 5 minutes to allow the seasoning to penetrate.

13. Pat the fish dry with paper towels. Rub each fillet with 1 teaspoon of the canola oil. Broil, rotating the baking sheet after 4½ minutes for even cooking, to medium-well, about 7 minutes total.

14. To serve, warm the mole. Spoon 3 to 4 tablespoons into each of four shallow bowls or deep serving plates. Set a piece of mahi mahi on top and finish each plate with a spoonful of the squash purée.

EXTRA CREDIT: BANANA LEAVES

At the restaurant, we line the serving plates for this dish with a banana leaf. It's an Indian thing to use banana leaves as plates, not Mexican. But there's a lot of overlap between ingredients in Indian and Mexican cuisines—spices, nuts, seeds, and chiles—so the banana leaf just made sense. It's a cool presentation to try at home, too.

· BROILED POMPANO ·
WITH COCONUT-CILANTRO SAUCE
AND BOK CHOY

SERVES 4 AS AN ENTRÉE

This is an adaptation of one of my signature dishes for the home kitchen. The heart of the recipe is a coconut milk sauce, spiced with cumin, red mustard seeds, curry leaves, coriander, and cumin. These vibrant flavors work well with pompano because it's such a full-flavored fish. Serve over steamed jasmine rice.

You can remove the skin from the pompano if you like, but the tender skin eats fine. If you do remove the skin, broil the fish skinned side *down*; the other side (the bone side) is more attractive for presentation. Pompano is not always available but dorade, which is farmed, and porgy make good substitutes.

FOR THE COCONUT-CILANTRO SAUCE

2 teaspoons canola oil

½ teaspoon black or brown mustard seeds (see Guide to Unusual Ingredients, page 400)

6 curry leaves, stacked in a pile and thinly sliced crosswise

1 teaspoon thinly sliced shallot, sliced crosswise

1 medium clove garlic, sliced

1½ teaspoons slivered seeded red finger chile

1 teaspoon minced peeled fresh ginger

½ teaspoon ground toasted coriander seeds

½ teaspoon ground toasted cumin seeds

1½ cups Low-Stress Chicken Stock (page 16) or store-bought low-sodium chicken stock

1 cup unsweetened coconut milk

1 tablespoon slivered fresh cilantro

FOR THE BOK CHOY

1¼ pounds bok choy

2 tablespoons canola oil

Fine sea salt and freshly ground black pepper

¼ cup unsalted dry-roasted peanuts

1 teaspoon unsalted butter

2 tablespoons minced shallot

2 teaspoons slivered seeded finger chile

2 teaspoons minced peeled fresh ginger

2 teaspoons slivered fresh cilantro

FOR THE POMPANO

4 boneless pompano fillets (skin optional; about 5 ounces each)

Fine sea salt and freshly ground black pepper

4 teaspoons canola oil

recipe continued on next page

1. For the sauce, heat a medium saucepan over medium-high heat. Add the canola oil and heat until it shimmers Add the mustard seeds, cover, and heat until the mustard seeds pop, about 45 seconds. Add the sliced curry leaves and cook, stirring often, 30 seconds. Add the shallot, garlic, chile, and ginger and cook 1 minute, stirring occasionally. Add the coriander and cumin and cook, stirring often, until fragrant, 15 to 20 seconds.

2. Add the chicken stock, bring to a boil, reduce the heat, and simmer gently for 10 minutes to reduce slightly and allow the flavors to come together.

3. Add the coconut milk and cook until it comes to a simmer, just shy of a boil, about 3 minutes. Do not let it boil. Off the heat, stir in the cilantro. Set aside at room temperature.

4. For the bok choy, trim the stems. Cut the leaves from the stems, stack them in a pile, and slice crosswise into strips about ¼ inch wide. Slice the stems on the bias about ¼ inch thick. Set the leaves and stems aside separately.

5. Place a 12-inch skillet over medium heat. Add the oil and heat until fluid enough to coat the bottom of the pan when swirled. Add the bok choy stems and cook without coloring, 3 minutes. Season with 1 teaspoon salt and ½ teaspoon pepper. Stir in the peanuts and cook 30 seconds.

6. Push the bok choy to the back of the pan. Tilt the front of the pan toward you a bit so that only the front edge of the pan is on the heat. Add the butter and the shallot, chile, and ginger; cook until fragrant, about 15 seconds. (This keeps the butter from spreading out and browning in the pan.) Return the pan flat on the heat and stir everything together. Add the sliced bok choy leaves and cook, stirring frequently, until wilted, 1½ minutes. Remove the pan from the heat and stir in the cilantro. Set aside.

7. Adjust the rack to 2 to 3 inches from the element and preheat the broiler to high. Line a baking sheet with aluminum foil. On the foil, sprinkle the fillets on one side (skinless side, if your fillets are skin-on) with salt and pepper. Let stand 5 minutes to allow the fish to absorb the seasoning.

8. Pat the fish dry with paper towels. Rub each fillet on both sides with 1 teaspoon olive oil and turn them skin side up if there is skin; otherwise, "bone"-side up. Broil, rotating the baking sheet about halfway through for even cooking, until the pompano is cooked

through and you see that the flesh is opaque, 4 to 6 minutes. (Pull the baking sheet out from the broiler so that you can lift the fillets to see when the fish is cooked.)

9. Return the sauce to a light simmer. Divide the bok choy among four shallow serving bowls or deep serving plates. Divide the sauce among the bowls, spooning it around the bok choy. Place a fillet on top of the bok choy in each bowl.

8.

STEAMED FISH

The next technique I want to introduce is steaming, a method of cooking over simmering liquid. Although it's not something I see a lot of people do at home, it's a great technique for cooking fish, in terms of both flavor and ease. (My wife likes it because you can cook with no fat.) At its simplest, the value of steaming is that it's all about the pure flavor of the fish. You're not adding anything—you're not browning in a skillet to create a crisp, intensely flavored crust; you're not poaching in a liquid that adds its own flavor accents. You're not glazing under the broiler or infusing flavor from a braising liquid. You just taste fish. And like baking, braising, and broiling, it's generally stress free. Once the fish is in the steamer, no manipulation is involved until it's time to take it out.

If you're new to steaming, Steamed Cod 101 with Ginger, Soy, and Chinese Broccoli (page 214) is a good starter recipe. Cod fillets are simply seasoned, placed in the steamer and steamed until cooked through, then served with a quick soy-ginger sauce and sautéed Chinese broccoli. You can replace the cod with any lean fish fillet. It's wonderful with black sea bass. When you get into more involved recipes like Steamed Black Sea Bass with Spinach, Soybeans, and Miso Broth (page 227), or Flounder Barigoule with Artichokes and Potatoes (page 221), you'll find that the steaming itself is just as straightforward; there are just more steps to complete for the sauce and vegetable garnish.

But let's say you do want to infuse your fish with some additional flavor. Steaming allows you to do that, too, and very delicately. Start with Branzino 101 Steamed on a Bed of Herbs and Lemon (page 213). The fish picks up subtle flavor from the lemon slices and herbs on which it's steamed. Again, you can vary this recipe with your favorite fish. Serve with lemon wedges, a drizzle of olive oil, and a sprinkle of coarse salt, or hot sauce, or any of the oils or vinaigrettes in the book. And you're done.

Another way to introduce flavor is to steam the fillets with vegetables and seasonings in a foil packet. This classic method is called *en papillote* in French and *al cartoccio* in Italian. Typically, parchment paper is used in this preparation, but I find aluminum foil much easier to fold. In Snapper in a Bag, on page 219, the fish is wrapped in aluminum foil with red bell pepper, carrots, and scallion, a little wine, and a drizzle of olive oil, and baked. The snapper cooks in its own juices, trapped by the packet, creating a fresh, tasty combination in which no flavor is lost. It looks elaborate but it's quite convenient since all the ingredients are neatly wrapped in the packet for easy serving and cleanup. You may recognize this technique from the recipe for Whole Roasted Branzino with Mushrooms, Spinach, and Fennel-Chile Vinaigrette (page 144) in Chapter 5, Baked and Roasted Fish; for that recipe, the branzino cooks most of the way through in the foil, but the foil is opened during the final phase of the cooking to allow the skin to develop color and a roasted flavor.

BEST FISH FOR STEAMING

Lean white fish such as cod, halibut, black sea bass, snapper, branzino, and grouper do very well in the steamer. I don't steam meaty fish like swordfish, tuna, cobia, and most of the Hawaiian varieties; to my mind, they're better on the stovetop or grill, under the broiler, or in the oven where they can get some color. And this is the only chapter where you'll find skate, an unusual fish that is superb steamed because the steamer makes it especially easy to skin and bone (Chilled Skate Salad with Zucchini and Lemon, page 232).

THREE STEPS TO STEAMING

1. Bring about 1 inch water to a boil in the bottom of a steamer pot.

2. Place the fish in a single layer in the perforated steamer basket. Place over the boiling water and cover the pot. (Cut wide, thin fillets like snapper, flounder, and branzino in half crosswise and then stack them, the skin side of each half to

the outside, so they fit more easily in the steamer.)

3. When the fish is cooked, turn off the heat. Uncover the steamer carefully, using oven mitts, and standing back—steam can burn badly. Carefully remove the fish with a spatula to serving plates.

EQUIP YOURSELF: STEAMING

You'll need a steamer to try this technique. Here are a few options.

• I use a 12-inch, perforated steamer insert that is sold separately and nests in my 8-quart pot. It's large enough to hold 4 wide fillets.

• A bamboo steamer works, too.

• Collapsible steamer baskets do not work unless you're desperate; they don't hold enough fish to be practical and once they're opened, they're not flat.

• You'll also need a metal or plastic spatula for removing the fish from the steamer.

· BRANZINO 101 STEAMED ·
ON A BED OF HERBS AND LEMON
SERVES 4 AS AN ENTRÉE

This very simple recipe can be varied with any fish fillet. Branzino fillets are relatively thin so I cut them in half crosswise and sandwich them to better fit inside the steamer. The halves sort of meld together during cooking. Count on 8 to 10 minutes per inch for thicker fillets. Serve with Olive Oil Crushed Potatoes (page 370).

Four 7-ounce boneless, skinless branzino fillets

Fine sea salt and freshly ground black pepper

2 small lemons, sliced crosswise ⅛ inch thick

4 sprigs fresh basil

6 sprigs fresh thyme

8 sprigs fresh parsley

Lemon wedges, for serving

Coarse sea salt, for serving

1. Cut the branzino fillets in half crosswise. On a plate or a sheet of aluminum foil, season the fillets on both sides with salt and pepper. Let stand 5 minutes to allow the seasonings to penetrate.

2. Bring about 1 inch of water to a boil in the bottom of a steamer pot. Set aside 8 lemon slices and cover the bottom of the steamer basket with the remaining slices. Make a bed of the basil, thyme, and parsley on top of the lemon. Stack the fillet pieces in pairs and place the pairs in a single layer on top of the herbs. Top with the reserved 8 lemon slices.

3. Place the steamer basket in the pot, cover, and steam until the branzino is cooked through, about 4 minutes. Remove the fish from the steamer basket with a spatula to four serving plates. Serve with lemon wedges and coarse salt.

· STEAMED COD 101 ·
WITH GINGER, SOY,
AND CHINESE BROCCOLI

SERVES 4 AS AN ENTRÉE

This recipe came to me through Parkin Lee, a regular customer at the restaurant. It was handed down to him from his mother, clearly an excellent cook. Her recipe called for a seasoning liquid called "fish soy" that I've replaced with a mixture of soy sauce and fish sauce. This preparation is delicious with any lean white fish. Chinese broccoli is available at Asian markets but if you have broccolini instead, go for it. Prepare it just as you would the Chinese broccoli: cut the stems on an angle and cut large buds in half. Yu-choy (page 398) is also a good substitute.

FOR THE JASMINE RICE

1 cup jasmine rice

1 teaspoon fine sea salt

FOR THE COD

Four 6- to 8-ounce boneless, skinless cod
    fillets, about 1 inch thick

Fine sea salt and freshly ground black pepper

8 ounces Chinese broccoli

6 scallions

1-inch piece peel-on fresh ginger

2 tablespoons fish sauce

¼ cup soy sauce

2 teaspoons slivered seeded finger chile

1 tablespoon plus 1 teaspoon canola oil

1. For the jasmine rice, combine the rice, 2 cups water, and the salt in a medium saucepan. Bring to a simmer, reduce the heat to low, cover, and simmer until the rice is tender, 18 minutes. Let stand off the heat with the lid ajar for a few minutes before serving.

2. Meanwhile, for the cod, on a plate or a sheet of aluminum foil, sprinkle the cod on both sides with salt and pepper. Let stand 5 minutes to allow the seasonings to penetrate.

3. Pull the leaves off the broccoli stems; set aside the leaves. Trim the base of the stems. Slice the stems, one at a time, about ¼ inch thick on a long bias. Pile up the leaves and chop into wide (about 2-inch) pieces. Set leaves and stems aside separately.

4. Cut the scallion greens from the whites. Cut both into thin slices on a long bias; set aside together.

5. Scrape the skin off the ginger with the edge of a spoon. Cut the ginger into thin slices; cut the slices into thin slivers. Set aside.

6. Combine the fish sauce, soy sauces, and 2 tablespoons water in a small bowl; set aside.

7. Bring about 1 inch water to a boil in the bottom of a steamer pot. Place the fish in the steamer basket and sprinkle each fillet with ½ teaspoon slivered chiles. Place on top of the simmering water, cover, and steam until the fish is cooked through, 8 to 10 minutes.

8. Meanwhile, heat in a large skillet over high heat. Add 1 tablespoon of the oil and heat until it shimmers. Add the broccoli stems, season very lightly with salt, and turn the heat down to medium. Cook, stirring often, for 2 minutes. Add the leaves, give it a stir, and cook 1 minute. Transfer to a bowl or a dish.

9. Turn the heat to medium-high. Add the remaining 1 teaspoon oil and heat until fluid enough to coat the bottom of the pan. Add the ginger and scallions and cook, stirring often, about 1 minute. Add the soy–fish sauce mixture and remove the pan from the heat.

10. To serve, scoop a spoonful of rice onto each of four serving plates. Spoon one-quarter of the broccoli on top of each mound of rice and place a fillet on top of each. Spoon the ginger-scallion sauce over.

· CHILLED COD SALAD 101 ·
WITH PRESERVED
LEMON–SOUR CREAM DRESSING

SERVES 4 AS AN ENTRÉE

I really dig the flavor of preserved lemons. A little bit, chopped up, elevates a simple recipe like this one to something quite sophisticated and wonderful. Cod steams nicely, and it stays moist even when it's chilled as in this salad. And the dressing is a standard sour cream–buttermilk mix—the preserved lemon makes it pop.

FOR THE COD

Four 5-ounce boneless, skinless cod fillets (about 1 inch thick)

Fine sea salt and freshly ground black pepper

FOR THE DRESSING

¼ cup sour cream

½ cup low-fat buttermilk

1½ tablespoons chopped Preserved Lemons (page 25), rind only (about 1 lemon quarter)

2 teaspoon sugar

¼ teaspoon fine sea salt

FOR THE SALAD

1 head romaine lettuce (about 1 pound), cut crosswise into 1-inch ribbons, then cut into 1-inch squares

½ head radicchio (4 ounces; cut through the root end), thinly sliced crosswise

½ medium bulb fennel (cut through the root end), trimmed, thinly shaved crosswise on a Japanese mandoline (about 1 cup gently packed)

3 medium carrots, shaved into thin coins on a Japanese mandoline (about 1 cup)

¼ cup raw pine nuts

Fine sea salt and freshly ground black pepper

1. On a plate or a sheet of aluminum foil, season the cod on both sides with salt and pepper. Let stand 5 minutes to allow the seasonings to penetrate.

2. Bring about 1 inch water to a boil in the bottom of a steamer pot. Place the fish in the steamer basket. Place on top of the boiling water, cover, and steam until the fish is cooked through, 8 to 10 minutes. Remove to a plate and let cool to room temperature. Cover and refrigerate until well chilled.

3. For the dressing, in a medium bowl, combine the sour cream, buttermilk, preserved lemon, sugar, and salt and whisk until well blended. Cover and refrigerate until you're ready to serve.

4. For the salad, in a large bowl, toss together the romaine, radicchio, fennel, carrots, pine nuts, 1 teaspoon salt, and pepper to taste. Add the dressing and toss to coat.

5. Divide the salad among four deep serving plates or shallow bowls. Flake the chilled cod into large chunks and divide among the salads, arranging the chunks attractively among the leaves.

· SNAPPER IN A BAG ·

SERVES 4 AS AN ENTRÉE

This traditional technique, called *en papillote*, is an ingenious way to steam fish in its own juices while making a sauce and vegetable garnish at the same time. Since it cooks with very little fat, the dish is light and healthy but doesn't lack for flavor. Here, snapper fillets are buried between layers of fennel, carrots, red bell pepper, and scallion, then folded into packets and baked. You can vary fish, vegetables, and herbs to your taste. The key is to slice the vegetables very thin so that they cook at the same rate as the fish. (If possible, slice the fennel and carrots on a Japanese mandoline.) Thicker fillets will take a bit more time to cook—if you want to peek, remove the packet from the oven, unfold one long side and lift the foil. If the fish isn't done to your liking, just wrap it back up and bake another 5 minutes. Make sure to serve the juices that collect at the bottom of the packets—the flavors are all captured there.

Four 6-ounce boneless red snapper fillets (about ½ inch thick)

Fine sea salt and freshly ground black pepper

1 medium bulb fennel, trimmed

1 red bell pepper, halved through the stem, stem, seeds, and ribs removed, thinly sliced lengthwise

4 medium carrots, peeled, thinly sliced on the bias (preferably on a Japanese mandoline)

4 scallions (white and green parts), thinly sliced on the bias

1 tablespoon slivered fresh Italian parsley

1 tablespoon slivered fresh basil

2 tablespoons extra virgin olive oil

2 tablespoons dry white wine

1. Preheat the oven to 400°F. On a plate or a sheet of aluminum foil, season the fish on both sides with salt and pepper. Let stand 5 minutes to allow the seasonings to penetrate.

2. Thinly slice the fennel crosswise (on a Japanese mandoline, if possible) to yield crescent-shaped slices (see Kitchen Notebook, page 220). Place in a large bowl. Add the red bell pepper, carrots, scallions, parsley, basil, olive oil, and wine. Toss to coat the vegetables.

3. Cut four sheets of aluminum foil, each about the size of a cookie sheet. Spread about one-quarter of the vegetable mixture over the center of one sheet of foil. Place 2 snapper fillets on top, skin side up. Cover with another quarter of the vegetable mixture. Repeat with a second sheet of foil and the remaining vegetables and fillets. Divide any juices left

recipe continued on next page

in the bowl over the two. Cover each with another sheet of foil. Fold in all in edges about ½ inch, then fold in again, ½ inch, to seal completely. Place both packets on a baking sheet and bake 18 minutes.

4. Remove the baking sheet from the oven. Cut open the packets with kitchen scissors. (Be careful; the escaping steam will be hot.) Use a large spatula to carefully transfer each fillet with some of the vegetables to a deep serving plate or shallow serving bowl. Pour the juices over.

KITCHEN NOTEBOOK: ANATOMY OF A FENNEL BULB

It's vastly easier to slice fennel on a mandoline if you prepare the bulb so that it fits easily on the slicer. To do this, imagine that the bulb is your hand. Hold your hand in front of you with your fingers (the fennel stalks) pointing up. You want to cut the fennel in half so that you cut between your middle and index fingers rather than through all five fingers. This will yield narrower halves that are easier to fit on a mandoline. You can also quarter the bulb if that makes it easier to slice. (See also Kitchen Notebook: Slicing Fennel, page 242.)

· FLOUNDER BARIGOULE ·
WITH ARTICHOKES AND POTATOES

SERVES 4 AS AN ENTRÉE

This light spring or summer dish is a play on artichokes *à la barigoule*, a Provençal dish of artichokes stewed in a white wine–vegetable broth with bacon, garlic, and good amount of olive oil. Artichokes make a great backdrop for the subtle flavor of steamed flounder, but any lean white fish fillet will benefit from this combination. I replace the traditional bacon with linguiça, a Portuguese sausage that adds a hit of tanginess to the dish. The artichoke hearts take a little time to prepare, but the preparation isn't difficult.

FOR THE BARIGOULE

½ lemon

4 large artichokes

½ cup extra virgin olive oil

¼ cup sliced (¼ inch) linguiça sausage (see Kitchen Notebook, page 222) or bacon lardons

½ cup thinly sliced shallots (about 2 large), sliced crosswise

1 small carrot, cut into ¼-inch dice (about ¼ cup)

½ medium stalk celery, cut into ¼-inch dice (about ¼ cup)

2 large cloves garlic, sliced

1 sprig fresh thyme

1 sprig fresh basil

1 bay leaf

5 medium fingerling potatoes, peel-on, sliced into ⅓-inch-thick coins

½ cup dry white wine

Fine sea salt and freshly ground black pepper

1 teaspoon fresh lemon juice

FOR THE FLOUNDER

1½ to 1¾ pounds boneless, skinless flounder fillets

Fine sea salt and freshly ground black pepper

4 teaspoons unsalted butter, softened

4 teaspoons minced fresh chives

1. For the barigoule, half fill a large bowl with cold water. Squeeze in the juice of one lemon half; add the juiced half to the bowl. Working with 1 artichoke at a time, break off and discard the outer leaves, bending them back and pulling them down toward the stem until they break off at the base. Continue until you reach the inner pale yellow cone of leaves. With a paring knife, trim the bottom of the stem. Cut off all of the outer dark green from the base and stem until you hit the pale flesh. Dip it in the lemon water to

recipe continued on next page

keep the artichoke from blackening. Cut off and discard the top two-thirds of the cone of the artichoke leaves. Spread open the leaves and pull out the purplish inner leaves to expose the fuzzy choke. Scrape out the choke with a melon baller or spoon. Drop into the bowl of lemon water to prevent from discoloring while you clean the remaining artichokes. Cut the artichoke hearts in sixths and return to the lemon water.

2. Place a medium saucepan over medium-low heat. Add the olive oil and heat until fluid enough to coat the bottom of the pan when swirled. Add the linguiça or bacon and cook without coloring to render the fat, about 2 minutes. Add the shallots, carrot, celery, garlic, thyme, basil, and bay leaf. Increase the heat to medium and cook without coloring, stirring often, for 3 minutes. (If the sausage starts to brown, reduce the heat.)

3. Add the potatoes and cook, stirring often, for 2 minutes, until slightly translucent

4. Drain the artichoke hearts and add to the barigoule. Stir for 30 seconds. Add the wine and 2 cups water. Bring to a boil, reduce the heat, and simmer, partially covered, stirring occasionally, until tender when pierced with a small knife, 20 minutes. Season with 1 teaspoon salt, a pinch of pepper, and the lemon juice. Fish out and discard the bay leaf.

5. Meanwhile, bring 1 inch water to a boil in the bottom of a steamer pot. On a plate or a sheet of aluminum foil, season the flounder fillets on one side with salt and pepper and let stand a few minutes to allow the seasonings to penetrate.

6. When the barigoule has cooked for about 15 minutes, cut the fillets in half crosswise and stack the halves one on top of another to make four stacks. Brush the top of each stack with 1 teaspoon of the softened butter. Place the stacks in a single layer in the steamer basket and sprinkle each with 1 teaspoon chives. Place over the boiling water, cover, and steam until the flounder is cooked through, 4 to 5 minutes.

7. To serve, remove the bay leaf and thyme and basil sprigs from the barigoule; discard. Spoon the barigoule solids into the centers of four deep serving plates or shallow serving bowls. Place a stack of flounder on top and pour the broth from the barigoule around.

KITCHEN NOTEBOOK: LINGUIÇA

The Portuguese pork sausage linguiça is a nice alternative to bacon; it adds an interesting rich, smoky dimension to soups and stews. I was introduced to linguiça long ago by a high school friend, Luis Nobre. His Portuguese family owns a restaurant, Sol-Mar, in Newark, a city that boasts one of the largest Portuguese populations in the world outside Portugal. When I was working with Floyd Cardoz, I discovered that linguiça also features in the cuisine of Goa, a state on the west coast of India, where Floyd grew up. Goa used to be a Portuguese colony and Portuguese influence is still strong there. I buy fantastic linguiça from my friend's Newark sausage maker, Herminio Lopes. It's also available retail by mail order (see Guide to Unusual Ingredients, page 399).

 **EXTRA CREDIT:**

RESTAURANT PRESENTATION

Choose wider flounder fillets and cut them in half lengthwise on an angle to obtain 2 triangular pieces. Lay the halves end to end, overlapping the ends by 2 to 3 inches. Roll the fillets into a cylinder and secure with a toothpick. (Thinner fillets needn't be cut in half; just overlap the ends and roll.) Place the rolls on end in the steamer, brush each roll with 1 teaspoon softened butter, sprinkle with 1 teaspoon minced chives, and steam 8 to 9 minutes. Remove from the steamer and remove the toothpicks. Divide the fish cylinders among the plates, setting the cylinders on end. Spoon the barigoule solids around the cylinders and pour over the broth from the barigoule.

· STEAMED HALIBUT ·
WITH CURRY LEAF VINAIGRETTE
SERVES 4 AS AN ENTRÉE

Curry leaves (page 397) give this vinaigrette a uniquely pungent, aromatic flavor. Try it with basil if you don't have the curry leaves; basil won't give you the same flavor but it will still be delicious. The garlic is blanched three times to soften its flavor, then poached in a ginger-chile broth sweetened with an unrefined Indian sugar called jaggery. Don't let this additional step or the exotic ingredients discourage you. This vinaigrette makes steamed halibut—pretty much any fish, actually—taste fantastic. Guaranteed. And it's very good with steamed bok choy.

FOR THE VINAIGRETTE

½ cup garlic cloves (from about 1 large head), peeled and halved lengthwise

Three ⅛-inch-thick coins peel-on fresh ginger

¼ finger chile, cut lengthwise, seeds removed

2 tablespoons jaggery or light brown sugar

1½ tablespoons rice vinegar

¼ teaspoon fine sea salt

½ cup firmly packed fresh curry leaves, basil leaves, or Thai basil leaves, plus 4 sprigs for garnish (optional)

½ cup canola or other neutral oil

FOR THE HALIBUT

Four 7- to 8-ounce boneless halibut fillets (1 to 1¼ inch thick)

Fine sea salt and freshly ground black pepper

1. For the vinaigrette, bring a small saucepan of water to a boil. Add the garlic, return to a boil, and boil 30 seconds. Drain the garlic in a fine-mesh strainer and rinse under cold running water. Fill the saucepan again with water, bring to a boil, add the garlic, and boil 30 seconds. Drain and rinse the garlic. Repeat once more; drain and rinse the garlic.

2. Combine the blanched garlic, ginger, chile, and sugar in a small saucepan. Add water to cover by about ½ inch. Bring to a boil, reduce the heat, and simmer very gently until there's no resistance when you bite down on a piece but the garlic still holds its shape, or the garlic is tender when pierced with the tip of a small knife, 20 to 25 minutes (the garlic should be covered by water during cooking; add more if needed). Transfer the garlic and cooking liquid to a container, cover, and refrigerate until cold.

3. Discard the ginger and chile from the chilled garlic. Drain the garlic, saving the cooking

liquid. Transfer the garlic to a measuring cup and add enough of the cooking liquid to equal ½ cup; you will probably need all the liquid. In a blender, combine the garlic and its cooking liquid, the vinegar, salt, curry leaves, and 2 tablespoons of the oil. Puree until smooth. (If you have a variable-speed blender, start the machine on low speed until the mixture catches, then increase to high speed.) With the blender running (on medium-high or high speed, if you have a variable-speed blender) drizzle in the remaining 6 tablespoons oil to emulsify. Scrape the vinaigrette into a container and chill until you're ready to serve.

4. On a plate or a sheet of aluminum foil, sprinkle the halibut on both sides with salt and pepper. Let stand 5 minutes to allow the seasonings to penetrate.

5. Bring about 1 inch water to a boil in the bottom of a steamer pot. Place the fish in the steamer basket, place on top of the boiling water, cover, and steam until the fish is cooked to medium-well, about 8 minutes.

6. Spoon the sauce onto each of four serving plates. With a spatula, remove the fish to the plates, setting the fillets on top of the sauce. Garnish with a sprig of curry or basil leaves, if using.

KITCHEN NOTEBOOK: BLANCHED GARLIC

I usually blanch the garlic the day before to ensure that it's well chilled; if warm, it will darken the beautiful light green color of the vinaigrette.

· STEAMED BLACK SEA BASS ·
WITH SPINACH, SOYBEANS, AND MISO BROTH

SERVES 4 AS AN ENTRÉE

This dish builds on the concept of a miso soup and highlights two of my favorite ingredients: black sea bass and miso. I like the sweetness of the bass, and it has a beautiful texture with a nice fat content. Miso is a fascinating ingredient with a rich, intense flavor that I love. It is complemented here with lemongrass, fresh ginger, shallot, and shiitake mushrooms.

FOR THE SOYBEANS

1 cup dried soybeans

1 teaspoon fine sea salt

FOR THE MISO BROTH

2½ teaspoons canola oil

½ medium shallot, thinly sliced (about 2 tablespoons)

1 clove garlic, sliced

¼-inch piece fresh ginger, peeled and sliced into thin coins

1½ teaspoons slivered seeded finger chile

½ stalk lemongrass, cut lengthwise, white part only, trimmed and thinly sliced crosswise (about 2 tablespoons)

3 fresh shiitake mushrooms, caps only, sliced ¼ inch wide

¼ cup dry white wine

¼ cup white miso (see page 400)

¼ teaspoon fine sea salt

1½ teaspoons fresh lemon juice

FOR THE SEA BASS AND SPINACH

Four 6- to 8-ounce boneless, skin-on black bass fillets (½ to ¾ inch thick)

Fine sea salt and freshly ground black pepper

1 tablespoon canola oil

1 pound spinach, heavy stems removed, or one 11-ounce bag spinach, rinsed well and dried

1. In a bowl, soak the soybeans in 1 quart water overnight.

2. Drain the soybeans, rinse, and place in a medium saucepan with 2 quarts fresh water. Bring to a boil and boil 2 minutes. Reduce the heat and simmer until tender, about 1¼ hours. Add the salt and set the soybeans aside to cool in the cooking liquid.

recipe continued on next page

3. For the miso broth, heat a medium saucepan over medium heat. Add the canola oil and heat until fluid enough to coat the bottom of the pan. Add the shallot, garlic, ginger, and chile. Cook without coloring, stirring often, 2 minutes. Add the lemongrass and shiitakes and cook, stirring often, 3 minutes, until the mushrooms soften. Add the wine and simmer until it has almost completely evaporated, about 2 minutes. Add 2 cups water, the miso, salt, and lemon juice. Bring to a boil, reduce the heat, and simmer, uncovered, until the flavors meld, 10 minutes. Remove from the heat and set aside. Do not strain.

4. On a plate or a sheet of aluminum foil, season the fish on both sides with salt and pepper. Let stand 5 minutes to allow the seasonings to penetrate.

5. Bring 1 inch water to a boil in the bottom of a steamer pot. Cut the fillets in half crosswise and stack the two halves one on top of the other. Place in the steamer basket. Place over the boiling water, cover, and steam until cooked through, 10 to 12 minutes.

6. Drain the soybeans; you should have about 2 cups beans. Place a large pot over medium heat. Add the oil and the soybeans and cook, stirring often, to warm, 1 minute. Add the spinach, ½ teaspoon salt, ⅛ teaspoon pepper, and ¼ cup water. Raise the heat to medium-high and cook, stirring often, until the spinach has wilted, about 3 minutes.

7. To serve, divide the spinach mixture among four shallow serving bowls. Return the broth to a simmer. Place one stack (two halves) of bass on top of the vegetables in each bowl. Pour ½ cup broth (including solids) into each bowl around the fish.

8. Let the remaining broth cool. Pour into a container, cover, and refrigerate for soup.

· STEAMED GROUPER ·
WITH INDIAN-SPICED
BLACK BEAN SAUCE AND MANGO

SERVES 4 AS AN ENTRÉE

Steaming is one of my favorite ways to cook grouper. Here it's sauced with a black bean purée delicately sweetened with coconut water (not milk) and seasoned with the North Indian spices of a *dal* (a bean or lentil stew). The fish is served on sautéed yu-choy, a tasty Asian green, with lotus root for crunch and mango for a sweet hit of the tropics. Chinese broccoli or broccolini make good substitutes for the yu-choy.

FOR THE SAUCE

½ cup dried black beans

Fine sea salt

2 teaspoons canola oil

1 tablespoon sliced shallot (1 small)

¼-inch piece fresh ginger, peeled and sliced

1 clove garlic, sliced

2 teaspoons slivered seeded finger chile

1½ cups coconut water (see page 397)

⅛ teaspoon ground cumin

⅛ teaspoon ground coriander

¼ teaspoon garam masala (optional)

1 teaspoon fresh lime juice

FOR THE YU-CHOY

1 pound yu-choy, stems trimmed

One 4-ounce piece lotus root

1 mango (ripe but firm enough to slice)

FOR THE GROUPER

Four 6- to 8-ounce boneless, skin-on grouper fillets

Fine sea salt and freshly ground black pepper

2 tablespoons canola oil, for serving

1. For the sauce, place the black beans in a bowl with cold water to cover and set aside to soak overnight.

2. Drain the beans and transfer to a medium saucepan. Add 5 cups fresh water, bring to a boil, reduce the heat, and simmer until tender, 45 minutes to an hour. Add 1 teaspoon salt and set aside to cool in the cooking liquid.

3. Drain the beans, saving the cooking liquid. Measure out ½ cup beans; set aside. Return the rest to the cooking liquid, cover, and refrigerate to add to salads and soups.

recipe continued on next page

4. Place a medium saucepan over medium heat. Add the oil, shallot, ginger, garlic, and chile, and cook without coloring, stirring often, for 1½ minutes. Add the cooked black beans, the coconut water, cumin, coriander, garam masala, if using, lime juice, and ¾ teaspoon salt. Bring to a boil, reduce the heat, and simmer 5 minutes. Pour into a blender. If your blender has a removable plug, remove it. Holding a folded kitchen towel over the top to steady the lid and to prevent the hot sauce from splashing upwards, blend until the sauce is smooth. Transfer to a container and set aside at room temperature.

5. For the yu-choy, cut the leaves from the stems. Cut the leaves crosswise into ½-inch-wide strips; set aside in a bowl. Slice the stems on the bias about ⅛ inch thick; set aside in another bowl.

6. Fill a medium bowl with cold water for the lotus root (once peeled, the root will brown if exposed to air). Trim the ends and peel with a vegetable peeler. Cut the root in half lengthwise, then cut it crosswise into ¼-inch-thick half-moons, placing them in the water as you work.

7. Bring 1 inch water to a boil in the bottom of a steamer pot. Drain the lotus root, place in a steamer basket on top of the boiling water, cover, and steam until tender, about 7 minutes. Set the lotus root aside but leave the water in the steamer pot.

8. Peel the mango with a paring knife. Set the mango on one end on a cutting board and cut the flesh off each side of the large flat seed with a chef's knife. Cut the flesh lengthwise into ¼-inch-wide slices. Cut the slices into ¼-inch-wide strips; set aside in a bowl.

9. For the fish, on a plate or a sheet of aluminum foil, season the grouper on both sides with salt and pepper. Let stand 5 minutes to allow the seasonings to penetrate.

10. Meanwhile, return the water in the steamer pot to a boil, adding more water if needed for 1 inch. Place the grouper in the steamer basket on top of the boiling water, cover, and steam until cooked through, about 8 minutes.

11. To serve, heat a large pot over medium heat. Add the oil and heat until it shimmers. Add the yu-choy stems and cook without coloring, stirring often, 3 minutes. Add the lotus root and cook, stirring often, 1 minute. Add the yu-choy leaves, 1 teaspoon salt, and ⅛ teaspoon pepper and cook, stirring often, until the leaves wilt, about 2 minutes. Fold in the mango strips until well mixed. Remove from the heat. Warm the sauce in a small saucepan.

12. When the fish is cooked, spoon one quarter of the sauce onto each of four deep serving plates or shallow serving bowls. Divide the vegetables among the plates, spooning them on top of the sauce. Remove the grouper from the steamer with a spatula and place on top of the vegetables.

· CHILLED SKATE SALAD ·
WITH ZUCCHINI AND LEMON
SERVES 4 AS A LIGHT ENTRÉE

Skate presents a challenge because its unique structure makes it difficult to remove the raw meat from the bone-like cartilage. Steaming solves this problem because once cooked, the meat comes right off. You can also buy skate fillets cleaned of skin and cartilage, but get it on the "bone," if you can: Some of the cartilage melts as it cooks, adding flavor to the meat. This is a great cold lunch dish—light but with a lot of flavor. It's easy to make at home, no fuss, and it goes well with a chilled glass of rosé.

One 2-pound skin-on skate wing on the bone, trimmed of the frilly cartilage that edges the outer 1 inch, or 1 pound boneless, skinless skate fillet (2 pieces)

Fine sea salt and freshly ground black pepper

1 large zucchini, trimmed, sliced into thin rounds (preferably on a Japanese mandoline; about 3 cups)

Finely grated zest and juice of 1 lemon (about 3 tablespoons juice)

¼ cup extra virgin olive oil

1 tablespoon gently packed slivered fresh oregano leaves

2 tablespoons gently packed slivered Italian parsley leaves

Warm baguette, for serving

1. On a plate or a sheet of aluminum foil, sprinkle the skate on both sides with salt and pepper. Let stand 5 minutes to allow the seasonings to penetrate.

2. Bring about 1 inch water to a boil in a steamer pot large enough to hold the skate in a single layer. If the skate is on the bone, place the skate in the steamer basket over the boiling water, cover and steam 20 minutes. If using fillets, fold each into thirds and steam 6 minutes. Remove from the steamer to a plate with a spatula. Cover and refrigerate until chilled.

3. For skate steamed on the bone, peel the skin off one side of the chilled meat with your fingers. Slide a butter knife between the meat and the cartilage to loosen the meat, then use the knife to slide the meat off. Flip the skate and repeat the process on the other side. Flake into long strips into a bowl with a fork or fingers. If working with fillets, simply flake with a fork or your fingers. Refrigerate, covered.

4. In a large bowl, combine the zucchini, lemon zest and juice, olive oil, ¾ teaspoon salt, ⅛ teaspoon pepper, the oregano, and parsley. Toss well to coat the zucchini. Let marinate at room temperature for 10 minutes, tossing occasionally.

5. Gently fold the flaked skate into the zucchini mixture. Divide among four serving plates. Serve with a warm baguette to sop up the vinaigrette.

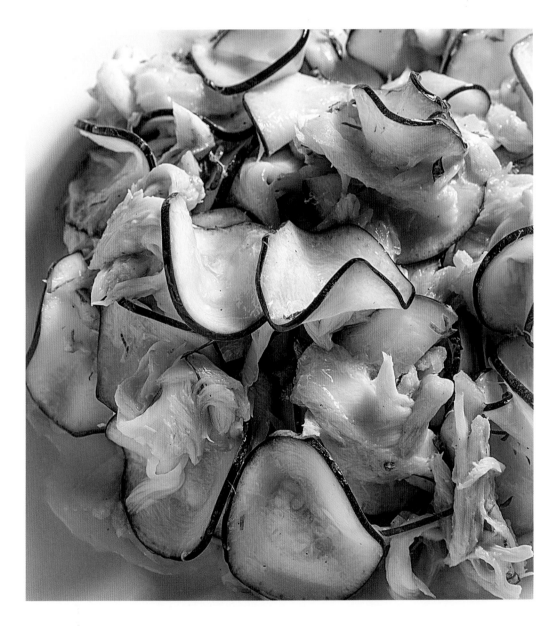

9.

POACHED FISH

Poaching means cooking fish in just enough simmering liquid to cover. It's a terrific way to add flavor and accentuate the natural sweetness of fish. As long as you keep the liquid at a gentle simmer, you don't have to worry about even delicate-fleshed fish falling apart or sticking.

Poaching is a nice alternative to the concentrated flavors that you get from browning a piece of fish on the grill, under the broiler, or in a skillet because it highlights the pure flavor of the fish by keeping it clean and sweet.

Poaching is a good way to cook fish that will be served cold. Chilling typically mutes the flavor of food, but flavors introduced by the poaching liquid will keep the fish tasting vibrant. And poached fish stays moist even after it's chilled.

So what goes into a poaching liquid? You can go as simple or as complicated as you like. I like using a classic court bouillon, a vegetable broth acidulated with white wine (see page 64), because

the combination of seasonings is a great accent to the natural flavor of the fish. A court bouillon doesn't take long to make (after all, it means "short boil" in French because it only cooks for 20 minutes).

But this chapter will start you out with recipes that use a quick court bouillon of water, wine, and herbs (Poached Salmon 101 with Salsa Verde on page 239 and Poached Halibut 101 with Fennel and Orange Salad on page 241). For the quick version, once you bring the ingredients to a simmer, you're ready to add the fish. Sometimes even simpler is better. I prefer not to mess with the flavor of black sea bass, for example, so I poach it in just salted water with a little wine. Feel free to use that poaching liquid for any fish.

You may have heard of fish poached in olive oil. I like to poach swordfish this way (see page 246) because it keeps the fish insanely moist and adds just the subtlest taste of the oil. When you're working with oil in such quantity, make sure you have a deep-fry thermometer (see below) to help you maintain a consistent temperature.

Beer is another option for poaching, and although you can cook lobsters in salted water, I like the flavor of beer, particularly wheat beer, with clams and lobster. (The Lobster Boil on page 250 falls someplace between poaching and steaming because the lobsters aren't entirely covered by the beer.) Unlike braising liquids, poaching liquids aren't usually served—they're too acidic to taste pleasant. The lobster boil is one of the few instances where you consume the poaching liquid. My homemade gefilte fish is another. In both cases, the liquid is not overly acidic.

BEST FISH FOR POACHING

Poaching is a good way to cook most varieties of fish, from delicate white-fleshed flounder, snapper, cod, halibut, and sea bass to oilier varieties. (The acid in a poaching liquid is a nice way to balance the fat in salmon.) I like to poach fillets, but poaching is also an excellent technique for small whole fish like sea bass, branzino, farm-raised striped bass (see page 252), and snapper. With small fish like these, you don't need a big fish poacher; a 12-inch-diameter pot is sufficient for one fish. Shellfish—lobsters, shrimp, and scallops—also taste great poached.

Serve poached fish with any of the vinaigrettes in this book, one of the herb oils, a mayonnaise, or my homemade hot sauce (start with the recipes in Chapter 1, Basics, beginning on page 10).

EQUIP YOURSELF: POACHING

- When you think of poaching, you may see one of those giant fish poachers in your future. But you don't need one unless you're planning on poaching a really big fish. (And I wouldn't—I'd grill a large fish for a crowd.)
- You do need pots and deep skillets wide enough to hold the fish along with the liquid to cover it. I use a 12-inch straight-sided skillet to poach fillets.
- A deep 12-inch-diameter pot is large enough to poach most whole small fish if you cut off the tail fins.
- A skimmer, spider, or slotted spoon for removing the fish from the poaching liquid.
- A digital deep-fry thermometer for poaching in olive oil.

· POACHED SALMON 101 ·
WITH SALSA VERDE

SERVES 4 AS AN ENTRÉE

Salsa verde is a classic cold Italian sauce of chopped fresh herbs and olive oil. There are as many versions as there are cooks. I add a puréed roasted green bell pepper; it's one more step but it's worth it. The sauce tastes fresh, like a pesto, and the roasted pepper adds a smoky background flavor. For a slightly different taste, try substituting a poblano pepper, or a finger chile if you want heat. Save the stems from the herbs you pick for the salsa verde and use them in the quick court bouillon.

FOR THE SALSA VERDE

1 green bell pepper

Extra virgin olive oil or canola oil, for roasting the pepper

1 tablespoon white wine vinegar

½ cup extra virgin olive oil

¼ cup gently packed fresh Italian parsley leaves, plus 4 small sprigs, for garnish (optional)

¼ cup gently packed fresh basil leaves, plus 4 small sprigs, for garnish (optional)

1 tablespoon gently packed fresh oregano leaves, plus 4 small sprigs for garnish (optional)

¼ teaspoon fine sea salt

FOR THE QUICK COURT BOUILLON

1½ cups dry white wine

Stem from 1 sprig fresh Italian parsley

Stem from 1 sprig fresh basil

Stem from 1 sprig fresh oregano

FOR THE SALMON

Four 6- to 8-ounce boneless, skinless salmon fillets, about 1½ inches thick

Fine sea salt and freshly ground black pepper

1. For the salsa verde, lightly rub the bell pepper all over with oil. If you have a gas burner, turn the heat to high, place the pepper directly on the burner and roast it, turning with tongs as the skin blackens, until the skin of the pepper is blackened all over. Make sure you blacken the top and bottom of the pepper, too. This should take about 5 minutes, total. (If your burners are electric, instead preheat the oven to 400°F. Place the oiled pepper on a baking sheet and roast, turning from time to time, until the skin is blistered all over, about 40 minutes.)

recipe continued on next page

2. Place the pepper in a bowl and cover with plastic until cool enough to handle, at least 5 minutes. Place the cooled pepper on a paper towel and scrape off all of the blackened skin with a paring knife. Cut the pepper in half through the stem end, cut out the stem, and scrape out the seeds. Coarsely chop the pepper.

3. Place the pepper in a blender. Add the vinegar and olive oil and purée until almost smooth. Add the parsley, basil, and oregano and blend. (If you have a variable-speed blender, start on low until the mixture catches, and then increase to high.) Stop the blender and scrape down the sides about halfway through. Set the sauce aside.

4. For the quick court bouillon, in a deep 12-inch skillet or pot deep enough to hold the liquid and the fish in a single layer, combine 2 quarts water, the wine, and the parsley, basil, and oregano stems. Cover and bring to a simmer.

5. Meanwhile, on a plate or a sheet of aluminum foil, season the salmon fillets on both sides with salt and pepper and let stand 15 minutes to allow the seasonings to penetrate.

6. Add the salmon to the simmering liquid in a single layer and cook, uncovered, until the fillets firm up but the flesh is still slightly soft on the sides and the salmon is medium-rare, 6 to 8 minutes.

7. To serve, spoon some of the salsa verde onto each of four shallow serving bowls or deep serving plates. Remove the salmon from the skillet with a slotted spatula and set on top of the salsa verde. Garnish with the herbs, if using.

KITCHEN NOTEBOOK: PEELING ROASTED PEPPERS

Scraping the blackened skin off the pepper is a little more work than peeling under running water but I recommend it because the water removes the flavor as well as the skin.

· POACHED HALIBUT 101 · WITH FENNEL AND ORANGE SALAD

SERVES 4 AS AN ENTRÉE

I like halibut for poaching because it stays firm and doesn't flake apart, so it's easy to handle. Its sweet flavor is highlighted here by the natural sweetness of the orange and fennel in the salad. I serve the fish hot, but this works very well as a cold summer dish, if you prefer. You can cut the fennel and orange well ahead of time for the salad, but don't dress it with the vinegar and oil until just before serving; the dressing will wilt the fennel. Try this dish with cod, black bass, and striped bass, too.

FOR THE QUICK COURT BOUILLON

1½ cups dry white wine

1 sprig fresh Italian parsley

1 sprig fresh basil

FOR THE FENNEL-ORANGE SALAD

1 medium bulb fennel, trimmed

1 navel orange

¼ cup plus 1 teaspoon extra virgin olive oil

1 tablespoon plus 1 teaspoon red wine vinegar

Fine sea salt and freshly ground black pepper

1 tablespoon slivered fresh mint leaves (from about 1 sprig)

1 tablespoon slivered fresh basil leaves (from about 1 sprig)

FOR THE HALIBUT

Four 6- to 8-ounce boneless, skinless halibut fillets (about 1 inch thick)

Fine sea salt and freshly ground black pepper

1. For the quick court bouillon, in a deep 12-inch skillet or another pot wide enough to hold the fish in a single layer and deep enough to hold the liquid, combine 2 quarts water, the wine, parsley, and basil. Cover and bring to a simmer; remove from the heat and set aside.

2. For the salad, prepare the fennel: Imagine that the bulb is your hand. Hold your hand in front of you with your fingers (the fennel stalks) pointing up. You want to cut the fennel in half so that you cut between your middle and index fingers rather than through all five fingers. This will yield narrower halves that are easier to fit on a mandoline. (You can also

recipe continued on next page

quarter the bulb if it makes it easier to slice.) Thinly slice crosswise (on a Japanese mandoline, if possible; see Kitchen Notebook, below) to yield crescent-shaped slices. Place in a medium bowl.

3. Finely grate the orange zest into the fennel, preferably with a Microplane. With a chef's knife, cut both ends off the orange. Stand the orange on one end on a cutting board and cut off the bitter white pith. Working over the bowl with the fennel to catch the juice, cut between the membranes of the orange with a paring knife to release the segments. Cut the segments in half and add to the bowl. Squeeze the juice from the membrane into the bowl and discard the membrane. Add the olive oil, vinegar, 1 teaspoon salt, ⅛ teaspoon pepper, the slivered mint, and basil. Toss to coat.

4. Meanwhile, for the halibut, on a plate or a sheet of aluminum foil, season the fillets on both sides with salt and pepper. Let stand 15 minutes to allow the seasonings to penetrate.

5. Return the court bouillon to a simmer. Add the halibut and cook until the fillets firm up and the fish is cooked through, 4 to 5 minutes. Remove the fillets to a plate with a slotted spatula.

6. To serve, divide the salad among four serving plates. Set a fillet on top of each and drizzle the remaining dressing from the salad over the fish.

KITCHEN NOTEBOOK: SLICING FENNEL

Don't cut out the core when you're slicing fennel on the mandoline. The core keeps the slices from falling apart; the whole thin slices give the salad volume and make an attractive, sort of frilly presentation. (See also Kitchen Notebook, page 220.)

· POACHED BLACK SEA BASS 101 ·
WITH PIQUILLO PEPPER AIOLI

SERVES 4 AS AN ENTRÉE

To maintain the delicate sweetness of black sea bass, I poach it quite simply in water seasoned with a small amount of white wine. Roasted piquillo peppers, which are a little less sweet than roasted red bell peppers, add a warm, tangy flavor to this bright, brick-orange sauce. It will highlight the flavor of almost any poached or steamed fish; we serve it with shrimp cocktail at the restaurant.

FOR THE PIQUILLO PEPPER AIOLI

1 large egg yolk (see Kitchen Notebook, page 22)

One 7-ounce jar piquillo peppers (14 peppers), drained

¼ teaspoon fine sea salt

Pinch of freshly ground black pepper

¾ teaspoon sherry vinegar

¼ cup canola oil

FOR THE SEA BASS

Four 6-ounce boneless, skin-on black sea bass fillets (½ to ¾ inch thick)

Fine sea salt and freshly ground black pepper

2 cups dry white wine

1. For the aioli, in a blender, combine the egg yolk, peppers, salt, pepper, and vinegar and purée until smooth. (If you have a variable-speed blender, start on low speed and work up to high.) With the blender running, drizzle in the oil. Taste for salt and pepper and adjust if necessary. Transfer to a container, cover, and chill.

2. For the bass, on a plate or a sheet of aluminum foil, season the fillets on both sides with salt and pepper. Let stand 15 minutes to allow the seasonings to penetrate.

3. Meanwhile, for the poaching liquid, in an 8-quart pot or a deep skillet wide enough to hold the fish in a single layer and deep enough to hold the liquid, combine 10 cups water, the wine, and 4 teaspoons salt. Cover and bring to a boil.

4. Add the fish to the poaching liquid and reduce the heat so that the water simmers gently. Poach until the fish is cooked through, about 8 minutes.

5. To serve, spoon some of the aioli into four shallow serving bowls or deep serving plates. Remove the fish from the steamer with a slotted spatula and place each fillet on top of the aioli in each bowl.

· OLIVE OIL–POACHED SWORDFISH 101 · WITH CAPONATA

SERVES 4 AS AN ENTRÉE

Poaching in olive oil produces an incredibly moist, tender texture—so tender, that I cook swordfish all the way through rather than to medium, as I usually do. Unlike deep-frying, you're cooking at a very low temperature (170°F). No crust develops, so you end up with the delicious, natural flavor of the fish. It's great with caponata. The key is to keep the oil at a consistent temperature for which you'll need a deep-fry thermometer (page 237). It's a no-brainer but you do need to babysit the process. Ask your fishmonger to cut thicker, smaller steaks that will fit comfortably into a 12-inch skillet, allowing for a little room between them.

Four 6- to 8-ounce skinless swordfish steaks (about 1¼ inches thick)

Fine sea salt and freshly ground black pepper

5 cups extra virgin olive oil (see Kitchen Notebook, opposite)

Sicilian-Style Eggplant Caponata (page 367), for serving

4 small basil sprigs, for garnish (optional)

1. Pull the fish out of the refrigerator about 1 hour before you plan to cook it—you want it at room temperature so that it cools the oil as little as possible. On a plate or a sheet of aluminum foil, season the fish on both sides with salt and pepper. Let stand 15 minutes to allow the seasonings to penetrate.

2. Pat the fish dry with paper towels. Line a baking dish with paper towels.

3. Pour the oil into a deep 12-inch skillet. Heat over low heat until the temperature reaches 170°F on a deep-fry thermometer. (Don't worry if the temperature is slightly higher—up to 185°F—because the fish will bring the temperature down.) Slide the fish into the oil in a single layer. Cook over low heat, monitoring the temperature frequently and adjusting the heat as needed, turning it up if the temperature drops below 170°F, and even pulling the pan off the heat if necessary to cool. Every now and then tilt the pan to move the oil a bit and distribute the heat, and stir the oil with the thermometer as you take its temperature to adjust for hot and cool spots. Cook until the swordfish is cooked through, about 15 minutes.

4. Remove the swordfish from the oil to the paper towel–lined baking dish with a slotted spatula to drain. Gently scrape off any blobs of white protein that have accumulated on the steaks. Serve with the caponata and garnish with basil sprigs, if using.

📖 KITCHEN NOTEBOOK: EXTRA VIRGIN GOLD

Five cups of extra virgin olive oil is an investment. After cooking, let it cool, then strain through a fine-mesh or cheesecloth-lined strainer into a freezer container, leaving the dregs with water or impurities behind in the pan. Cover and store it in the freezer until you're ready to poach another batch of fish.

· POACHED SCALLOPS 101 ·
WITH PEA SHOOTS, SUGAR SNAPS, WALNUTS, AND ORANGE VINAIGRETTE

SERVES 4 AS AN ENTRÉE

Poaching is a nice way to appreciate scallops. Served cold, their sweet flavor really pops against an orange vinaigrette. We get very large, beautiful scallops (U10) at the restaurant. If you find yourself with smaller scallops (20–30 count), check them at 3 minutes.

At the restaurant, where I have access to all sorts of greens, I garnish this with sorrel, chervil, the flowering tips of Thai basil flowers, and really cool live micro pea shoots from Good Water Farms in East Hampton, Long Island. If you can get hold of sorrel, chervil, and Thai basil leaves, you'll enjoy a similar, herbaceous spring flavor.

1¼ to 1½ pounds large (preferably U10) scallops (tough white side muscles removed)

Fine sea salt

6 cups Classic Court Bouillon (page 64), Quick Court Bouillon (page 241), or water

8 ounces sugar snap peas, strings removed

4 cups gently packed large pea shoot leaves (3 ounces; from about 6 ounces pea shoots on the stem)

½ cup raw walnut pieces

Freshly ground black pepper

½ cup Orange Vinaigrette (page 20)

¼ cup gently packed torn sorrel leaves (optional)

¼ cup gently packed fresh chervil (optional)

¼ cup gently packed torn fresh Thai basil leaves (optional)

1. On a plate or a sheet of aluminum foil, season the scallops on both sides with salt. Let stand 15 minutes to allow the salt to penetrate.

2. In a medium saucepan, bring the court bouillon to a boil. Add the scallops, bring to a simmer, and simmer until the scallops are firm and cooked to medium-rare, about 4 minutes. Let cool in the poaching liquid.

3. Meanwhile, bring a pot of salted water to a boil and prepare an ice bath by filling a large bowl with ice and water. Add the sugar snap peas to the boiling water and cook 1 minute. Drain, then drop into the ice bath. When they're cold, drain and pat dry on paper towels.

4. To serve, combine the cooked sugar snap peas, the pea shoots, and walnuts in a large bowl. Season with ¼ teaspoon salt and pepper. Drizzle 6 tablespoons of the dressing around the rim of the bowl. Gently fold the salad into the dressing (see Kitchen Notebook, below). Divide the salad among four shallow serving bowls or deep serving plates.

5. Cut the scallops in half to make thinner disks. Put the scallops in the salad bowl, add the remaining 2 tablespoons dressing, and toss lightly to coat. Divide the scallop halves between the bowls, tucking them into the salad in each bowl. Garnish with torn sorrel leaves, chervil, and basil, if using.

KITCHEN NOTEBOOK: DRESSING THE SALAD BOWL

It may sound weird, but the best way to dress your salad is to dress the bowl. Put the greens in the bowl, drizzle the dressing around the rim, and then fold the greens into the dressing. This way, you don't weigh down delicate greens by dumping the dressing on top. And it's easier to evenly distribute the dressing through the greens. Additionally, the greens are dressed faster, which means that you handle them less so there's less chance of bruising.

· LOBSTER BOIL 101 ·
WITH CLAMS, CORN, AND POTATOES

SERVES 4 AS AN ENTRÉE

I don't know where the idea of shellfish steamed in beer came from but I've been doing clams that way for ages. You're probably going to be cooking lobster in the summertime, hopefully by the shore. Lobster tastes fine with a cold beer so why not cook it with beer, too. Your favorite lager will taste good in this; with its acidity, wheat beer is even better. You'll need a 4- to 5-gallon pot with a lid to hold lobsters, potatoes, and corn.

1 pound small red potatoes, scrubbed and halved

7½ cups beer (five 12-ounce cans or bottles)

4 ears corn, husked and snapped in half

Four 1¼-pound live lobsters

16 littleneck clams, scrubbed

12 tablespoons (1½ sticks) unsalted butter

1. Put the potatoes in a 4- to 5-gallon pot. Add the beer and bring to a simmer. Cover and cook until potatoes are about halfway cooked, 10 to 15 minutes.

2. Add the corn. Cut the rubber bands off the lobster claws and add the lobsters. Cover and cook until the lobsters are almost cooked through, 12 to 15 minutes. To check, remove a lobster from the pot with tongs and place on a cutting board. Bend back the pincer on one claw to check the flesh, which should be opaque (see Kitchen Notebook, opposite).

3. Add the clams, cover, and continue to simmer until the clams open, 1 to 2 minutes more.

4. Remove the lobsters from the pot with tongs and place on a big platter. Remove the clams, potatoes, and corn with a spider, skimmer, or slotted spoon and pile them up on the platter, too.

5. While everything is still steaming hot, melt the butter in a small saucepan. Divide among four ramekins. Fill four more ramekins with poaching liquid. Serve butter and poaching liquid at each place setting along with lobster crackers for cracking the claws, a big bowl for the shells, and plenty of napkins.

The easiest way to tell if a whole lobster is cooked through is to remove it from the pot, oven, or grill, and wiggle the pincer on one claw. When the lobster is cooked correctly, you should be able to pull the pincer and the attached piece of cartilage easily out of the claw. And you'll get a look at the flesh inside the claw—when underdone, the flesh is translucent; when the lobster is cooked, the flesh will be opaque.

· POACHED WHOLE STRIPED BASS ·
WITH BASIL-GARLIC COMPOTE

SERVES 4 AS AN ENTRÉE

Two-pound farm-raised striped bass are a perfect size for poaching because two will fit easily in a deep 12-inch-diameter pot. Poaching in a classic court bouillon will also mitigate the sometimes muddy flavor of the farmed fish, which are a hybrid of striped bass and white bass. The fish are easily recognizable by the look of their stripes: they are not as bold as the unbroken stripes on a wild striper, and the stripes toward the belly edge look more like dashes than stripes. Two fish will serve four average or two very hungry appetites. Make this with a Classic Court Bouillon or the Quick Court Bouillon, below. Serve with a salad of sliced tomatoes dressed with extra virgin olive oil, vinegar, salt and pepper.

FOR THE BASIL-GARLIC COMPOTE

2 heads garlic, cloves separated, skin-on

1 cup extra virgin olive oil

½ cup gently packed fresh basil leaves

1 tablespoon white wine vinegar

¼ teaspoon fine sea salt

⅛ teaspoon freshly ground black pepper

FOR THE STRIPED BASS

Two 2-pound farmed striped bass, scaled and
gutted, fins, tails, and gills removed

3 quarts Classic Court Bouillon (page 64) or
Quick Court Bouillon (page 241)

1. For the compote, preheat the oven to 225°F. Place the garlic cloves in a small ovenproof pot with a lid. Add the olive oil and heat over medium heat until the oil begins to bubble. Cover, place in the oven, and bake until the garlic is meltingly tender and has turned a warm tan, about 1½ hours. Let cool.

2. With a slotted spoon, remove the garlic cloves to a cutting board; save the oil. Pop the garlic cloves out of their skins and measure ¼ cup; chop to a paste and place in a medium bowl. (Refrigerate the remaining garlic; mash into vinaigrettes or mayonnaise for sandwiches and chicken and tuna salads.) Press the basil leaves together into a loose pile on a cutting board and thinly slice; crosscut the pile 4 times to shorten the slices but leave some texture. Add to the garlic paste. Add ¼ cup of the oil from the garlic. (Store the remaining oil, covered, in the refrigerator for use in vinaigrettes.) Stir in the vinegar, salt, and pepper. Set aside.

3. In a 12-inch-diameter pot deep enough to hold the court bouillon, bring the court bouillon to a simmer. Place the fish side by side in the pot. Cover and simmer until the fish are cooked through, about 10 minutes. Test by lifting a fish out of the pot with a large spatula and placing on a cutting board. Use a paring knife to make a small horizontal cut at the backbone. The flesh should lift easily from the bone but will still be slightly translucent; the fish will continue to cook a bit after removing from the heat.

4. Use a fork and serving spoon to fillet the fish (see page 382). Use the fork and spoon to lift and place 1 fillet onto each of four serving plates. Spoon one quarter of the basil-garlic compote to the side of each fillet.

· NOT YOUR MOTHER'S GEFILTE FISH ·

SERVES 4 AS AN ENTRÉE

I like to do something special at Oceana to celebrate all the holidays. I didn't grow up with gefilte fish but when I began cooking fish professionally, I got curious and did some research. The word *gefilte* is a Yiddish word, meaning "stuffed." Historically, the minced fish was stuffed into fish skin for cooking. This sounded worth checking out, so I tried a version of the recipe below, rolling narrow cylinders of ground, seasoned fish in salmon skin. It looks like a sushi roll and tastes like a tender seafood sausage. It's served at the restaurant sliced on the bias, in a horseradish-infused broth. At home, I don't bother with the salmon skin. I simply scoop small spoonfuls of the fish into the simmering broth.

Traditionally, gefilte fish is made with a combination of pike, whitefish, and carp. I leave out the carp because its flavor can be muddy. Pike and whitefish are often available during Passover season, or you can use a combination of striped bass and halibut. This is a little bit of a production so I recommend making the broth a day ahead.

For the cleanest cut when grinding the fish, chill the grinder attachment or the bowl and blade of your food processor in the freezer for about 15 minutes before you use them. Chill the fish, too.

FOR THE BROTH

7 cups Fish Fumet (page 13)

1¾ cups grated peeled fresh horseradish

1 tablespoon fresh lemon juice

1¾ teaspoons fine sea salt

FOR THE GEFILTE FISH

2 teaspoons canola oil

2 tablespoons finely diced onion (¼-inch dice)

2 tablespoons finely diced carrot (¼-inch dice)

6 ounces boneless, skinless pike fillets, chilled 15 minutes in the freezer

6 ounces boneless, skinless whitefish fillets, chilled 15 minutes in the freezer

1 large egg yolk

2 tablespoons slivered fresh Italian parsley

1 tablespoon finely sliced fresh chives

½ teaspoon fine sea salt

FOR SERVING

1 tablespoon canola oil

½ cup sliced leek coins (white part only), separated into rings and washed well

½ cup thinly sliced carrot coins

1 teaspoon fine sea salt

20 fresh Italian parsley leaves

1. For the broth, in a medium pot, combine the fumet, horseradish, lemon juice, and salt. Bring to a simmer and cook 30 minutes. Set aside without straining. (You should have about 5 cups liquid.)

2. For the fish, heat a medium saucepan over medium heat. Add the oil, the onion, and carrot and cook without coloring for 2 minutes. Remove to a medium bowl and set aside to cool to room temperature.

3. Meanwhile, grind the fish through the small plate of a chilled meat grinder. Or cut into ½-inch dice and pulse in the chilled food processor until coarsely ground. (Do not purée.) Add to the cooled vegetables along with the egg yolk, parsley, chives, and salt and stir to blend. Cover and refrigerate until you're ready to cook.

4. To serve, heat a 12-inch skillet or an 8-quart pot over medium heat. Add the oil, the leek, carrot, and salt. Cook without coloring, stirring often, 3 minutes. Strain the reserved broth into the pan and bring to a gentle simmer. Simmer 2 minutes. Using a small spoon, scoop up a rounded teaspoonful of the fish mixture, then use a second spoon to scrape the fish off the spoon in a small ball and into the simmering broth; you should have 20 balls. (Alternatively, you can roll the mixture into small balls with your hands and place them on a plate or baking sheet until you're ready to poach them; just be careful not to overwork the fish.) Poach gently for 3 minutes.

5. With a slotted spoon, place 5 fish balls in each of four deep serving plates or shallow bowls. Add about a cup of hot broth to each plate or bowl and garnish each with 5 parsley leaves.

10.

GRILLED FISH

Vacationing on Long Beach Island with my family, I'd been fishing all week for striped bass, casting off the beach with surf clams as bait. Striped bass are territorial and you can usually expect to find a few feeding among the rock jetties. Surf clams roll in and bust up on the rocks, and the bass come in to feed on them. It was the last day of my vacation and I hadn't caught anything of significance. I was on my way out to the beach when my wife asked, with good reason, "What are you going to do if you catch something? We're going home today." I said I probably wouldn't hook anything anyway. "So why are you bothering to go fishing?" she asked. Good question. What can I say—I just love to fish.

After an hour or so of fishing with no result, there I was, casting out with my last piece of clam, and bang, I get this big chomp on the line. It was a monster 36-inch striped bass. And the question remained: What do I do with this thing?

I cleaned it, cut off the head and tail so that it would fit in the cooler, and we drove home with it. I filled the cavity with lemon slices and herbs, and seasoned it. I had no idea how long the fish would take to cook so I wrapped it in foil to protect the exterior from overcooking and make the fish easier to handle. I put it on the grill. It barely fit. But it was delicious. And my wife forgave me.

That's the great thing about grilling. It's versatile and it's fun! Grilled food tastes awesome. You're cooking outdoors. The kitchen stays clean, the oven stays off, and the grill is easy to clean. Although some fish is more challenging than others, you can put almost anything on the grill. You can cook whole fish, steaks, and fillets. Lobster, scallops, clams, and squid work well on the grill, and it's the easiest way I know to cook a really big fish like my bass. Smaller fish are even easier.

I grill a lot when I'm home, usually scallops, salmon, halibut, striped bass, grouper, and snapper fillet—fish that cook quickly when I need to get dinner for the family on the table. But grilling is also the perfect way to answer the question of what to cook for a crowd during the summer when everyone wants to be outside anyway. Don't worry about fancy sauces—lemon, olive oil, and hot sauce are just fine with grilled fish. Fresh salsas are such a wonderful accompaniment that I've given you a few recipes in this chapter, too. The charred flavor of the fish jibes with the combination of sweet, sour, and herbal notes in the salsas.

With apologies to purists, when I say grill, I mean propane gas. I'm all for the right way to grill, which is over wood or lump charcoal. Depending on your grill, the wood or charcoal may burn hotter, and they impart a flavor that can't be beat. But at home, the reality is that as a parent, I find it easier to fire up the gas grill for dinner. I'll show you how to use wood chips to give the food some of that woodsy flavor.

The keys to foolproof grilling are a clean grill to prevent sticking and off-flavors, getting the right temperature, and avoiding flare-ups.

CLEANING AND PREPARING THE GRILL

Before grilling, preheat the grill and scrub the grill grates well with a wire grill brush. Oil the grill grates: Fold several sheets of paper towels into a rectangle about 3 inches long by 1 inch wide. Put about 1 tablespoon canola or vegetable oil in a dish. Put the folded paper towels in the dish to allow them to soak up the oil. (You want them saturated with the oil but not dripping.)

Immediately before you put the fish on the grill, holding the oil-soaked towels with tongs, wipe them over the clean, hot grates. Discard the oily towels when you've finished grilling.

After grilling, leave the grill on high for a few minutes to burn off any remaining bits of food. Scrub the grates with the wire brush and turn off the grill.

TIMING AND TEMPERATURE

Grilling times and temperature will vary depending on the type of fish, its den-

sity or flakiness, and its thickness. Meaty, dense fish like swordfish will take longer to cook than lighter, flakier fish like snapper and grouper. The recipes in this chapter are, with some exceptions, written to grill over high heat. But you'll need to take your particular grill into consideration. Start over high heat, but if the fish is browning too fast, lower the heat to medium-high. I sometimes work with two zones of heat: I heat half the grill to high, half to low. I start the fish on high but if I find it browning up too quickly or if it's a very thick piece of fish, once I get my crosshatch pattern (see Making a Crosshatch Pattern, page 262), I move it to finish over low heat. If you find the grill flaring up on high, the two-level approach is a good way to go. Just keep shifting the fish to low as it flares up.

BEST FISH FOR GRILLING

Meaty fish such as tuna, wahoo (ono), mahi mahi, swordfish, cobia, opah, and monchong are ideal for grilling because they hold together well and are easy to handle.

Salmon is also excellent on the grill but be aware that with its high fat content, the fat will melt and cause flare-ups if the heat is too high; just move it to the lower heat.

Skin is tasty on the grill because it gets crisp. Start the fish skin side down and grill until the skin begins to get crisp and releases easily from the grill grates.

Delicate, flakey fish like cod and halibut pose more of a challenge because they fall apart easily. They won't give you trouble if you use a grill basket (see Equip Yourself, opposite). Without a grill basket, make sure to allow several inches between each piece of fish so that you have plenty of room to maneuver your spatula.

Small whole fish (up to 3 pounds) work well on the grill, which crisps the skin, but they take a little practice. Oceana was the first place I was professionally responsible for turning out whole grilled fish on a regular basis. When I started, I thought it was best to use grill baskets to keep the fish from sticking. I'd suggest the same to you. Once we got comfortable handling the fish at the restaurant and became meticulous about keeping the grill grates clean and well-oiled, we graduated to cooking without the baskets. You might, too, but the baskets are more foolproof.

- You'll need a sturdy wire grill brush for cleaning the grill.

- I use a wide metal spatula for turning more delicate fish and fish with skin, because tongs will tear up the skin and fish.

- You'll need a pair of tongs to oil the grill. If you're careful, you can use tongs with denser fish such as mahi mahi, swordfish, and scallops, but their sharp edges can cut into the flesh. You're almost always better off with a spatula. I do use tongs to pick up the edge of a fillet or the head of a whole fish, to make it easier to slide the spatula underneath.

- Buy a grill basket that encloses the fish between two sides of the basket and allows you to flip the fish without having to manipulate it. They're inexpensive and come in a variety of shapes and sizes. A 5 by 12-inch basket works well for fillets, steaks, and small whole fish. Some have detachable handles, which may make it easier to close the cover of the grill. (The cover of my grill is notched to accommodate a rotisserie spit, and the handle of my grill basket fits in that notch.) Oil the grill basket or spray with nonstick spray to prevent the fish from sticking to it.

- Wood chips add a nice smoky flavor. Soak them for 10 minutes in water to cover, drain, and put them in an aluminum pie tin or a sheet of aluminum foil. Place on a corner of the grill to heat for a few minutes before you add the fish.

- When you can't get outside, ridged grill pans on the stovetop are surprisingly effective at creating a charred crust. There are a lot of grill pans out there; mine is cast iron. The most practical pan, unless you never cook for more than two, is a rectangular griddle-type pan that fits across two burners. A caution when using these pans: they *will* smoke up your house unless you maintain an even, moderate heat. Heat the pan over high heat for about 5 minutes. Reduce the heat to medium. Lightly oil the ridges as if you were cooking on an outdoor grill. Place the fish on the pan and cook as you would on the grill. A 1-inch-thick or less piece of fish should cook fine this way. For thicker fillets, you may need to cover the pan: Place the fish on the pan and cook to make a crosshatch pattern on one side, flip it, then cover the pan with a double layer of aluminum foil (when we get in a bind for time in the restaurant, we speed things up by overturning a pot over the food on the grill).

That professional-looking diamond cross-hatch pattern that we make in a restaurant kitchen isn't just for show. It encourages even cooking and ensures that the grill marks don't get hammered into the flesh of the fish as it sits in one spot for 4 to 5 minutes. (Squid is not really going to show a crosshatch pattern, but it's important to keep it moving on the grill.)

To make a crosshatch pattern, place your fish on the grill at an angle to the grates. (If you lay it straight on the grates, you'll get squares, not diamonds.) Let the fish cook until it's marked with rich brown lines. This will take 2 to 4 minutes, depending on your grill. Then turn the fish 90 degrees and cook 2 to 4 minutes more, until you've got your crosshatch. Flip the fish, and do the same on the other side until the fish is cooked.

· GRILLED MAHI MAHI 101 ·
WITH HOT SAUCE VINAIGRETTE

SERVES 4 AS AN ENTRÉE

This vinaigrette is killer with pretty much any kind of fish, but full-flavored mahi mahi stands up particularly well to it. You will have leftover vinaigrette; it tastes amazing on salads.

Four 6- to 8-ounce fillets boneless, skinless
  mahi mahi (¾ to 1 inch thick)

Fine sea salt

4 teaspoons extra virgin olive oil

Hot Sauce Vinaigrette (page 20)

1. Preheat a gas grill to high. Scrub the grill grates with a grill brush. On a plate, season the fish on both sides with salt and let stand 5 minutes to allow the seasoning to penetrate.

2. Pat the fish dry with paper towels. Rub each fillet all over with 1 teaspoon oil.

3. Oil the grill grates. Place the fish on the grill over high heat at an angle to the grates and cook 2 minutes to mark. Turn 90 degrees with a spatula to make a crosshatch pattern and cook 2 minutes more. Flip the fish with the spatula, and cook 2 minutes more. Turn 90 degrees with the spatula and cook until the fillets are cooked through to medium, about 2 minutes more.

4. Place a fillet on each of four serving plates with the spatula and serve with the vinaigrette.

· STRIPED BASS 101 WITH GRILLED CORN ·
AND RED ONION SALAD

SERVES 4 AS AN ENTRÉE

Striped bass is a summer catch that's perfect on the grill, particularly if you're a fan of crisp skin. And given that you're heating the grill anyway, it's easy to grill up some corn and red onion for a summer salad. Epazote is an herb that grows wild in Mexico. It adds a distinctive peppery, minty flavor to Mexican dishes—you either love it or hate it—and I love it in this salad. There's no real substitute, but that doesn't mean you can't use whatever you've got on hand; Italian parsley, basil, and tarragon are all tasty.

FOR THE SALAD

4 ears corn, husked

Extra virgin olive oil

Fine sea salt and freshly ground black pepper

2 medium or 1 large red onion, peeled

Finely grated zest and juice of 2 limes

2 teaspoons slivered seeded finger chile

¼ cup loosely packed fresh cilantro leaves

¼ cup loosely packed, coarsely chopped fresh epazote (optional)

Fine sea salt and freshly ground pepper

FOR THE STRIPED BASS

Four 7- to 8-ounce boneless, skin-on striped bass fillets (1½ to 1¾ inch thick)

Fine sea salt and freshly ground black pepper

4 teaspoons extra virgin olive oil

1. For the salad, preheat a gas grill to high. Scrub the grill grates with a grill brush.

2. On a baking sheet, rub each ear of corn with 1 teaspoon olive oil and sprinkle all over with salt and pepper. Slice the onion crosswise about ⅓ inch thick, taking care that the slices don't fall apart into rings. Place the slices in a single layer on the baking sheet and rub with 1 teaspoon olive oil. Sprinkle one side with salt and pepper.

3. Oil the grill grates. Place the corn and onion slices on the grill over high heat. Grill the onion slices until lightly charred and tender, turning halfway through with a metal spatula, 4 to 5 minutes total. Remove to the baking sheet with a metal spatula. Continue cooking the corn, turning as the kernels blister and brown, until the color of the corn has brightened from a pale to a vibrant yellow speckled with brown, and the skins of the kernels are popping, 5 to 7 minutes total; remove to the baking sheet. Let the vegetables stand until cool enough to handle.

recipe continued on next page

4. Stand an ear of corn on a cutting board, holding it by the skinny end. Cut down the length of the cob with a chef's knife to cut off a row of kernels. Give the ear a turn and cut off another row of kernels. Continue in this way to remove all of the kernels from all of the ears. Place the kernels in a large bowl and discard the cobs. Dice the onion into pieces about the same size as the corn kernels (see Kitchen Notebook, below). Add the onion to the corn. Add the lime zest and juice, the chiles, ¼ cup olive oil, the cilantro, epazote if using, ½ teaspoon salt, and ⅛ teaspoon black pepper. Stir well. Taste for seasoning. Set aside until you're ready to serve.

5. For the striped bass, on a plate or a sheet of aluminum foil, season the fish on both sides with salt and pepper. Let stand 5 minutes to allow the seasonings to penetrate.

6. Pat the fish dry with paper towels. Rub each fillet with 1 teaspoon oil. Oil the grill grates. Place the fish skin side down on the grill over high heat at an angle to the grates and cook 3 minutes to mark. Turn 90 degrees with a spatula to make a crosshatch pattern and cook until the skin is good and crisp, 2 to 3 minutes more. Flip the fish with the spatula and cook 4 minutes more. Turn 90 degrees with the spatula and cook until the fillets are cooked through, 3 to 5 minutes more.

7. To serve, divide the salad between four serving plates. Place the fillets on top of the salad with the spatula.

KITCHEN NOTEBOOK: A QUICK CHOP

When cutting the grilled onion slices into ⅓- to ½-inch dice, you don't want to get too hung up on perfection. Just place the onion slices in a shallow pile on the cutting board. Slice crosswise at ⅓- to ½-inch intervals; turn the cutting board or your body so the knife is at a 90 degree angle to the first cut, and cut again at ⅓- to ½-inch intervals.

· GRILLED BLUEFISH 101 ·
WITH TOMATILLO SALSA

SERVES 4 AS AN ENTRÉE

This recipe offers a cool combination of summertime flavors when bluefish and tomatillos are at their prime. Bluefish is delicate and has a tendency to fall apart so it should be handled as little as possible on the grill; don't attempt a crosshatch pattern. If you've never worked with fresh tomatillos, they taste pretty much like green tomatoes and their bright, acidic flavor offsets the richness of a fatty fish like bluefish. You may find them in the market other times of the year, but in season, the skins are thin and tender and there's no need to peel. Just throw the ingredients in the blender and you're done. Out of season, score an "x" in the bottom of each tomatillo and simmer in boiling water for 30 seconds; remove with a slotted spoon, transfer to a bowl of ice water to chill, and peel with a small knife.

FOR THE BLUEFISH

Four 6- to 8-ounce skinless bluefish fillets, bloodlines removed (about ½ inch thick)

Fine sea salt and freshly ground black pepper

2 tablespoons extra virgin olive oil

1 tablespoon sherry vinegar

2 cloves garlic, crushed with the side of a chef's knife

2 large sprigs fresh cilantro

Lime wedges, for garnish

FOR THE TOMATILLO SALSA

6 medium tomatillos (4 ounces), papery skins removed, rinsed

½ clove garlic

1-inch piece green finger chile, seeds removed, chopped

Fine sea salt

6 tablespoons extra virgin olive oil

1 tablespoon fresh lime juice

½ cup loosely packed fresh cilantro leaves

1 teaspoon cumin seeds, toasted over medium heat until aromatic (2 to 3 minutes) and cooled, or ½ teaspoon ground cumin

1 teaspoon ground coriander

¼ teaspoon freshly ground black pepper

1. For the bluefish, on a plate or a sheet of aluminum foil, season the fillets on both sides with salt and pepper. Let stand 5 minutes to allow the seasonings to penetrate. Meanwhile, mix the oil, vinegar, garlic, and cilantro in a glass baking dish large enough to hold the fillets (they don't need to be in a single layer).

recipe continued on next page

2. Add the bluefish to the marinade and turn to coat. Refrigerate 1 hour. Most of the marinade will be absorbed.

3. For the salsa, coarsely chop the tomatillos and place in a food processor. Add the garlic, chile, and ¼ teaspoon salt and pulse until the tomatillos are coarsely puréed. Add the olive oil, lime, and cilantro, and pulse to medium-fine. Transfer to a bowl and season with the cumin and coriander, salt to taste, and the pepper. It will be a loose sauce.

4. Preheat a gas grill to high. Scrub the grill grates well with a grill brush, then oil the grates. Place the fillets on the grill over high heat and cook 2 minutes. Use a spatula to carefully flip the fillets and grill until cooked through, about 2 minutes more.

5. To serve, spoon some of the sauce into each of four deep serving plates or shallow serving bowls. Place a fillet on each with the spatula.. Garnish with lime wedges.

· SWORDFISH 101 ·
WITH GRILLED ASPARAGUS,
ASPARAGUS SALAD,
AND BALSAMIC REDUCTION

SERVES 4 AS AN ENTRÉE

This spring recipe has a lot of moving parts but they're all easy to accomplish. You'll need a Japanese mandoline (see Equip Yourself, page 140) to slice the asparagus for the salad. If you have the time while cooking this dish, don't discard the asparagus stalks; use them in a purée (see Extra Credit, page 270).

FOR THE BALSAMIC REDUCTION

2 cups balsamic vinegar

FOR THE SWORDFISH

Four 7- to 8-ounce swordfish steaks (with or without skin; about 1 inch thick)

Fine sea salt and freshly ground black pepper

4 teaspoons extra virgin olive oil

FOR THE ASPARAGUS SALAD

1 bunch jumbo asparagus (about 1 pound)

2 tablespoons extra virgin olive oil

Fine sea salt and freshly ground black pepper

FOR THE GRILLED ASPARAGUS

2 bunches jumbo asparagus (about 2 pounds, total), woody ends snapped off

2 tablespoons extra virgin olive oil

Fine sea salt and freshly ground black pepper

1 teaspoon balsamic vinegar

1. For the reduction, place the vinegar in a small saucepan and simmer until thickened and reduced to about ¼ cup. Transfer to a container and set aside.

2. For the fish, preheat a gas grill to high. Scrub the grill grates with a grill brush. On a plate or a sheet of aluminum foil, season the fish on both sides with salt and pepper. Let stand at least 5 minutes to allow the seasonings to penetrate.

3. Meanwhile, for the asparagus salad, trim the woody ends (about 2 inches) from the asparagus. Take one end of a stalk in the thumb and forefinger of each hand and flex the stalk; where it stops bending is where the tough, woody part starts. Save the ends of

recipe continued on next page

the stalks for purée, if you like. Shave the asparagus lengthwise into long, thin slices on a Japanese mandoline. Set aside.

4. For the grilled asparagus, drizzle the asparagus with the oil and season with salt and pepper. Oil the grill grates. Place the spears so they won't fall through the grates and grill, turning once or twice with tongs for even cooking, until lightly browned and tender when pierced with a paring knife, 4 to 5 minutes. Remove with tongs to a serving bowl. Drizzle with the balsamic reduction and set aside.

5. For the fish, scrub the grill grates again and oil them. Pat the fish dry with paper towels. Rub each steak with 1 teaspoon oil. Place the fish on the grill over high heat at an angle to the grates and cook 2 minutes to mark. Turn 90 degrees with a spatula to make a cross-hatch pattern and cook 2 minutes more. Flip the fish with the spatula and cook 2 minutes more. Turn 90 degrees with the spatula and cook until the steaks are cooked to medium, 1 to 3 minutes more.

6. To serve, toss the sliced asparagus with the olive oil and season with salt and pepper. Place the fish on four serving plates. Top each with one quarter of the asparagus salad. Arrange the grilled asparagus to the side of the fish. Drizzle the balsamic reduction around the plate.

 EXTRA CREDIT: ASPARAGUS PURÉE

To kick this dish up a notch, save the ends of the asparagus stalks for an asparagus purée.

1. Trim and discard the very ends—the whitish parts—of the reserved stalks. Slice the green part of the stalks ½ inch thick.

2. Prepare an ice bath in a large bowl.

3. Place a medium saucepan over medium heat. Add 1 tablespoon extra virgin olive oil and heat until fluid enough to coat the bottom of the pan when swirled. Add 1 sliced shallot and cook without coloring, stirring often, until the shallot is translucent, 2 to 3 minutes. Add the sliced stalks and cook without coloring, stirring often, about 2 minutes more. Add 1 tablespoon butter and ½ cup chicken stock. Bring to a simmer and cook until the asparagus is tender, 3 to 5 minutes. Transfer to a bowl and chill in the ice bath.

4. When cold, purée in a blender until smooth. Season to taste with salt and pepper. Strain through a fine-mesh strainer.

5. To serve, spoon the purée onto the serving plates and set the grilled swordfish steaks on top. Add the asparagus salad, grilled asparagus, and balsamic reduction as in step 6 of the recipe. (The purée may also be thinned with more chicken stock for soup.)

To take this dish a step further for extra extra credit, peel the green stalks of the asparagus for grilling as we did at Le Louis XV for a more sophisticated presentation: Make a "collar" by scoring a line around each trimmed stalk with a paring knife, about 1 inch from the bottom. Starting at the scored line and working toward the end of the stalk, use the knife to peel off the skin. Then grill the asparagus as in step 4.

· GRILLED SALMON 101 ·
WITH ROASTED BRUSSELS SPROUTS, BACON, AND MAPLE

SERVES 4 AS AN ENTRÉE

The combination of sweet and sour plus a smoky, meaty element like bacon, prosciutto, or duck confit elevates the humble Brussels sprout to something great. They're delicious with salmon—the flavor of the sprouts is pretty bold and salmon will hold up to it. For this as for all salmon recipes, I recommend heating part of the grill to low so that you can move the salmon to lower heat if you get a flare-up.

FOR THE BRUSSELS SPROUTS

1½ pounds Brussels sprouts, trimmed and halved through the root end

½ teaspoon fine sea salt

3 tablespoons canola oil

2 slices thick-cut bacon (2½ to 3 ounces), cut into ¼-inch dice or ¼-inch crosswise strips (about ½ cup)

½ cup diced shallot (¼-inch dice; about 1 large)

¼ cup sherry vinegar

3 tablespoons maple syrup

Freshly ground black pepper

FOR THE SALMON

Four 6- to 8-ounce boneless, skinless salmon fillets (about 1½ inches thick)

Fine sea salt and freshly ground black pepper

1 teaspoon canola oil

1. For the Brussels sprouts, preheat the oven to 400°F. Place the Brussels sprouts on a baking sheet and toss with the salt and oil to coat. Arrange in a single layer and roast until browned and tender when pierced with a knife, 25 to 30 minutes.

2. Meanwhile, cook the bacon in a medium saucepan over low heat, stirring often, until the fat is rendered and the bacon browns lightly, about 5 minutes. Add the shallots and cook without coloring until tender, about 5 minutes. Add the vinegar and maple syrup and simmer until thickened (do not reduce to a glaze), about 5 minutes.

3. Add the Brussels sprouts to the saucepan. Season with pepper and toss to coat with the maple syrup–vinegar mixture. Remove from the heat. Turn the oven heat down to 200°F. Keep the Brussels sprouts warm in the oven.

4. Meanwhile, preheat a gas grill to high, heating a second zone to low. Scrub the grill grates with a grill brush.

5. On a plate or a sheet of aluminum foil, sprinkle the salmon on both sides with salt and pepper. Let stand 5 minutes to allow the seasonings to penetrate.

6. Pat the fish dry with paper towels. Coat each fillet with ¼ teaspoon oil. Oil the grill grates. Place the salmon on the grill over high heat at an angle to the grates and cook 2 to 3 minutes to mark. Turn the salmon 90 degrees with a spatula and cook 2 minutes more to make a crosshatch pattern. Flip the salmon carefully with the spatula (if it flames up, move it to low heat) and continue cooking to medium-rare, 2 to 3 minutes more.

7. Divide the sprouts among four serving plates. Place a steak on each with the spatula.

· CHARRED SQUID 101 ·
WITH ROSEMARY AND
RED PEPPER FLAKES

SERVES 4 AS AN ENTRÉE

I cook squid in its thin skin because the skin has good flavor, turns an attractive deep reddish-purple color, and shows off the grill marks. But if you prefer, peel it off or ask the person at the fish counter to do it for you. Optimally, the squid should marinate at least 1 hour but it will pick up a good amount flavor even if you've only got 5 to 10 minutes. Salt the squid sparingly; the flesh tastes mildly salty on its own.

2 pounds cleaned squid (skin-on if possible), tentacles and bodies with wings cut apart

Needles from two 6-inch sprigs fresh rosemary, chopped

1 teaspoon Aleppo pepper or red pepper flakes

Finely grated zest of 1 lemon

¼ cup extra virgin olive oil

Fine sea salt

Celery-Arugula Salad (page 293, optional)

1. Line a baking sheet with paper towels. Place the squid in a single layer on the baking sheet, cover with another layer of paper towels, and blot well to pat the squid dry.

2. Sprinkle the bottom of an 8 by 8-inch baking dish (or similar-size vessel) with the rosemary, Aleppo pepper, and grated zest. Add the olive oil. Add the squid and toss, rubbing with your hands to coat the squid with the seasonings. Cover and let stand at room temperature for 1 hour, or refrigerate overnight.

3. Preheat a gas grill to high. Scrub the grates well with a grill brush, then oil the grates.

4. Sprinkle the squid very lightly with salt. Set a cooling rack on a baking sheet and set the baking sheet beside the grill. Place the squid tentacles and bodies on the grill over high heat. Cook the tentacles, turning with tongs every 30 seconds or so for even cooking, until the skin darkens to a purplish-red and the flesh is opaque, 3 to 4 minutes total. Remove the tentacles with tongs to the cooling rack. At the same time, cook the bodies until the skin begins to blister and darken, about 1 minute. Turn 90 degrees to make a crosshatch pattern and cook 1 minute more. Flip the bodies with tongs, tilting them to drain the liquid that has accumulated inside; cook until the flesh turns

opaque, about 5 minutes total. Remove the bodies to the rack to drain as each piece is cooked.

5. Place one quarter of the squid tentacles and bodies on each of four serving plates. Serve with the salad if you like.

· GRILLED COBIA 101 ·
WITH PINEAPPLE SALSA

SERVES 4 AS AN ENTRÉE

Cobia is like "swordfish light"—it's a rich fish but not quite as full-flavored as swordfish. So if you're normally a flounder person, working your way into fuller-flavored varieties of fish, cobia is a great way to bridge the gap. It's beginning to be farmed, too, so it's showing up more regularly. But if you find yourself in the area from the Carolinas to Florida, that's where they're catching cobia wild and that's what you want to be eating.

FOR THE PINEAPPLE SALSA

1 ripe pineapple

Two ¼- to ⅓-inch-thick slices cut crosswise from a medium red onion

½ cup extra virgin olive oil, plus extra for grilling

Fine sea salt and freshly ground black pepper

¾ teaspoon coriander seeds or ½ teaspoon ground coriander

¼ teaspoon whole Tellicherry peppercorns or ⅛ teaspoon freshly ground black pepper

3 allspice berries or ⅛ teaspoon ground allspice

Finely grated zest and juice of 1 lime

½-inch piece peeled fresh ginger, finely chopped

¼ finger chile (cut lengthwise), seeds removed, slivered

2 teaspoons honey

¼ cup slivered fresh cilantro leaves

FOR THE COBIA

Four 6- to 8-ounce boneless, skinless cobia fillets (about 1 inch thick)

Fine sea salt and freshly ground black pepper

4 teaspoons extra virgin olive oil

1. Preheat a gas grill to high. Scrub the grill grates with a grill brush then oil the grates.

2. For the salsa, cut off the top and skin of the pineapple with a chef's knife, cutting deeply to remove the prickly "eyes." Quarter the pineapple lengthwise. Cut the core from one quarter and cut the quarter lengthwise into ¼- to ⅓-inch-thick slices. (I serve the rest of the pineapple for dessert.)

3. Place the pineapple slices on the grill over high heat, flipping once, and grill until lightly charred, about 1 minute on each side. Remove to a plate with a metal spatula. Rub the onion slices with about 1 teaspoon oil and sprinkle with salt and pepper. Grill the onion

recipe continued on next page

slices, turning halfway through with a metal spatula, until lightly charred and tender, 4 to 5 minutes total. Remove to the plate and let cool. Do not turn off the grill.

4. If using whole spices, toast the coriander, peppercorns, and allspice in a small skillet over medium heat until aromatic, 2 to 3 minutes. Grind in a spice grinder (see Equip Yourself: Spice Grinder, below); set aside.

5. Cut the cooled pineapple into ¼-inch dice and place in a bowl. Cut the onion slices into ¼-inch dice and add to the pineapple. Add the lime zest and juice, the ginger, chile, ½ cup olive oil, the honey, ground spices, and ¼ teaspoon salt. Stir gently to mix. Fold in the cilantro. Taste for salt and adjust if necessary. Set aside until you're ready to serve.

6. On a plate or a sheet of aluminum foil, season the fish on both sides with salt and pepper. Let stand 5 minutes to allow the seasonings to penetrate.

7. Pat the fish dry with paper towels. Scrub the grill grates again with a grill brush. Oil the grill grates. Rub each fillet with 1 teaspoon oil. Place the fish on the grill over high heat at an angle to the grates and cook 3 minutes to mark. Turn 90 degrees with a spatula to make a crosshatch pattern and cook 3 minutes more. Flip the fish with the spatula and cook 3 minutes more. Turn 90 degrees with the spatula and cook until the steaks are cooked to medium, 1 to 3 minutes more.

8. Divide the salsa among four serving plates. Place a fillet on each with the spatula and serve.

EQUIP YOURSELF: SPICE GRINDER

You can usually get away with using ground spices but for some recipes, like this salsa and the mole on page 201, toasting and grinding whole spices is worth the effort. The flavor is better. A coffee grinder works well, but make it a "dedicated" spice grinder; if you also use it for coffee beans, the flavor of the coffee will permeate the spices.

· GRILLED SCALLOPS 101 ·
WITH PEACH SALSA

SERVES 4 AS AN ENTRÉE

I'm kind of a peach fanatic. New Jersey peaches are not as famous as the Georgia peach and maybe I'm just feeling a little bit of New Jersey pride, but I think they taste just as terrific. I planted a tree in my front yard—it's still too young to bear fruit but I'm waiting. In the meantime, not far from my house there are orchards where you can pick your own peaches in season, from about the middle of July through August. Every year we take the kids peach picking and I always go overboard and come home with too much fruit. Salsa is the answer to all that abundance. The peaches should ripen until they're no longer hard but not be so ripe that they'll mush apart when you're working with them. The really ripe ones are best eaten over the sink, juice dripping off your chin.

I like to make this with very large (U10) scallops but you can use smaller scallops—just make sure the total number is divisible by four plates.

FOR THE PEACH SALSA

1 pound peaches (about 3 medium), peeled (see Kitchen Notebook, page 280), halved, pitted, and cut into ¼-inch dice

1-inch piece peeled fresh ginger, minced

1 red finger chile, halved lengthwise, seeds removed, slivered

Finely grated zest and juice of 2 limes

2 tablespoons extra virgin olive oil

1 tablespoon honey

¾ teaspoon fine sea salt

¼ cup gently packed basil leaves (preferably Thai basil; 4 to 5 sprigs)

FOR THE SCALLOPS

1½ pounds sea scallops (preferably U10), tough white side muscles removed

1 tablespoon extra virgin olive oil

Fine sea salt and freshly ground black pepper

1. For the salsa, combine the peaches, ginger, chile, lime zest and lime juice, olive oil, honey, and salt in a medium bowl. Mix well. Let stand a few minutes to macerate. Cut the basil leaves in thin slices; turn your body and cross-cut the slices a few times to coarsely chop. Fold into the salsa.

2. For the scallops, preheat a gas grill to high. Scrub the grill grates with a grill brush. In a bowl, toss the scallops with the olive oil and a large pinch each of salt and pepper. Let stand 5 minutes to allow the seasonings to penetrate.

recipe continued on next page

3. Oil the grill grates. For U10 scallops: Place the scallops on the grill over high heat and cook 3 minutes. Turn 90 degrees with a metal spatula and cook 1 minute more to make a crosshatch pattern. Flip the scallops with the spatula and cook 2 minutes more. Turn 90 degrees and cook until the scallops are medium-rare, about 1 minute more. (For smaller scallops, proceed in the same way but cook 2 minutes on the first side instead of 3 minutes; cook 1 minute on the second side instead of 2 minutes.)

4. Divide the salsa among four serving plates. With the spatula, place one quarter of the scallops on top of the salsa on each plate and serve.

KITCHEN NOTEBOOK: PEELING PEACHES AND TOMATOES

You don't need to peel the peaches for this salsa but you'll get a better result if you do. Peel with a vegetable peeler. Or bring a saucepan of water to a boil and prepare an ice bath by filling a large bowl with ice and cold water. Score the peaches with an X on the pointy end. Drop the peaches in the boiling water for about 20 seconds, or until the skin begins to loosen. Remove with a spider, skimmer, or slotted spoon and drop into the ice bath. The peel should come off easily with a paring knife. The same method works for peeling ripe tomatoes.

EXTRA CREDIT: THAI BASIL

Thai basil is another summer crop that grows so easily, it's almost like a weed. At the end of the season, I just stop picking it and let the flowers go to seed, and the seeds fall into the earth. The plants come back the next year without replanting. If you're into that, there is a variety of Thai-style basils out there. Look in a seed catalog or at a farmers' market. I'm partial to the purple Thai basil and pungent holy basil.

· SALMON BURGERS ·
WITH PICKLED RED ONIONS
AND HORSERADISH AIOLI

SERVES 4 AS AN ENTRÉE

I make this with wild coho salmon, which has a full, meaty flavor and it cooks up with a bright orange color. Coho is lean, however, so if you use it, be particularly careful to cook the burgers to medium-rare or they will be dry. Otherwise, farm-raised salmon is a fine substitute and the texture is more forgiving than coho. If you have the time, the onions are best made the day before.

FOR THE PICKLED RED ONIONS

2 medium red onions, sliced crosswise into thin rounds

2 cups red wine vinegar

1 cup sugar

FOR THE HORSERADISH AIOLI

1 cup Homemade Mayonnaise (page 21), or good-quality store-bought mayonnaise

1 tablespoon plus 1 teaspoon white prepared horseradish, excess liquid pressed out with clean fingers

FOR THE SALMON BURGERS

2 pounds boneless, skinless salmon fillet, pin bones removed

Fine sea salt and freshly ground black pepper

1 teaspoon canola oil

4 hamburger buns

2 tablespoons unsalted butter, softened or melted

1 cup loosely packed arugula leaves, for serving

1. For the onions, place in a heatproof bowl. In a small saucepan, bring the vinegar and sugar to a boil, stirring occasionally to dissolve the sugar. Pour over the onions—they should be entirely submerged (choose a smaller container, if necessary). Cover and let stand at least 1 hour or overnight to cool completely to room temperature. Set aside.

2. For the aioli, whisk the mayonnaise with the horseradish in a bowl. Refrigerate until you're ready to serve.

3. For the burgers, if you have a grinder attachment for your standing mixer, cut the salmon into long strips and chill the salmon and the grinder attachment and small-hole plate in

the freezer for 15 minutes. Grind the salmon into a chilled bowl. Or cut the salmon into small dice and chill in the freezer for 15 minutes along with the bowl and blade of the food processor. Pulse until coarsely ground. Do not overwork. Shape the ground salmon into 4 equal patties about 3½ inches in diameter. Place on a plate, cover, and refrigerate.

4. Preheat a gas grill to high. Scrub the grill grates with a grill brush. Season the patties on both sides with salt and pepper. Brush each side with ¼ teaspoon canola oil.

5. Oil the grill grates. Place the burgers on the grill over high heat and cook 1½ minutes to mark. Turn 90 degrees with a spatula to make a crosshatch pattern and cook 1½ minutes more. Flip the patties with the spatula and cook 1½ minutes more. Turn 90 degrees with the spatula and grill until the burgers are cooked to medium-rare, about 1½ minutes more.

6. Lightly rub the cut sides of the buns with the butter. Reduce the heat on one zone of the grill to medium-low. Toast the buns over medium-low heat until marked, 30 to 45 seconds. Turn 90 degrees with a spatula to make a crosshatch pattern and toast about 30 seconds more.

7. Serve the burgers in the buns with the aioli, onions, and arugula.

· CLAMS 101 ON THE GRILL ·

SERVES 2 AS AN APPETIZER

If you're going to be firing up the grill anyway, it's easy to pop open some clams on the grill before dinner. The clams will produce a decent amount of juice, which is tasty to drink or sop up with bread.

12 littleneck clams, scrubbed

4 tablespoons (½ stick) unsalted butter, melted

Crusty bread, for serving (optional)

1. Preheat a gas grill to high. Scrub the grill grates with a grill brush.

2. Place the clams on the grill and cook until they open. Begin checking after 2½ minutes; they should all open within 5 minutes. Remove with tongs to a bowl, careful to hold them level so you don't lose the juice.

3. Serve the clams with a small bowl of the melted butter. Spoon a little of the butter onto each clam before eating. Serve with bread for sopping up the juice and butter, if you like.

· GRILLED STURGEON WITH AGGHIOTTA ·

SERVES 4 AS AN ENTRÉE

This is a riff on *agghiotta*, a traditional Sicilian dish of swordfish braised in tomato with olives. I've adapted it to grilled sturgeon, adding a caponata-like sauce made with eggplant, vinegar, raisins, and tomato that goes perfectly with meaty, assertive fish like sturgeon or swordfish. This is a dish to make in the late summer when beefsteak tomatoes are in season. You can use any size baby eggplant—anything from 2 to 4 to 5 inches long. The roasting time will increase with the size of the eggplant.

FOR THE AGGHIOTTA

1¼ pounds baby eggplant, trimmed

¼ cup extra virgin olive oil

Fine sea salt

½ cup golden raisins

¼ cup white wine vinegar, plus more if needed

½ slender carrot, peeled and cut into ½- to 1-inch chunks

½ onion, cut into chunks

½ large stalk celery, cut into 1-inch dice

¼ small bulb fennel, cut into 1-inch dice

2 small cloves garlic, halved

1-inch piece finger chile, seeds removed slivered

Freshly ground black pepper

2 beefsteak tomatoes (about 1½ pounds), cored and cut into large dice

½ cup Fish Fumet (page 13) or store-bought low-sodium chicken stock

¾ cup quartered pitted green olives, preferably Picholine

1 tablespoon slivered fresh Italian parsley

1 tablespoon slivered fresh basil

FOR THE STURGEON

Four 6- to 7-ounce boneless, skinless sturgeon fillets (about 1 inch thick)

Fine sea salt and freshly ground black pepper

4 teaspoons extra virgin olive oil

1. For the agghiotta, preheat the oven to 350°F. Line a baking sheet with aluminum foil.

2. Pierce each eggplant 3 times with a paring knife so that the steam escapes and the eggplant cooks evenly. In a bowl, toss the eggplants with 1 tablespoon of the oil and ⅛ teaspoon salt. Place on the baking sheet and bake until the skin of the eggplants is lightly browned and wilted and the flesh is tender but not mushy when pierced with a paring knife, 20 to 25 minutes for small eggplant, 45 to 50 minutes for larger eggplant. Set aside to cool. Leave the oven on.

recipe continued on next page

3. Place the raisins in a small saucepan and add the vinegar. Bring to a boil. Remove from the heat and set aside to plump at least 10 minutes.

4. Combine the carrot, onion, celery, fennel, garlic, and chile in the bowl of a food processor and pulse to finely chop. Remove to a bowl.

5. Place the tomatoes in the bowl of the food processor and pulse to chop coarsely; set aside.

6. Place an ovenproof saucepan over medium heat. Add the remaining 3 tablespoons oil and heat until fluid enough to coat the bottom of the pan when swirled. Add the chopped vegetable mixture and cook without coloring, stirring often, until the raw taste of the vegetable cooks out, 10 to 15 minutes. Season with ¼ teaspoon salt and ⅛ teaspoon black pepper.

7. Add the chopped tomatoes and bring to a boil. Add the fumet or stock and simmer gently until the agghiotta reduces to the consistency of a loose sauce, 15 to 20 minutes.

8. Stir in the olives. Drain the raisins, saving the vinegar. Holding back 2 tablespoons of the vinegar, add the rest, plus the raisins, to the agghiotta and return to a boil.

9. Cut eggplant into 1-inch lengths. (Smaller eggplants—2 to 3 inches—may be braised whole.) Add to the agghiotta and stir gently to coat. Season with ¼ teaspoon salt. Taste for vinegar and add a little more if you think it's needed.

10. Partially cover with an ovenproof lid or a parchment round (see Kitchen Notebook, opposite) and braise in the oven until the sauce is reduced and thickened, 30 to 40 minutes. Taste for salt and pepper and adjust if necessary. Set aside while you cook the fish.

11. For the fish, preheat a gas grill to high. Scrub the grill grates with a grill brush. On a plate, season the fish on both sides with salt and pepper and let stand 5 minutes to allow the seasoning to penetrate.

12. Pat the fish dry with paper towels. Rub each fillet all over with 1 teaspoon oil. Oil the grill grates. Place the fish on the grill over high heat at an angle to the grates and cook 3 to 4 minutes to mark. Turn 90 degrees with a spatula to make a crosshatch pattern and cook 3 to 4 minutes more. Flip the fish with the spatula and cook 3 minutes more. Turn 90 degrees and cook until the fillets are cooked through, about 3 minutes more.

13. Place a fillet on each of four serving plates with the spatula. Stir the parsley and basil into the agghiotta and serve with the fish.

KITCHEN NOTEBOOK: MAKING A PARCHMENT PAPER CARTOUCHE

At the restaurant, we braise eggplant the traditional way, covered with a parchment round called a cartouche. The advantage to the cartouche is that it allows for evaporation during cooking so that the sauce reduces somewhat around the eggplant while preventing the eggplant from scorching. (A lid, partially covering the eggplant, will also do the job.)

Cut a piece of parchment as wide as the saucepan. Fold in half. Fold in half again to make a square. Now locate the inside point of the fold (this is the center of the sheet of paper) and place your finger there. Fold the square in half diagonally. Continue folding diagonally into increasingly slender wedges. Hold this multilayered wedge-shaped paper over the saucepan so that the point is right in the center of the pot. Mark with your finger where the paper hits the edge of the pot. Cut the paper there with scissors. Unfold your paper—it will be in the shape of a circle the size of your pan.

· GRILLED SWORDFISH ·
WITH BLACK OLIVE BAGNA CAUDA
AND GRILLED ESCAROLE

SERVES 4 AS AN ENTRÉE

I really dug the Italian crudité dip called *bagna cauda* (a serious step up from French onion dip) when I was introduced to it in Nice. It's a classic recipe from the Piedmont region, which is just across the border into Italy. Bagna cauda means "warm bath" because garlic and anchovies are simmered in warm butter and olive oil. These flavors taste great with a meaty fish like swordfish. Olives add another dimension. And for a cleaner taste, I've replaced the butter with extra virgin olive oil and added fresh herbs and tomato, elements of the Provençal *sauce vierge* I learned in Alain Ducasse's kitchen. So this is really a melding of Provence and Piedmont, with a nice piquant taste. Easy to make at home; just make sure to cut all of the ingredients equally small so that no single flavor dominates.

The swordfish can be replaced with cobia, mahi mahi, tuna, and most firm-fleshed Hawaiian fish such as opah and wahoo (ono).

FOR THE BLACK OLIVE BAGNA CAUDA

2 large cloves garlic, finely minced

¾ cup extra virgin olive oil

1 oil-packed anchovy fillet (preferably in extra virgin olive oil), drained and mashed to a purée

½ medium plum tomato, core and seeds removed, cut into ¼-inch dice

¼ finger chile, cut lengthwise, seeds removed, finely diced

2 tablespoons thinly sliced pitted black olives (preferably Alphonso)

1 tablespoon red wine vinegar (preferably cabernet sauvignon vinegar; see page 404)

¼ teaspoon fine sea salt

¼ cup slivered fresh basil, cross-cut into short pieces

¼ cup slivered fresh Italian parsley

FOR THE SWORDFISH

Grilled Escarole (page 366)

Four 6- to 8-ounce swordfish steaks (with or without skin; about 1 inch thick)

Fine sea salt and freshly ground black pepper

2 teaspoons extra virgin olive oil

1. For the bagna cauda, place the garlic and about half of the oil in a small saucepan. Place over medium-low heat and cook without coloring until the garlic sizzles lightly and the

recipe continued on next page

oil is hot, about 5 minutes. Add the anchovy and cook 30 seconds. Add the diced tomato and cook 1 minute. Add the diced chile and cook 1 minute more. Stir in the olives and the vinegar and remove from the heat. Season with the salt. Add the remaining oil and let cool to room temperature. When cool, stir in the slivered basil and parsley.

2. For the swordfish, preheat a gas grill to medium-high. Scrub the grill grates with a grill brush and oil the grates.

3. Grill the escarole according to the recipe and remove to a serving platter. Increase the grill heat to high. On a plate, season the swordfish on both sides with salt and pepper. Let stand 5 minutes to allow the seasonings to penetrate.

4. Pat the fish dry with paper towels. Coat each steak with ½ teaspoon oil. Scrub and lightly oil the grill grates again. Place the swordfish on the grill over high heat at an angle to the grates and grill 2 to 3 minutes to mark. Turn the steaks 90 degrees with a spatula and cook 2 minutes more to make a crosshatch pattern. Flip the steaks carefully with the spatula and cook 2 minutes more. Turn the steaks 90 degrees and cook to medium, 1 to 3 minutes more.

5. Place a steak on each of four serving plates with the spatula and serve with the bagna cauda and grilled escarole.

· GRILLED WHOLE DORADE ·

SERVES 2 AS AN ENTRÉE

Introduce a Greek flavor palette by stuffing the whole dorade with parsley, dill, and mint, or stick to a classic Italian combination with parsley, thyme, and oregano. If this is your first time grilling a whole fish, I recommend using a grill basket.

Two 1½-pound whole dorades, scaled, gutted, fins and gills removed

Fine sea salt and freshly ground black pepper

8 thin slices lemon

4 sprigs fresh Italian parsley

4 sprigs fresh dill

4 sprigs fresh mint

2 teaspoons extra virgin olive oil

Coarse salt, for serving

Lemon wedges, for serving

1. Preheat a gas grill to high. Scrub the grill grates well with a grill brush.

2. With a sharp knife, score the skin of each fish along one side of the backbone from behind the head to the tail. Turn the fish over and repeat the operation on the other side. Then cut 3 evenly spaced slashes on a 45-degree angle through the skin and almost to the bone, on both sides of the fish. Repeat with the second fish. On a baking sheet, season the fish with salt and pepper all over, including inside the cavity. Line each cavity with 4 lemon slices and 2 sprigs each of parsley, dill, and mint. Let stand 5 minutes to allow the seasonings to penetrate.

3. Pat the fish dry with paper towels. Rub each fish all over with 1 teaspoon olive oil.

4. Oil the grill grates. Place the fish on the grill over high heat at an angle to the grates. Reduce the heat to medium. Grill 4½ minutes to mark. One fish at a time, use tongs to lift the head of a fish and carefully slide a large metal spatula under the body. Turn the fish 90 degrees to make a crosshatch pattern. Grill 4½ minutes more.

5. Using tongs and spatula as above, carefully flip both fish and cook 4½ minutes. Turn each fish 90 degrees with the spatula and cook until the skin is crisp and the fish is cooked through, 4 to 4½ minutes more. The flesh along the back of the fish should begin to separate from the bone and a paring knife or cake tester stuck into the thickest part of the fish should encounter no resistance.

6. Use the spatula to remove the fish to a platter. Let stand 5 minutes before serving. Fillet the fish as shown on page 382. Serve with coarse salt and lemon wedges or flavored oil.

· GRILLED OCTOPUS ·
WITH A RAGOUT OF
BLACK-EYED PEAS AND TOMATO

SERVES 4 AS AN ENTRÉE

This is a version of one of the recipes I cooked for my audition as executive chef at Oceana. I topped a bean ragout with grilled shrimp and it got me the job. But when I put the dish on the menu, I decided that octopus, more interesting and unusual than shrimp, would better serve the style of the restaurant. (If you prefer, the method for grilling shrimp is on page 74.) The octopus braises for a long time until tender, then it's grilled to a smoky char. I use a fancy Spanish cabernet sauvignon vinegar (see Guide to Unusual Ingredients, page 404) to season the ragout—great, if you can get it. Otherwise, a good-quality red wine vinegar will do the trick. A salad of celery leaves and arugula is a good way to use the celery leaves we all have hanging around in the produce drawer of the fridge.

This recipe is not terribly hard but it is too time consuming to make in one day, unless that's all you're doing that day. The tomato confit and octopus can be made one or two days in advance, and the black-eyed peas can be cooked ahead and refrigerated in their cooking liquid. The day you're planning to serve, make the ragout and the salad, grill the octopus, and assemble.

FOR THE BLACK-EYED PEA AND TOMATO RAGOUT

1 cup dried black-eyed peas

Fine sea salt

2 tablespoons extra virgin olive oil from the
   tomato confit

2 cloves garlic from the tomato confit, sliced

1 shallot from the tomato confit, sliced

1 cup chopped peeled drained tomato confit
   pieces (5 to 6)

1 cup octopus cooking liquid

1 cup black-eyed pea cooking liquid

1 teaspoon good-quality red wine vinegar

1 tablespoon slivered fresh Italian parsley

1 tablespoon slivered fresh basil, preferably
   Thai basil

FOR THE TOMATO CONFIT

2 pounds plum tomatoes (about 9)

Fine sea salt

2 shallots, halved

2 cloves garlic, halved

1 sprig fresh basil (optional)

1 sprig fresh rosemary (optional)

1 sprig fresh Italian parsley (optional)

1 sprig fresh thyme (optional)

3 to 4 cups extra virgin olive oil

FOR THE OCTOPUS

½ cup extra virgin olive oil from the tomato confit

2 cloves garlic, thinly sliced

2 shallots, thinly sliced

1 tablespoon fennel seeds

1 teaspoon red pepper flakes

1 small sprig rosemary

4½ pounds octopus, eyes and beak cut out, rinsed well under cold running water

½ cup dry white wine

1 cup Fish Fumet (page 13), Low-Stress Chicken Stock (page 16), store-bought low-sodium chicken stock, or water

Extra virgin olive oil, for grilling and serving

FOR THE CELERY-ARUGULA SALAD

1 or 2 pieces tomato confit, peeled and chopped

Finely grated zest of 1 lemon

1 teaspoon red wine vinegar

1 tablespoon extra virgin olive oil from the tomato confit

Fine sea salt and freshly ground black pepper

2 cups gently packed arugula

¼ cup celery leaves (yellow inner leaves only)

¼ cup halved, slivered, pitted green olives, preferably Picholine

1. For the ragout, in a bowl, cover the black-eyed peas with cold water by about 3 inches. Cover and set aside to soak overnight.

2. For the tomato confit, preheat the oven to 275°F. Core the tomatoes and cut them in half lengthwise. Scoop out the seeds with a finger and discard. Sprinkle the cut sides of the tomato with salt. Arrange the tomatoes, cut side down, in a single layer in a baking dish. Add the shallots and garlic. Strew the basil, rosemary, parsley, and thyme sprigs over the top, if using, and pour in enough olive oil over to come about three-quarters of the way up the sides of the tomatoes. Cover with aluminum foil and bake until the tomatoes are soft to the touch but not falling apart, and the skins pull away, about 2½ hours. Let the tomatoes, garlic, and shallots cool in the oil. If you're making this ahead of time, transfer to a container, cover, and refrigerate (see Extra Credit, page 295).

3. For the octopus, preheat the oven to 350°F. Place a large ovenproof pot over medium heat. Add ½ cup oil from the confit and heat until fluid enough to coat the bottom of the pot when swirled. Add the sliced garlic and shallots and cook without coloring, stirring often, until translucent, about 2 minutes. Add the fennel seeds and pepper flakes and cook, stirring often, until the fennel seeds turn golden, about 1 minute. Add the rosemary and cook 15 seconds. Add the octopus and cook, stirring often, until the skin turns dark reddish-purple and the flesh firms up, about 5 minutes.

4. Add the wine and boil 1 minute to reduce it a bit. Add the fumet and bring to a boil. (The liquid should cover the octopus by about one-half; the octopus will exude lots of liquid during cooking.) Cover the pot with aluminum foil, place in the oven, and braise until the flesh is tender enough to release the tines of a kitchen fork easily, 1½ to 2 hours.

5. Remove from the oven and let octopus cool in braising liquid. Measure and set aside 1 cup of braising liquid for the ragout. Set octopus aside in remaining liquid.

6. While the octopus is cooling, drain and rinse black-eyed peas. Transfer to a medium saucepan and add fresh water to cover by about 3 inches. Bring to a boil, reduce the heat, and simmer until the peas are tender, about 25 minutes to 1 hour, depending on the age of the beans. Add 1 teaspoon salt and set aside to cool in the cooking liquid. (If not using immediately, refrigerate the peas in the cooking liquid.)

7. Drain the black-eyed peas, saving 1 cup of the cooking liquid. (The liquid will add flavor and body from the starch to the ragout.) Heat 2 tablespoons of the oil from the tomatoes in a medium saucepan over medium heat until fluid enough to coat the bottom of the pan. Add the sliced garlic and shallot from the confit, the chopped tomatoes, the peas, the reserved cooking liquids from the octopus and peas, and water as needed to cover the peas by 1 inch. Bring to a boil and simmer vigorously until the peas break down and the liquid thickens around them, about 10 minutes. Smash some of the peas on the side of the pan with a heatproof spatula and continue cooking until the peas are suspended in a thickened, creamy liquid, 1 to 2 minutes more. If the ragout sticks to the pan, add a little water. Remove from the heat. Stir in the vinegar and season to taste with salt.

8. Meanwhile, preheat a gas grill to high. Scrub the grill grates with a grill brush. Remove the octopus from the braising liquid; discard the liquid. Pat dry on paper towels. Cut the head from the legs. Cut the head into thin slices and stir into the ragout. Keep the ragout warm over low heat.

9. For the salad, combine the chopped tomato confit, lemon zest, vinegar, the olive oil, salt and pepper to taste in a medium bowl; set aside.

10. Cut the octopus legs into 4- to 5-inch sections. Place on a baking sheet and rub with 1 tablespoon olive oil.

11. Oil the grill grates. Place the octopus leg sections on the grill over high heat on an angle to the grates and grill 2 minutes to mark. Turn 90 degrees with a spatula and grill to make a crosshatch pattern, 1 to 2 minutes more. Flip the legs with the spatula and grill until the legs are warmed through, 2 to 4 minutes more depending on the thickness of the legs. Return to the baking sheet and drizzle lightly with olive oil.

12. To serve, stir the slivered parsley and basil into the ragout. Add the arugula, celery leaves, and olives to the salad dressing and toss to coat. Spoon the ragout into each of four deep plates or large, shallow bowls. Divide the octopus leg sections among the plates, arranging them on top of each serving of ragout. Top each with one-quarter of the salad.

EXTRA CREDIT: TOMATO CONFIT

Leftover tomato confit will last a couple of weeks in the refrigerator. Turn it into an easy sauce or vinaigrette by coarsely chopping the tomatoes with shallot and garlic. Whisk in some vinegar and olive oil (ratio of 1 part vinegar to 3 parts oil), salt, and pepper.

· LOBSTER BARBECUE ·

At Oceana, I serve this Indian-spiced barbecue sauce on a surf and turf dish with swordfish and short ribs. But the sauce is dynamite with grilled lobster, too. This is a delicious meal to serve to friends and family on the weekend when you have a little time to cook. Serve with a pot of grits, some wilted spinach, and a couple of watermelon mojitos. Try the leftover sauce with grilled swordfish or steak.

FOR THE BARBECUE SAUCE

½ teaspoon ground cinnamon

¼ teaspoon ground ginger

1 teaspoon Colman's mustard powder

1 teaspoon smoked paprika

1 teaspoon freshly ground black pepper

½ teaspoon ground cumin

½ dried New Mexico chile, with seeds

½ dried chipotle meco chile, with seeds

2 tablespoons canola oil

1 red onion, cut into ⅛-inch dice

3 cloves garlic, minced

One 28-ounce can whole peeled plum tomatoes (preferably organic), puréed with their juice

7 tablespoons firmly packed light brown sugar

3 tablespoons plus 1 teaspoon tamarind paste

3 tablespoons plus 1 teaspoon malt vinegar

2 cups Low-Stress Chicken Stock (page 16) or store-bought low-sodium chicken stock

1¾ teaspoon fine sea salt

FOR THE LOBSTER

Four 1¼-pound live lobsters

Fine sea salt

4 teaspoons extra virgin olive oil

1. For the sauce, combine the cinnamon, ginger, mustard, paprika, pepper, and cumin in a small bowl. Add 2 tablespoons water and stir to a paste; set aside.

2. In a dry skillet, toast the New Mexico and chipotle chiles over medium-high heat until fragrant, swirling the pan constantly so that they do not burn, about 3 minutes. Let cool, then finely grind in a spice grinder; set aside.

3. Place a medium saucepan over medium heat. Add the canola oil and heat until fluid enough to coat the bottom of the pan when swirled. Add the onion and cook without coloring, stirring often, until translucent, 4 to 5 minutes. Add the garlic and cook without coloring, stirring often, about 1 minute. Add the spice paste and cook, stirring often, until fragrant, about 1½ minutes. Add the puréed tomatoes, brown sugar, tamarind, vinegar, and the ground chiles. Bring to a boil, reduce the heat and simmer over medium heat until the sauce thickens, about 45 minutes.

4. Add the chicken stock and return to a boil. Remove from the heat and set aside.

5. Heat a gas grill to medium heat for the lobster halves; heat a smaller zone of the grill to medium-high for the claw sections.

6. Pull off the lobster claws and knuckles in one piece, split the lobsters in half lengthwise, crack the claws, and remove the vein and the grain sac from the head (see page 390).

7. Place the lobster halves and claws on a baking sheet. Season the tail meat lightly with salt, and drizzle each tail half with ½ teaspoon olive oil. Scrub the grill grates with a grill brush.

8. Lightly oil the grill grates. Place the lobster halves on the grill over medium heat; place the claws over medium-high heat. Grill for 8 minutes. Flip the claws. Brush each lobster tail half with 2 teaspoons of the barbecue sauce. Continue grilling 4 minutes more. Brush each tail half with 1 teaspoon of the barbecue sauce. Grill 5 minutes more, until a skewer inserted into the lobster meat comes out warm to the touch.

9. Remove lobster halves and claws to a serving platter. Serve the barbecue sauce on the side. Cover and refrigerate leftover sauce for up to 1 week. Delicious on steak, burgers, and grilled shrimp!

11.

FRIED FISH

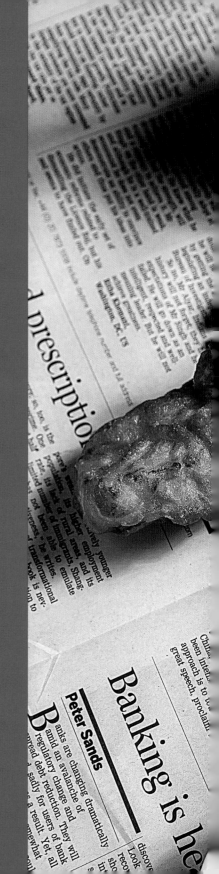

I thought about leaving this chapter out of the book. Who deep-fries fish at home? Well, I do. Not often—fried food is something we mostly eat out at a clam shack on vacation at the shore. But on Christmas Eve, I fire up my turkey fryer out in the backyard and cook a big batch of calamari for the Feast of Seven Fishes. It's a cool way to cook for a crowd—some years, I've fed 20 to 30 people when cooking this traditional Italian holiday meal for family and friends.

And from a taste perspective, deep-frying is also one of *the* great ways to enjoy seafood. Forget greasy and heavy. Deep-frying actually highlights the natural flavor of fish. Think about it: You're essentially steaming the fish inside its crisp crust, so the fish stays moist and its delicate taste comes through cleanly. As a bonus, you get to enjoy the contrast between the soft flesh and the crisp shell. If you maintain your oil at the right temperature—and deep-fry thermome-

ters have made this job much easier—the crust will be dry, light, and very probably a lot less greasy than the fare at your favorite clam shack.

This chapter covers two related frying techniques. The first is shallow-frying, also called pan-frying. Shallow-frying is an effective way to develop a golden crust on relatively thinner fish. This method uses a whole lot less oil than deep-frying—you only need enough to come about halfway up the sides of the fish—and cooks in a skillet. Start with Venetian-Style Bluefish 101 with Raisins, Green Olives, and Pine Nuts (page 307). The bluefish fillets are dredged in flour, then fried, to create a very light crust. Then try Pan-Fried Flounder 101 with Braised Greens and Warm Cherry Tomato Vinaigrette (page 309), and Pan-Fried Crab Cakes with Wasabi Aioli (page 321), both fried with a golden crust of panko breadcrumbs—Japanese breadcrumbs that fry up super crunchy, crunchier than standard breadcrumbs.

The second technique is deep-frying, which means frying in a big pot or electric deep-fryer (see Equip Yourself, page 304) in enough oil to cover. With the help of a deep-fry thermometer, you bring the oil up to the temperature noted in the recipe, immerse the food, and cook until golden brown outside, cooked through inside. The fish is usually coated in something before frying to give it crunch. Deep-frying is a good method for cooking fish fillets (page 319), scallops (page 316), clams (page 315), calamari (page 313), and even lobster, for General Tsao's Lobster (page 327).

The cooking temperature of the oil is determined by the size and density of the fish. Clams, for example, which are small and cook quickly, are fried at a higher temperature than fish fillets or even scallops, which, though small, have dense flesh.

The biggest concern I hear from home cooks about deep-frying is splattering oil; their next concern is what to do with the oil when they're finished. Splattering can be minimized by using a deep pot or an electric deep-fryer. If you fry a lot, I'd recommend that you save and reuse the oil as long as there are no off-flavors or odors. Strain it through a fine-mesh strainer or cheesecloth, leaving any sediment behind. Let it cool, then taste it—it should taste pleasant. If it does, pour it into a sealable plastic container (a gallon plastic milk container, for example) and store in the refrigerator. If you don't fry often, let the oil cool completely, pour it into a sealable plastic container and throw it out. Recycling centers in some areas also accept cooking oil. Do not dispose of it down the drain as it may clog the drain.

BEST FISH TO FRY

Lean white fish fillets such as flounder, cod, and hake are more suitable for deep-frying than meaty fish such as swordfish, shark, and tuna. Shellfish, of course, are a traditional deep-fry treat.

CRUSTS AND BATTERS FOR FRYING

Part of the fun of deep-frying is choosing among a variety of different breading and crust options. In this chapter, I show you how to work with five types of coatings: flour alone, a "chicken-fried" coating, cornmeal, dried breadcrumbs, and panko breadcrumbs. Then we'll do two batters: a beer batter for Fish and Oven-Fried Chips (page

319), and an egg white–cornstarch batter for General Tsao's Lobster (page 327).

Coating follows different procedures, depending on the elements. But the bottom line is that when you've got a liquid element—buttermilk or egg—along with your dry element(s), frying will go more smoothly if you set yourself up correctly.

Let's start with a flour-egg-breadcrumb coating. It has the most steps, but it will best demonstrate the concept. You'll find it used in the recipes for Pan-Fried Flounder 101 (page 309) and Fried Sea Scallops 101 (page 316). You'll do a version in Chapter 12, Seared and Sautéed Fish, too.

The first thing to do is get three shallow containers. Deep plates will work, as will baking dishes, pie pans, and shallow bowls. Line the three containers up on the counter, one next to the other. You'll also need a fourth container, preferably a large plate, baking dish, or baking sheet, for the finished coated product. Put the flour in the first container, the eggs in the middle, and the breadcrumbs in the third. Dredge the fish in the flour, turning it over and patting the flour all over the fish with one hand to coat evenly and completely. Use that same hand to pick up the fish, gently shake off the excess flour, and place it in the egg. Using your other hand (this is now your messy hand), dip the fish in the egg to coat completely. Drop the fish into the breadcrumbs. Now use your dry hand to scoop some of the breadcrumbs over the fish. Once the fish is covered, use that dry hand to turn it in the breadcrumbs and pat the breadcrumbs over. Still with your dry hand, move the fish to the container for the finished products, placing the pieces in a single layer, not touching. This way, you only get the fingers of one hand messy; the other hand stays dry and clean. After you've breaded the first piece of fish, use your dry hand for dredging subsequent pieces in the flour.

For a recipe in which the fish is simply dredged in flour (check out the Venetian-Style Bluefish 101 with Raisins, Green Olives, and Pine Nuts on page 307), you'll need just one container, only flour, and one dry hand. For a cornmeal coating (see Fried Sea Scallops on page 316), it's two containers: one for buttermilk, one for cornmeal; one messy hand for the buttermilk and one clean, dry hand for the cornmeal. For Chicken-Fried Blowfish with Cajun Aioli (page 323), it's two containers: flour and buttermilk; one dry hand, one messy.

For batter-frying, you just dip the fish in the batter, shake off the excess, and slide the fish into the hot oil. Easy!

After coating it, you want to get the fish in the oil as soon as possible so that the crust doesn't get soggy. That said, fish may be coated 10 or up to 15 minutes before frying, and sometimes even longer.

THIRTEEN EASY STEPS TO PERFECT DEEP-FRYING

1. An electric fryer makes things easy because you get maximum control over the temperature of the oil (see Equip Yourself, page 304). Otherwise, use a deep pot to prevent oil from splattering or bubbling over.

2. Line a baking dish or rimmed baking sheet with a double layer of paper towels to absorb the oil from the fried fish.

3. Fill the fryer or pot with about 3 inches of oil. I like canola oil but vegetable, safflower, and peanut oil are also appropriate for frying. You could use less oil, if need be—2 inches is enough—but the temperature will drop more radically when you add the fish. More oil will allow you to more easily maintain a constant temperature.

4. Heat the pot of the oil over medium-high heat, checking it every now and then with your deep-fry thermometer, until it reaches the temperature specified in the recipe. There will be hotter areas and cooler areas when you put the thermometer in the oil, stir it around so that you get a correct reading. It's okay if the oil registers 5° or 10°F more than you want—it will cool with the addition of the food. If you're using an electric fryer, set the temperature as needed. Check it with a thermometer the same way, even if the fryer has a temperature control.

5. If possible, cut the fish to uniform size so that all of the pieces cook in the same time.

6. Coat the fish.

7. Add the pieces one by one, or in the case of squid and clams, a few at a time. (This keeps the oil from bubbling up furiously and prevents the temperature from dropping too quickly.) Hold the fish close to the oil and gently drop it in; dropping it from a height will cause splattering.

8. Don't overcrowd the pot. Too much food will cool the oil. And you need enough space for the oil to circulate around the fish so that the pieces don't stick to one another. Cook in batches. You can keep the batches warm in a 200°F oven (preheat it while the oil comes up to temperature), or just plan on feeding people as the food comes out of the oil. (Deep-frying promotes a casual atmosphere anyway.) Remember that breaded fish will stay very hot for longer than you expect so it can sit for 5 minutes, no problem.

9. Once you've added the fish, begin taking the temperature of the oil again and adjust the heat as needed to keep the oil within range of the correct temperature. It's going to go up and down—that's normal. Just stay on top of it.

10. After about 30 seconds, move the food around gently with your spider or skimmer (see Equip Yourself, page 237) or slotted spoon to keep the pieces from sticking to one another.

11. When the fish is golden brown and has cooked for the amount of time noted in the recipe, bring your paper towel–lined baking dish over to where you're frying and remove the fish in batches to the baking dish with the spider, skimmer, or slotted spoon. Shake the dish a little to blot all surfaces, or blot the top of the fish with a second layer of paper towels. Serve the fish immediately or put it in the oven to keep hot.

12. Take the temperature of the oil again and heat it until it comes back up to temperature. Cook your next batch the same way.

13. When you cook coated fish, some of the coating will inevitably fall off in the pot, and if you're cooking several batches, it may eventually start to get too brown. This will give your oil a strong, unpleasant flavor. If you feel confident, you can *very carefully* pour the oil through a fine-mesh strainer into a clean pot to strain out the burned bits. Put the oil back over the heat or return it to the fryer and continue. An all-metal, fine-mesh skimmer, sold at Asian groceries, can be used to clean the oil in a turkey fryer: when you see brown bits in the oil, skim in a circular motion a couple of times to remove. To clean the skimmer, turn the skimmer over and tap on the lip of a baking dish to knock the crumbs off.

EQUIP YOURSELF: FRYING

• A moderate investment will buy you an electric deep-fryer that holds the oil at a constant temperature and may have a timer as well. Look for a fryer with a thermometer control. Less-expensive models may only heat to a single temperature; more expensive models have thermometer controls, so are worth it.

• Not interested? You need a big, deep pot, preferably with a heavy bottom.

- Wooden-handled wire-mesh spiders, so called because the wire "spoon" part looks like a spider web, are inexpensive; they're available at Asian markets.
- A skimmer (a large, flat round perforated metal "spoon" attached to a long handle) will also work, as will a large slotted spoon, though the latter won't hold much fish at one time.
- You'll need a long-stemmed deep-fry thermometer that clips to the edge of the pot.
- Shallow bowls, deep plates, or baking dishes for breading; baking dishes or baking sheets for draining the cooked food.
- Paper towels for absorbing oil.
- If you fry a lot for a crowd and can cook outside, you may want to think about buying a turkey fryer kit. It's just a burner with a hose that attaches to a propane tank, with a kettle on top of the burner. A long-stemmed thermometer clips to the side of the kettle. You fill the kettle with oil and the fryer does the rest; the thermometer makes it easy to gauge when the heat should be adjusted to maintain optimal temperature. Where you set up the fryer is important. You want a level area as far from the house as possible for safety—a patio, for example, or a level grass area out back. Not a wooden deck, which is flammable. Break open a couple of big cardboard boxes and lay them on the ground under the fryer to absorb oil. And make sure your spider or skimmer fits inside the mouth of the fryer. I found out too late that mine did not.

MAYONNAISE-BASED SAUCES FOR DEEP-FRYING

All deep-fried food can be served simply and sensationally with just lemon wedges. For something extra, try one or several of the following.
- Tartar Sauce (page 313)
- Spicy Aioli (page 346)
- Roasted Red Pepper Aioli (page 22)
- Horseradish Aioli (page 282)
- Cajun Aioli (page 323)
- Wasabi Aioli (page 321)
- Piquillo Pepper Aioli (page 244)

· VENETIAN-STYLE BLUEFISH 101 ·
WITH RAISINS, GREEN OLIVES,
AND PINE NUTS

SERVES 4 AS A LIGHT ENTRÉE

This is a very traditional preparation for mackerel called *filetto di sgombro en saor* that I've adapted for bluefish. Similar to the Spanish escabeche, the fish is coated in flour, shallow-fried in olive oil, then marinated in a sweet (raisins) and sour (vinegar) marinade. This type of preparation is found throughout Italy for both fish and vegetables; raisins, pine nuts, and onions make it recognizably Venetian. I had a lot of fun with this dish when I made it on *The Martha Stewart Show* where she was celebrating Doctor Seuss: "One fish, two fish, red fish, blue fish." Serve it to the Doctor Seuss aficionados in your life as a nice, light summer lunch. It's convenient because you make it the day before.

FOR THE BLUEFISH

Eight 3-ounce boneless, skinless bluefish fillets, bloodline removed (about ½ inch thick)

Fine sea salt and freshly ground black pepper

1 cup all-purpose flour

½ cup extra virgin olive oil

FOR THE MARINADE

2 cups extra virgin olive oil

1 red onion, quartered through the root end and thinly sliced crosswise

2 cloves garlic, thinly sliced

1 cup white wine vinegar

¼ cup golden raisins

¼ cup thinly sliced (crosswise) pitted green olives (preferably Picholine)

¼ cup raw pine nuts

Fine sea salt and freshly ground black pepper

¼ cup gently packed slivered fresh Italian parsley

¼ cup gently packed slivered fresh basil

FOR SERVING

6 cups gently packed mixed greens, or a 6-ounce bag

1. For the bluefish, line a baking dish with a double layer of paper towels. On a plate, season the bluefish on both sides with salt and pepper. Let stand a few minutes to allow the seasonings to penetrate. Pat dry with paper towels.

2. Place the flour in a shallow bowl, deep plate, or baking dish.

recipe continued on next page

3. Heat ½ cup olive oil in a large skillet over medium-high heat until a pinch of flour sizzles when dropped into the oil.

4. Working in batches, dredge the bluefish pieces in the flour to coat. Shake off the excess and slide into the oil, adding as many pieces as will fit comfortably in the pan without crowding. Cook until lightly golden, about 1 minute. Turn with a spatula and cook until lightly golden on the second side. Remove to the paper towel–lined baking dish to drain.

5. For the marinade, heat 2 cups olive oil in a large skillet over medium heat. Add the onion and garlic and cook without coloring, stirring often, for 1 minute. Add the vinegar, golden raisins, olives, and pine nuts. Bring to a simmer and remove from the heat. Season to taste with salt and pepper.

6. Arrange the fish in a single layer in a 9 by 13-inch baking dish. Pour the hot marinade over. Cover with plastic wrap and refrigerate overnight.

7. The next day, let the fish stand at room temperature for at least 1 hour. Sprinkle with the parsley and basil.

8. To serve, divide the greens among four deep serving plates or shallow serving bowls. Add two pieces of bluefish to each plate and spoon some of the marinade over the fish and greens.

· PAN-FRIED FLOUNDER 101 ·
WITH BRAISED GREENS
AND WARM CHERRY TOMATO VINAIGRETTE

SERVES 4 AS AN ENTRÉE

A crunchy, golden panko crust adds a dimension of contrasting texture and flavor to soft-fleshed flounder. The cherry tomato vinaigrette provides a bright accent and color that complements both fish and greens. I like a mix of tender young leaves for braising (you may find a packaged mix at your supermarket) but larger leaves are fine, too—they'll just take a little longer to cook. Flounder fillets may be long and narrow; if necessary, cut them in half crosswise to make it easier to fit them in the pan. The vinaigrette can be served warm or cold (I prefer it warm) and can be made ahead, refrigerated, and reheated over medium heat.

FOR THE BRAISED GREENS

1 pound mixed greens such as mustard greens, tatsoi, purple kale, baby or standard spinach, kale, Swiss chard, Tuscan kale, and escarole (4 quarts gently packed)

2 tablespoons extra virgin olive oil

2 cloves garlic, sliced

¼ teaspoon fine sea salt

¼ cup store-bought low-sodium chicken stock or water

FOR THE WARM CHERRY TOMATO VINAIGRETTE

¼ cup extra virgin olive oil

8 ounces cherry tomatoes, stems removed, halved (quartered if large)

¼ teaspoon fine sea salt

1 tablespoon fresh lemon juice

1 tablespoon gently packed slivered fresh basil

FOR THE FLOUNDER

1⅓ pounds boneless, skinless flounder fillets, halved crosswise if long and narrow

Fine sea salt and freshly ground black pepper

½ cup all-purpose flour

2 large eggs

2 cups panko breadcrumbs

1 cup canola oil

1. For the greens, if using larger greens, cut or strip out any tough stems and tear the leaves into 3- to 4-inch pieces. Place an 8-quart pot over medium heat. Add the olive oil

recipe continued on next page

and garlic and cook without coloring, stirring often, 1½ minutes. Add the greens, season with the salt, and raise the heat to high. Cook, stirring often, until the greens start to wilt, about 2 minutes. Add the stock or water, cover, and cook until the greens wilt completely, about 1 minute for small, tender greens, 7 to 10 minutes for larger leaves. Uncover and cook to evaporate most of the moisture, about 30 seconds more. Set aside, uncovered, at room temperature.

2. For the vinaigrette, warm the oil in a 10-inch skillet over medium heat. Add the tomatoes and cook, stirring occasionally, about 5 minutes. You want the tomatoes to warm up and begin to let go their juices but not really cook. Remove from the heat and stir in the salt, lemon, and basil. Set aside at room temperature.

3. For the flounder, line a baking dish with a double layer of paper towels. Place the flour in a shallow bowl, deep plate, or baking dish. In a second shallow bowl, whisk the eggs with a fork until blended (see Kitchen Notebook, opposite); set the bowl next to the flour. Place the breadcrumbs next to the egg in another shallow bowl, deep plate, or baking dish. Place a baking sheet or another baking dish at the end of the line.

4. Working in batches, dredge the flounder pieces in the flour to coat. With one hand, shake off the excess and place the fish in the egg. Use the other hand to dip the fish in the egg to coat, shake off the excess, and place the fish in the breadcrumbs. Use your dry hand to coat the fish in breadcrumbs and remove to the baking sheet or baking dish. Repeat, using your dry hand for the flour and breadcrumbs and your now-messy hand for the egg coating. Place the coated fillets in a single layer, not touching one another.

5. Heat the oil in a large skillet over medium-high heat (you should have about ¼ inch oil) until the oil sizzles when you dip a corner of the fish into the oil. Add as many flounder pieces as will fit comfortably in the pan without crowding and cook until golden brown, about 1 minute. Turn with a spatula and cook until golden brown on the second side. Remove to the paper towel–lined baking dish to drain.

6. Warm the braised greens and spoon them onto four serving plates. Divide the flounder among the plates, placing the fish on top of the greens. Divide the vinaigrette between the plates, spooning it over the fish.

KITCHEN NOTEBOOK: BEATING EGGS FOR COATINGS

For a smooth coating, beat the egg(s) with a fork until the white and yolk have blended to a smooth consistency. Test this by lifting the fork from the egg. Before beating, the egg will fall in blobs. When beaten correctly, it should fall in a smooth, thin ribbon.

· CRISPY CALAMARI 101 ·
WITH TARTAR SAUCE

SERVES 4 AS AN ENTRÉE, 6 TO 8 AS AN APPETIZER

The breading for this calamari dish, a mix of flour and finely ground graham cracker crumbs, is straight from the Union Square Cafe kitchen. You can't beat it. The graham cracker crumbs help brown the squid and add a subtly sweet crunch.

FOR THE TARTAR SAUCE

1 large egg yolk (see Kitchen Notebook, page 22)

Finely grated zest and juice of 1 lemon

1 tablespoon plus 1½ teaspoons Dijon mustard

2 tablespoons finely chopped cornichons or pickles, plus 1 tablespoon pickle liquid

1 cup grapeseed or canola oil

1 tablespoon chopped, drained capers (in brine)

1 tablespoon thinly sliced fresh chives

1 tablespoon chopped fresh dill

1 tablespoon slivered fresh Italian parsley

Pinch of piment d'Espelette (see page 402), Aleppo pepper, or cayenne pepper

FOR THE SQUID

3 quarts vegetable oil

¾ cup all-purpose flour

¼ cup finely ground graham cracker crumbs (about 4 square crackers)

1 pound cleaned squid with skin, bodies cut crosswise into ⅓-inch-wide rings, tentacles left whole

1 cup seltzer water

Fine sea salt

1 lemon, halved

1. For the tartar sauce, combine the egg yolk, lemon zest and juice, mustard, cornichons or pickles, and pickling liquid in a medium bowl. Add the oil in a thin stream, whisking constantly to emulsify. The sauce should not be too stiff; add a little water, as needed. Stir in the chopped capers, chives, dill, parsley, and piment d'Espelette, Aleppo, or cayenne pepper. Cover and refrigerate until you're ready to serve.

2. In a large, deep pot, heat the oil over high heat until it registers 375° to 385°F on a deep-fry thermometer. Line a baking sheet with a double layer of paper towels and place it near the stove.

recipe continued on next page

3. While the oil is heating, in a medium bowl, stir together the flour and graham cracker crumbs to blend. Put the squid in another medium bowl, pour the seltzer over and let stand 5 minutes. Drain in a fine-mesh strainer and shake to remove excess seltzer.

4. When the oil is hot, put about half of the squid in the flour-crumb mixture. Stir and toss with your hand to coat the squid.

5. Pick up about a quarter of the squid, shake off the excess coating, and gently add it to the hot oil a few pieces at a time. Continue this way to add the rest of the coated squid. The oil will bubble with steam and become cloudy. Wait for 30 to 40 seconds for that initial steam to disperse; the oil will become clear again. Then stir with a spider, skimmer, or slotted spoon and cook until the squid is crisp and lightly browned, 30 to 60 seconds more. The interior of the squid should be tender; if undercooked, it will be slightly gooey. Remove in batches to the paper towel–lined baking sheet with the spider, skimmer, or slotted spoon, gently shaking the squid over the oil to remove excess. Sprinkle the cooked squid with salt.

6. Repeat to coat and cook the second batch, waiting for the oil to come back up to temperature before adding more squid.

7. Squeeze lemon over all of the squid, arrange on a platter, and serve with the tartar sauce.

· FRIED CLAMS 101 ·

SERVES 4 AS AN ENTRÉE, 6 TO 8 AS AN APPETIZER

The clams served in clam shacks in the Northeast are traditionally whole-belly steamer clams. Littlenecks are a nice variation. They're a bit firmer than steamers, and they come out of the oil still moist with some chew and a crunchy cornmeal-textured exterior. Ask your fishmonger to shuck them for you and give you the clams with the juice. (Freeze the juice for soup.) Or open and shuck them yourself; see page 388.

3 quarts canola oil or as needed, for deep-frying

2 cups finely ground white or yellow cornmeal

40 shucked littleneck clams, drained

½ cup low-fat buttermilk

Fine sea salt

Lemon wedges, for serving

1. In a large pot, heat the canola oil over medium-high heat until it registers 375°F on a deep-fry thermometer. While the oil is heating, set a baking sheet on the counter for the breaded clams. Line a baking dish with a double layer of paper towels to drain the fried clams and place it near the stove.

2. Put the cornmeal in a shallow bowl, deep plate, or small baking dish. Place 10 of the drained clams in another bowl. Add the buttermilk and toss to coat. Working in batches, use one hand to remove a handful of the clams from the buttermilk, shaking off excess liquid. Place in the cornmeal. Toss with your other hand to coat. Remove to the baking sheet and spread the clams in a single layer. Repeat until all the clams are breaded, using your messy hand for the clams in buttermilk and your dry hand for the cornmeal coating.

3. When the oil reaches 375°F, pick the clams up by the small handful and carefully place in the oil, one by one, holding them close to the oil and dropping them gently. Add about half of the breaded clams to the oil. After about 30 seconds, move the clams around gently with a spider, skimmer, or slotted spoon to prevent them from sticking to one another. Continue frying, taking the temperature of the oil and adjusting the heat as needed, until the clams are golden brown, about 50 seconds total. Remove to the paper towel–lined baking dish with the spider, skimmer, or slotted spoon and toss gently.

4. Adjust the heat as necessary to return the oil to 375°F. Repeat to fry the rest of the clams. Serve hot with lemon wedges.

· FRIED SEA SCALLOPS 101 ·

SERVES 4 AS AN ENTRÉE

This crisp, light breadcrumb coating is perfect for scallops. The scallops should be cooked in two batches but they may be breaded all at once. Make sure to cook them medium-rare. Serve with lemon and Tartar Sauce or one of the other creamy mayonnaise-based sauces in the book.

3 quarts canola oil or as needed for frying

1½ pounds large (U15) sea scallops (about 20), tough white side muscles removed

Fine sea salt and freshly ground black pepper

⅓ cup all-purpose flour

2 large eggs

1 cup dried breadcrumbs

Tartar Sauce (page 313), or any of the mayonnaise-based sauces listed on page 305, for serving

Lemon wedges, for serving

1. In a large, deep pot, heat the canola oil over medium-high heat until it registers 330°F on a deep-fry thermometer. Line a baking dish with a double layer of paper towels and place it near the stove.

2. While the oil is heating, in another baking dish, season the scallops on both sides with salt and pepper.

3. Place the flour in a shallow bowl, deep plate, or baking dish on the counter. In a shallow bowl, whisk the eggs with a fork (see Kitchen Notebook: Beating Eggs for Coatings, page 311); set the eggs next to the flour. Place the breadcrumbs next to the egg in another shallow bowl, deep plate, or baking dish. Place a baking sheet next to the breadcrumbs to hold the breaded scallops.

4. Toss 2 of the scallops in the flour to coat. Shake off the excess with one hand and drop them in the egg. Toss with your other hand to coat the scallops with egg. Remove the scallops with your messy hand and place them in the breadcrumbs. Use your dry hand to coat them with the breadcrumbs and remove them to the baking sheet, placing the scallops in a single layer. Continue to coat all of the scallops.

5. When the oil reaches 330°F, carefully place half of the scallops in the oil one by one, holding the scallops close to the oil and dropping them gently. After about 30 seconds,

move the scallops around gently with a spider, skimmer, or slotted spoon to prevent them from sticking to one another. Continue frying, taking the temperature of the oil and adjusting the heat as needed, until the scallops are golden brown and a cake tester inserted into the scallops feels warm but not hot when placed below your lip, about 2 minutes total. Smaller scallops will cook faster. Start testing them after 1½ minutes. Remove to the paper towel–lined baking dish and toss gently.

6. Adjust the heat as needed to return the oil to 330°F. Fry the rest of the scallops.

7. Serve immediately with the tartar sauce and lemon wedges.

· FISH AND OVEN-FRIED CHIPS ·

SERVES 4 AS AN ENTRÉE

This is a classic. The batter is light and crisp, leavened with beer. In the restaurant, I serve this on plates lined with a folded page from the iconic British newspaper *Financial Times*—a nod to the traditional newspaper wrapping at chipperies. No reason not to do the same at your home, if you like, with the newspaper of your choice. The potatoes are baked, which is easier than making french fries at home. And they're actually closer in cut and texture to traditional British chips, which are moist—not crisp—wedges of potato. If you have one, a nonstick baking sheet is perfect for the fries.

To get fish and chips on the plate at the same time, start the fish when the potatoes are a few minutes away from being cooked. Turn off the oven, crack the door and put the first batch of fish in the oven to stay warm with the potatoes while you fry the second batch.

The batter may be made and refrigerated up to 1 day ahead.

FOR THE OVEN-FRIED CHIPS

Canola oil, for the baking sheet (optional)

3 large russet potatoes (about 3 pounds), scrubbed

2 tablespoons canola oil

Fine sea salt and freshly ground black pepper

FOR THE BATTER

1 cup all-purpose flour

1 cup rice flour

⅔ cup lager beer

2 teaspoons honey

FOR THE FISH

2 quarts canola oil or as needed, for frying

Four 7- to 8-ounce pieces boneless, skinless hake or cod fillets (½ to ¾ inch thick)

¼ cup rice flour, for dusting

Tartar Sauce (page 313), for serving

Malt vinegar, for serving

1. For the chips, preheat the oven to 400°F. If your baking sheet is not nonstick, oil it and set aside. Peel the potatoes and cut them in half lengthwise. Slice each half lengthwise into 4 or 5 wedges about ½ inch thick, depending on the size of the potato. Place in a bowl and toss with the canola oil, 1½ teaspoons salt, and pepper to taste. Spread over the baking sheet in a single layer. Bake, stirring them twice during baking for even cooking, until crisp and golden brown on the outside and tender when pierced with a paring knife,

recipe continued on next page

about 45 minutes. When the chips are cooked, turn off the oven, crack open the door, and leave the fries in the oven to stay warm.

2. For the batter, combine the all-purpose and rice flours in a medium bowl. Add ⅔ cup water, the beer, and honey and whisk until smooth. Set aside on the counter. (If you're making it ahead, cover and refrigerate. Let it come back to room temperature before using it; you may have to whisk it to recombine.)

3. For the fish, heat the canola oil in a deep 4-quart pot over medium-high heat until it registers 375°F on a deep-fry thermometer. Line a baking sheet with a double layer of paper towels; place it next to the stove to drain the fried fish.

4. While the oil is heating, cut the fish fillets in thirds so that you end up with 12 "fingers," each 3 to 4 inches long and about ¾ inch wide. On a plate, season the fish on both sides with salt and pepper. Let stand 5 minutes to allow the seasonings to penetrate.

5. Pat the fish dry with paper towels. Spread the rice flour on a plate and set it next to the batter. Dredge about half of the fish in the rice flour to coat. Shake off the excess with one hand. With your other hand, dip in the batter, shake off the excess, and slide the fish into the oil. Let cook about 30 seconds. Gently move the fish around with a spider, skimmer, or slotted spoon to keep the pieces from sticking together. Check the temperature of the oil; it will have dropped. Increase the heat to bring the temperature just to 350°F, then reduce the heat to maintain that temperature, adjusting the heat as needed throughout the frying process.

6. Cook the fish until golden brown, about 6½ minutes total. Remove the fish with a spider, skimmer, or slotted spoon to the paper towel–lined baking sheet. Place in the oven to keep warm while you fry the rest of the fish.

7. Place the fish on a serving platter and sprinkle with salt. Wait a couple of minutes before serving because the fish will continue steaming inside its crust for several minutes. Or tell your guests to crack open a piece and let the steam escape before devouring. Serve with the chips, tartar sauce, and malt vinegar.

· PAN-FRIED CRAB CAKES ·
WITH WASABI AIOLI

SERVES 4 AS AN ENTRÉE

At a restaurant with a name like Oceana, how do you not have a crab cake on the menu? Still, I wanted something a little different, and lighter than the classic mix of crab, mayonnaise, and breading. I borrowed the idea of a light fish mousse from Floyd Cardoz at Tabla. Sofrito gives the cakes a depth of flavor that doesn't hit you over the head; it just makes the cakes taste great. Panko breadcrumbs add a satisfying crunch. At the restaurant, we shape the cakes into cylinders and deep-fry them. At home, it's easier to make traditional cakes and shallow-fry. Serve with a green salad and wasabi aioli.

FOR THE CRAB CAKES

2 tablespoons extra virgin olive oil

½ medium onion, chopped (about ½ cup)

5 cloves garlic, minced (about 2½ tablespoons)

1 medium plum tomato, core and seeds removed, cut into ¼-inch dice (about ½ cup)

1 pound lump crabmeat, picked through, bits of shell and cartilage removed

Fine sea salt and freshly ground black pepper

1¼ cups panko breadcrumbs

4 ounces boneless, skinless lean white fish such as halibut, cod, flounder, striped bass, snapper, or black bass

1 large egg yolk

Finely grated zest of 1 lemon

1 tablespoon fresh lemon juice

1 tablespoon slivered fresh Italian parsley

2 tablespoons minced fresh chives

6 tablespoons canola oil

FOR THE WASABI AIOLI

1 cup Homemade Mayonnaise (page 21) or good-quality store-bought mayonnaise

1 tablespoon fresh lime juice

1 teaspoon finely grated lime zest

¼ teaspoon fine sea salt

1 tablespoon wasabi paste

1. For the crab cakes, place a small saucepan over medium heat. Add the olive oil and heat until fluid when the pan is swirled. Add the onion and garlic cook without coloring, stirring often, until the onion is translucent, about 5 minutes. Add the diced tomato and cook until it breaks down to a paste, about 15 minutes. Spread the sofrito over a baking sheet or baking dish and cool to room temperature.

recipe continued on next page

2. In a bowl, season the crabmeat with ¾ teaspoon salt and ⅛ teaspoon pepper. Let stand a few minutes for the seasonings to penetrate. Line a baking dish with aluminum foil, dust with breadcrumbs, and set aside.

3. Combine the fish and the egg yolk in a food processor and pulse until blended. Scrape into a medium bowl. Add the cooled sofrito, the lemon zest and juice, parsley, and chives. Stir until well mixed. Fold in the crabmeat.

4. Spread the panko on a plate. Form the crab mixture into 4 equal cakes about 4 inches in diameter and 1 inch thick. Gently turn the cakes in the panko to coat, patting the panko onto the cakes to adhere, and place in the foil-lined baking dish. Cover and refrigerate for 1 hour to allow the cakes to firm up.

5. Preheat the oven to 400°F. Place a 12-inch ovenproof skillet over medium heat. Add the canola oil and heat until the oil sizzles when a corner of a cake is dipped into the oil. Carefully add the crab cakes to the pan in a single layer. Cook until nicely browned, about 4 minutes. Turn the cakes with a spatula and cook 1½ minutes more. Place the skillet in the oven and bake until the cakes are warmed through when tested with a cake tester, 4 to 5 minutes.

6. For the wasabi aioli, in a medium bowl, whisk the mayonnaise with the lime juice and zest, salt, and wasabi to blend.

7. Serve the crab cakes with the aioli.

· CHICKEN-FRIED BLOWFISH ·
WITH CAJUN AIOLI

SERVES 2 AS AN ENTRÉE

At the height of a fried chicken craze a couple of years back in fine-dining restaurants in Manhattan, I had some fun with the trend by creating a seafood recipe made exactly the same way I make fried chicken. Blowfish—which coincidentally are called chicken of the sea—have a meaty flesh that is perfect for this purpose. The double-dip coating yields the characteristic flakey, textured crust. Ask your fishmonger to bone the blowfish tails for you, leaving the tail fin. Once fried, they look like giant butterflied shrimp.

FOR THE CAJUN AIOLI

1 teaspoon Blackening Spice (page 23)

1 cup Homemade Mayonnaise (page 21), or good-quality store-bought mayonnaise

FOR THE BLOWFISH

½ cup low-fat buttermilk

Needles from 1 small (4- to 5-inch) sprig fresh rosemary

1 clove garlic, crushed with the side of a chef's knife and peeled

Freshly ground black pepper

4 boneless blowfish tails, with tail fins (10 to 11 ounces total)

1 cup all-purpose flour

1 teaspoon Blackening Spice (page 23)

3 quarts canola oil or as needed, for frying

Lemon wedges, for serving

1. For the aioli, stir the blackening spice into the mayonnaise. Cover and refrigerate until you're ready to serve.

2. Pour the buttermilk into a medium bowl. Add the rosemary needles, garlic, and black pepper to taste. Stir to blend. Add the blowfish tails. Cover and refrigerate 1 hour.

3. With a fork, stir together the flour and blackening spice in a deep plate, shallow bowl, or small baking dish. Transfer about half of the mixture to another bowl and set aside; you'll use it later. Place a large plate, platter, or baking sheet next to the seasoned flour to hold the coated blowfish.

4. Use one hand to remove the blowfish, one at a time, from the marinade. Carefully pick off the rosemary needles with the fingers of your other hand but do not wipe off the

recipe continued on next page

buttermilk. Place in the seasoned flour. Use your drier hand to dredge the fish in the flour and shake off the excess. Place the blowfish on the plate in a single layer. Set aside the remaining seasoned flour in its container. Let the coated blowfish stand until the buttermilk is almost entirely absorbed by the flour and the coating is tacky, about 25 minutes.

5. Meanwhile, in a large, deep pot, heat the canola oil over medium-high heat until it registers 330°F on a deep-fry thermometer. Line a baking dish with a double layer of paper towels and place it near the stove.

6. Add the unused seasoned flour to the used flour. Dredge the blowfish, one at a time, in the flour as above and return them to the plate.

7. When the oil has reached 330°F, carefully place the blowfish in the oil, one by one, holding them close to the oil and dropping them gently. After about 30 seconds, move the fish around gently with a spider, skimmer, or slotted spoon to prevent them from sticking to one another. Continue frying, taking the temperature of the oil and adjusting the heat as needed, until the blowfish are golden brown and cooked through, about 4 minutes. Remove to the paper towel–lined baking dish with the spider, skimmer, or slotted spoon and toss gently.

8. Sprinkle with salt and serve with the aioli and lemon wedges.

· GENERAL TSAO'S LOBSTER ·

SERVES 4 AS AN ENTRÉE

Given that I like spicy food in general, and that my go-to favorite for Chinese takeout is General Tsao's chicken, this recipe was inevitable. This is a really great dish to share with a group of people. If you want to do it up a little at home, get several take-out containers from your local Chinese restaurant and dish it up in those with black sticky rice. My publisher, Louise Burke, loves this dish—so much, that she made sure I put it in the book.

This recipe has a lot of steps, so I recommend doing some of them ahead. You can make the sauce several days ahead and refrigerate it. The batter can be made a day ahead, and the lobsters can also be cooked, shelled, and cut up the day before.

If you have time, use the lobster heads for an easy lobster broth (see Extra Credit, page 329) to use in place of water in the General Tsao sauce. Note that sticky rice is made without seasoning or lemon juice; the lobster sauce is highly seasoned enough.

FOR THE LOBSTER
Four 1¼-pound live lobsters

FOR THE SAUCE

1 tablespoon canola oil

3 cloves garlic, sliced

2 tablespoons minced peeled fresh ginger

⅓ cup sugar

¼ cup plus 2 tablespoons soy sauce

4½ teaspoons sweet chili sauce (preferably Mae Ploy brand)

1 teaspoon toasted sesame oil

2 tablespoons rice vinegar

1 tablespoon cornstarch

FOR THE BATTER

4 large egg whites

2 teaspoons fish sauce

2 teaspoons soy sauce

1 cup cornstarch

2 quarts canola oil for deep-frying, plus 1 tablespoon for cooking the scallions

¼ cup raw unsalted cashews

6 scallions (white and green parts), sliced on the bias into pieces about 2 inches long

4 teaspoons slivered fresh cilantro

Black Sticky Rice (page 373), freshly cooked (omit salt, pepper, and lemon juice)

recipe continued on next page

1. For the lobster, prepare an ice bath by filling your sink with ice and cold water. Bring 6 to 8 quarts water to a boil in a large pot. Add the lobsters to the boiling water (no need to remove the rubber bands). Boil 5 minutes. With tongs, remove the lobsters from the pot and place them in the ice bath to stop the cooking and cool them.

2. When the lobsters are cool, shell them, including claws and knuckles (see page 392). Cut the tail meat in half lengthwise, devein it, then cut it crosswise into thirds. If large, cut the claws in half crosswise. Cover and refrigerate the lobster meat until ready to cook.

3. For the sauce, heat a 10-inch skillet over medium heat. Add the oil, the garlic and the ginger and cook without coloring, stirring often, 3 minutes. Add 1¼ cups water, the sugar, soy sauce, sweet chili sauce, sesame oil, and rice vinegar. Bring to a boil and boil 2 minutes. In a small bowl, stir ¼ cup cold water with the cornstarch until blended to make a slurry. Whisk the slurry into the sauce and boil for 1 minute to thicken it. Remove from the heat and set aside. Transfer to a container, cover, and refrigerate if not using soon.

4. For the batter, whisk the egg whites with the fish sauce, soy sauce, and cornstarch in a medium bowl. Cover and refrigerate if not using soon.

5. When you're ready to finish the dish, stir the lobster pieces into the batter to marinate for 15 minutes. (If the batter has been refrigerated, it will be very stiff and dry. Just stir; it will loosen up.)

6. Meanwhile, heat the 2 quarts canola oil in a deep 6- to 8-quart pot until it registers 325°F on a deep-fry thermometer. Preheat the oven to 200°F. Line a baking sheet with paper towels.

7. With a skimmer or slotted spoon, gently lower the cashews into the oil and cook until golden, about 1¼ minutes. Remove to the baking sheet with the skimmer or slotted spoon; set aside.

8. Increase the heat under the pot and heat the oil until it registers 375°F on a deep-fry thermometer.

9. With your fingers, remove the lobster from the batter one piece at a time, shaking off the excess, and gently lower the piece of lobster into the oil. Add as many pieces as will fit comfortably without touching; don't crowd the pan or you'll lower the temperature of the oil too much. Fry until the batter is golden brown and crisp, about 1½ minutes for each batch.

Remove the cooked lobster with the skimmer or slotted spoon to the paper towel–lined baking sheet to drain. Place in the oven to keep warm while you cook the remaining batches.

10. Place a large pot over medium heat. Add the 1 remaining tablespoon canola oil and the scallions and cook without coloring, stirring, often, until softened 1 to 2 minutes. Add the sauce and cook to warm it through. Add the cashews, cilantro, and lobster. Gently toss the lobster with the sauce to coat.

11. To serve, spoon some black sticky rice into the center of each of four serving plates. Spoon the lobster and sauce over.

EXTRA CREDIT

· LOBSTER BROTH ·

MAKES 3 CUPS

Making a broth is a good way to extract the essence from lobster heads and legs that would otherwise be discarded. Use the broth in sauces like General Tsao's or to add extra flavor to soups and pasta. Freeze any extra until you need it.

4 lobster heads with legs   3 tablespoons canola oil

1. Remove but don't discard the carapace (the shell that covers the head) from each head. Remove and discard the small translucent stomach sac. Remove and set aside the light green tomalley and the roe, if there is any. Cut the carapaces into quarters with kitchen scissors. Cut the heads in half lengthwise with a knife, then in half again crosswise.

2. Place a medium pot over medium-high heat. Add the canola oil and heat until it shimmers. Add the carapaces, heads, and legs and cook until the legs and carapaces turn bright red and smell like lobster, 2½ to 3 minutes. Stir often with a wooden spoon, scraping the bottom. Take care not to let the bottom of the pot burn.

3. Add the reserved tomalley and roe and cook, stirring constantly, 30 seconds.

4. Add 6 cups water. Bring to a boil, reduce the heat, and simmer 30 minutes.

5. Strain the broth through a fine-mesh strainer into a large bowl. Use immediately or transfer to a container, seal, and freeze.

12.

SEARED AND
SAUTÉED FISH

T I've saved sautéing to the end of the book because it's an elegant, professional technique and it seems like the right way to finish up. And after seven other chapters of cooking methods, you're ready! Sautéing can be as simple as seasoning fillets, blotting them dry with paper towels, and cooking them on both sides in a pan with a little hot oil. A bit of butter can be added for flavor and color, too. The name of the game is to create a caramelized, crusty exterior that delivers a concentrated layer of flavor and textural contrast. Take a few minutes more to make a pan sauce with mustard (page 337), Marsala wine (page 348), or lemon juice and parsley (page 342), and you've got a quick but very classy and exceptionally delicious dish.

There's a perception out there that sautéing is challenging for the home cook and that's not untrue. Cooking goes quickly and you're manipulating delicate fish in a hot pan. It's important to get the temperature of your oil and pan right so that the fish neither sticks nor overbrowns. But I give you tips below for handling these issues so that you can have some fun and sauté like a pro.

Are there fish that lend themselves better than others to sautéing? Definitely. If you love crisp skin, sautéing is a great way to cook skin-on fillets like striped bass, trout, and snapper. In a hot pan, you can drive the moisture out of the skin very effectively to give the skin that dry, crisp texture we love.

Sautéing is traditionally an excellent way to cook thin fillets like trout, fluke, and flounder, because they'll cook all the way through on top of the stove. Recipes in this chapter will show you how to cook thicker fillets so that the interior of the fish is cooked through by the time the exterior is nicely caramelized. Sautéing is also a fantastic way to cook shrimp.

Sautéing is theoretically less advisable for dense, meaty fish like mahi mahi, cobia, and wahoo. These fish are typically grilled, broiled, or roasted because they're too thick to cook all the way through on top of the stove before the exterior overcooks. But here's where restaurant technique has something to offer home cooks. In the restaurant, we do something called "searing," which means browning the fish on top of the stove in a very small amount of fat. Then the fish goes into a hot oven in the pan to finish cooking. This is a no-brainer in a restaurant, of course, because we've got the ovens going all night. But even if it sounds like a pain, it's worth turning your oven on at home, too. For two reasons: First, baking is easier than sautéing. So once you've developed that caramelized exterior, you get the fish in the oven and you're home free. Second, the less time the hot fat spends on top of your stove, the less splattering you'll have

to clean up. I cook Blackened Swordfish (page 339), whole Dover sole (page 348), striped bass (page 353), and thick fillets of cod and halibut this way.

Once you get the technique down, you may want to try something I do at home when I'm prepared to cheat a little and want to limit the splattering of hot fat. I heat the pan and oil on top of the stove as if I were sautéing. I open the oven door. With one hand, I hold the pan over the oven door. With the other hand, I swoop the seasoned fish into the pan and quickly slide the pan into the oven. I let the fish cook until browned on one side, then remove the pan to the stovetop and flip the fish with a spatula. The pan goes back into the oven to finish cooking to the desired doneness.

FLOUR AND OTHER COATINGS FOR SAUTÉED FISH

Fillets may be dredged in flour before sautéing to prevent them from sticking to the pan. Fish with high moisture content, such as sole, flounder, halibut, cod, snapper, and sea bass, are often treated this way. Flour encourages browning and helps create a crust quickly; this is particularly helpful when you're working with thin fillets that may otherwise cook through before they brown. Some chefs

use Wondra, a precooked flour. You may want to give it a try—it results in a very smooth, even coating.

To dredge fillets in flour, scatter the flour on a plate or baking dish. Place the fish on the plate. Pick the fish up by one corner between your thumb and forefinger and flip it in the flour. Flip the fish a couple of times, patting the flour evenly over the fish, until it's completely and evenly coated. Holding the fish by the corner, gently shake off the excess, then gently place the fillets in the pan.

Cornmeal makes a dynamite crust, too, with more texture than flour, and with good flavor (try Cornmeal-Crusted Redfish 101 wtih Spicy Aioli, page 346). The fish is brushed with egg first to help the cornmeal stick. Sliced almonds are another option (as in Almond-Crusted Red Snapper 101, page 344) for a nutty, delicately crunchy layer.

TIPS FOR KEEPING FISH FROM STICKING

• Pat the fish dry very well with paper towels before sautéing.

• Coat the fish in flour, cornmeal, or almonds to create a crust.

• Choose a skillet large enough that the fish will fit in comfortably in a single layer.

• Make sure there's enough oil. Sautéing differs from shallow-frying in that it's done in only enough oil to lightly coat the bottom of the pan. (For shallow-frying, there should be enough oil to come about halfway up the sides of the fish.) But if there's too little oil, your fish may stick. Follow the recipes in this chapter until you get a sense of what enough oil looks like and then you can wing it.

• Don't crowd the pan; make sure there's enough space—½ inch is good—between the fillets so that moisture doesn't get trapped and steam the fish.

• If the heat is too low, the fish will stick. You want to heat the pan first for a few minutes over medium-high to high heat (there are some exceptions—I cook tuna over medium, for example). Then add the oil and heat until it shimmers; gently shake the pan and note the "waves" of oil that form. When those waves smooth out, if the oil is hot enough, you'll see lines shimmering in the oil.

• Another trick for knowing if your pan is hot enough is to gently dip one corner of the fish into the hot pan; the oil should sizzle.

• Recipes for large, thin fillets are written for two servings so that all the fish fits comfortably in one large pan. If you want to cook for four, double the ingredients and use two pans. Or cook in batches, holding the first batch in a 200°F oven to keep warm. For the pan sauce, double the ingredients but make it in only one of the pans.

• Start the fish over high heat so that it starts browning quickly.

• Continue cooking the fillets for 1 to 2 minutes over high heat, until the crust starts to form. Then turn the heat down to medium or medium-high. Cook until the fillet is well browned and the flesh turns opaque around the edges.

• You can add a little butter at this point for flavor and browning; swirl to melt.

• Turn the fillets with a spatula and cook until the second side is well browned and the fillets are cooked through (see Kitchen Notebook, page 251).

• Drain on a paper towel–lined plate or baking dish.

TIPS FOR SAUTÉING THICK FILLETS

• Thick fillets are sautéed over lower heat so that the exterior doesn't overcook before the interior cooks through. Start the fillets on medium-high heat. Sauté the fish on both sides for 2 to 3 minutes to brown, adjusting the heat as needed to keep the fish browning nicely.

• Salmon is best medium-rare, so unless you have a monster-thick fillet, you will be able to get it to medium-rare on the stovetop. For really thick fillets, it's easiest to finish them in a 400°F oven once browned on both sides.

• For fillets 1 inch thick and thicker, you can brown edges and ends, too: stand the fillets on edge, leaning them against one another as needed for stability, and cook until browned. Then flip and cook the other edges. Test for doneness (see page 8).

• Drain on a paper towel–lined plate or baking dish.

• Most of the cooking will be done on the skin side. Start the fillets skin side down on medium-high heat. Press down gently with a metal spatula to prevent curling and maintain contact between skin and pan. Cook about 2 minutes, then turn the heat down to medium. The longer you can keep the skin over the heat, the drier and crisper it will get. So adjust the heat to keep browning without burning. And give it a little patience. It might seem as if the skin is sticking, but if you give it some time, it will eventually release. (If you're wondering whether to cook your fish skin-on, check the Fish-ionary to find out whether the skin is edible. If it is, it will crisp up nicely when sautéed.)

• Once the skin side is good and brown, turn the fillets and cook until the second side is browned. Thin fillets will be pretty much cooked through at this point; the flesh side need just be "kissed" by the heat.

• Finish thicker fillets in a 400°F oven. (See Is It Done Yet?, page 8.)

• Drain on a paper towel–lined plate or baking dish.

EQUIP YOURSELF: SAUTÉING

• The best pan to use for sautéing is one that's large enough to hold the fish in a single layer with about ½ inch between the pieces. A heavy-bottomed pan will help prevent burning the fish. I'm assuming you're using stainless steel, or an anodized aluminum pan. A nonstick pan is another option.

• Cast-iron skillets are also an option. They're an even distributor of heat, very inexpensive, and they will take your fish from stovetop to oven. Cast iron requires seasoning and maintenance, but if that's your thing, it may be a good choice for you. A well-seasoned cast-iron pan is essentially nonstick.

• You'll also need a metal spatula for flipping the fish, or plastic if you're using nonstick.

· SAUTÉED TROUT FILLETS 101 ·
WITH MUSTARD-RIESLING SAUCE

SERVES 2 AS AN ENTRÉE

Trout is sautéed almost entirely skin side down and flipped at the end of cooking just to "kiss" the flesh side. Rich enough to enjoy the acidity of mustard, trout pairs well with a sauce that offsets the spicy mustard with a riesling wine. Choose a riesling that is on the sweeter side; I use a Mosel Riesling Kabinett. The sauce works equally well with Dover sole, salmon, arctic char, and other rich fish. Serve with braised red or green cabbage (try the recipe on page 185 but leave out the spices).

3 boneless, skin-on trout fillets (15 to 16 ounces total)

Fine sea salt and freshly ground black pepper

3 tablespoons canola oil

1 teaspoon plus 1 tablespoon extra virgin olive oil

1 tablespoon chopped shallot

½ cup riesling or other fruity white wine

1 teaspoon Dijon mustard

1 tablespoon whole-grain Dijon mustard

¼ cup Low-Stress Chicken Stock (page 16) or store-bought low-sodium chicken stock

1. Trim the tail ends of the fillets to a V shape, starting the cut about 3 inches above the tip of the tail on each side. (The meat at the end of the tail is so thin that it will overcook. Most of what you'll be trimming is skin. This also makes for an attractive presentation.)

2. Line a baking sheet with a double layer of paper towels. On another baking sheet, season the fillets on one side with salt and pepper and let stand a few minutes to allow the seasonings to penetrate. Pat dry very well with paper towels.

3. Place a 12-inch skillet over high heat. Add the canola oil and heat until it shimmers. Gently lay 1 fillet, skin side down, in the pan, placing the edge closest to you down first so as not to splatter yourself with hot oil. Turn the heat down to medium. Press down firmly along the length of the fillet with a spatula for about 15 seconds, to prevent the fillet from curling. You don't want to mash the fish; just apply gentle, even pressure. (Pull the pan off the heat if your hand gets too hot.) Gently place the other 2 fillets, one at a time, the same way, pressing down on the second to prevent curling before adding the third. (If necessary, the third fillet can be cut in half to fit the pan.) Cook the fillets until you see that the belly (thin) side of the fillets is cooked through and has turned opaque.

recipe continued on next page

(This will happen sequentially because the fillets were started sequentially.) Flip the fillets skin side up and cook to just "kiss" the other side, about 30 seconds. Remove each fillet to the paper towel–lined baking sheet as it's cooked. After all the fish is cooked, pour off any fat remaining in the pan (into the trash, not the sink).

4. Off the heat, add 1 teaspoon of the olive oil to the pan. Add the shallot and cook until fragrant, about 30 seconds. (There should be enough residual heat in the pan to cook; if not, return to medium heat.)

5. Add the wine and return to medium heat. Add the Dijon mustard and swirl the pan to combine. Add the whole-grain mustard and stir to blend. Bring to a simmer and cook to reduce the sauce by about one-half, about 1 minute.

6. Add the chicken stock, swirl to combine, and simmer to thicken and reduce by about one-half, about 30 seconds. Drizzle in the remaining 1 tablespoon olive oil, swirling the pan to emulsify as if you were making a hot vinaigrette. Remove from the heat.

7. Cut one fillet in half if you haven't already. Spoon sauce on each of two serving plates and arrange 1½ fillets on top of the sauce on each.

· BLACKENED SWORDFISH 101 ·

SERVES 4 AS AN ENTRÉE

This is my version of the dish made famous by Paul Prudhomme. The fish is dredged in a mixture of spices, sautéed briefly to make sure the spices cook, then baked in the oven to cook through. (Very thin swordfish steaks can be cooked entirely on top of the stove.) We want to blacken—not burn—the spices, so the fish is sautéed on medium-high heat, not cranked up to high. Serve with something mild like braised greens (page 309) because the flavor of the blackening spice will overpower everything—in a good way!

Four 7- to 8-ounce swordfish steaks (with or
without skin)

Fine sea salt

¼ cup Blackening Spice (page 23)

4 tablespoons canola oil

1. Preheat the oven to 400°F. Cover a baking sheet with aluminum foil.

2. On a plate or a sheet of aluminum foil, season the swordfish on both sides with salt. Let stand 5 minutes to allow the salt to penetrate.

3. Spread the blackening spice on an unlined baking sheet. Dredge both sides of the swordfish in the mix.

4. Place a 12-inch skillet over medium-high heat. Add 2 tablespoons of the oil and heat until it shimmers. Gently shake the excess spice mix off two of the fillets, and gently lay them in the pan, placing the edge closer to you down first so as not to splatter yourself with hot oil. Sear about 10 seconds; flip with a spatula and sear 10 seconds on the second side. Remove with a spatula to the foil-lined baking sheet. Wipe out the pan with paper towels to prevent any spices remaining in the pan from burning. Repeat with the remaining 2 tablespoons canola oil to sear the remaining two steaks on both sides; place the steaks on the foil-lined baking sheet.

5. Put the baking sheet in the oven and bake until the steaks begin to firm up, 3 to 3½ minutes. Flip with the spatula and bake until the steaks are cooked through to medium, 3 to 3½ minutes more. Place each steak on a serving plate.

· SHRIMP SCAMPI 101 ·
WITH PRESERVED LEMON

SERVES 2 AS AN ENTRÉE

People ask me what "shrimp scampi" means and I have to chuckle because *scampi* is simply the Italian word for Dublin Bay prawns or langoustines—a variety of shellfish that's closer to the lobster family than the shrimp. So what you're really saying is "shrimp prawn," or "shrimp langoustine." In any event, the name refers to a very simple Italian-style shrimp sauté with a garlic, white wine, and butter pan sauce. My version is jazzed up with chopped preserved lemon, which gives this classic a unique accent with almost no extra work.

Some of the best shrimp in the United States come through New Orleans, see Fishionary, page 423. Serve with crusty, warm bread to soak up the garlicky goodness.

Rind from 1 quarter Preserved Lemons (page 25), soaked in cold water to cover at least 20 minutes or overnight

24 medium shrimp (about 12 ounces), shelled, tails left on, deveined (see page 385)

Fine sea salt and freshly ground black pepper

3 tablespoons extra virgin olive oil

3 cloves garlic, minced

¼ cup dry white wine

3 tablespoons unsalted butter, softened

Leaves from 1 sprig fresh oregano, coarsely chopped (about 1 teaspoon)

Warm baguette, for serving

1. Drain the preserved lemon. Cut out the pulp with a small knife. Cut it in half lengthwise, then thinly slice crosswise.

2. Butterfly the shrimp, cutting deeply along the length of the back, almost in half, until the shrimp can be opened up like a book but the halves are still connected. On a baking sheet or platter, season the shrimp on both sides with salt and pepper. Let stand a few minutes to allow the seasonings to penetrate. Blot the shrimp well with paper towels.

3. Place a 10- to 12-inch skillet over high heat. Add 1 tablespoon of the oil and heat until it shimmers. Gently lay half the shrimp in the pan (they don't need to lie flat) and cook, without stirring, for 30 seconds. Give the pan a little shake to move the shrimp around, then cook 30 seconds more. Toss again. The shrimp will have curled up. Spread them out in a single layer with a spatula or tongs. Continue cooking until the shrimp are mostly opaque with a little translucence in the center, 1½ minutes total.

4. Remove the pan from the heat. Remove the shrimp to a plate. Add another 1 tablespoon oil to the pan and sauté the rest of the shrimp the same way. Remove to the plate.

5. Off the heat, add the remaining 1 tablespoon oil and the garlic. (As long as the garlic is sizzling, there's enough residual heat in the pan to cook; if not, replace over the heat.) Cook the garlic until aromatic, about 40 seconds.

6. Add the preserved lemon and the wine. Return the pan to high heat and cook until the pan is almost dry, about 1 minute. Add the butter and stir over the heat to emulsify.

7. Return the shrimp to the pan with any juices that have accumulated on the plate and cook over high heat to rewarm, about 1 minute. Add the oregano and stir. Divide among four serving plates and serve with warm bread.

· FILLET OF FLOUNDER 101 MEUNIÈRE ·

SERVES 2 AS AN ENTRÉE

This is your basic technique for sautéing any thin flatfish fillet such as flounder, fluke, gray sole, lemon sole, and petrale sole. I flour the fillets and add a little butter about halfway through cooking for better browning and flavor. The classic recipe (called *meunière*, meaning "miller's wife" because the fish is coated in flour) is sauced with nut-brown butter, lemon juice, and parsley, but you can change the flavor profile with lime, orange, or even yuzu juice. As far as accompaniments for a meunière preparation, you want to keep it simple so as not to distract from the delicate flavor of the lemon and brown butter. Serve with Thyme and Honey–Glazed Carrots (page 374), or plain steamed asparagus or broccoli.

14- to 16-ounces boneless, skinless fluke fillets

Fine sea salt and freshly ground black pepper

¼ cup all-purpose flour

3 tablespoons canola oil

2 teaspoons plus 3 tablespoons unsalted butter

¼ cup gently packed slivered fresh Italian parsley

2¼ teaspoons fresh lemon juice

1. Pat the fillets dry with paper towels. On a baking sheet, sprinkle one side of each fillet with salt and pepper. Let stand a few minutes to allow the seasonings to penetrate. Line a baking sheet with paper towels to drain the fish.

2. Spread the flour over a plate. Dredge the fillets in the flour, flipping them a few times and patting the flour over the fillets to create an even, thin layer.

3. Place a 12-inch skillet over high heat. Add the oil and heat until it shimmers and almost smokes. Gently shake off the excess flour and gently lay the floured fillets side by side in the pan, placing the edge closest to you down first so as not to splatter yourself with hot oil, and allowing a little space between them. (Larger fillets will fit best in the center of the pan; smaller fillets on the sides.) Cook for about 1 minute to allow the crust to form, then turn the heat down to medium-high. Cook until the fillets are golden brown and are opaque around the edges, about 1 minute more. Add the 2 teaspoons butter to the pan, swirl gently to melt, and cook 1 minute more.

4. Turn the heat down to medium. Flip the fillets gently with a spatula and cook until the fillets are cooked through, 2 to 3 minutes more. Remove the fillets to the paper towel–lined baking sheet.

5. Drain the fat from the pan and wipe out the pan if there are any burned bits on the bottom. Otherwise, add the remaining 3 tablespoons butter to the pan and heat over medium heat, swirling, 15 to 30 seconds. The butter will be foamy and as the foam subsides, the butter will begin to turn a golden brown color. Remove from the heat. Add the parsley, lemon juice, and ⅛ teaspoon salt and swirl to combine.

6. Divide the fillets between two serving plates, overlapping the fillets on each plate. Spoon the sauce over.

KITCHEN NOTEBOOK: CUT TO FIT

Your fillets are probably going to be different sizes and shapes. Cut them as needed so that you have two relatively equal portions.

· ALMOND-CRUSTED RED SNAPPER 101 ·

SERVES 4 AS AN ENTRÉE

Here's a simple way to give snapper fillets an elegant crust that will make you look like a pro. This recipe uses more oil than a normal sauté because the fat must reach the level of the almonds in order to cook them evenly. Butter also helps the almonds brown. These nutty, buttery fillets taste great with Grilled Escarole (page 366) or Sugar Snap Peas with Preserved Ginger, Chile, and Mint (page 375). Black sea bass is a good substitute for snapper.

You won't use all the almonds, but discard the leftovers; they will have been tainted by egg and fish.

Four 7-ounce red snapper fillets (with or without skin; about ½ inch thick)

Fine sea salt and freshly ground black pepper

2 large eggs

2 tablespoons all-purpose flour

1½ cups blanched, sliced almonds

6 tablespoons canola oil

2 tablespoons unsalted butter

Lemon wedges, for serving

1. Preheat the oven to 400°F. Line a baking sheet with paper towels to drain the fish.

2. On a plate or a sheet of aluminum foil, season the fillets on both sides with salt and pepper. Let stand 5 minutes to allow the seasonings to penetrate.

3. In a shallow bowl, beat the eggs and flour with a fork until blended and the mixture forms a smooth ribbon when the fork is lifted from the bowl (see Kitchen Notebook: Beating Eggs for Coatings, page 311); set aside. Spread the almonds on a baking sheet and place next to the egg wash.

4. Place two 12-inch ovenproof skillets over medium-low heat. Add 3 tablespoons oil and 1 tablespoon butter to each pan and heat, swirling to melt the butter.

5. While the fats are heating, pat the fish dry with paper towels. Coat the fillets: Holding a fillet between the thumb and pointer finger of one hand, brush the flesh side with the egg wash (if your fillets are skinless, either side is fine—brush only one side). Place on the almonds on the baking sheet, egg-washed side down. Repeat with the remaining fillets, placing them next to one other without touching. Press the fish lightly to get the almonds to adhere.

6. When the butter has melted, gently lay two fillets in each pan, almond crust down, placing the edge closest to you down first so as not to splatter yourself with hot oil. Cook until the almonds are golden brown, 3 to 4 minutes, shaking the pan gently a couple of times to keep the fillets moving. Place in the oven and bake 7 minutes.

7. Carefully remove both pans from the oven, flip the fish with a spatula, and return to the oven for 1 minute more, until the snapper is cooked through.

8. Remove the fillets to the paper towel–lined baking sheet to drain briefly.

9. Place each fillet on a serving plate and serve with lemon wedges.

· CORNMEAL-CRUSTED REDFISH 101 ·
WITH SPICY AIOLI

SERVES 4 AS AN ENTRÉE

Redfish is one of those fish that goes by a variety of names. In the Gulf, I've heard it called redfish; off the Carolina coast, channel bass. Its official name is red drum. Whatever you call it, it's delicious coated with a crunchy cornmeal crust and dipped in a sweet and spicy aioli. You may need two skillets for this, depending on the size of the fillets. Or cook them in two batches, adding more oil to the pan for the second. Striped bass or snapper make good substitutes. The correct regional accompaniment to this dish is Fried Green Tomatoes (page 377). If you're like me, you'll add some hot sauce.

FOR THE SPICY AIOLI

⅔ cup Homemade Mayonnaise (page 21) or good-quality store-bought mayonnaise

⅓ cup sweet chili sauce (preferably Mae Ploy brand)

FOR THE REDFISH

Four 6- to 8-ounce boneless, skinless redfish fillets (about ¾ inch thick)

Fine sea salt

2 large eggs

2 tablespoons all-purpose flour

½ cup finely ground yellow or white cornmeal

2 teaspoons Blackening Spice (page 23)

3 tablespoons canola oil

Lemon wedges, for serving

Fried Green Tomatoes (optional)

1. For the aioli, stir together the mayonnaise and chili sauce in a small bowl. Cover and refrigerate until you're ready to serve.

2. For the fish, on a plate or a sheet of aluminum foil, season the fish on both sides lightly with salt only. Let stand a few minutes to allow the salt to penetrate. Pat dry on paper towels.

3. In a shallow bowl, beat the eggs and flour with a fork until blended and the egg wash forms a smooth ribbon when the fork is lifted from the bowl (see Kitchen Notebook, page 311). Set a baking dish next to the egg wash. In the baking dish, combine the cornmeal and blackening spice and mix with a fork. Line a baking sheet with paper towels to drain the fish.

4. Place a large skillet over medium-high heat. Add the oil and heat until it shimmers.

While the oil is heating, coat the fillets: Holding a fillet between the thumb and pointer finger of one hand, brush both sides with the egg wash. Place the fillet on the cornmeal. Repeat with the remaining fillets, placing them next to one another without touching. Swirl the baking dish gently so the cornmeal dusts up over the fillets. Flip the fillets to dredge the other side in the cornmeal.

5. Gently lay the fillets in the pan, placing the edge closest to you down first so as not to splatter yourself with hot oil. Cook 1 minute to set the crust. Turn the heat down to medium and cook until golden brown, about 3 minutes more. Flip the fillets with a spatula and cook until the other side is golden brown and the fish is cooked through, about 3 minutes more. Remove to the paper towel–lined baking sheet to drain briefly.

6. Serve with the spicy aioli, lemon wedges, and fried green tomatoes, if you like.

· DOVER SOLE ON THE BONE ·
WITH MARSALA SAUCE

SERVES 2 AS AN ENTRÉE

Dover sole is a splurge. But occasionally, a splurge is so worth it. The flesh is firm, moist, meaty, and delicate. It's delicious sautéed and served with a pan sauce, either this one or the classic sauce meunière (as prepared in Fillet of Flounder 101 Meunière, page 342). Don't want to spend so much? You'll like this recipe with any whole scaled flatfish (it's very difficult to skin flatfish other than Dover sole; remove the skin after cooking). If you're not inclined to fillet the fish in the kitchen before serving, don't worry: a fair number of guests at the restaurant ask that Dover be served on the bone so you're in good company. Serve with boiled green beans or Garlicky Spinach (page 189) and some crusty bread to sop up the sauce.

Two 14- to 16-ounce Dover sole, skinned, head and tail removed, fins trimmed (cleaned weight 8 to 9 ounces each)

Fine sea salt and freshly ground black pepper

¼ cup all-purpose flour

3 tablespoons plus 1 teaspoon canola oil

3 to 4 ounces cremini mushrooms, wiped clean, stems trimmed, sliced ¼ inch thick (about 1 cup)

1 tablespoon chopped shallot

½ cup dry Marsala wine

½ cup Low-Stress Chicken Stock (page 16), or store-bought low-sodium chicken stock

1 tablespoon unsalted butter

1. Preheat the oven to 400°F. Line a baking sheet with paper towels for draining the cooked fish.

2. Pat the sole dry very well with paper towels. On a baking sheet, sprinkle on both sides with salt and pepper. Let stand 5 minutes to allow the seasonings to penetrate. Pat the fish dry again with fresh paper towels.

3. Spread the flour over a plate. Dredge one of the sole in the flour, flipping it a few times and patting the flour over the fish to create an even, thin layer.

4. Place a 12-inch ovenproof skillet over high heat. Add the 3 tablespoons oil and heat until it shimmers.

5. Gently shake off the excess flour and gently lay the floured fish across one half of the pan,

recipe continued on next page

placing the edge closest to you down first so as not to splatter yourself with hot oil. Dredge the second fish, shake off the excess flour, and gently lay it in the pan next to the first fish, allowing room between the two. Let cook about 1 minute. Shake the pan gently—enough of a crust should have formed that the fish will glide in the pan. Turn the heat down to medium-high and cook until golden brown, 3 to 4 minutes. Turn the heat down a bit more if the fish are browning too quickly.

6. Carefully flip the fish with a spatula. Turn the heat to high and cook 1 minute to begin to form a crust on the other side. Place the pan in the oven and bake until the fillets separate easily at the center line when you insert the edge of your spatula along the line and lift gently, about 10 minutes. Remove the fish with the spatula to the paper towel–lined baking sheet to drain. Turn off the oven and crack the oven door. Return the fish to the oven to stay warm while you make the sauce.

7. Wipe out the skillet with paper towels if there are any burned bits on the bottom. Otherwise, place the pan over high heat. (Careful—the handle is very hot.) Add the remaining 1 teaspoon canola oil. Add the mushrooms and sprinkle with ¼ teaspoon salt and a pinch of pepper. (Salting immediately will draw moisture from the mushrooms, helping them to cook more quickly; moisture will also pick up any caramelized pan juices.) Cook, removing the pan from the heat every now and then to toss, until the mushrooms start to brown, 2 to 3 minutes.

8. Add the shallot and cook 30 seconds. Off the heat, add the Marsala. Return to the heat, bring to a boil, and boil until the sauce is reduced by about one half, 1 to 2 minutes. Remove the pan from the heat, add the butter, and swirl to emulsify the butter into the sauce.

9. Place the fish on two serving plates and spoon the sauce over.

KITCHEN NOTEBOOK: SAUTÉING WHOLE FLATFISH

It is possible to cook a whole fish on the bone entirely on top of the stove, but I finish this in the oven because the bone will slow the cooking and I want to make sure that it's thoroughly cooked. On top of the stove, you run the risk of the fish browning too much before it cooks through. With a fish as pricey as Dover sole, don't take the chance.

· SAUTÉED PIKE ·
WITH ROASTED CAULIFLOWER, CAPERS, OLIVES, AND CURRANTS

SERVES 4 AS AN ENTRÉE

Pike is a fish that benefits from a little color, so it's perfect for sautéing. Cut the cauliflower florets very small so that they meld with the pine nuts, olives, capers, and currants for a mixture that's more of a sauce or relish than a side dish. (Try broccoli cooked this way, too.) Roast the cauliflower first and let it marinate with the other ingredients while you cook the pike. I like Banyuls vinegar for its oxidized flavor but sherry vinegar, or even red wine vinegar, will work just fine. If you can't find pike, substitute striped bass.

FOR THE ROASTED CAULIFLOWER

1 head cauliflower (about 2 pounds), trimmed of leaves

5 tablespoons extra virgin olive oil

Fine sea salt and freshly ground black pepper

2 tablespoons large capers (preferably salted, not brined), soaked at least 2 hours or overnight, drained, and coarsely chopped

2 tablespoons raw pine nuts, chopped

2 tablespoons sliced pitted green olives (preferably Picholine)

2 tablespoons currants, soaked 15 minutes in hot water and drained

¾ teaspoon dried oregano

1 tablespoon Banyuls vinegar, sherry vinegar, or red wine vinegar

FOR THE PIKE

Four 6- to 8-ounce boneless, skinless pike fillets (½ to ¾ inch thick)

Fine sea salt and freshly ground black pepper

4 teaspoons extra virgin olive oil

1 tablespoon unsalted butter

1. Preheat the oven to 450°F.

2. For the roasted cauliflower, cut the cauliflower into very small florets (½ to 1 inch); cut the stems and core into cubes of a similar size. Place in a large bowl. Add 2 tablespoons of the olive oil, ¾ teaspoon salt, and ¼ teaspoon pepper and toss to coat. Spread over a baking sheet and roast, stirring 2 or 3 times for even cooking, until tender with golden-brown edges, 25 to 30 minutes.

3. While the cauliflower is roasting, combine the remaining 3 tablespoons olive oil, the

recipe continued on next page

capers, pine nuts, olives, currants, oregano, and vinegar in the same bowl. When the cauliflower is cooked, scrape it into the bowl. Season with ¼ teaspoon salt and a little more pepper and toss to coat; set aside to marinate while you cook the fish.

4. For the pike, on a plate or a sheet of aluminum foil, sprinkle the fish on both sides with salt and pepper. Let stand 5 minutes to allow the seasonings to penetrate.

5. Pat the fish dry with paper towels. Line a baking sheet or baking dish with paper towels to drain the fish.

6. Place a large skillet over high heat. Add the oil and heat until it shimmers. Gently lay the pike fillets in the pan in a single layer, placing the edge closest to you down first so as not to splatter yourself with hot oil. Cook, without moving them, for 30 seconds. Reduce the heat to medium and continue cooking until the fillets are nicely browned and cooked about halfway, about 2½ minutes total. Off the heat, add the butter to the pan and swirl the pan to melt the butter. Flip the fillets with a spatula. Return the pan to the heat and cook until the pike is cooked through, about 4½ minutes total. If you see the butter begin to brown before the pike is almost cooked through, reduce the heat to low.

7. Remove the fillets with a spatula to the paper towel–lined baking sheet to drain briefly.

8. Place each fillet on one of four serving plates. Spoon the cauliflower alongside.

· CRISP-SKINNED STRIPED BASS ·
WITH TOMATO-BASIL RISOTTO

SERVES 4 AS AN ENTRÉE

This recipe demonstrates the method for sautéing a thick fillet by searing and finishing in the oven. I serve it with a risotto made with full-flavored summer tomatoes from my garden. Just core and purée—no need to skin, seed, or strain. Canned tomatoes work fine off-season. I like vegetable purées for risotto. They add flavor, of course, but the hidden benefit is that the vegetable fiber creates a creamy texture without finishing with lots of butter. That means a lighter dish with intense tomato and basil flavors.

The timing is a little tricky, but doable! To get fish and risotto on the table at the same time, start cooking the fish when you begin adding stock to the risotto. Though the risotto should be stirred as constantly as possible, it's fine to let the stirring go periodically as necessary to handle the fish.

FOR THE STRIPED BASS

Four 6- to 8-ounce striped bass fillets (about 1 inch thick)

Fine sea salt and freshly ground black pepper

3 tablespoons canola oil

FOR THE TOMATO-BASIL RISOTTO

2 teaspoons extra virgin olive oil, plus extra for drizzling

2 teaspoons unsalted butter

1 tablespoon chopped shallot

2 large cloves garlic, minced

1½ cups Carnaroli rice

Fine sea salt and freshly ground black pepper

½ cup dry white wine

1 pound fresh tomatoes, cored, coarsely chopped, and puréed, or one 14.5-ounce can whole peeled tomatoes (preferably organic), puréed with their juice

4 cups Low-Stress Chicken Stock (page 16) or store-bought low-sodium chicken stock, heated and held at a bare simmer

¼ cup grated Parmesan cheese

½ cup gently packed torn fresh basil leaves

1. For the fish, preheat the oven to 400°F. On a plate or a sheet of aluminum foil, season on both sides with salt and pepper. Let stand 5 minutes to allow the seasonings to penetrate while you start the risotto.

2. For the risotto, heat a 10- to 11-inch-diameter pot or skillet over medium-low heat. Add the oil and butter and heat until the butter melts. Add the shallot and garlic and cook with-

recipe continued on next page

out coloring, stirring often with a heatproof spatula, until aromatic, 30 to 60 seconds. Add the rice and cook without coloring, stirring often, until it smells lightly toasted, 2 minutes. Season with 1 teaspoon salt, and pepper to taste.

3. Remove the pot from the heat and add the wine. Return to the heat and simmer, stirring constantly, about 1 minute or until the wine reduces enough that when you draw a line through the center of the rice with your spatula, the remaining liquid returns only very slowly to refill the space. This is key: This is your indication throughout the cooking process that's it's time to add more liquid.

4. Add about one half of the tomato purée and simmer, stirring constantly, until reduced as in step 3. Add the remaining tomato purée and simmer, stirring constantly, until reduced as in step 3.

5. While the purée reduces, pat the fish very dry with paper towels, making sure to blot the skin particularly well.

6. When the tomato purée has reduced, add ½ cup of the simmering chicken stock. Cook, stirring and scraping down the sides of the pot often with the spatula, until reduced as in step 3. Add another ½ cup chicken stock and repeat. Continue adding the stock in ½-cup increments, stirring constantly and adding stock only when the liquid is reduced as in step 3. You'll use about 3½ cups stock total. Taste a few grains of rice; it is done when it has lost the chalky center but still has tooth. This should take 16 to 18 minutes once you start adding the stock.

7. Meanwhile, once you have added that first ½ cup stock to the risotto, take a quick break from stirring and get started cooking the fish. Place a 12-inch ovenproof skillet over medium-high heat. Add the canola oil and heat until it shimmers. Gently lay the fish in the pan skin side down, placing the edge closest to you down first so as not to splatter yourself with hot oil, and pressing down gently with a spatula to prevent curling. Cook until the skin has crisped up, 4 to 5 minutes. Turn the fish skin side up and reduce the heat to medium. Continue cooking to brown the flesh side, 4 to 5 minutes more. Place the skillet in the oven and bake the fish until well done, about 5 minutes more.

8. When the risotto is cooked, take it off the heat, and stir in the Parmesan cheese and the basil.

recipe continued on next page

9. Divide the risotto among four deep plates or shallow bowls. If it has dried out a bit while waiting for the fish to cook, stir in a little hot stock before serving. Set the fish on top and drizzle the rice with a little olive oil.

KITCHEN NOTEBOOK: RISOTTO

I start my risotto with a small amount of butter and olive oil. The combination gives the rice better flavor than either fat alone.

· WILD ALASKAN SALMON · WITH CHANTERELLES, CORN, AND CHERRIES

SERVES 4 AS AN ENTRÉE

Here's a method for sautéing salmon fillets to medium-rare entirely on top of the stove. The recipe takes advantage of some of my favorite summer ingredients, pairing wild king salmon and a quick, easy relish of cooked chanterelle mushrooms and corn, tossed with fresh cherries. The salmon fillets can be skinless or skin-on; it's a matter of taste. And if you can't get wild salmon, the recipe will work exactly the same with farm-raised salmon.

Four 6- to 8-ounce boneless wild king salmon fillets (with or without skin), pin bones removed

Fine sea salt and freshly ground black pepper

2 ears corn, husked

4 teaspoons extra virgin olive oil

5 to 6 ounces fresh chanterelle mushrooms, wiped clean, stems trimmed, cut into 1- to 1½-inch pieces (about 2 cups; see Kitchen Notebook, page 358)

⅔ cup halved pitted fresh sweet, red Bing cherries

1 teaspoon slivered fresh Italian parsley

1 tablespoon canola oil

1. On a plate or a sheet of aluminum foil, season the fillets on both sides with salt and pepper. Let stand 5 minutes to allow the seasonings to penetrate. Line a baking sheet with paper towels, to drain the cooked fish.

2. Meanwhile, set an ear of corn on end on the cutting board and cut off the kernels with a chef's knife. Repeat with the second ear of corn; set the kernels aside and discard the cobs.

3. Place a 12-inch skillet over medium heat. Add the olive oil and heat until it shimmers. Add the mushrooms, 1 teaspoon salt, and a pinch of pepper. Cook about 2 minutes without stirring. Add the corn and turn the heat to high. Add ⅛ teaspoon salt and cook, stirring often, until the corn begins to brown and the color deepens, and it no longer tastes raw, about 2 minutes. Remove the pan from the heat. Add the cherries and parsley and stir to combine. Scrape into a bowl and set aside. Wipe out the pan with paper towels.

4. Place the pan back on the stove over medium-high heat. Add the canola oil and heat until it shimmers. Pat the fillets dry with paper towels. Place the fillets in the oil and cook

recipe continued on next page

until nicely browned on one side, about 2 minutes. Flip and cook until well browned on the other side, about 2 minutes. Turn the fillets on their edges, leaning against each other to stay upright if necessary, and cook 1 to 2 minutes to brown the edge. Flip onto the other edge and brown 1 to 2 minutes. Test for doneness (see page 8); the salmon should be medium-rare. Remove to the paper towel–lined baking sheet to drain briefly.

5. Return the pan to medium heat. Add the corn mixture and heat to warm through.

6. Divide the corn mixture among four serving plates and place a salmon fillet on top of each.

KITCHEN NOTEBOOK: MUSHROOMS

Hedgehog mushrooms have a similar texture to chanterelles and make a good substitute.

· SEARED TUNA ·
WITH RED WINE SAUCE
AND SUNCHOKES

SERVES 4 AS AN ENTRÉE

A friend of mine assures me that this sauce would even taste good with rocks. I don't know about that, but it tastes great with tuna and roasted sunchokes. Sunchokes, also called Jerusalem artichokes, are deplorably underappreciated. Knobby like fresh ginger, with a light pinkish skin, they're crisp and sweet if you eat them raw, and they take on a nutty taste when cooked. If you like, you can make the sauce the way we do at the restaurant with a brown fish stock (see Extra Credit, page 361), which gives it another rich dimension of flavor. Either way, it can be made ahead and held at room temperature, covered, for an hour or two. Choose a red wine that doesn't have a prominently oaky flavor and rewarm the sauce over low heat but do not boil or it will separate. This sauce is also delicious with salmon and other full-flavored fish.

FOR THE RED WINE SAUCE

2 heads garlic, broken into cloves (skin-on)

1 tablespoon extra virgin olive oil

Fine sea salt

One 750-milliliter bottle dry red wine

1½ teaspoons sugar

1 pound unsalted butter, cut into ½-inch chunks and softened to room temperature

FOR THE SUNCHOKES

Nonstick cooking spray

2 pounds sunchokes, washed well but not peeled

¼ cup extra virgin olive oil

2 teaspoons fine sea salt

Freshly ground black pepper

4 ounces arugula (1½ quarts not packed)

FOR THE TUNA

Four 7- to 8-ounce tuna steaks (about 1 inch thick)

Fine sea salt and freshly ground black pepper

1 tablespoon canola oil

1. For the sauce, preheat the oven to 400°F. In a small baking dish, toss the garlic cloves with the oil and ½ teaspoon salt. Cover with foil and roast 45 minutes. Set aside until cool enough to handle.

recipe continued on next page

2. Meanwhile, simmer the wine in a saucepan until reduced to ¾ cup, about 25 minutes.

3. Pop the garlic cloves out of the skins into a bowl and mash with a fork. (You should have about 3 tablespoons garlic paste; a little more or less is fine.) Place the garlic in a blender. Add the reduced wine (it must be hot—return to a simmer if it has cooled), the sugar, and 2 teaspoons salt. Purée to blend. With the blender running, add the butter a little at a time until the sauce is emulsified. (If you have a variable-speed blender, blend on medium-high speed.) Transfer to a small pot, cover, and set aside at room temperature.

4. For the sunchokes, preheat the oven to 450°F. Line a baking sheet with aluminum foil and spray with nonstick cooking spray.

5. Cut the sunchokes on an angle into 1-inch pieces, rolling them slightly after each cut to achieve oblique pieces.

6. Toss the sunchokes with the olive oil, salt, and pepper to taste in a large bowl. Spread in a single layer on the baking sheet and roast until golden brown and tender, about 30 minutes. Remove to a bowl, add the arugula, and toss so that the hot sunchokes wilt the arugula.

7. On a plate or a sheet of aluminum foil, season the tuna on both sides with salt and pepper. Let stand 5 minutes to allow the seasonings to penetrate.

8. Pat the tuna dry with paper towels. Place a 12-inch skillet over medium heat. Add the oil and heat until it shimmers. Gently lay the tuna in the pan, placing the edge closest to you down first so as not to splatter yourself with hot oil. Sear until the bottom quarter of the steak turns opaque, about 2 minutes. Stand on one edge and cook until the edge is opaque, about 40 seconds. Stand on each of the other three edges and cook until opaque, about 2 minutes total. Turn to the final side and cook to medium-rare, about 1 minute more. Cooking time should be about 5 minutes total. (For rare tuna, sear 1½ minutes on the first side, 1½ minutes total for the edges, and about 45 seconds on the second side.)

9. To serve, gently warm the sauce over low heat. Spoon sunchokes in the center of each of four deep serving plates or shallow serving bowls. Place a spoonful of sauce to the side. Lean the tuna steaks on the sunchokes, with one edge in the sauce.

EXTRA CREDIT: BROWN FISH STOCK

To make a brown fish stock, prepare the ingredients listed in the recipe for Fish Fumet on page 13. But after rinsing and soaking the bones, pat them dry and refrigerate on a cooling rack in the refrigerator overnight to dry completely. Lightly coat the bones with canola or grapeseed oil, place in a large roasting pan, and roast in the oven at 450°F until browned all over, 10 to 12 minutes. Place the pan on the stovetop, over two burners on medium-high heat. Add 1 cup of the water from the fumet recipe, bring to a simmer and cook, scraping the bottom of the pan to pick up the browned bits. Continue on with the fumet recipe as written.

For the red wine sauce, bring 2 cups of the brown fish stock to a boil and reduce to ¼ cup. Blend into the sauce before adding the butter.

· SOFT-SHELL CRAB SALTIMBOCCA · WITH GARLICKY SPINACH

SERVES 4 AS AN ENTRÉE

This recipe was inspired by one of my early restaurant jobs before cooking school, working as a line cook at a red-sauce joint in New Jersey. One of our mainstays, like every other Italian-American restaurant in New Jersey, was saltimbocca, a classic Italian dish of thinly sliced veal topped with a whole sage leaf, prosciutto, and Fontina cheese. It's kind of a mix-and-match dish—we made it with veal or chicken. It's pretty good with halibut, too, but it's terrific with soft-shell crabs.

8 slices prosciutto

Eight 5-ounce soft-shell crabs, cleaned

8 fresh sage leaves

6 tablespoons extra virgin olive oil

8 thin rectangular slices Fontina cheese (½ ounce each)

1 cup dry white wine

2 tablespoons unsalted butter, cut into 2 equal pieces

Garlicky Spinach (see page 189)

1. For the crabs, preheat the oven to 400°F. Lay a slice of prosciutto on your cutting board so that one short side is at the bottom. Place a crab crosswise on its back on top of the prosciutto, about 2 to 3 inches from the bottom edge. Place a sage leaf on top of the crab. Fold the bottom edge of the prosciutto up and over the crab. Roll the crab away from you to wrap it in the prosciutto. Place seam side down on a baking sheet. Repeat to wrap the remaining crabs.

2. Place 2 large ovenproof skillets over medium-high heat. Add 3 tablespoons oil to each pan and heat until it shimmers. Add the crabs seam side up (you want the presentation side to be flat in the pan) and cook until the prosciutto is nicely browned and the claws turn orange, 2 to 3 minutes. Stand back while the crabs cook; their high water content means that they have a tendency to really pop. Flip the crabs with a spatula. Center a piece of cheese on each crab and put both skillets in the oven. Bake until the cheese melts, 2 to 3 minutes.

3. To serve, divide the spinach among four serving plates. Place 2 crabs on top of the spinach on each plate.

4. Add the wine to one of the pans and simmer vigorously to reduce by about one half. Reduce the heat to medium. Add the butter and swirl the pan over the heat to emulsify the butter into the wine. Pour over the crabs.

13.

VEGETABLE SIDES

· GRILLED ESCAROLE ·

SERVES 4 AS A SIDE

Escarole is a sturdy bitter green that is most often braised or stewed. So when Guy Jones, a farmer at Blooming Hill Farm in Washingtonville, New York, where I buy some of my produce, told me that he loves escarole grilled, I had to try his recipe. It's excellent. Serve it hot, or make it ahead to eat at room temperature. It's especially good with grilled swordfish and bagna cauda (page 289) but will complement any firm, full-flavored fish like striped bass or salmon, grilled, broiled, or sautéed for crisp skin.

1 head escarole (about 1 ½ pounds)	¼ cup extra virgin olive oil
2 tablespoons white wine vinegar	Fine sea salt and freshly ground black pepper

1. Remove any browned or wilted leaves from the escarole. Quarter the head lengthwise and trim the stem ends so that the quarters remain intact. Rinse well to remove the grit between the leaves. Spin dry.

2. Place the quarters in a large baking dish or platter. Drizzle with the vinegar, oil, and salt and pepper to taste. Let marinate at room temperature for about 1 hour, turning the escarole in the marinade every now and then to make sure the seasonings penetrate.

3. Preheat a gas grill to medium-high. Scrub the grill grates with a grill brush.

4. Lightly oil the grates. Place the escarole on the grill and grill, flipping once, until charred on the edges and wilted, and a paring knife pierces the escarole with no resistance, 2 to 3 minutes each side.

 GOES GREAT WITH: Grilled Swordfish with Black Olive Bagna Cauda; Almond-Crusted Red Snapper 101; Charred Squid 101 with Rosemary and Red Pepper Flakes.

· SICILIAN-STYLE EGGPLANT CAPONATA ·

SERVES 4 AS A SIDE

This version of caponata is a little different from the usual because it's made without raisins or currants. It's delicious the day it's made and excellent made a day ahead, but it will also hold for several days in the refrigerator. Salting the eggplant helps it to cook evenly without absorbing a lot of oil. Canned tomatoes work perfectly well in this recipe, but in season, I use fresh. I prefer caponata at room temperature but it is also tasty hot or cold.

1 eggplant (1 to 1¼ pounds), peel-on, trimmed and cut into 1-inch dice (5 to 6 cups)

1 teaspoon fine sea salt

¼ cup plus 2 tablespoons extra virgin olive oil

2 cloves garlic, sliced

1 oil-packed anchovy fillet (preferably extra virgin olive oil), drained and finely minced

½ small onion, halved through the root end, sliced crosswise

¼ red finger chile, cut lengthwise, seeds removed, slivered

½ medium stalk celery, halved lengthwise and sliced crosswise (½ cup)

One 14.5-ounce can tomatoes (preferably organic), puréed with their juice (1¾ cups), or 1 pound ripe tomatoes, cored, coarsely chopped, and puréed

1 teaspoon sugar

2 tablespoons red wine vinegar

2 tablespoons large capers (preferably salted, not brined; see Kitchen Notebook, page 368), soaked at least 2 hours or overnight, drained, rinsed and coarsely chopped

⅓ cup coarsely chopped pitted green olives (preferably Picholine)

1 tablespoon slivered fresh basil

1 tablespoon slivered fresh Italian parsley

1. Preheat the oven to 350°F. In a bowl, sprinkle the diced eggplant with the salt. Rub the salt into the eggplant and let stand 15 minutes. Blot dry on paper towels.

2. On a baking sheet, toss the eggplant with ¼ cup of the olive oil. Spread out in a single layer and bake until lightly browned and softened, about 30 minutes. Set aside.

3. Place a large saucepan over medium heat. Add the remaining 2 tablespoons olive oil and heat until fluid when the pan is swirled. Add the garlic and cook, stirring often, until light golden brown, about 2 minutes. Add the anchovy and cook until fragrant, 10 to 15 seconds. Add the onion and cook, stirring often, until the onion is softened and light gold, 5 to 6 minutes. Add the chile and cook until fragrant, 30 seconds. Add the celery and cook without coloring, stirring often, until just softened, about 3 minutes.

recipe continued on next page

4. Add the tomato purée and simmer until thickened and reduced by about one-half, 10 to 12 minutes. Add the sugar, vinegar, capers, and olives. Add the eggplant and gently fold in with a rubber spatula. Simmer gently 4 to 5 minutes to meld the flavors. Stir in the basil and parsley. Serve immediately or cover and refrigerate.

GOES GREAT WITH: Olive Oil–Poached Swordfish 101 with Caponata; Grilled Whole Dorade; Charred Squid 101 with Rosemary and Red Pepper Flakes; Branzino 101 Steamed on a Bed of Herbs and Lemon; New Jersey Baked Fish 101.

KITCHEN NOTEBOOK: CAPERS

In a recipe like this one, where whole capers feature so prominently, I prefer salted to brined capers. They have a purer flavor; brined capers taste primarily of the brine. Look for the large capers produced on the island of Pantelleria, off the coast of Sicily.

· GREEN BEANS WITH SOFRITO ·

SERVES 4 AS A SIDE

The ingredients in this recipe are almost identical to those in the stracotto on page 158. The difference here is that the beans are simply boiled, then tossed with a sofrito. The stracotto, on the other hand, relies on long cooking to infuse the beans with the flavor of the sofrito; the beans end up very delicious but very cooked. So if you want your beans to taste of those flavors and still have a little bite left in them, this preparation is for you.

Fine sea salt

1¼ pounds green beans, stem ends trimmed

2 tablespoons extra virgin olive oil

½ cup Sofrito (page 24)

Freshly ground black pepper

1. Bring 5 quarts water to a boil in a large pot. Add 3 tablespoons salt. Add the beans and boil until they are just cooked through but still have some bite, 4 to 5 minutes. Drain in a colander.

2. Return the pot to the stove and dry over medium heat. Add the olive oil and the drained beans and stir to coat the beans with the oil. Add the sofrito and cook, stirring often, 2 to 3 minutes, to meld the flavors. Season to taste with salt and pepper.

GOES GREAT WITH: New Jersey Baked Fish 101; Broiled Cod 101 with Fulton Fish Market Glaçage; Poached Whole Striped Bass with Basil-Garlic Compote.

• OLIVE OIL CRUSHED POTATOES •

SERVES 4 TO 6 AS A SIDE

I'm not fond of classic mashed potatoes. Never was as a kid, and I'm still not. So I was glad to discover this recipe in Alain Ducasse's kitchen at Le Louis XV. Made with olive oil and chicken stock, it's a lot lighter and cleaner than the classic. It's easy, and goes great with any kind of fish. Here's a recipe where I really recommend using homemade chicken stock. You can really taste the difference.

2¾ pounds large Yukon gold potatoes (about 4)

Fine sea salt

¾ cup Low-Stress Homemade Chicken Stock (page 16) or store-bought low-sodium chicken stock

6 tablespoons extra virgin olive oil

2 tablespoons slivered fresh Italian parsley

Freshly ground black pepper

1. Put the potatoes in a large pot and add cold water to cover by about 2 inches. Add 2 table-spoons salt, bring to a boil, reduce the heat, and simmer until you encounter no resistance when you pierce the potatoes with a paring knife, 40 to 45 minutes. Drain, let stand until cool enough to handle and peel with a paring knife. Return the peeled potatoes to the pot.

2. Meanwhile, bring the stock to a simmer in a small saucepan.

3. Crush the potatoes with a fork to a coarse texture (you want ¼- to ½-inch chunks). Add the hot stock, olive oil, parsley, 1¾ teaspoons salt, and pepper to taste. Stir with the fork to combine but leave the potatoes chunky.

GOES GREAT WITH: Roasted Lobster 101 with Basil-Garlic Butter; Branzino 101 Steamed on a Bed of Herbs and Lemon; Shrimp Scampi 101 with Preserved Lemon.

· BRAISED BELGIAN ENDIVE ·

SERVES 4 AS A SIDE

Unlike the classic endive gratin, which is blanketed with a creamy sauce, this is a very light preparation moistened with a vegetable broth. The endive halves, which do not brown at all, are placed cut side up in the baking dish to allow the broth to penetrate. The broth is lightly sweetened to balance the bitterness of the endive. Delicious with any fairly plain baked or sautéed fish.

2 tablespoons fine sea salt

4 heads endive, halved lengthwise, stem ends trimmed

2 tablespoons extra virgin olive oil

3 cloves garlic, sliced (about 1 tablespoon)

½ medium onion, cut into ¼-inch dice (about ½ cup)

1 small carrot, cut into ¼-inch dice (about ⅓ cup)

1 stalk celery, cut into ¼-inch dice (about ½ cup)

1 sprig fresh thyme

1 bay leaf

½ cup dry white wine

½ cup champagne vinegar

1 tablespoon sugar

1. Place a cooling rack on a baking sheet; set aside. Preheat the oven to 350°F. While the oven is heating, bring 1 gallon water to a boil in a large pot. Add the salt. Add half of the endive and cook for 1 minute. Remove with a slotted spoon and place cut side down on the rack. Cook the remaining endive halves and remove to the rack, cut side down.

2. Place a large saucepan over medium heat. Add the olive oil, garlic, and onion and cook without coloring, stirring occasionally, until the onion is translucent, about 5 minutes. Add the diced carrot and celery and cook without coloring, stirring occasionally, about 5 minutes. Add the thyme and bay leaf and cook, stirring occasionally, until aromatic, about 30 seconds.

3. Add 1 cup water, the white wine, champagne vinegar, and sugar and bring to a boil.

4. Arrange the endive, cut side up, in a single layer in a 9 by 13-inch baking dish. Pour the contents of the saucepan over. Cover with aluminum foil and bake until the endive is very tender when pierced with a paring knife, about 1 hour. Fish out and discard the bay leaf. Serve the endive with the juices.

GOES GREAT WITH: Dover Sole on the Bone with Marsala Sauce; Grilled Whole Dorade; Lemon Sole 101 with Ben's All-Purpose Seasoning Mix.

· SUMMERTIME SUCCOTASH ·

SERVES 4 TO 6 AS A SIDE

Succotash was originally a Native American dish of corn and shell beans. The combination was adopted by American settlers, and in time, it came to have a variety of regional variations. I like to take advantage of the season and use everything that is fresh and delicious—corn, shell beans, green beans, okra, tomatoes, and sugar snap peas.

1½ cups shelled fresh cranberry beans, from about 1½ pounds beans in the shell (see Kitchen Notebook, opposite)

Fine sea salt

2 tablespoons canola oil

1 medium red onion, cut into ½-inch dice (about 1 cup)

3 cloves garlic, thinly sliced

½ finger chile, cut lengthwise, seeds removed, slivered

1 large sprig fresh thyme

2 cups tomato purée from about 2 ripe beefsteak tomatoes, cored, coarsely chopped, and puréed, or one 14.5-ounce can whole peeled tomatoes (preferably organic), puréed with their juices

1½ cups fresh corn kernels (cut from about 2 large ears corn)

1½ cups sliced trimmed okra (⅓-inch-thick slices)

¾ cup trimmed, halved (crosswise) green beans

¾ cup stringed, halved (crosswise) sugar snap peas

Fine sea salt and freshly ground black pepper

1. Bring a large pot of water to a boil. Add the cranberry beans and simmer until tender, about 10 minutes. Drain, saving ¼ cup of the cooking liquid.

2. Place a medium saucepan over medium heat. Add the canola oil, onion, garlic, and chile and cook without coloring, stirring occasionally, until the onion is translucent, about 3 minutes. Add the thyme and cook until aromatic, about 15 seconds. Add the tomato purée and stir well. Cook, stirring often 3 minutes.

3. Add the cooked cranberry beans and reserved cooking liquid and simmer 3 minutes more. Add the corn, okra, string beans, sugar snap peas, 1 cup water, 2 teaspoons salt, and a pinch of pepper and cook uncovered over medium heat, stirring occasionally, until the cranberry beans are beginning to fall apart but still have texture, about 15 minutes.

GOES GREAT WITH: Grilled Bluefish 101 with Tomatillo Salsa; Grilled Mahi Mahi 101 with Hot Sauce Vinaigrette; Chicken-Fried Blowfish with Cajun Aioli.

KITCHEN NOTEBOOK: DRIED CRANBERRY BEANS

Since this is such a late summer dish, I prefer to use fresh cranberry beans, which I'm seeing around more and more, even in my local supermarket. But if you can't find them, substitute dried cranberry beans: Soak 1 cup dried beans overnight in enough cold water to cover by about 1 inch.

The next day, drain the beans and rinse under running water. Place in a 3-quart saucepan and add 5 cups fresh water. Bring to a boil, reduce the heat and simmer until tender, about 40 minutes. Let stand off the heat for 5 minutes to allow the beans to absorb some of the cooking liquid. Drain, reserving about ¼ cup cooking liquid.

· BLACK STICKY RICE ·

SERVES 4 AS A SIDE

Black sticky rice is a nutty-flavored, deep burgundy–colored short grain rice. A squeeze of fresh lemon juice highlights its flavor.

1½ cups black sticky rice	Freshly ground black pepper
1 teaspoon fine sea salt	1 tablespoon fresh lemon juice

1. Place the rice in a medium bowl, cover with 1 quart water, and let soak at room temperature overnight.

2. Drain in a colander and rinse briefly under cold running water. Drain. Place the rice, salt, and 1 quart water in a 2-quart saucepan. Bring to boil and cook uncovered at a medium simmer, stirring occasionally, until the water is absorbed and the rice is tender, about 40 minutes. Season to taste with pepper and stir in the lemon juice.

GOES GREAT WITH: General Tsao's Lobster; Grilled Cobia 101 with Pineapple Salsa; Grilled Scallops 101 with Peach Salsa; Tamarind-Glazed Sablefish.

· THYME AND HONEY–GLAZED CARROTS ·

SERVES 4 AS A SIDE

A touch of honey brings out the natural sweetness in carrots; a drizzle of vinegar brings it back into check. The carrots are cut in what is called a "roll cut" by cutting on an angle, then rolling the carrot slightly on the cutting board after each cut to achieve an oblique shape; see page 378. It's a small refinement but it makes for an interesting presentation.

1½ pounds carrots, peeled	2 tablespoons honey
3 tablespoons extra virgin olive oil	2 tablespoons cider vinegar
Fine sea salt	1½ tablespoons unsalted butter
3 sprigs fresh thyme	Freshly ground black pepper

1. Cut the carrots on an angle into ¾-inch pieces, rolling the carrots slightly after each cut to form oblique pieces.

2. Place a 12-inch skillet (with a lid) over medium heat. Add the oil and the carrots and season with 1 teaspoon salt. Add the thyme and stir. Cover and cook, stirring frequently, until the carrots are tender, about 10 minutes. Remove from the heat.

3. Add the honey and vinegar and stir to combine. Add the butter and stir until the glaze is blended. Season to taste with salt and pepper. Remove the thyme before serving.

GOES GREAT WITH: Fillet of Flounder 101 Meunière; Sauteéd Trout Fillets 101 with Mustard Riesling Sauce; Cape Cod "Turkey"; Branzino 101 Steamed on a Bed of Herbs and Lemon.

· SUGAR SNAP PEAS ·
WITH PRESERVED GINGER,
CHILE, AND MINT

SERVES 4 AS A SIDE

Candied ginger and fresh mint brighten up sugar snap peas in this quick sauté. I recommend cooking the recipe in two batches; the cooking goes quickly enough that the first batch will stay warm while you cook the second.

4 teaspoons extra virgin olive oil	¼ cup candied ginger, cut into ⅛-inch dice
1 pound sugar snap peas, strings removed	4 teaspoons slivered, seeded finger chile
2 teaspoons fine sea salt	2 tablespoons slivered fresh mint

1. Heat a 12-inch skillet over high heat for 1 minute. Add 2 teaspoons of the oil and heat until just shy of smoking. Add about half of the peas and cook 1 minute, stirring or tossing constantly. Season with 1 teaspoon of the salt. Add 2 tablespoons of the candied ginger and 2 teaspoons of the chile. Cook 2 minutes more, stirring or tossing constantly.

2. Remove from the heat. Add 2 tablespoons water and stir or toss constantly for 30 seconds more. Stir in 1 tablespoon of the mint. Transfer to a serving bowl.

3. Return the pan to high heat and repeat steps 1 and 2 to cook the rest of the peas.

GOES GREAT WITH: Tamarind-Glazed Sablefish; Orange Chile–Glazed Tilefish; Steamed Cod 101 with Ginger, Soy, and Chinese Broccoli (as an alternative to broccoli); Steamed Halibut with Curry Leaf Vinaigrette; Almond-Crusted Red Snapper 101.

· ROASTED EGGPLANT PURÉE ·

SERVES 4 AS A SIDE (MAKES ABOUT 2 CUPS)

I always end up with more eggplant than I know what to do with in my garden at home. Which is not a hardship—Mediterranean, North African, and Indian cuisines offer lots of great eggplant dishes to choose from. Here's a very basic preparation—just four ingredients—that we serve at the restaurant with Grilled Swordfish with Black Olive Bagna Cauda (page 289). There's so much going on in that dish that the eggplant provides a welcome background flavor. But with a simpler fish recipe, you can jazz up the purée with fresh herbs, lemon, maybe some chiles. Or chill the purée, stir in some yogurt, lemon, and mint, and serve it as a cold sauce or dip.

2 medium eggplants (about 4 pounds total), trimmed

3 tablespoons extra virgin olive oil

Fine sea salt and freshly ground black pepper

1. Preheat the oven to 350°F. Cut the eggplants in half lengthwise. Deeply score the flesh on the diagonal at 1-inch intervals down to but not through the skin; score again on the opposite diagonal to make diamonds.

2. Place the eggplant halves in a single layer on a baking sheet, skin side down. Drizzle the flesh with 2½ tablespoons of the oil and season with 1 teaspoon salt and ¼ teaspoon pepper. Flip the halves over, cut side down, and drizzle with the remaining ½ tablespoon oil. Season with ½ teaspoon salt and ¼ teaspoon pepper. Roast the eggplant until very tender, about 30 minutes.

3. Remove from the oven and let cool. Scrape out the flesh with a spoon and purée until smooth in a food processor. Discard the skin. Season with more salt and pepper as needed.

GOES GREAT WITH: Grilled Swordfish with Black Olive Bagna Cauda and Grilled Escarole; Soft-Shell Crab Saltimbocca; Grilled Scallops 101 with Peach Salsa; Roasted Lobster 101 with Basil-Garlic Butter.

· FRIED GREEN TOMATOES ·

SERVES 4 AS A SIDE

Crunchy on the outside, juicy and mildly acidic inside, these are a southern classic.

3 quarts canola oil or as needed, for deep-frying

½ cup low-fat buttermilk

1 cup finely ground yellow or white cornmeal

2 large green tomatoes (about 1 pound), cored and sliced crosswise ⅓ to ½ inch thick

Fine sea salt and freshly ground black pepper

1. In a large, deep heavy-bottomed pot, heat the canola oil over medium-high heat until it registers 350°F on a deep-fry thermometer. Line a baking dish with a double layer of paper towels.

2. Pour the buttermilk into a shallow bowl or deep plate. Put the cornmeal in another shallow bowl or deep plate next to the buttermilk. Place a baking sheet next to the cornmeal to hold the coated tomato slices.

3. On a plate or a sheet of aluminum foil, season the tomato slices with salt and pepper. Use the fingers of one hand to dip each slice in buttermilk to coat. Shake off the excess, then place in the cornmeal; toss with your other hand to coat. Place on the baking sheet.

4. When the oil has reached 350°F, carefully place half of the coated tomato slices in the hot oil, one by one, holding them close to the oil and dropping them in gently. (Be particularly careful: because of the high water content of the tomatoes, the oil will bubble up as if it's boiling.) After about 30 seconds, move the slices around gently with a spider, skimmer, or slotted spoon to prevent them from sticking to one another. Continue frying, taking the temperature of the oil with the deep-fry thermometer and adjusting the heat as needed, until the tomatoes are golden brown outside and tender inside, about 3 minutes.

5. Remove to the paper towel–lined baking dish with the spider, skimmer, or slotted spoon and toss gently to drain. Repeat to fry the rest of the slices. Sprinkle with salt and let cool slightly before eating; the tomatoes will stay very hot for several minutes.

GOES GREAT WITH: Cornmeal-Crusted Redfish 101 with Spicy Aioli; Chicken-Fried Blowfish with Cajun Aioli; Fried Sea Scallops 101; Fried Clams 101; Almond-Crusted Red Snapper.

TECHNIQUES

MAKING ROLL CUTS FOR VEGETABLES

A roll cut, also called an oblique cut, is a technique for cutting long, cylindrical vegetables such as carrots into attractive, irregular shapes.

1. Make a diagonal cut to the stem end of the carrot. Keep the knife at the same angle, roll the carrot a quarter turn, and make another diagonal cut to produce an asymmetrical chunk.

2. Roll the carrot another quarter turn, and make another diagonal cut. Continue to cut the entire carrot.

REMOVING PIN BONES FROM A FISH FILLET

Most fillets contain small, thin, flexible bones called pin bones that run the length of the fillet at an angle to the flesh. They are best removed before cooking.

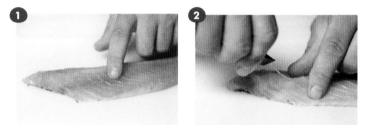

1. Run your fingertip over the fillet from the head end to the tail end to feel for the bones, gently lifting the ends of the bones so that they protrude from the flesh.

2. Use fish tweezers or needle-nosed pliers to grasp and pull out the bones. Pull toward the head end of the fillet; pulling straight up will tear up the flesh.

REMOVING PIN BONES FROM A STEAK SUCH AS SALMON OR COD

1. To find the pin bones in a steak, in your mind's eye divide the steak into two halves: the rounded half and the half that looks as if a V-shaped chunk has been taken out of it. The pin bones run in a horizontal line between the two halves.

2. Run your fingers along that line to feel for and then gently lift the bones. Pull out the bones on one side of the center bone with fish tweezers or needle-nosed pliers. Turn the steak 180° and repeat to remove the bones from the other half of the steak.

SKINNING A FISH FILLET SUCH AS BLACK SEA BASS

1. Lay the fillet, skin side down, on a cutting board. Starting about ½ inch from the tail end, slip the blade of the knife between the flesh and the skin, so that you can grasp the tail end of the skin with the other hand.

2. Hold the blade almost flat against the skin. Holding the skin firmly and tugging it gently from side to side, slide the knife blade along the length of the fillet.

3. Release the fillet completely from the skin.

REMOVING THE BLOODLINE FROM FISH FILLETS

The bloodline is a muscle that lies underneath the skin of the fish. It is usually darker in color—red to dark red, depending on the variety of fish—than the rest of the meat. Despite the name, the color is not actually caused by blood; the muscle simply contains a higher percentage of a protein called myoglobin. It is edible—many people enjoy it—but the flavor is stronger than the rest of the flesh. At the restaurant, we remove it.

1. On fillets such as striped bass, black bass, bluefish, and mahi mahi, the bloodline appears as a line down the center of the skin-side of the fillet. To remove the bloodline, first skin the fillet (see opposite page). Then, holding your knife at an angle, make a cut all the way down one side of the bloodline, just to the centerline of the fillet.

2. Turn the fillet 180°. Cut down the other side of the bloodline in the same manner. The bloodline will now be released on both sides but attached to the fillet along the centerline.

3. Starting about two inches from the tail end, pull up the two sides of the bloodline with one hand. Holding the knife flat, slide the blade between the bloodline and the flesh of the fillet. Slice toward the tail to free that end of the bloodline.

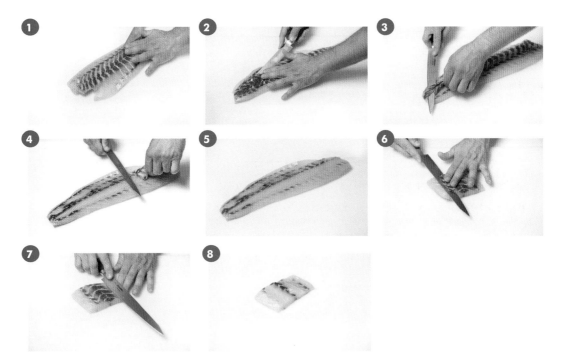

4. Then grasp the tail end of the bloodline with one hand, and turn the knife so that the blade faces the head end of the fillet. Gently pull up on the bloodline, slip the blade of the knife between the bloodline and the underlying flesh, and slide the knife toward the head end of the fillet to remove the bloodline in one piece.

5. The finished fillet may contain traces of bloodline; that's okay.

6. It's even easier to remove the bloodline from a portion of fillet. Starting at one side and holding the knife at an angle, slip the blade of the knife under the bloodline and slice to the centerline of the fillet.

7. Turn your knife and slide the blade under the other half of the bloodline and remove it.

8. The finished fillet may also contain traces of bloodline.

FILLETING A WHOLE COOKED FISH SUCH AS DORADE FOR SERVING

NOTE: This fish has been scored for grilling (see page 291) but the filleting technique will be the same regardless of cooking technique.

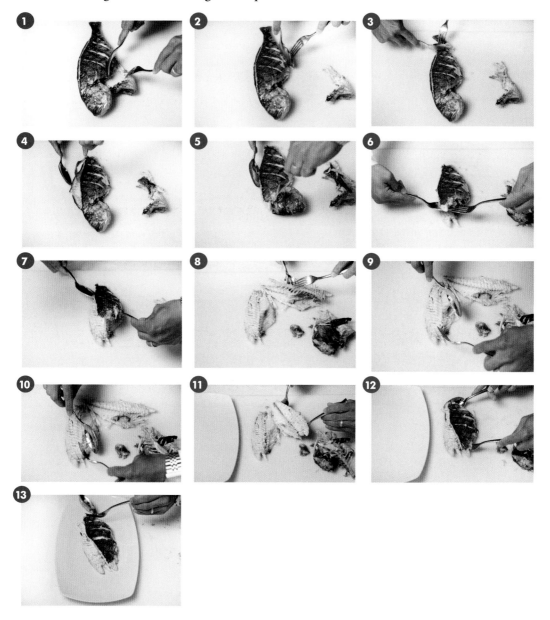

1. Cut behind the gill plate with a spoon and use a fork to pull off the boney, triangle-shaped piece behind the head.

2. A series of short bones lines the belly edge of the fish; press down with the edge of the spoon to separate the bones from the flesh. Pull the bones away with the fork.

3. Use the edge of the spoon to make a cut just above the tail; gently pull off the tail with the fork.

4. Starting at the head end and moving all along the length of the fish, insert the edge of the spoon about ¼ inch in from the top edge to loosen the small bones that line the top of the fish; pull them out with the fork.

5. Make a cut behind the head with the edge of the spoon and use the fork to pull off the head.

6. Starting at the head end, slide the spoon in between the backbone and the fillet to lift and loosen the top fillet.

7. Lift the top fillet off the bone. (It may come in pieces—that's fine, don't worry about it.)

8. Lift the bone off the bottom fillet in one piece.

9. Slide the spoon and fork underneath the long, curved bones on the belly side of the fillets; lift to remove them.

10. With the edge of the fork and spoon, pull out the pin bones that run along the centerline of the fillets.

11. If serving both fillets as a single serving, use the fork and spoon to flip one fillet on top of the other, skin side up.

12. Lift onto a serving plate.

13. And serve.

SLICING FISH FILLETS SUCH AS BLACK SEA BASS
FOR CRUDO AND SASHIMI

With a few exceptions, this technique may be used with any fish fillet. The size of the slices will vary depending on the size and shape of the fillet. The thinner the fillet, the more steeply the knife is angled.

1. Starting at the tail end of a skinned fillet, hold the knife at a steep angle—almost parallel to the cutting board.

2. Slice the fish about ¼-inch thick.

3. Adjust the knife to a shallower angle as you work up to the thicker part of the fillet.

PREPARING SEA SCALLOPS

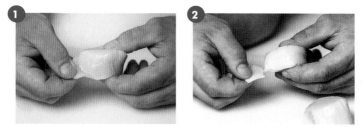

1. Check to see if a crescent-shaped muscle is attached to the side of the scallop; it will toughen when cooked. Just pull it off.

2. It will detach easily.

CLEANING SHRIMP

At home, I clean shrimp on a sheet of paper towel because clean-up is easy; just throw out the towel when you're done. I don't recommend rinsing the cleaned shrimp. You'll rinse off the flavor.

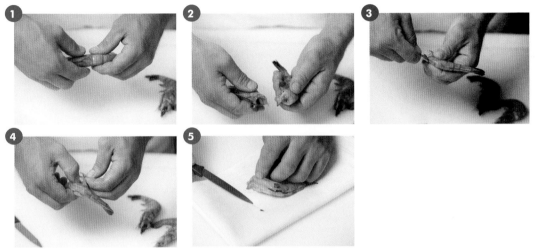

1. For head-on shrimp, hold the tail in one hand at the point where the tail meets the head. Hold the head in the other hand.

2. Twist to pull off the head.

3. Hold the tail in one hand, rounded side facing up. Pinch the blade of a paring knife, sharp edge facing up, between thumb and forefingers about 1 inch from the tip. Place the tip of the knife directly beneath the shrimp shell at the head end. Push gently to insert it into the flesh. Wiggle the blade with upward pressure to cut through the top of the shell. Continue this movement until you have split the shell along its entire length.

4. Pull off the shell and legs.

5. Place the shrimp on a napkin or paper towel; you'll see that you have made a shallow cut along the length of the tail. Use the point of the knife to separate the edges of the cut and scrape out the dark vein.

CLEANING SOFT-SHELL CRABS

If you're going to cook them immediately, ask your fishmonger to clean the crabs for you. But with a pair of kitchen scissors, it's easy to do on your own.

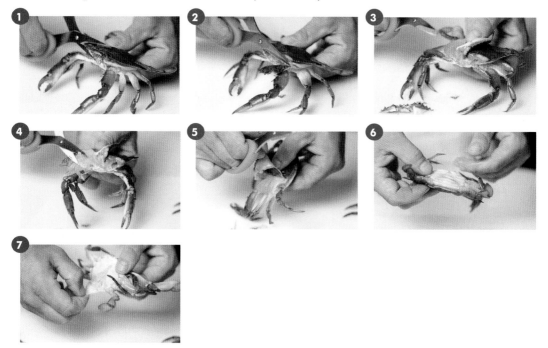

1. Hold the crab in one hand and cut off the front of the head.

2. Make the cut right behind the eyes.

3. Lift one side of the top "shell."

4. Cut out the spongy gills.

5. Repeat to cut out the gills on the other side.

6. Turn the crab over.

7. Pull open the tail flap, called the "apron" (opposite the head), and twist it off.

OPENING RAW OYSTERS

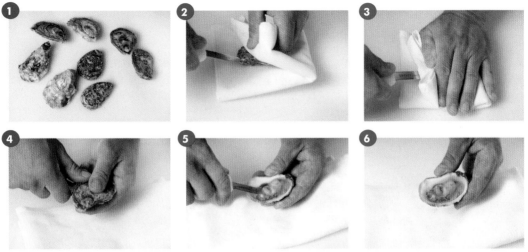

1. All varieties of oysters are opened with the same technique; this series demonstrates with East Coast oysters. Before opening, scrub oysters with a stiff brush under running water. Then, while opening, keep the oysters as level as possible so as not to lose the oyster liquor.

2. With a folded towel to protect your hands, place the oyster on a cutting board, cupped side down, with the hinge facing out. Steady the oyster with one hand while you work the blade of an oyster knife between the shell halves at the hinge.

3. Fold the towel over the oyster. Twist the knife to break the hinge.

4. Slide the knife against the top shell from the hinge to the opposite side to sever the adductor muscle at the top shell. Work carefully so as not to cut the flesh. Pull off the top shell.

5. Run the knife underneath the oyster to sever the adductor muscle where it attaches to the bottom shell to free the oyster completely.

6. If necessary, use the tip of your knife to remove any bits of broken shell or grit so that the oyster is nice and clean.

OPENING RAW CLAMS

Scrub clams with a stiff brush under running water before opening. Then, while opening, keep them as level as possible so as not to lose any juices.

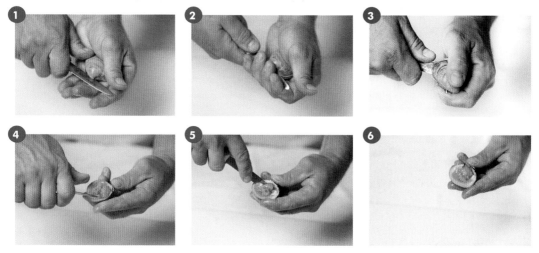

1. Cup a clam in one hand with the hinge facing out. Holding a clam knife in the other hand, work the edge of the blade into the hinge.

2. Twist the blade back and forth to break the hinge; you'll feel the clam pop open slightly.

3. Slide the tip of the knife against the top shell, turning the knife clockwise while turning the clam counterclockwise to sever the two adductor muscles at the top shell. Work carefully so as not to cut the flesh. Twist off the top shell.

4. Run the tip of the knife underneath the clam to sever the first adductor muscle.

5. And then sever the other adductor muscle at the bottom shell to free the clam completely.

6. If necessary, use the tip of your knife to remove any bits of broken shell or grit so that the clam is nice and clean.

SPLITTING A LIVE LOBSTER

This is the easiest way to split a live lobster.

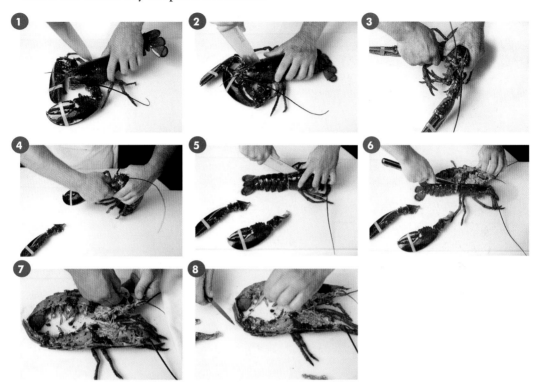

1. On a cutting board, hold the tail of the lobster with one hand. Find the center point of the horizontal line that bisects the head of the lobster. You'll see a slight indentation; place the point of a chef's knife there.

2. Press down on the tail with the palm of one hand to steady the lobster against the board. Drive the point of the knife through the head, down to the cutting board. This will kill the lobster immediately. Then cut down to split the head in half.

3. Grasp one "arm" (claw and knuckle) by the knuckle where it meets the body and twist to remove the claw and knuckle in one piece.

4. Repeat to twist off the second "arm" in one piece.

5. Replace the lobster on the cutting board. Insert the point of the knife at the center point where you began.

6. Cut down to split the tail in half.

7. Open out the two halves of the lobster as if you were opening a book. Note the light green–colored tomalley (liver) and, in this female lobster, the dark green roe. Leave them; both are delicious. But pull out the translucent stomach sac that lies behind the eyes; you'll find half the sac in each lobster half.

8. Pull out the long, stringy vein that runs from the stomach down the length of the tail. You may find parts of the vein in both tail halves.

BUTTERFLYING A LIVE LOBSTER

This is more challenging than the previous technique but great for a more impressive presentation or for stuffed lobster (see page 147).

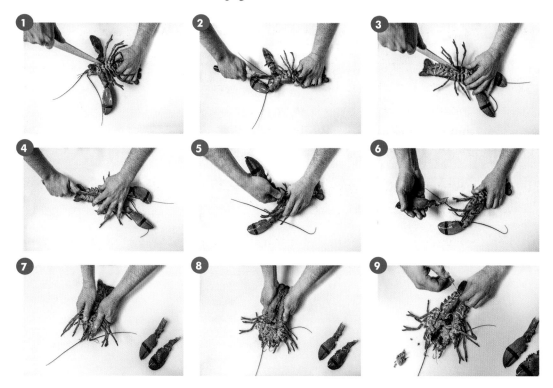

1. Place the lobster on a cutting board, underside facing up. Hold the lobster with one hand at the point where the tail meets the head. Place the point of the knife smack in the center of the head.

2. Drive the point of the knife into the head so that it reaches but does not penetrate the underside of the top shell. This will kill the lobster immediately. Cut down to split the head, still careful not to cut all the way through the top shell.

3. Turn the lobster 180°. Insert the tip of the knife at the center point where you began.

4. Cut down the length of the tail to split it, still careful not to cut all the way through the top shell.

5. Holding the lobster head in one hand, grasp one "arm" (claw and knuckle) by the knuckle where it meets the body.

6. Twist to remove the claw and knuckle in one piece; repeat to twist off the second "arm."

7. Arrange the lobster underside-up and head away from you. Place your thumbs on top, along the line where the legs meet the body. Place the tips of your fingers underneath along the centerline of the top shell. Now pull your thumbs apart, applying upward pressure with your fingertips to crack open the head of the lobster without breaking the halves entirely apart.

8. Move your hands down and crack open the tail half the same way; the two halves will still be connected by shell.

9. Pull out and discard the stomach sac that lies behind the eyes. Pull out the vein from the tails. Remove the rubber bands from the claws; you'll crack the claws after cooking, as on pages 393–94.

SHELLING A COOKED LOBSTER

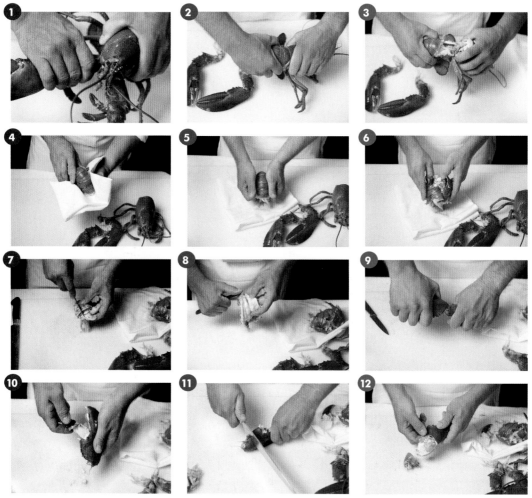

1. Grasp the head of the lobster in one hand and twist the "arm" (claw and knuckle) off the body with the other hand. Repeat to remove the second "arm."

2. Holding the head in one hand, twist the tail.

3. And remove the tail from the head.

4. Place a folded towel over the palm of one hand. Place the lobster tail on the towel with the back facing up. Placing your hands on either side of the tail, squeeze the tail between your hands, in the napkin, until you hear the bottom shell crack.

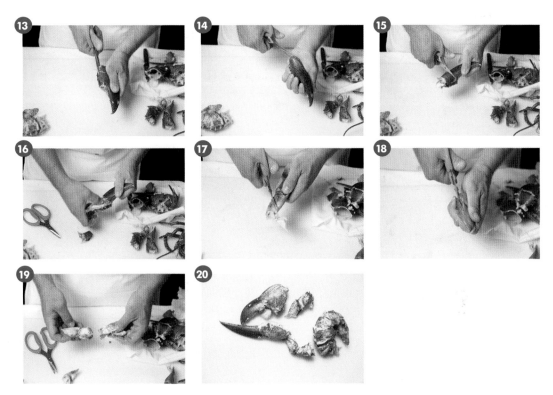

5. Now hook the fingertips of both hands under the edge of the shell on both sides.

6. Pull up with your fingertips to crack the top of the shell in half. Pull apart the shell and pull out the tail meat in one piece.

7. Cut down the curved side of the tail with a paring knife.

8. Separate the edges of the cut and remove the vein with the tip of a paring knife.

9. Twist the claws off the knuckles.

10. Bend the claw pincers (the "thumbs") back until they release, and pull off the pincers with the attached cartilage. From here there are two ways to shell the claws:

Method #1

11. Set the claw on edge on a cutting board, holding in one hand by the pointy end. Using the end of the blade closest to the handle, crack the other (wide) end of the claw with a chef's knife so that the blade penetrates about ¼ inch. Twist the knife; the shell will crack.

12. Pull the claw meat out of the shell.

Method #2: The "Window" Method

13. Holding the claw in one hand, cut along the "thumb" side of the claw from the bottom, where the knuckle was attached, to the top, where the "thumb" used to be.

14. Turn the claw over and cut along the other side about halfway to the tip of the claw. (Make sure to keep your thumb out of the way of the scissors, or protect your hand with a folded towel.)

15. Now cut across the claw to cut a "window" in the shell; remove the shell.

16. Pull out the claw meat in one piece.

17. Whichever method you used to shell the claws, now shell the knuckles. With kitchen scissors, trim the body end of the knuckle along the joint and discard that joint; there's no meat in it.

18. Use the tips of the scissors to cut the length of the knuckles. Turn the knuckles over and cut along the other side.

19. Lift off the shell and remove the meat.

20. Gently scrape any coagulated white albumen off the shelled meat for presentation.

Guide to Unusual Ingredients

Unless specifically noted, these ingredients can be found at your supermarket, local specialty food store, or online. I've indicated if ingredients can be found at Hispanic or Asian markets, and included favorite online sites, if available.

ALMONDS, MARCONA: A variety of Spanish almond with a shorter, rounder shape than California almonds. I like them for their sweeter, more delicate flavor. They are sold both raw and fried in olive oil; the recipes in this book use raw almonds.

BANANA LEAVES: The leaves of the banana plant are used in many cuisines for wrapping, cooking, and serving food. I sometimes use them to decorate my serving plates (see Extra Credit, page 204). Wash and trim the edges before using. Banana leaves are available frozen at Asian and Hispanic markets, and at melissas.com.

BEANS, ADZUKI OR RED: These small red beans originated in Asia. They are often sweetened to make a paste used in desserts. Adzuki beans can be found in Asian and natural-food markets.

BONITO FLAKES (*KATSUOBUSHI, IN JAPANESE*): Bonito flakes are thin-shaved bits of steamed, aged, air-dried bonito, a member of the mackerel family. The pale, tan-colored flakes are one of the main ingredients in the Japanese stock dashi (the other is kombu, page 403). Available at Japanese markets and Asian websites.

CAPERS: Capers are the green flowering buds of the caper bush, grown in the Mediterranean. They may be pickled and sold in brine; these are available at your supermarket and specialty stores. For some dishes, such as Roasted Cauliflower, page 351, I prefer to use large salted Italian capers, the most famous of which are produced on the island of Pantelleria, off the coast of Sicily. To use brined capers, simply drain them. Salted capers should be soaked at least 2 hours or overnight, then drained. In a pinch, substitute brined capers.

CHESTNUTS: Chestnuts, the fruit of the sweet chestnut tree that grows throughout the Mediterranean, are a staple of Italian cuisine. They're harvested during the fall. I love them. Fresh chestnuts must be shelled and peeled before cooking; it's much easier to order them shelled, cooked, peeled, and ready to go from D'Artagnan (dartagnan.com).

CHILES, DRIED: I use several varieties of dried chiles in this book: dried Thai bird chiles; New Mexico chiles; chipotle meco chiles; and two varieties of Mexican chiles for mole: mulato and pasilla. The red Thai bird chiles used in my chile oil are 1 to 2 inches long and very hot. Find them in Asian markets, or online (amazon.com), or substitute dried red cayenne chiles, sold in Asian and Indian markets and gourmet markets. New Mexico chiles are a dark red with medium heat; ancho chiles may be substituted. Grayish-tan chipotle meco are a type of chipotle chile (dried jalapeño chiles), with a medium heat. Mulato chiles are dark-colored, with fairly mild heat. If you can't find them, substitute dried ancho chiles. Dried pasilla chiles are long, narrow, black chiles. If you can't find them, substitute ancho or mulato chiles. Mulato and pasilla chiles are available at Mexican markets.

CHILES, FRESH: I use two varieties of fresh chiles in this book. The first is my staple, a 5- to 6-inch-long, finger-width, medium-spicy chile called a finger chile. You can use either red or green finger chiles in these recipes unless I specify a color. To prepare them, cut them in half lengthwise, remove the stem and seeds, and cut into slices or slivers; if you want more heat, leave in the seeds. If you can't find them, substitute half the amount in jalapeño chiles. I also use the larger poblano pepper, a relatively mild variety available in supermarkets. Prepare poblano peppers by cutting off the stem, then cutting the peppers in half lengthwise, scraping out the seeds, and cutting as called for in the recipe.

COCONUT MILK: Unlike the clear water contained in young coconuts, coconut milk is made by soaking grated coconut meat in hot water and straining. This is not something I'm recommending that you do yourself; good-quality coconut milk is sold in cans at supermarkets and Asian markets. I like Chaokoh brand. Don't confuse it with the thick, sweetened cream of coconut used in rum drinks.

COCONUT, UNSWEETENED DRIED: Do not confuse this dried shredded coconut with the moist, soft sweetened coconut strands used in baking. The unsweetened flakes are just that—unsweetened. Available at Indian and natural-food markets.

COCONUT WATER: This is the clear liquid contained in young coconuts. It has a mild, sweet flavor and is delicious to drink. Don't confuse it with creamy coconut milk (opposite). These days, coconut water is routinely available at supermarkets.

COD, SALT: Salt cod is fresh cod that has been preserved by salting and drying. Ask at your fish market for a block of "center cut" salt cod rather than a tail portion; the thicker center cut portions are generally less salty and more flavorful than the tail pieces. If you live in an area where there are Spanish and Portuguese markets, like Newark, New Jersey, or Fall River, Massachusetts, you're in salt cod heaven. Look for cod that is white, not yellow. Buy without skin, if possible—it's just easier to deal with. The bone is not too hard to pull out after cooking, but boneless is easier.

CRÈME FRAÎCHE: Crème fraîche is a tangy cultured cream. Unlike sour cream, it will not separate when boiled. If you can't find it, you can use heavy cream and add a squeeze of lemon to the sauce before serving. But, at home, I don't go crazy about it—I'll use sour cream in the recipe for Blackfish 101 Braised with Oyster Mushrooms, Crème Fraîche, and Tarragon (page 160), for example; the sauce is not as smooth as it would be with crème fraîche, but it tastes just fine.

CURRY LEAVES: Curry leaves are dark, slender leaves from the kari plant, a tree native to South India. Their pungent, aromatic flavor is a distinctive, irreplaceable element in the South Indian flavor palette. (Note that curry leaves have nothing to do with the spice mix called curry powder.) They are available fresh, frozen, and dried at Indian and some Asian markets. Fresh curry leaves have the best flavor. They'll last up to 2 weeks in the refrigerator. Or freeze them.

EDAMAME: Edamame are fresh young soybeans in the pod. Edamame in the pods are available at many supermarkets these days; try the freezer section. Or find them at Asian markets. To prepare edamame, steam or boil the pods for 3 to 4 minutes. Drain, and shell for recipes that call for the shelled beans. To serve whole, just sprinkle with salt. Eat the beans by biting down on the pods, then pulling the pods out, leaving the beans in your mouth.

EPAZOTE: This jagged-leafed herb is very common in Mexican cuisine, particularly in bean dishes. It grows wild throughout Mexico and southwestern areas of the United States; because it's so invasive, some people consider it a weed. It has a peppery, pungent flavor that I love. Look for fresh epazote in Mexican markets; order dried epazote at melissas.com.

GARAM MASALA: Garam masala is a spice mixture used in Northern Indian cuisine. Recipes vary but usually include cinnamon, bay leaf, cumin, coriander, green and black cardamom, peppercorns, and clove. Garam masala is available at Indian markets. Or substitute by roughly approximating the blend with equal parts ground cinnamon, ground black pepper, and ground allspice.

GINGER, CANDIED: Candied ginger is fresh ginger that has been peeled, sliced, and cooked in a sugar syrup. Once drained and dried, the slices are tossed in granulated sugar. Chopped, they add a sweet bite to savory dishes. (And on their own, whole slices make a tasty snack.) Candied ginger can be stored at room temperature in a sealed container for up to 3 months.

GOCHUJANG: Gochujang is a pungent, brick red, fermented chile-soy bean paste. Used as a condiment and seasoning, the spicy, savory, salty, slightly sweet paste is a staple ingredient in Korean cuisine.

GREENS, ASIAN: I call for three types of Asian greens in this book: bok choy, Chinese broccoli, and yu-choy. Bok choy is a variety of Chinese cabbage with wide, white stalks topped with crinkly, dark green leaves. Bok choy and miniature bok choy are available in supermarkets. Chinese broccoli is a leafy vegetable with thick stalks and large green leaves, with some broccoli-like buds. I prepare Chinese broccoli by separating the leaves and stalks, slicing both, and sautéing, adding the stems to the pan first because they take longer to cook (see page 214). Yu-choy (see page 229) looks similar to Chinese broccoli, but with more slender stems, and I prepare it the same way. Both are sold in Asian markets. Broccolini makes a good substitute.

HAM, BAYONNE: *Jambon de Bayonne* is a salted, aged, air-dried raw ham named for the port of Bayonne in southwest France, the region in which the ham is made. It is an essential element in regional Basque and Gascon cuisines in southwest France. Bayonne ham is available at specialty markets. D'Artagnan also produces a version that is sold online at dartagnan.com. Bayonne ham and prosciutto may be used interchangeably in my recipes.

HAM, PROSCIUTTO: A salted, aged, air-dried raw ham produced in several regions of Italy. Imported prosciutto is sold at specialty markets and some supermarkets. Good-quality prosciutto is also made in America these days and can be found at butchers, specialty markets, and online from laquercia.us. Convenient packaged sliced prosciutto is also available in delis and markets. Prosciutto and Bayonne ham may be used interchangeably in my recipes.

HEARTS OF PALM: Hearts of palm are the edible, ivory-colored inner cores of one of several varieties of palm trees. They are crunchy and slightly sweet, with a flavor that's similar to artichokes. The tubular hearts are obtained by cutting down a young tree, stripping off the bark and fibrous outer layers to get to the core, then cutting the core into sections. Fresh raw hearts, trimmed and ready to use, are available online through localharvest.org. You may find raw hearts of palm sealed in plastic at specialty stores or high-end supermarkets. Don't use canned hearts of palm; they are mushy and taste like the tin. If you can't get fresh hearts of palm, substitute water chestnuts.

JAGGERY: Jaggery is an unrefined Indian sugar that tastes similar to brown sugar but with even more flavor. Jaggery is sold at Indian markets. Light brown sugar makes a good substitute, as does piloncillo, available at Mexican markets.

KAFFIR LIME LEAVES: Kaffir limes are a variety of lime used in Southeast Asian cooking. The leaves add a distinctive aromatic flavor and fragrance. Nothing really replaces that flavor, but a couple of strips of lime zest or the grated zest of ½ lime will give a reasonable facsimile. Refrigerate fresh kaffir lime leaves for up to 2 weeks, tightly wrapped in plastic, or wrap and freeze for up to several months. Fresh kaffir lime leaves are available at Asian markets and online at importfood.com.

KIMCHEE: In traditional Korean cuisine, a spicy, pickled side dish. Though there are many, many varieties of kimchee, the most common in America is made with Napa cabbage.

LEMONGRASS: Lemongrass is a flavoring used in Southeast Asian cooking. It grows as a slender, fibrous, pale yellow stalk, of which only the bottom 3 inches are used. Cut off the tops, pull off the fibrous outer layer to get to the white core, and chop. Lemongrass is more and more available at supermarkets and certainly at Asian markets. Substitute grated lemon zest.

LINGUIÇA: A smoked Portuguese pork sausage seasoned with garlic and paprika. Linguiça is available at butcher shops in Portuguese neighborhoods and by mail order from Lopes Sausage Company in Newark, New Jersey, (973) 344-3063.

LOTUS ROOT: Lotus root sounds exotic and people may be too intimidated to try it. Don't be. It has more texture than flavor. Lotus root grows in connected links, looking like sausages. Each link averages 6 to 8 inches long and about 2 inches in diameter. To prepare the root, peel with a vegetable peeler or paring knife, slice, and store in water to keep it from browning until you're ready to cook. Then steam, boil, or stir-fry it for a nutty crunch in soups, stews, braises, and stir-fries. Or chill and add to salads. Lotus root is available at Asian markets

MAPLE SYRUP: Maple syrup is not graded by quality but rather by color, ranging from a pale to dark amber for Grade A, to a dark brown color for Grade B. Color corresponds to flavor: the darker the syrup, the stronger the flavor. I like Grade B maple syrup for cooking because of its rich, dark taste. (For more about maple syrup, check out www.deepmoun tainmaple.com.) Some of my favorite maple syrup is available online at www .sugarmanofvermont.com and www.deep mountainmaple.com.

MIRIN: A sweet wine used in Japanese cooking, not for drinking. You'll find it in the Asian section of your supermarket, and at Asian markets.

MISO: Miso is a thick paste made of fermented soybeans. There are several different varieties, each with a specific flavor

and texture. I use two types in this book: white and red. White miso, with a white-to-light-yellow color, is the most common miso, with the mildest flavor; it is typically used in miso soup. Red miso has a deeper, richer, nuttier flavor. Miso is available at Asian markets. Refrigerate after opening.

MUSHROOMS, HONSHIMEIJI: Honshimeiji mushrooms are a delicate, thin-stemmed cultivated Japanese mushroom with small caps, juicy flesh, and a mild, nutty flavor. They grow in clusters. They are prepared by trimming the dry edges from the bottoms and pulling the clusters apart. If you can't find them, substitute white, cremini, shiitake, and/or oyster mushrooms; just trim and quarter. On occasion I've seen them at the supermarket; otherwise they are available online from dartagnan.com.

MUSTARD SEEDS: I use yellow, and black or brown mustard seeds in this book. The black and brown seeds have a sharper, more pungent flavor than the lighter colored seeds, and are used often in regional Indian cuisines. Yellow mustard seeds are sold in supermarkets but you may have to look harder for black or brown seeds—a specialty store, or online.

NOODLES, GLASS: Also called vermicelli, cellophane noodles, and bean thread noodles, glass noodles are very thin, transparent noodles made from mung beans. Like rice noodles, they are soaked in hot water before a brief cooking. If they're not available at your supermarket, you'll find them at Asian markets.

OCTOPUS, COOKED (TAKO): Precooked octopus tentacles for Paejun (page 91) are sold at Japanese markets.

OIL, OLIVE: I use extra virgin olive oil, which is oil from the first cold pressing (without chemicals or heat) of high-quality olives. Olive oils have a tremendous range of flavor, like wine; I generally look for a fruitier oil, rather than one with a bite at the end. Since heat damages the flavor of the oil, I use a different oil for cooking than for dressing salads and for "finishing" (which means drizzling on finished dishes before serving). For cooking, I prefer a Spanish oil, a blend of Arbequina and Picual olives. For finishing, I prefer oils from Liguria, in Italy, such as Taggiasche oil. Two of my favorite brands are Ardoino and Raineri. I also use a Spanish oil, Nunez de Prado, for finishing, as well as Alziari, a brand made in Nice, in the south of France. In general, I recommend using a less expensive extra virgin oil for cooking. Save your money for an excellent finishing oil.

OIL, TOASTED SESAME: The sesame oil called for in this book, made from toasted sesame seeds, is a rich, golden-brown color; don't confuse it with light-colored (untoasted) sesame oil, which doesn't have the same flavor. Sesame oil is sold in supermarkets and Asian markets. Toasted sesame oil should be refrigerated after opening

OLIVES, ALPHONSO: Alphonso olives are large, soft purplish-black olives, cured in wine or a wine vinegar solution. Substitute Kalamata and Gaeta olives.

OLIVES, PICHOLINE: Picholine olives are small, firm green olives, typically grown in the south of France in Provence, the Côte d'Azur, and Languedoc. Substitute any good-quality green olive, except cocktail olives.

OLIVES, TAGGIASCHE: Taggiasche olives are small black olives from the region of Liguria, in Italy. Look for them online or at a specialty food market, or substitute Gaeta or Kalamata olives.

PEPPER, PIQUILLO: A small, sweet-tasting, bright red chile pepper traditionally grown in northern Spain. They are not spicy like a hot chile, but when roasted, they have a smoky, piquant flavor that is richer and deeper than roasted bell peppers. I use roasted, peeled, seeded, jarred piquillo peppers in Piquillo Pepper Aioli (page 244). The jarred peppers are available online at tienda.com.

PEPPERCORNS, TELLICHERRY: Tellicherry peppercorns have a finer, fruitier flavor than standard peppercorns; you taste flavor, not just heat.

PERNOD: A brand of the anise-flavored liqueur pastis made in France. Pernod is consumed as an aperitif and is a staple of Mediterranean French cuisine. Available at most liquor stores.

PIMENT D'ESPELETTE: *Piment d'Espelette* is French for the chile pepper cultivated in the French commune of Espelette in the Basque region of France; dried and ground, it essentially replaces black pepper in Basque cuisine. The orangey-red powder is a traditional ingredient in the Basque red bell pepper stew, piperade (see page 164). Aleppo pepper (a crushed Mediterranean chile), hot paprika, and cayenne pepper make good substitutes; if you use cayenne, use less.

PLANTAINS: A plantain is a starchy fruit that looks very much like a banana, but larger. Popular in Latin cuisines, plantains, unlike bananas, are always cooked. Plantains are cooked at varying stages of ripeness: green (at which point they are very bland), medium-ripe (at which point the skin turns yellow and the fruit sweet-

ens somewhat), and ripe, at which point the skin turns black and the fruit is sweet and soft. While ripe plantains peel like a banana, the green plantains used in this book must be baked before peeling (see page 197). Plantains are sold in supermarkets and Hispanic markets.

RICARD: A brand of the anise-flavored liqueur pastis made in France. Ricard is consumed as an aperitif and is a staple of Mediterranean French cuisine. Available at most liquor stores.

RICE, BLACK STICKY: Black sticky rice is a deep burgundy–colored, nutty-flavored, short-grain, glutinous rice grown in Asia. (In ancient China, a variety of black rice was so revered that only the emperor was allowed to eat it; thus it was called "forbidden rice.") It can be found at Asian markets, generally from Thailand.

RICE, CARNAROLI: Carnaroli rice is one of several Italian short-grain rice varieties used for risotto. You probably already know Arborio; Carnaroli and Vialone Nano are two others. I like Carnaroli best. Not to get too scientific on you, these varieties all contain different percentages of two different types of starches. One type helps to make the risotto creamy. The other helps keep the grains firm. Carnaroli contains a nice balance of the two. Unlike

Arborio, Carnaroli is unlikely to be sold at your supermarket but you'll find it online and at specialty stores.

RICE FLOUR: Rice flour is a powdery flour ground from short-grain rice, used in Asian cooking. It's available at Asian markets.

SAFFRON: Saffron is a brick-red colored spice, long used in Mediterranean cuisine. The stamen of the saffron crocus flower, it is sold in threads and powdered. I prefer the threads; though they will almost certainly be more expensive, they are likely to have more flavor than the powder. The threads must be soaked in hot water briefly to release flavor and aroma.

SAKE: Sake is a Japanese alcoholic beverage brewed from rice. There is a variety of styles. Look for a medium-dry sake such as junmai for my recipes. It is available at Japanese markets and most liquor stores.

SEA SALT: I use a fine sea salt from France in most of my cooking, La Baleine brand. When I'd like the texture of a coarser salt, I'll choose fleur de sel or sel gris de Guérande, both from France. The Hawaiian red sea salt, Alaea, is a coarse sea salt mixed with red volcanic clay. It adds a nice earthy, mineral flavor to foods. A great variety of sea salts, coarse and fine, are available at specialty food stores, and online at salt works.us. It's fun to taste a selection.

SEAWEED, KOMBU: Kombu is a variety of edible seaweed used in Japanese cooking, one of the two ingredients in the Japanese stock dashi (the other is bonito flakes, see page 395). It is also used in a traditional Japanese cure for fish (see Kombu-Cured Fluke, page 55). The sturdy, dark brown kelp is sold dried in thick strips or large sheets. Kombu is available at Asian markets.

SEAWEED, NORI: This black or dark green seaweed is best known for its use as wrapping for sushi. Nori comes in packages of thin sheets (I buy it in sheets that measure 8 by 7½-inches). It's available at Asian markets.

SEAWEED SALAD: This crunchy, pleasantly gelatinous salad, which we used to find exclusively in Japanese restaurants, is showing up in the refrigerator cases of fish markets and supermarkets. Made with strands of wakame seaweed, it's typically seasoned with sesame oil, soy sauce, sesame seeds, and rice vinegar for a crunchy, salty, slightly sweet side dish.

SHICHIMI TOGARASHI: Shichimi (which means "seven flavors" in Japanese: *shi* for seven, *ichimi* for flavor) togarashi (which means "chile pepper") is a blend of seven different ingredients: red chile pepper, sansho (a zesty Japanese spice), black and white sesame seeds, dried orange peel, nori flakes, and hemp seed. Different blends are more or less spicy. It is available at Japanese markets, where it may also be sold as togarashi.

SHRIMP, NEW ORLEANS: Wild-caught Gulf shrimp are some of the best shrimp I've eaten. They may be available at your fish market. Or order it from my shrimpers at (504) 228-8038 and split the order with friends—their minimum order is 20 pounds.

TAMARIND PASTE: Sticky, blackish tamarind pulp is contained, along with seeds, in the long, brown pods of the tamarind tree. Tamarind adds a sour, tangy flavor to the dishes. The pulp can be dried and pressed into cakes, or processed into a paste, which is much easier to use. Tamarind paste is sold at Asian, Indian, and Mexican markets.

VERJUS: Verjus (pronounced vair-JHOO) is the pressed juice of unripened grapes. Unlike wine, verjus is not fermented. Its flavor is a combination of sweet, somewhat acidic, and tart, but it's not nearly as tart as vinegar. If you can find it, I particularly like verjus from Wolffer Estate Vineyard on Long Island in New York.

VINEGAR, BANYULS: Banyuls vinegar is made from Banyuls wine, a fortified dessert wine made in southwest France. The flavor is slightly nutty, and resembles sherry vinegar, which can be substituted. Banyuls vinegar is available at specialty food stores, or online at amazon.com.

VINEGAR, RICE: This light-colored vinegar is lighter in flavor and acidity than most vinegars. You'll find it at your supermarket or Asian food stores. Don't confuse this with seasoned rice vinegar, with added salt and sugar.

VINEGAR, SPANISH CABERNET SAUVIGNON: An unfiltered vinegar made from cabernet sauvignon grapes, produced in Catalonia, Spain, and aged in oak. I use Forum brand, available at amazon.com.

WASABI PASTE: Almost all of what is sold as wasabi is not real wasabi. Wasabi is a root with flavor characteristics that are not dissimilar to horseradish but it's a different plant with a more fragrant flavor. It's difficult to grow and, as a result, expensive. Most wasabi paste is made from horseradish powder that has been tinted green and mixed with Chinese mustard. There's nothing wrong with it and you should feel free to go ahead and use it—it's just not wasabi. Look for real wasabi at Asian markets: grated wasabi in the freezer, powdered wasabi, or wasabi paste.

FISH-IONARY

Part of the fun of cooking seafood is the great variety. But all that variety can be confusing to cooks and frankly, while seafood classification and description is fascinating, it's complicated. Different fish are available in different parts of the country, and fish may be identified by several different names depending on where they're sold.

My goal here is to give you a general idea of what's out there and what it looks and tastes like so that you feel comfortable buying and cooking it. To make it easier to get your mind around so many different finfish, I've divided them into four categories based on the texture and fat content of the flesh. "Delicate lean white-fleshed fish" have the most delicate, fragile, flakey flesh and mildest flavor. "Firmer lean white-fleshed fish" are still lean, white, flakey, and mild-flavored, but are made of sturdier stuff. Some, like monkfish and blowfish, do not flake at all. "Richer, fuller-flavored fish" begin to have a stronger flavor due to their increased fat content. Their

color may be less white as a result of the fat content. Their texture may be more or less flakey and delicate—bluefish, for example, is fairly dark-fleshed and very delicate. "Meaty fish" are sturdy varieties that don't fall apart easily.

Shellfish are grouped by anatomical categories. The first category, bivalve mollusks, is a group of saltwater animals with two shells, including clams, mussels, oysters, and scallops. The second, crustaceans, is a group of animals, found in salt- and freshwater, that have segmented bodies covered by a shell. Crustaceans come in different shapes—shrimp, lobster, and crabs are crustaceans—but they're all considered to be made up of two parts: the head, which contains the organs, to which the "arms" are attached, and the tail, which is used for swimming. (This anatomy is easy to recognize in shrimp and lobsters—less so on crabs; their tail is very small and difficult to see.) The third category, cephalopods, include squid and octopus. Barely recognizable as shellfish, they are saltwater animals with eyes and arms or tentacles, with the ability to eject ink from a sac to defend themselves.

My hope is that these categories will not only help familiarize you with the fish, but also help you choose substitutes based on the freshest varieties available to you. All delicate fish, for example, are easiest to bake, broil, steam, and braise, but not so easy to grill unless you've got a grill basket. Sturdy meaty fish won't fall apart on the grill. Shrimp can replace lobster; mussels can replace clams; and squid can stand in for octopus.

Each entry includes my recommendation for degree of doneness—rare, medium-rare, cooked through. I find that most fish benefit from being cooked through, though some species, such as swordfish and halibut, have better texture and flavor when cooked less. I also let you know whether the skin is edible, and how the fish is sold—steaks, fillets, and/or whole fish. Most finfish contain pin bones—small, thin, flexible bones that run the length of the fillet. With some exceptions, it's best to remove pin

bones before cooking (see page 379), so I also point out the varieties that don't contain pin bones.

All the finfish you're working with can be divided into two categories: roundfish and flatfish. The size and shape of the fish determine the cuts you'll find at the market.

Roundfish have a relatively rounded shape, and swim vertically. Flatfish are wide and flat, and swim flat on their sides. Larger roundfish such as salmon and cod are cut into steaks and fillets. With the exception of halibut, which is large enough to be sold in steaks, flatfish are usually cut into fillets. Flatfish are bottom dwellers, typically found lying on the ocean floor. The skin on one side is usually a mottled brown or black that blends into the environment and serves as protective camouflage. (The specific color varies with the habitat.) The skin on the other side is usually white. Among the fish listed below, flounder, Dover sole, and halibut are flatfish; the rest are roundfish.

DELICATE LEAN WHITE-FLESHED FISH

These mild-tasting, lean species flake and fall apart easily during cooking. You'll need to handle them carefully, but they are delicious baked, braised, steamed, poached, deep-fried, and sautéed. These are also some of my favorite fish for broiling.

Cod and Hake

The cod family includes a wealth of saltwater species in both Pacific and Atlantic waters including Pacific and Atlantic cod, hake, haddock, pollock, and scrod (traditionally the market term for a small cod). For centuries, populations have subsisted on cod, which was salted and dried as salt cod (see page 397) to preserve it. All members of the family taste somewhat different, and some are firmer than others. But in all species, the flesh separates readily into large flakes. Cod and its family are sold in whole fish, fillets, and steaks. My favorite of the group is cod, which has the meatiest flakes. I recommend skinning cod before cooking.

Cod and hake are best cooked through.

Flounder

Flounder is a general name for a relatively small (compared to their much larger relative, halibut) flatfish. It encompasses several species of American flatfish including gray sole, lemon sole, petrale sole, fluke, plaice, and dab, found in Atlantic and Pacific waters. To complicate matters, these flounder are sold under different names. Lemon sole, for example, may also be called winter flounder and blackback; fluke is called summer flounder. The important thing for the cook is that these fish can be used interchangeably in the recipes in this book. Flounder fillets will be relatively small and thin (less than ½ inch thick is typical). Note that when I call for a fillet, I mean the long, narrow fillets that are actually half fillets, one quarter of each fish—a distinction your fishmonger will understand. The taste and texture are delicate. Some are firmer than others—experiment with what's available and find out what you like. Flounder may be cooked whole or filleted. I recommend skinning flounder before cooking.

Flounder is best cooked through.

Halibut

Halibut is the heftiest flatfish. It can grow to be quite large, but 30 to 40 pounds is typical. Fillets vary in thickness depending on whether they're cut close to the head or the tail; if cut near the head, you can get a nice size fillet 1 to 1½ inches thick. Halibut is also cut into steaks, with bone. Halibut is found in the North Atlantic and North Pacific waters. The meat is firm, light-flavored, and delicious. Halibut is available wild, seasonally. I can also recommend farm-raised halibut. I recommend skinning halibut before cooking.

Halibut is so lean that it tends to dry out, so it's best just barely cooked through.

Ocean Perch

These small (1- to 3-pound) saltwater fish are mild-flavored with moderately firm flakey flesh and delicate, edible pink skin. Ocean perch is sold as whole fish and fillets. The skin is edible.

Ocean perch is best cooked through.

Tilefish

The flesh of this Atlantic fish is sweet and moist. When cooked, it separates into large flakes almost like cod. Tilefish is typically marketed between 5 and 10 pounds and represents a very good value. New Jersey and Long Island are rich fishing grounds for the tilefish. Tilefish is sold in steaks and fillets. The rainbow-colored skin is edible.

Tilefish is best cooked through.

FIRMER LEAN WHITE-FLESHED FISH

These species are somewhat firmer and hold together better during cooking, making them easier to handle on the grill or in the skillet. Like the fish in the delicate category, they're also tasty baked, braised, broiled, steamed, poached, and fried.

Blackfish

Also called by its Native American name, tautog, the skin of this firm, mild-flavored, lean fish is typically dark gray or black. Blackfish is found along the Atlantic coast from Cape Cod to North Carolina, and is most abundant during the summer. It is sometimes mistaken for black sea bass, which it resembles. It typically runs from 3 to 6 pounds and is sold as whole fish and fillets. The skin is edible.

Blackfish is best cooked through.

Black Sea Bass

If I had to choose a favorite fish, this would be it. The flavor is sweet and delicate, and the texture is moderately firm. The skin is mostly black until it is scaled, and then it shows a black-and-white fishnet pattern. It is found along the Atlantic coast from Maine to Florida. It varies in size but you're likely to find it in the 1½- to 2-pound range. Sea bass is sold as whole fish and fillets. The delicate skin is edible. (Note that the word "bass" may refer to a variety of unrelated fish, both fresh- and saltwater. Neither Chilean sea bass nor striped bass, for example, is in the same family as black sea bass.)

Black sea bass is best cooked through.

Blowfish

The blowfish, officially called Northern puffer, that are caught off the Atlantic coast during the summer months is in the same family as the deadly pufferfish (fugu) enjoyed in Japan. Like fugu, it can inflate itself into a ball when threatened. Fortunately, our East Coast species isn't poisonous. Blowfish is built like monkfish, which is to say a big head and a single, thick, cartilaginous backbone. Also called sea squab and chicken of the sea, blowfish is small (5 to 8 inches) with a soft, mild-flavored, meaty flesh. The rough skin is inedible and is removed before cooking. Blowfish has no pin bones.

Blowfish is best cooked through.

Dover Sole

Despite its name, this European flatfish bears little resemblance to North American soles and flounders. The delicious flesh is delicate, yet firmer than flounder, and holds up better when cooked. Dover sole is narrower than flounder. It is sold whole, and weighs about 1 pound apiece. It is expensive in Europe and even more so in the States. Dover sole is excellent cooked on the bone or in fillets. I recommend removing the skin, which is peeled rather than cut off, before cooking.

Dover sole is best cooked through.

Grouper

Grouper belongs to a large family of saltwater fish that also includes black sea bass. It varies a lot in size (it can grow to be very, very large) and skin color. It is fished off the coast of Florida, the Gulf of Mexico, and in the Caribbean, as well as in the Pacific. Grouper flesh is mild, moderately firm, and flakey. Small grouper may be sold whole and in fillets; larger fish are sold in fillets. The skin of smaller groupers is edible; the skin of larger fish is tough.

Grouper is best cooked through.

John Dory

John Dory is a delicious saltwater fish, highly prized and expensive in Europe. It is also called Saint Peter's fish because of the round black spots, which are supposed to be the fingerprints of Saint Peter, on the skin on either side of its flattened body. The flesh is very white, and the texture is tight. Whole John Dory runs 3 to 5 pounds. It is sold as whole fish and fillets, and can be substituted for flounder in the recipes in this book. I recommend removing the skin before cooking.

John Dory is best cooked through.

Monkfish

Monkfish is an unusual-looking fish with a big, ugly head and large mouth with lots of sharp teeth. The meat, which is in the tail section, is very white and firm with a meaty, tight texture that is often compared to lobster, though the taste is not at all similar. Like blowfish, the monkfish tail is composed of a single cartilaginous backbone. Monkfish is fished along the Atlantic coast from South America to Newfoundland, and in Europe. Monkfish is sold as whole tails with the bone, or fillets. The tails with bone run from 1 to 5 pounds. The skin is inedible and must be removed before cooking. Monkfish have no pin bones.

Monkfish is best cooked through.

Pike

Pike is a freshwater fish found in North American streams and lakes, as well as in Europe. Along with whitefish and carp, it is traditionally used in gefilte fish (page 254). The mild, white, flakey flesh contains a lot of small bones, which should be removed with tweezers before cooking. I also recommend removing the skin.

Pike is best cooked through.

Sea Robin

Sea robin is a close cousin of gurnard, one of the boney fish classically used in French bouillabaisse and other Mediterranean seafood soups, stews, and dishes. Its long pectoral fins look a little like bird wings. Little used in the United States, it's a great fish, abundant along the Eastern Seaboard, with firm, lean, tight, flavorful flesh. Sea robin typically weighs 1 to 3 pounds. The tail can be filleted before cooking, or cooked on the bone. The skin is edible.

When we cook sea robin for staff meal at the restaurant, we gut and scale the fish, cut off the fins and gills, then roast the whole fish, head on. We pick them up by the heads and eat them like chicken drumsticks. Fantastic!

Sea robin is best cooked through.

Skate

Skate is a diamond-shaped fish with wide pectoral fins, called "wings," and a long, skinny tail. The wings are the edible part. They are thick near the core of the fish and thin out at the edges. Like rays and sharks, to which skates are related, skate is cartilaginous; it doesn't have true bones. Because it is cartilaginous, it should be eaten as soon as possible, before it becomes ammoniac. Each wing is comprised of a layer of cartilage sandwiched between two fillets. The meat is firm and fine-grained, and separates into long, thin strips when cooked. Skate is sold on the bone with skin, or filleted and skinned. I prefer to steam it on the bone. The skin is not edible. Skate have no pin bones.

Skate is best cooked through.

Red Snapper

There are hundreds of species of snappers. Red snapper is one of the most famous and desirable. (But this shouldn't deter you from trying other species: In Florida, hog snapper and mutton snapper are greatly appreciated.) With red skin and flesh that is firm, lean, mild-flavored, and moderately flakey, red snapper is fished off the southern Atlantic coast of the United States, in the Gulf of Mexico, and in the Caribbean. It can grow to be very large but market size averages 2 to 8 pounds. Snapper is sold in whole fish and fillets, and the skin is edible. On the West Coast, the abundant species of Pacific rockfish may be substituted for snapper in the recipes in this book.

Red snapper is best cooked through.

Hybrid Striped Bass

This farm-raised fish is not a true striped bass but rather a hybrid of striped bass and white bass. The mild flavor and more delicate texture are different enough from the wild fish that it's best to simply consider the farm-raised species on its own merits, as a different fish. Hybrid striped bass is easily recognizable by its stripes, which, unlike on the wild fish, look broken. The whole fish usually weighs between 1 and 2 pounds. Unlike the wild fish, hybrid striped bass is available year-round, as whole fish and fillets. The thin skin is edible.

Hybrid striped bass is best cooked through.

Whitefish

Whitefish is a silver-skinned freshwater fish found in lakes and streams throughout North America. A member of the salmon family, its flesh is relatively fat, firm, white, and mild-flavored. Whitefish is one of the trio of fish traditionally used in gefilte fish (carp and pike are the other two). Market size ranges from 2 to 6 pounds. It is sold whole, in fillets, and smoked. The skin is edible.

Whitefish is best cooked through.

These richer, full-flavored species vary in texture but they have a higher oil content than the fish in the previous two catego- ries. They are delicious baked, broiled, sautéed, and grilled.

Bluefish

Bluefish is a silver-skinned fish found on the Atlantic coast of the United States from Cape Cod to Florida. The moder- ately fat flesh is flakey and soft. The flavor is relatively strong, though if you taste it the day it's caught, you may be surprised at how mild it can be. The key to cook- ing bluefish is to marinate the fillets in vinegary marinade to soften the flavor— the vinegar cuts the fat. The skin and dark, strong-tasting bloodline should be removed. Bluefish can grow to be quite large. But market weight is between 1 and 2 pounds for smaller bluefish called "snappers," and up to about 10 pounds. Bluefish is sold in whole fish and fillets.

Bluefish is best cooked through.

Branzino

Branzino, the Italian name for an excel- lent European bass, is esteemed through- out Europe for its delicious flavor and meaty texture. It is now farm-raised in a variety of locations throughout Europe, making good-quality branzino available at reasonable prices. The farm-raised fish ranges from 1 to 2 pounds. The flesh is white and firm, and the skin is edible. Sold as whole fish and fillets.

Branzino is best cooked through.

Dorade

Dorade is another prized European fish (*daurade* or *dorade* in French; *orata* in Ital- ian) that is now farm raised. The flesh is moderately firm and mild-tasting. Whole dorade weigh 1 to 1½ pounds each. It is sold as whole fish and fillets. The skin is edible. Porgy, a related wild fish with the same general body shape, is a good substi- tute for dorade. The flesh is not as sweet as a dorade, but it is a good value. Don't con- fuse dorade with dorado, another name for mahi mahi.

Dorade is best cooked through.

Pompano

This excellent fish is a member of the jack family, as is hamachi (also called yellowtail). It has a flat body (for a roundfish) with the smooth, silver skin characteristic of jacks, and firm, rich, full-flavored flesh. Pompano is an Atlantic fish, found off the coast of the Carolinas, Florida, and the Gulf of Mexico. The whole fish typically weighs between 1 and 1½ pounds. Pompano is sold as whole fish and fillets. The skin is edible.

Pompano is best cooked through.

Redfish

This is the fish that Paul Prudhomme made famous with his blackened redfish recipe. Also called red drum and, when over 10 pounds in weight, channel bass. Redfish is found in the southern Atlantic as far south as the Gulf of Mexico and is typically sold in the 1- to 2-pound range, though sometimes larger. The flesh is lean, mild-flavored, and firm. Redfish is sold as whole fish and fillet. The skin is edible.

Redfish is best cooked through.

Trout

Trout is a member of the salmon family and, unless you catch it yourself, your trout is almost certainly farm-raised. Trout is moderately fatty, with a delicate flavor and soft flesh. It is sold as whole fish (ask your fishmonger to fillet for you), weighing a little less than 1 pound. The skin is edible.

Trout is best cooked through.

MEATY FISH

The flesh of these species is darker-colored, moderately to quite fatty, with a sturdy texture that makes it perfect for grilling.

Cobia

Wild cobia, which looks a little like a shark, is found throughout the world in temperate and tropical waters such as the Caribbean and off the coast of the Carolinas down to Florida. The flesh is white, firm, and flavorful. I like to think of it as "swordfish light," because while it is rich, it's not as full-flavored as swordfish. It is also farm-raised, so it is becoming more available. I recommend removing the skin before cooking. Because of the size of the fish, the fillets will not have pin bones. Cobia is sold as steaks and boneless fillet.

Cobia is best cooked to medium.

Hamachi

A member of the jack family, hamachi is also called yellowtail. It is prized by sushi chefs for its soft, smooth, buttery flesh and delicate flavor. Most hamachi is farm-raised in Japan and exported in fillets. Hamachi is best known raw, at sushi bars, but it is equally delicious cooked. I recommend removing the skin before cooking.

Hamachi is best cooked rare to medium-rare.

Hiramasa

Hiramasa is a firm, creamy-textured fish related by species to hamachi, which it resembles. But I find hiramasa to have a somewhat lighter mouthfeel. Most hiramasa you're likely to find is farm-raised in Australia. Like hamachi, hiramasa is best known raw, in sushi bars, but it's also very good cooked. I recommend removing the skin before cooking.

Hiramasa is best cooked rare to medium-rare.

Mackerel

The mackerel family is large and includes tuna, bonito, and mahi mahi, as well as a few different varieties called mackerel. Whether you're on the East Coast, in which case you're probably getting Atlantic (also called Boston), Spanish, or king mackerel, or on the West Coast, in which case it's likely to be Pacific mackerel, most mackerels have a high fat content which means that their flesh is rich and full-flavored. Except for the larger king mackerel, market weight of whole mackerel is 1 to 7 pounds. I use one of the smaller varieties in my recipe for Mackerel Sujime (page 57). Mackerel is sold as whole fish and fillets. The skin is edible.

Mackerel is best cooked to medium-rare.

Mahi Mahi (Dolphinfish)

Mahi mahi is another member of the mackerel family, found along the Atlantic coast, primarily in Florida, and off the coasts of Central and South America. Also called dolphinfish and dorado, it has no relationship to dolphins, the mammals. The flesh is firm, white, and mild-flavored, with a low fat content. Although mahi mahi can grow to be very large, market weight for whole fish is 8 to 20 pounds. They are sold in fillets. Their thick, silvery skin is best removed before cooking. The bloodline should be trimmed because it can be strong-tasting. Because of the size of the fish, mahi mahi fillets will have no pin bones.

Mahi mahi is best cooked to medium-well.

Moonfish (Opah)

Moonfish, called opah in Hawaii where it is fished, is distinctive for its round (full-moon) shape. Its skin is pink with white spots that resemble moons. The firm, meaty, pinkish flesh is moderately fatty and turns white when cooked. The flavor is delicate. Moonfish is sold in fillets because it's such a big fish; anywhere between 20 and 200 pounds is usual. I recommend removing the skin before cooking. Because of the size of the fish, the fillets will not have pin bones.

Moonfish is best cooked through.

Monchong

The pinkish-white meat of this Hawaiian fish, also known as big scale pomfret, has a high fat content and a firm, meaty texture. The flavor is mild. Market weight is 12 pounds or more. Monchong is sold in fillets. I recommend removing the skin before cooking. Because of the size of the fish, the fillets will not have pin bones.

Monchong is best cooked through.

Sablefish (Black Cod)

Despite its name, sablefish or black cod has nothing to do with the cod family. With its high fat content, the silky flesh is much richer than cod. You may have only eaten it smoked, but sablefish is delicious fresh, too. When cooked, it's luxuriously unctuous and silky. Sablefish is found in Pacific waters, from California north to

Alaska. Though the fish can grow to be quite large, market weight is from about 5 to 10 pounds. Sablefish is sold in fillets.

The skin, which is dark gray to black, is best removed before cooking. Sablefish is also farm-raised.

Sablefish is best cooked through.

Salmon

The salmon sold in your fish market belongs to one of two species: Pacific or Atlantic. All the Atlantic salmon sold in the United States is farm-raised in Norway, Scotland, Ireland, Canada, or Chile, to name a few of the several places around the world where the salmon farming industry has successfully taken hold. The orange flesh of farm-raised Atlantic salmon has a moderately high fat content, full flavor, and a silky texture. Because it is farm-raised, excellent-quality Atlantic salmon is available year-round at good prices.

Some Pacific salmon is farm-raised but in smaller quantities than the Atlantic species. Wild Pacific salmon is also available seasonally. Five species of Pacific salmon are sold in the United States: king (also called Chinook), coho, sockeye (also called red salmon because of its deep red flesh), chum, and pink salmon. Found from California north to Alaska, the five species are available from spring through fall, with the season peaking during the summer months. King salmon is the largest of the Pacific species, running from 15 to something in excess of 30 pounds. It is a full-flavored fish with a high fat content, and carries the highest price tag. The meat is usually a deep orange color, but you may also come across white or ivory king salmon, which has a similar flavor. Coho and sockeye salmons have a moderately high fat content. Chum salmon are less expensive than the previous three, with very pale pink flesh and a low fat content; chum salmon is often canned. Pink salmon is the smallest and least expensive of the five species, with a low fat content; it is almost always found canned.

Salmon is sold as whole fish, fillets, and steaks. Salmon skin is edible.

All species of salmon are best cooked to medium-rare.

Shark

There are a number of shark species sold in the United States, and they're all very tasty. Shark is a moderately lean, firm, white fish with a texture that resembles swordfish but is even meatier. Because it is cartilaginous, it should be eaten as soon as possible, before it becomes ammoniac. Shark is usually sold in fillets (usually called steaks, though they're boneless). It's best to remove the tough skin before cooking. Because of the size of the fillets, shark will have no pin bones.

Shark is best cooked through.

Wild Striped Bass

For folks like me who fish in the Northeast, there is no more iconic catch than striped bass fished off the rocks around Montauk, New York, at the height of summer. Wild striped bass is an Atlantic fish also found in the Chesapeake Bay, and off the coast of Virginia, Maryland, and New York during spring, summer, and fall. Also called the striper and, in the mid-Atlantic, rockfish, the fish is easily recognized by the dark stripes that mark its silvery skin. The flesh is firm, lean, and very flavorful. It's delicious cooked and raw. Wild striped bass can grow to be very large but market weight is typically 6 to 15 pounds. Wild striped bass is sold as whole fish and fillets, and the skin is edible.

Wild striped bass is best cooked through.

Sturgeon

Most people think of sturgeon as a smoked fish. But it's also sold fresh—most of what you find is farm-raised, essentially as a result of the caviar industry. It's a prehistoric-looking creature, but the pinkish meat has a good, full flavor, and it's so firm and meaty that it almost eats like chicken or pork. Sturgeon has a high fat content so it won't dry out even when cooked. The farmed fish range from 8 to 20 pounds. Sturgeon is usually sold skinless, in steaks and fillets, and has no pin bones. The tough skin is inedible.

Sturgeon is best cooked through.

Swordfish

Swordfish is a very large fish regularly caught in the 200- to 300-pound range, and can weigh far more. It is named for the long, flat "sword" that protrudes from its head. Swordfish is fished off the coast of New England, Florida, California, and the Gulf of Mexico. The fatty, white meat is firm with a full, delicious flavor. Large swordfish are usually cut crosswise into pieces called "wheels." The wheels are quartered lengthwise, and cut crosswise into slices. These slices, usually called steaks even though they are boneless, are roughly triangle-shaped. Some steaks will include a strip of belly meat, which is fatter than the rest of the steak and delicious. There will be a darker area of bloodline on one side; if the fish is fresh, the bloodline will be a deep red color, not brown. This meat has a stronger flavor than the white but it's perfectly edible, if you like it. If not, cut it off before or after cooking.

Steaks may be cooked with or without skin, but remove the skin before eating. Because of the size of the fish, swordfish steaks will have no pin bones.

Swordfish is best cooked to medium except when poached in olive oil, when it's better cooked through.

Tuna

Tuna is a member of the mackerel family. There are several species, many of which grow to be very large, like swordfish. Tuna are fished in temperate and tropical waters around the world. The fat content varies among species but they are all delicious. Bluefin tuna is the largest and the most expensive; its red flesh has the highest fat content. You may only have encountered it at sushi restaurants, but if you find it in your fish store, it's also excellent cooked. Most of the tuna sold in the United States is red-fleshed yellowfin, which along with bigeye tuna (called ahi tuna in Hawaii), is leaner. Albacore tuna is very light-colored: you probably know it canned as "white tuna," but it's sometimes available fresh, too. Don't confuse it with escolar, a different fish that may also be called white tuna.

Tuna is sold in boneless steaks. They will be roughly triangle-shaped with a dark area of bloodline that is stronger-tasting than the rest of the meat, but entirely edible, if it appeals to you. The tough skin is not edible. Because of the size of the fish, tuna steaks will have no pin bones.

Tuna is best cooked rare to medium-rare, except when poached in olive oil, when it's better to cook it through. If you're hesitant to try fish on the rarer side, tuna is a great starter fish—try it both medium-rare and rare and see how you like it.

Wahoo (Ono)

Wahoo, also called ono (which means "good to eat" in Hawaiian), is a member of the mackerel family. The meat is pale pink to gray when raw but turns white when cooked. The flesh is lean, firm, and meaty and the flavor is milder than some other fish in the mackerel family. Wahoo can grow to be quite large but market weight ranges between 8 to 30 pounds. Wahoo is sold in fillets. I recommend removing the skin before cooking.

Wahoo is best cooked through.

SHELLFISH: BIVALVE MOLLUSKS

Clams

You'll find a variety of clams in markets, but generally clams can be divided into two types: hard-shell and soft-shell. The difference is just what it sounds like. I have recipes for both types in this book. Though they have different names—quahogs or chowder clams, cherrystones, top necks, and littlenecks—hard-shell clams all belong to the same species. The names refer to size, with quahogs being the largest and littlenecks the smallest. Tough quahogs are best used in chowders, as their other name implies. Cherrystones and littlenecks can be used interchangeably in recipes for steamed clams, pastas, raw clams, and other dishes that require a tender clam. These clams are an East Coast product, available down the Eastern Seaboard from Canada into Florida.

Soft-shell clams (which include steamers) are found buried in tidal mudflats on both the Atlantic and Pacific coasts of the United States. They can be recognized by their thin, flexible shells that are easily broken, and their slender, protruding necks. I don't eat soft-shell clams raw; I like to steam them like hard-shells, and they're traditional for fried clams. Their flesh is softer than that of hard-shell clams.

Clams should be alive when you cook them, and hard-shells should be tightly closed. Test gaping hard-shell clams by pressing the shells closed or immersing them in cold water; if they stay closed, they're fine. If not, throw the clams away. Scrub hard-shell clams well with a stiff brush, such as a potato brush, before cooking.

The shells of soft-shell clams, however, will be slightly open. Test their aliveness by touching the neck; it should move slightly. There's no need to scrub, but give the clams a good rinse. Throw away any clams—hard- or soft-shell—with broken shells.

Soft-shell clams may contain a lot of of mud and sand because they live in the mud. To purge them of sand and mud, rinse, then put them in a container with cold water to cover and enough salt to taste like seawater. Add a small handful of cornmeal and refrigerate for 1 to 2 days. As the clams ingest the cornmeal, they'll purge themselves of the sand. You may also find soft-shell clams that have been raft-purged, which means that they have been held out of the mud in a net or cage in the water for long enough to purge. (See page 388 for instructions on opening raw clams.)

Mussels

You'll find two types of mussels in the market: a shiny black-shelled species called the blue mussel, and the larger, green-brown New Zealand green-lipped mussel. They can be used interchangeably in recipes and their flavor is very similar. Thread-like beards protrude from the mussel shell to attach the mussel to its environment (rocks and piers). Remove beards with a sharp yank just before cooking.

While blue mussels may be available wild, both species are also cultivated. The cultivated mussels are an excellent product; easy to prepare because they're very clean, with none of the mud that wild mussels may contain. And cultivated mussels often have no beards at all. All they need is a good scrub with a stiff brush, such as a potato brush.

Mussels should be tightly closed and alive when you cook them. Squeeze together the shells of any mussels that are gaping and throw away any that don't close.

Oysters

Despite a profusion of names, there are just five major species of oysters harvested in the United States: the East Coast oyster (also called Atlantic); the Pacific oyster; the Kumamoto oyster; the European flat oyster (also called Belon); and the Olympia oyster. Of the five, the East Coast and Pacific varieties are the most abundant. Recipes in this book can be made with either.

Atlantic and Pacific oysters are named for the specific area in which they are harvested, because their flavor is enormously affected by the nutrients in the waters where they grow. East Coast oysters are grown up and down the Atlantic coast from Canada to the Gulf Coast: Glidden Point (from Maine), Moonstone (Rhode Island), Fisher's Island and Blue Point (New York), Chincoteague (Virginia), and Apalachicola (Florida) are names of a few of the more common East Coast oysters. Most East Coast oysters are cultivated.

Most oysters grown in Pacific waters are Kumamoto oysters and Pacific oysters with names like Hama Hama (from Hood Canal, Washington), Totten Inlet (Puget Sound, Washington), and Fanny Bay (British Columbia). All are cultivated.

The tiny Olympia oyster also grows wild in the Pacific. A small number of round, flat European flat oysters are cultivated on both coasts.

Unless you're buying them already shucked (see page 387), oysters must be alive, with shells tightly closed.

Sea Scallops

Scallops are shucked at sea because they spoil quickly, so it's rare to find them sold in the shell. What you see at your fish counter is the large, meaty muscle that opens and closes the shell. (Sometimes the pink or orange roe is attached; it is edible and a delicacy.) The only cleaning required before using is to remove the tough white muscle you'll find on the side of most scallops.

Recipes in this book are for sea scallops, which are available year round. (Bay and calico scallops are smaller species and not used in this book.) Most sea scallops in the United States are harvested wild off the Atlantic coast.

When buying sea scallops, it is important to ensure that you are buying what in the industry are called "dry scallops." Because scallops spoil so quickly, they are sometimes dipped in a phosphate chemical dip that acts as a preservative and causes the scallops to absorb liquid. Untreated dry scallops have a better flavor and brown better in the pan and under the broiler. It's easy to spot the difference: Untreated scallops are ivory- to beige-colored and the texture is a little sticky; soaked scallops are very white, slick-textured, and are usually sitting in liquid.

Scallops, like shrimp, are sometimes sold by the number to the pound. The smaller the number, the larger the scallop. U10 or U15 indicates fewer than 10 or 15 scallops to the pound. In some of the recipes in this book, size is important and I recommend a count per pound. Otherwise, you can use whatever size you come up with. Just remember that smaller scallops will cook more quickly than large scallops.

Sea scallops are best cooked to medium-rare.

SHELLFISH: CRUSTACEANS

Shrimp

Shrimp are sold in a range of sizes, head off, shelled and shell on. Most of what you'll find is farm-raised, and good quality. I love wild-caught Gulf shrimp for their wonderful, full flavor. I buy them direct from seventh-generation shrimpers Kay and Ray Brandhurst of Four Winds Seafood in Louisiana. The name of the business belies the scale of the operation— it's just Ray and Kay. Ray calls from their shrimping boat to give Kay a report on the catch he's bringing in. Kay contacts chefs like me and retailers immediately so that the shrimp on Ray's boat today can be in my kitchen tomorrow. If you're cooking for a crowd (their minimum order is 20 pounds), they will ship to you; see Guide to Unusual Ingredients, page 404.

Shrimp may be sold in sizes ranging from large (with names like colossal, super colossal, and jumbo) to small or cocktail. Since these size designations are not consistent among retailers, my recipes call for shrimp the way they're described in the industry: by the number of pieces to the pound. Most of my recipes call for large shrimp (16 to 20 shrimp to the pound, designated 16–20), or medium (21–30). For my shrimp cocktail in the restaurant, I use a larger shrimp designated U15, meaning fewer than 15 shrimp to the pound. Use what you can find, and remember that smaller shrimp cook faster than larger shrimp.

If you buy the shrimp in the shell, you will need to shell and devein them (see page 385).

Shrimp are best cooked through.

Lobster

Two types of lobsters are sold in the United States. There is the clawed American lobster that I use in my recipes, harvested in the North Atlantic and sold live from lobster tanks. Lobsters without claws are a different, warm water species called spiny or rock lobster; they are almost always found frozen, as "lobster tails." I don't use them in this book.

Clawed lobsters must be alive when you buy them and they should be lively. Traditional wisdom is that lobsters should be very energetic. But their liveliness also depends on the temperature of the water in which they're stored. I keep the water in my lobster tank at the restaurant between 36° and 38°F because colder water preserves lobsters better, but colder water also makes them less active. So while your lobster need not be super energetic, it should not be droopy, and the eyes should look alive.

The recipes in this book call for 1¼-pound lobsters, which is a fairly common size, though you'll also find them larger, 1½ pounds and up to 5 pounds. (See pages 389 to 394 for instructions on preparing lobsters for cooking, and shelling cooked lobster.)

Lobster is best cooked through.

Crab (Blue Crab, King Crab)

There are a great number of edible crabs in the world. In the United States, the most commonly available are blue crabs from the Atlantic, Dungeness crab from the West Coast, king crab from Alaska, and stone crab from Florida. I use only blue crab and king crab in the recipes in this book.

Blue crabs are sold whole, live, and as picked crabmeat. The meat is very delicate and shreds easily. For crab cakes (see page 321), you'll want to buy the picked meat. Ask for jumbo lump crabmeat, sold in chunks. Whole blue crabs must be alive and lively. Soft-shell crabs are blue crabs that have shed their hard shells; the soft "shells" that remain are edible. Soft-shell crab season is from May through September. Like the hard-shell version, soft-shell crabs must be alive when you buy them. (See page 386 for instructions on cleaning soft-shell crabs.)

King crab is a much larger crab; it weighs up to several pounds. The legs are sold cooked and frozen, with the shell cracked so that you can get to the firm meat easily. Thaw in the refrigerator and use immediately.

Squid

Better known by its Italian name, calamari, squid has an appealing, mild flavor, and is tender when correctly cooked. Squid bodies and tentacles are sold fresh, cleaned, with and without the thin, purplish skin, or frozen. I like the skin; it adds color and flavor. But if you don't, it's easy to strip off before cooking. I like to grill the bodies whole or cut them in rings to deep-fry or sauté. The tentacles may be cooked whole unless they're really large, in which case, cut them in half.

Squid is best cooked through, but don't overcook it as it will toughen.

Octopus

Octopus is mild-flavored and like squid, very tender when cooked correctly. The weight of an octopus can vary between 2 and 10 pounds. Raw whole octopus is usually sold cleaned and frozen but you may find it fresh, particularly around the Christmas holidays. Thaw frozen octopus in the refrigerator before cooking. Octopus legs may also be purchased cooked (see Guide to Unusual Ingredients, page 401).

Octopus is delicious grilled but it must be braised or poached first to tenderize it. Cooking time varies wildly depending on the octopus.

Octopus is best cooked through.

Acknowledgments

To my family and friends: My wife, Christine, has been my rock. You had faith in me when I was just a young cook, and you've sacrificed greatly—still do!—during the long hours and through all the adventures of this culinary journey. Thank you for being there during the tough times as well as the good times.

Few things in this world give me more joy than sharing the gifts of cooking, gardening, and fishing with our children, Nathaniel, Caroline, and Catherine. I love you guys. My mom and dad, Liz and Bill, were definitely not expecting me to turn into a chef; thank you for your support, for encouraging my choices, and for allowing me to live at home for a lot longer than we thought I would. My mother- and father-in-law, Barbara and Joel Trella, also deserve my gratitude for welcoming me into their family and supporting me and Christine as we build our own.

Thank you to my sister, Becky, and the rest of my family and friends for their continuing encouragement and love. Cristina and Victor Mosquera provided a family recipe, friendship, and good times at their table.

And a special thank-you to my friends Carlos Jimenez and Deborah Sinclaire, who, in sharing in this voyage, have truly become family.

To the folks in the restaurant business who have supported my journey: The Livanos family—John, Nick, Bill, and Corina—and Paul McLaughlin took a risk when they offered a young chef his first shot as executive chef in the Big Apple. You gave me a stage on which to shine! You stood with me as I grew, you let me take chances, and perhaps most meaningfully you trusted me. Thank you for all the opportunities and for allowing me the freedom to write this book. I am proud to work with a family with such values as yours.

Chef Floyd Cardoz opened my eyes to a new cuisine and made me a better cook; finally, he taught me to be a chef. Thank you for sharing all you did with me and for holding me to the highest standards.

Rozanne Gold and Michael Whiteman have been invaluable sources of guidance and advice. I am blessed to have you share your wisdom with me.

Christian Delouvrier, Alain Ducasse, Franck Cerutti, and Jean-Jacques Rachou led me to new heights of possibility in the kitchen. Michael Romano, Danny Meyer, and their partners at USHG gave me a world of opportunities and a lifetime of life lessons. Thank you all.

At Oceana: I am grateful to the entire kitchen team. You put your careers in my hands. It is a responsibility I do not take lightly, and I am proud and thankful for all you do, every day. I'm particularly indebted to my executive sous chef, John Dugan, and my chef de cuisine, Matt Howard. John was my right-hand-man recipe tester and photography assistant. Matt's dedication to managing my kitchen while he helped with testing and photography allowed me to focus my energies on *School of Fish*. This book could not have been written without you two.

Executive Sous Chef Matt Adler, Sous Chefs Masahiro Miura, Brendan McNulty, Aaron Watson, Moshe Grundman, and Ethan Koelbel, and cooks Albino Hernandez and Yelena del Mundo also gave generously of their time. A big gracias to my cook, Maria Gonzalez, for sharing her family recipe. You are the unsung hero of my kitchen; you stand tall among your peers.

Gracias to my fish butcher, Javier Flores, for taking such great care with our fish. Also to my fabulous fish buyer, Adam Kolenberg, who scours the Fulton Fish Market nightly for the best fish in the city; your passion for buying the highest quality fish equals my passion for cooking it. And to one of our favorite guests, Parkin Lee, thanks for sharing your mother's recipe.

To the people who helped make this book: Stephanie Lyness, my coauthor, truly brought the best out of me, made my voice clear, and simply let me cook. Thank you for doing such a great job of translating what I do in the kitchen and for teaching me how to write a book.

I cannot thank Noah Fecks enough for making my food look so beautiful. You're a wizard with a camera and so much fun to be around. And you did an awesome job keeping up on ten-hour-plus photo shoots! Thanks to Paul Wagtouicz for assisting behind the lens and for eating as much cod as you did, and to Jeffrey Heaney at Bauscher USA for generously providing the beautiful plates for the shoot.

Thanks to my agent, David Black, and to Sarah Smith and David Larabell at The David Black Agency for taking care of business.

Finally, to my publisher, Louise Burke, thank you for your confidence and your appreciation of my General Tsao's Lobster. You've assembled an awesome team at Gallery Books. Publisher Jen Bergstrom and editor Trish Boczkowski have cared for the book and raised it well. Thank you for that; and for the good times and the laughter.

• BEN POLLINGER •

INDEX

———